D1562593

FRONTIERS OF SUPERCOMPUTING

FRONTIERS OF
SUPER-
COMPUTING

edited by

N. METROPOLIS, D.H. SHARP
W. J. WORLTON, & K.R. AMES

UNIVERSITY OF CALIFORNIA PRESS
Berkeley   Los Angeles   London

University of California Press
Berkeley and Los Angeles, California

University of California Press, Ltd.
London, England

Library of Congress Cataloging in Publication Data

Supercomputer conference proceedings.
  Papers presented at a conference co-sponsored by the Los Alamos
National Laboratory and the National Security Agency.
  1. Supercomputers—Congresses. I. Metropolis, N. (Nicholas), 1915-.
II. Los Alamos National Laboratory. III. United States. National Secur-
ity Agency.
QA76.5.S8947   1984   001.64   84-28010
ISBN 0-520-05190-4

Printed in the United States of America

1 2 3 4 5 6 7 8 9

CONTENTS

Preface

For many years, scientific computing has been a major factor in maintaining U.S. leadership in several areas of science and technology and in the application of science to defense needs. Electronic computers were developed, in fact, during and after World War II to meet the need for numerical simulation in the design and control of military technology. Today, scientists and engineers are using supercomputers to solve ever more complex and demanding problems; the availability of supercomputers ten thousand times faster than the first electronic devices is having a profound impact on all branches of science and engineering—from astrophysics to elementary particle physics, from fusion energy research to aircraft design. The reason is clear: supercomputers enormously extend the range of problems that are effectively solvable. However, several factors have combined to place the discipline of scientific computing in a critical position. These factors involve both scientific and societal issues.

Although the last 40 years have seen a dramatic increase in computer performance, the number of users and the difficulty and range of applications have been increasing at an even faster rate, to the point that demands for greater performance far outstrip the improvements in computer systems. For example, to achieve an increase in resolution by an order of magnitude in a three-dimensional, time-dependent problem would require an increase of speed by a factor of 10^4—far in excess of the increases projected to be available in the next few years. The result is that difficult problems are typically undercomputed relative to the scientific requirements. Of comparable importance is the fact that the broadened community of users is demanding improvements in software that will permit a more comfortable interface between user and machine.

Ways to meet these needs are on the horizon, but to exploit these opportunities will require scientific progress on several fronts. Computers, as we have known them for the past 20 to 30 years, are about as fast as we can make them. The demand for greatly increased speed can be met only by a radical change in computer architecture—from a single serial processor, whose logical design goes back to Turing and to von Neumann, to a computer consisting of an aggregation of many intercommunicating parallel processors that can perform independent operations concurrently. This latter approach, which can be enabled by the remarkable development of reliable large-scale integrated circuits, will entail fundamental changes in logical design, languages and operating systems, algorithms, and, indeed, in numerical mathematics itself.

Although massively parallel machines hold great promise for the future, the importance of measures to more effectively use available hardware cannot be overemphasized. These measures include the development of better numerical algorithms and better software for their implementation. Improved software could also greatly reduce the time needed to translate difficult problems into a machine-computable form. Since the introduction of computers, improvements in software have increased the productivity of users by at least two orders of magnitude. If another order of magnitude can be realized within the next decade, then practice in many fields of science and technology will be revolutionized.

Supercomputing is unusual in the rapidity with which progress in the field will affect vital national needs in the areas of security and economics. For example, the skill and effectiveness with which supercomputers can be used to design new and more economical civilian aircraft will determine whether there is employment in Seattle or in a foreign city. Computer-aided design of automobiles is playing an important role in Detroit's effort to recapture its position in the automobile market. The speed and reliability with which information can be processed will bear on the effectiveness of our national intelligence services. It is thus a matter of concern that traditional U.S. leadership in supercomputer technology is being challenged by robust foreign competition.

What conditions are necessary for a conducive climate for further rapid develpment and application of supercomputers in the U.S.? What scientific issues must be resolved to make the revolutionary step to massively parallel supercomputers? How can individual efforts in computer architecture, software, and programming languages best be coordinated for this purpose?

To address these and other critical issues, the Los Alamos National Laboratory and the National Security Agency co-sponsored a conference on the "Frontiers of Supercomputing," held in Los Alamos on August 15-19, 1983. The papers in this proceedings were presented at that conference. The essays have been organized into sections dealing with national and industry perspective, advanced architecture, Los Alamos and supercomputing, software, algorithms and applications, and national priorities and supercomputing. A very broad spectrum of interests and points of view is represented. Collectively, the work represents impressive national strengths in supercomputing, including a vigorous supercomputer industry, innovative academic research on parallel architecture and software, and a strong base of research on increasingly ambitious and realistic applications. A point on which there was wide agreement was that it is imperative for the U.S. to maintain its leadership in all aspects of supercomputing, and that the key to this lies in effective collaboration among industry, the universities, and government users.

We would like to thank K. Speierman, Chief Scientist, NSA, who had the idea for the Conference and D. M. Kerr, Director of the Los Alamos National Laboratory, and Lt. Gen. L. D. Faurer, Director of National Security Agency, for their support. We would like to acknowledge the members of the Organizing Committee, C. W. Bostick, K. R. Braithwaite, B. L. Buzbee, B. W. Keadle, N. H. Krikorian, J. T. Pinkston, and G-C. Rota, with special thanks to P. G. Salgado, Executive Administrator of the Organizing Committee. We would also like to acknowledge Linda Randolph, who was the liaison between the organizing committee and IT Division and the visitor contact; Nancy L. Bazzel for manuscript assistance; and Nathana Haines for editorial assistance.

N. Metropolis
D. H. Sharp
W. J. Worlton
K. R. Ames

Welcome to Los Alamos

D. M. Kerr
Los Alamos National Laboratory
Los Alamos, New Mexico

Ladies and gentlemen, I'm pleased to welcome you to this conference on the frontiers of supercomputing. I can think of few better places to be in the middle of August than Los Alamos, and I compliment you on your decision to spend a week in these cool mountains during what has been a very hot summer elsewhere in the country. More important, I compliment you on your recognition that supercomputing is a topic of vital interest to this country and that it merits your attention and attendance here. There are many frontiers that exist in relation to supercomputing today. One is an intellectual frontier, where sophisticated creative thinking is required in order to make progress in pushing back this frontier.

This topic also deals with the frontier of national policy. To maintain international leadership in this important field, new government policies, new corporate policies, and new collaborative arrangements may be required among universities, industry, national laboratories, and government agencies. Both frontiers create stimulating challenges.

I think it is fitting that this conference is held in Los Alamos. It was the computational needs of our nuclear weapons development that provided the drive for the first high-speed computing capability. That need has now been joined by many other needs for such capability, ranging from the needs of organizations analyzing massive amounts of data, such as oil companies, to the advanced graphics used in Hollywood's current productions. The key concern motivating this conference has been to maintain U.S. leadership in an area that is vital to so many areas of the nation's future, and particularly, to its national security. I applaud the vision of the National Security Agency in providing support for this conference, financially, organizationally, and intellectually. Its role has been key in making it possible for this conference to occur, and we appreciate their efforts. We have one key goal: that is, to mix the ideas that flow from universities and business with the policy perspective of government officials so that a focused intellectual exchange may stimulate further rapid advances in research and development of supercomputers.

We also hope this focus will help develop government policies that will maximize the efforts necessary to push forward the frontiers of supercomputing. The people here are leaders from universities, government, national laboratories, and business, and I am confident they will respond to the challenge posed by this conference. I welcome you to Los Alamos and to what promises to be a stimulating week for all of us.

Before I introduce our keynote speaker, I am pleased to have the opportunity of introducing a special guest, who has recognized the importance of this conference and is visiting with us today. Senator Jeff Bingaman was elected to the United States Senate by New Mexicans last year and has already established a pattern of thoughtful analysis of these key issues. We are pleased that he could spend some time here with us this morning, and I should, in introducing him, mention what his background is. He was born in El Paso but soon moved to Silver City, New Mexico. Senator Bingaman went to Harvard to do his undergraduate work and received a law degree from Stanford University. He was in private law practice in New Mexico and then in public law practice as our Attorney General for 4 years prior to 1982, when he successfully ran for the United States Senate. Another important factor from the point of view of this conference and the Los Alamos National Laboratory is that he is a member of the Senate Armed Services Committee and serves on their Subcommittee on Tactical Warfare and the Subcommittee on Manpower and Personnel. Senator Bingaman, we are pleased to have you with us this morning.

I would like now to introduce our keynote speaker. And while he is in fact the newly appointed president and chief executive officer of the Microelectronic and Computer Technology Corporation, you might also think of him as the physical embodiment of this interesting confluence of private sector needs, government needs, and where the policy really makes a difference in terms of what may happen.

Admiral Inman is a native Texan, returning next week to become a Texan again, having spent a distinguished career in the United States Navy, serving most recently as Chief of Naval Intelligence, subsequently and not consecutively, as the Director of the National Security Agency, and his final government post as Deputy Director of Central Intelligence. He also was the man who very publicly and openly dealt with a major issue of 2 or 3 years ago, and in fact, an issue still today, that had to do with public ciphers, research in universities on encryption techniques, and how the interests of national security and open research might be dealt with in our society. He has never been reticent about important issues. He has volunteered, for example, to serve as the director of the Arms Control Association, he is a member of the Association of Former Intelligence Officers and a senior fellow of the Hoover Institution. In all of his professional career and private life, he has been outspoken in support of what he has seen to be the right direction for this country to take in dealing with very difficult problems. It is a pleasure to introduce him this morning as our keynote speaker to deal with this very difficult problem of supercomputing and electronics research.

Keynote Address

Supercomputer Leadership: A U.S. Priority

Admiral B. R. Inman
Microelectronics and Computer Technology Corporation
Austin, Texas

When one reflects on the use of computers in this country, it is a natural pairing of Los Alamos and the National Security Agency. Although NSA's part has often been shrouded in secrecy in the past, the fact that the first Cray came here and that the second went to NSA is only one of the many symbols of the fact that both have pressed research in mathematics out ahead of the rest of the country. And it's been particularly fun for me over the last few hours to see a lot of admired colleagues from NSA in the audience. Hopefully, they're not identified just as Department of Defense attendees. But that's an old in-house joke.

Earlier, I had intended to speak at some length about the Microelectronic and Computer Technology Corporation (MCC). You've read a lot about it in the press, and perhaps we'll have a little time for questions to talk about it before it's time for you to move on to the important agenda you have ahead of you.

Some time ago I appeared on a television program in which a new book was being promoted. The book put forth the view that supercomputers offer great dangers to this society. I eventually became sufficiently frustrated during the discussion to liken the situation to children so afraid of the dark that they were afraid to ever go out and look and see the stars that were there. I think those who go about this critical challenge of defining the next generation of supercomputers are going to be challenged constantly. Why does this country need to proceed, to stay at the leading edge of technology in so many areas, but particularly in the area of computing? I hope to at least arm you with some arguments. You may discard them. You're also free to use them if they are of any benefit at all.

What are the challenges and opportunities that will face us in this world in the 1990s? The challenge primarily is going to take two major forms: military and economic. And we're going to have to learn to balance both of those and to do it effectively if we're going to take advantage of the opportunities that the rest of this century offers.

Let me begin with the military side. We will primarily concentrate in the years ahead, as we have in the past decade, on the Soviet Union. But we're going to be worrying about instability in the Third World, political/military clashes, Arab/Israeli unsettled issues, and about Libya and North Korea. Mostly, we will focus on the evolving Soviet challenge—many components of it; on the strategic side, steady, sustained improvement in their strategic offensive forces. They are going a little slower at deploying new improvements right now than they have previously, and they may be deliberately holding back to see where there are some additional arms control opportunities. It may also be that they have technical difficulties that have encouraged them to hold back a little in the normal cycle we've seen of rolling out the next generation of strategic weapons systems. It is clear that there is an agressive research and development program in defensive weapons systems, and there are areas where we've not proceeded in our own effort with sufficient detail to be very comfortable that we can make confident judgments about what progress they may or may not achieve in that area. But I would have to tell this group that I'm much more concerned, looking out over the next 15 years, about the evolving mobility of Soviet conventional forces than I am about changes in the strategic ones, because I believe that for any Soviet leadership, use of nuclear weapons is still going to be an act of desperation, not an early policy decision.

We have watched, over the past 18 years, following the ouster of Khrushchev, an increase in investment to solidify support by a new Politburo, an annual steady investment in Soviet defense capabilities, left largely to the Defense Ministry to allocate. And we have steadily watched not a growth in numbers—in fact, even perhaps a slight reduction in numbers—but an incredible change in the capability of conventional forces to be deployed, to go to fight, and to stay for far longer periods of time. The changes have occurred in air, land, and sea forces, and there are some advantages—not many—but there are some that accrue to their system of government, where a Merchant Marine is entirely owned by the government and can be marshalled to support those military efforts very quickly indeed.

But it is the evolving attitude about the use of force away from their periphery that concerns me at least as much as the changing capabilities. Nineteen seventy-five was a watershed year with the decision that November to move 15 000 Cuban troops and massive quantities of Soviet arms, by air and by sea, halfway around the globe to Angola in a 2-

week time frame. I won't dwell on how we tried to deal with the matter. We don't seem to be very good at learning our own lessons of history. Two years later, they proceeded with another effort in Ethiopia, and others have followed—Yemen, Kampuchea, Laos, and then their own use of force in Afghanistan. But when one stands back, while 1975 was a watershed about being willing to use force a very long distance away, the current old Bolsheviks have been very cautious about using that evolving power where there was a prospect for direct conflict with the U.S. and its allies.

What about the 1990s, when there will be almost a total change of the senior leadership for reasons of age and health? We may be fortunate. Because they've grown up in the Khrushchev-inspired era of the Communist Party being the world's largest bureaucracy and enjoy their privileged positions, having risen to dominance in the Politburo, largely through service in heavy machine industries and other areas that have benefited from this heavy investment in the defense structure in their own climbs to position of power, and therefore, they will be cautious about risking a privileged position. But there is at least as much danger that they will be more arrogant without the memory that the current old Bolsheviks have of Germans on the banks of the Volga, and therefore, will be far more willing to use military force when they see opportunity. What will drive that interest? Their inability to compete economically. The economy continues to be just this side of a total disaster. But it has nonetheless steadily produced very slight improvements in the consumer side year after year for 20 years throughout a sustained major military buildup. The principal problems—corruption and central planning—may now be under attack. I do not see a possibility of a turnaround on the economic side that would let them be a part of the great economic competition during the rest of the century. But I believe it is likely to be sufficiently successful that they can sustain their level of investment in their defense establishment without interruption. That means they will look to the outside world in their feeling of inferiority about great power status. But because of their inability to take part in, participate in, enjoy, and compete economically, they will look for opportunities for use of their burgeoning military power.

What is that economic challenge going to look like that they will be watching? It's going to be marked by very intense competition—for markets, for raw materials, for natural resources. Most of that competition for markets is going to take place West to West, inside the countries, within the economies of the U.S. and its principal military allies, with all the strains on alliances that that has to offer. But a lot of the competition will gradually evolve, particularly into the 1990s, for markets and for raw materials and natural resources out in the Third World. If that Third World were stable, then one could look at the economic competition as something relatively easy to manage. But I'm afraid we're going to see the trend of continued instability. Only in Asia with the Association of Southeast Asian Nations and South Korea and Taiwan has there been sufficient political stability and economic growth to offer a reasonable prospect of continued stability. In fact, we may find there the new element in the economic competition that we'll find in the rest of this century.

For much of the rest of the Third World, we're going to have to contemplate how we can encourage political stability at the same time that we help bring them into a potentially great economic boom. Balancing and managing these economic opportunities to keep the alliances coherent, while limiting opportunity and temptation for the Soviets to use their mobile military power, is going to be the principal challenge with which we will have to deal. But it isn't just a world of challenge. It is a world of great opportunity, if we only look for it and take advantage of it.

The prospect of encouraging world stability, I think, is reasonably there if we lead and help share economic prosperity. To do that, to be able to bring about some balance about how we approach military challenge and a clear, sharp, long-term focus for the economic policies that will keep an alliance coherent, the number one requirement is a consensus on national security policy in this country. And a broad understanding that national security policy involves diplomacy, foreign aid, arms control, the structure of force levels of our defense forces and their deployment, and international trade will be needed. We must address all of those coherently in long-range planning if we are, in fact, to be in a position to take advantage of economic opportunities.

What's going to lead that economic boom? I believe the real leadership for it will come from the information-handling industry, which in 1981, worldwide, had revenues of about $325 billion, with 5 million jobs; in the U.S. alone, some $136 billion in revenues and 2 million jobs. We're not going to replace the basic industries. They're going to remain very critical. But we can help lead the way they're automated and become more productive and focus on retraining people who must operate the modernized facilities. But if we really seize the opportunity in the information-handling industry, we have a potential for providing excellent jobs for those entering the work force in these next 15 years, if we have prepared them along the way to be able to take positions in an adult world. If one looks at the current growth in the information-handling industry, growing at 15% a year with just a reasonable effort to keep it rolling, that's a worldwide trillion-dollar annual revenue in the early 1990s—easily 15 million jobs. Half of that clearly should be in this country, if we invest now in the research and development, in the infrastructure that will sustain it, and prepare to manufacture high-quality products and market them in a way that insures that we compete as we have demonstrated we can at times in the past.

We are not well prepared to fully seize the opportunities that are here. In many cases, being prepared takes long-term planning. And we make short-term decisions. In 1963, cost effectiveness was the great catch-word in looking at the national security budget; looking for ways to reduce investment, and by 1964, to pay for the commitment in Viet Nam. We decided it wasn't cost effective for the Department of Defense to make unconstrained grants for graduate education unless it was directly related to supporting design of a weapons system. If you stand back and examine the great economic boom of the 1940s and 1950s, you will find that the GI bill and unconstrained grants for graduate studies that came from organizations like the Office of Naval Research fueled much of the education. But to be cost effective, we dried up a lot of that in the mid-1960s. And it was at a point in time when the National Aeronautics and Space Administration's investment was beginning to decrease. Industry did not pick it up. No one else picked it up. And beginning in 1968, you can chart the drop in graduate students in the U.S. in sciences and math. The size of our educational institutions didn't really drop because foreign students came to take advantage of the opportunity. And we have, probably usefully over the long term for these Western economies, educated a great many of the bright graduate students who are now fueling the competitiveness of our allies. One of the early challenges that we have as a country is to again spur substantially greater investment in the graduate schools in science and mathematics, recognizing that a great deal of that has been done by the Defense Advanced Research Projects Agency over the last decade. Even quietly, the Office of Naval Research and its counterparts have still found some ways to play, but not nearly to the degree that the country can both absorb and very usefully benefit from. And as we look at where we find qualified graduate students, we must begin with the basic education systems across the country, insuring that we are producing students going into schools who have the fundamental background to permit them to take advantage of the educational opportunities they will have.

Simply because we have not invested in that graduate level education to the degree we should have for the last 25 years, we have to find new approaches, and that is why, following the model of the Electric Power Research Institute of some years ago and the Semiconductor Research Cooperative, we are evolving the MCC, where we pool talent from competing companies, accepting the wisdom of that part of the Japanese model and evolving it to our own intense free enterprise system, but recognizing we simply cannot afford, if we're going to meet the challenges, and certainly not if we're going to seize the opportunities, to continue to have a great many people recreate the same basic technologies across a large number of companies.

What are the U.S. needs? What do we need to do to try to seize the opportunities and to meet the challenges? Well, it won't surprise you that for the near term, finding again a consensus on national security policy is the first requirement. It isn't going to be easy to do, and I'll offer a tough suggestion for our Congressional leadership along the way. We have to draw the Congress and Executive together in the process and force long-range planning. As long as we're addressing problems on a year-to-year basis, we will never move on any kind of broad scale to address problems in a long-range way. Shifting to 3-year authorizations will be very painful, but I know of no other early way to produce a long-term focus on problems rather than an annual short-term look.

We need some modifications in the antitrust laws of this country to recognize that we are not dealing with the 1890s to 1910 and rapacious industrialists plundering U.S. society. But there is some genius in the antitrust laws that we want to sustain. Competition at the market place works in Japan, just as it works here. And so when we turn to modifications, we don't want to deal with everybody who's got a problem (often through their own mismanagement), but to make those changes that signal to industry that we want them to pool scarce resources for research; we want them to invest in long-range research, and we are prepared to give them tax credits or other write-offs to encourage the investment they ought to be making. The system of focus on quarterly profits, in fact, does not stimulate such investment. The antitrust laws should encourage the broadest sharing of research and not try to postulate what products might come out 6 to 10 years from now against what projected market share. Rather, the focus should be on how fast we can insure that the technology that's developed is placed in the hands of other U.S. corporations, particularly small companies, to insure competition at the market place.

Government must define its needs. What we don't need is another plan on how to invest in technology without any clear sense of how government will use it. We need now for the federal government to define what they see as the government needs in supercomputing, in other uses of information handling, and in telecommunications to finally provide us with something that would approach the quality of communications the government needs and clearly could afford if it had the right priority. That's going to have to be done across the government. The needs of the intelligence community are to deal with Soviet mobility, not just with Soviet forces on the Eurasian land mass. The key priorities for making political decisions are (1) being able to sort through incredible volumes of information and at the earliest point recognize preparation for movement of substantial forces outside Soviet borders and (2) the ability to follow burgeoning instability in Third World countries themselves. As one thinks about defensive systems, a critical problem is how to sort through, at a very early stage, incredible volumes of information to be able, within matters of seconds, to track individual elements of millions of moving events.

The next point is a harder one in the near term; that's investment in education. I'm not persuaded that substantial federal investment is the answer, though clearly some encouragement is necessary. Where does it need to come? It needs to come in the areas that you define as government needs, where it is unlikely that the commercial sector will see a market to pick up. And the same is true for your supercomputer needs: in defining now what your own needs are, in recognizing those areas where there will be a market and letting them be driven by the commercial market place, but letting the government invest in areas where the needs are likely to be predominantly those of the government.

There are also opportunities that we've not really begun to address in retraining the work force. We do know from our experience in the military that you can take an individual who is barely literate and, with computer-aided education, train him to become a first-class engine mechanic. The National Automobile Dealers' Association has spent a great deal of time putting together standards for adequate repair of automobiles, but there has been no great rush to retrain people with basic mechanical skills to do that. Wouldn't it be nice to be able to get your automobile repaired well and quickly?

For the long term, we have to push the frontiers of research and development. Computers are going to be at the leading edge. I hope that this week you'll define what the broad elements of that program ought to look like. Many of you already know what MCC has set out to do, but that's only part of the competition. I think it's a very important part. To identify the talent and get the talent applied to the problems, both by the competing companies for MCC and among the universities, and insure that we recognize that, if we are really going to seize the opportunities of the 1990s, we are going to have to make some priorities, and those priorities are going to have to be increased investment at the university level in engineering and computer science departments. And we're going to have to beef up our long-term approach to education.

The key to success is the collaboration of government, academia, and the private sector. When we've had this collaboration in this country, it's normally been stimulated by fear of or the reality of military threats from the outside. We need to encourage that collaboration now for our long-term economic well being if we are to avoid repetition of the lessons of the past. When we shied away from collaboration for fear that we might damage academic freedom or that we would somehow suppress competitiveness at the market place, the alternative seemed to be trade barriers, which ultimately leads to breaking up of alliances. The 1990s can be an extraordinarily exciting time for all of us. But the challenges are there, and if we don't manage them and manage them effectively, then we are likely to find ourselves in the 1990s at a time of some very intense military confrontation. And on that cheerless note, let me send you off to the exciting events you have ahead of you.

1

Supercomputers:
A Congressional Perspective

Senator Jeff Bingaman
Washington, D. C.

I appreciate the chance to address this conference this morning and to join in welcoming you to New Mexico and to Los Alamos. You have set an extremely ambitious goal for this week, as I understand the statement of purpose of the conference. Let me just quote from that. It is "to define directions and national priorities that are required to assure effective advancement in computer science and retention of the U.S. lead in supercomputing during the 1990s."

I share the view that is implicit in the statement of the conference's purpose, which is that it is essential for the U.S. to retain its lead in this area. If we do not do so, it could have severe repercussions, both for our national security and for our economic competitiveness in world markets. That is so because the next generation of computers, with its ability to reason with enormous amounts of information, promises to revolutionize not only our weapons but also our society in general.

I am sure it is clear to all of us that the challenge to our predominance in computer science and technology is coming from Japan. The Ministry of International Trade and Industry (MITI) National Superspeed Computer Project and MITI's Fifth-Generation Computer Project are really the reason we are gathered here today. The remarkable success that the Japanese have had in the semiconductor industry in the last decade lends credence to their ability to achieve the ambitious goals that they have set for themselves in these projects as well. Without the challenge of Japan, I doubt whether we would be considering changes in the decentralized and possibly uncoordinated way in which we have developed our information-processing industry thus far.

The big question for this conference, as I see it, at least from a Congressional perspective, is what is the proper role of government in our national effort to compete with the Japanese challenge in the next generation of computers. We in Washington are currently spending a great deal of time, as most of you know , debating in general terms about the issue of industrial policy. The question is sometimes put in terms of whether or not we should have an industrial policy. But I believe the real question is whether we are to have a successful industrial policy. Today we have an industrial policy. We have one that focuses on supporting industries with the power to lobby in Washington; steel, automobiles, textiles, and agriculture are a few examples. Of these industries, perhaps only the agricultural policy has been a success and promises to continue to be one.

I regard this conference as an attempt to define an industrial policy for this critical industry—one that will have the support of a broad consensus of industry, of government, and of academia. It is conceivable to me that you will decide that, with the remarkable changes that have already been made within government and industry, we are now on the right track. I am here speaking about the Semiconductor Research Cooperative (SRC), which is designed to funnel industry money into university research laboratories to develop new semiconductor devices. I am speaking about Admiral Inman's Microelectronics and Computer Technology Corporation (MCC), of which we will hear more in a few moments. I am speaking of the Defense Advanced Research Project Agency's (DARPA's) Fifth-Generation Supercomputer Program, which is proposed to grow from a $50 million effort today to a several-hundred-million-dollar program in the late 1980s. If these initiatives are coupled with the individual efforts of computer firms, with the ongoing support of the National Science Foundation for our university computer science departments, and with the efforts of the Department of Energy (DOE), the National Security Agency (NSA), the National Aeronautics and Space Administration (NASA), and the Armed Services as consumers of the most advanced computers, perhaps we are on the right track.

But it is equally conceivable to me that much more needs to be done. Professor Edward Feigenbaum of Stanford, in his recently published book, *The Fifth Generation*, recounts all of these efforts and yet concludes that the U.S. is, in his words, "trailing along in disarrayed and diffuse indecision" in this field. He calls for a bolder step—the establishment of a national center for knowledge technology, which would support basic research in a broad range of information and knowledge technologies, "from telecommunications to publishing, from new computer designs to new curriculum designs for our schools."

I am not sure I would go as far as Professor Feigenbaum, but it does seem clear to me that much depends on how we as a nation put meat on the bones of SRC, MCC, and DARPA's strategic computing program. We do need a coordinated national effort, and I believe that the Congress will respond enthusiastically to a program that has backing among the people in this room. We in the Congress would like to be out front for a change, helping those vibrant industries, such as the computer industry, compete in world markets, instead of focusing merely on bailing out industries once they get into trouble.

Let me clarify that the issue of computer predominance in the world has not received wide attention within the Congress. The Senate Armed Services Committee did not even discuss the DARPA strategic computing program, which is at the heart of our governmental effort. This program was buried in a larger line item in DARPA's budget entitled "Strategic Technology," and was therefore assigned to the Strategic Warfare Subcommittee. The subcommittee staff, in fact, quietly cut the program by $10.5 million as a way to save money for higher priority strategic programs—something that I discovered only 2 weeks ago during the House-Senate conference on the defense authorization bill.

On the House side, I would say you are in better shape. The House Armed Services Committee has a Research and Development Subcommittee whose staff director, Tony Battista, has taken an intense interest in this technology. The House Armed Services Committee stated in its report on the Department of Defense (DoD) authorization bill that its members believed "every effort should be made to maintain" the U.S. lead in computer technology. But from my conversations with Tony during the conference, I know he is concerned about the lack of a comprehensive plan, at least one that has been announced, within DARPA to conduct the fifth-generation computer effort.

The House-Senate conference, therefore, fenced the funds for the supercomputer program, pending receipt of that comprehensive plan from the Secretary of Defense. At the same time, the conferees restored the budget for the program to the higher level approved by the House. My staff has since been in touch with Bob Cooper and Bob Kahn at DARPA and has been assured that a comprehensive plan is nearing completion within DARPA. My hope is that their plan will reflect a broad consensus within the computer science community and that funding for the program will receive support within the Pentagon in what will undoubtedly be an extremely competitive environment for funds in fiscal 1985.

I want to compliment the organizers of the conference for helping us focus national attention on the problem of our dwindling lead in this critical technology. Let me conclude by wishing you a very productive week, and I look forward to getting a report on your discussions. Thank you very much.

2

Technology Overview

J. A. Armstrong
IBM Thomas J. Watson Research Center
Yorktown Heights, New York

Introduction

This technology overview will be given from a system point of view; chips will not be considered apart from how they fit as parts of an eventual hardware system, consisting of chips plus means for packaging them. There will be little discussion of ring oscillators, since characterizing technologies by quoting ring oscillator numbers is like guessing who will win the Olympic Pentathlon from observations of the running event only. Furthermore, this review will not discuss supercomputer performance per se.

The technologies that will be considered are bipolar silicon, silicon very large-scale integration (VLSI), gallium arsenide (GaAs), and Josephson junction (JJ). Bipolar silicon is the current supercomputer technology; aggregations of silicon complementary metal oxide semiconductor (CMOS) or negative metal oxide semiconductor (NMOS) VLSI may be future candidates; GaAs field-effect transistor (FET) devices of various kinds are potential competitors for the silicon bipolar technology; and JJ technology is a potential novel solution to very high performance, large-scale computing. Only publicly available data have been used in the assessments that will be given.

To make clear what I mean by the system point of view in evaluating technologies, consider Fig. 1. It is an idealized schematic, but not an unrealistic view of the various time delays that make up the machine cycle in a large general-purpose computer. That the picture would differ somewhat for different high-performance or supercomputer configurations is not important for the points I wish to make. Note that the on-chip delay accounts for less than one-third of the cycle time, whereas

4

CONTRIBUTIONS TO CYCLE TIME

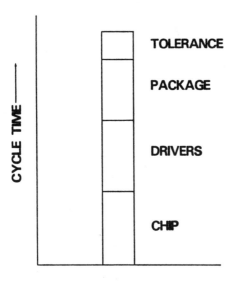

Fig. 1. Major delay components that determine the cycle time of a large system.

delays associated with drivers and packaging account for more than half.
Note further that if a particular chip technology were replaced by one 10
times faster on-chip, with the other parts of the overall system un-
changed, the system would be only 30% faster, despite the 10-fold
increase in on-chip performance. The moral is that *packaging is as
important as chips.*

It is also clear from Fig. 1 that system technologists should strive to
shrink all delays in about the same proportion as improvements in the
chip delay. If a level of packaging can be eliminated, so much the better.

Figure 1 also helps to illustrate the fact that when two systems are built
from dissimilar chip technologies, one of which is much faster than the
other, the system performances are likely to differ by a smaller factor
than the chip performance ratio.

Generic Technology Issues

Lithography

Figure 2 shows schematically the past and projected trends for average lithographic capability in manufacturing, worldwide. It shows that today lithography is practiced in a range from somewhat below 2 μm to around 3 μm. (There arc, of course, at any particular time, a few special cases that fall outside the average range.) Over the next decade, the average feature size will shrink at an average rate of about 13% per year. This evolution will take lithographic practice from almost exclusive reliance on optical tools to a product-and-task-dependent mix of full wafer,

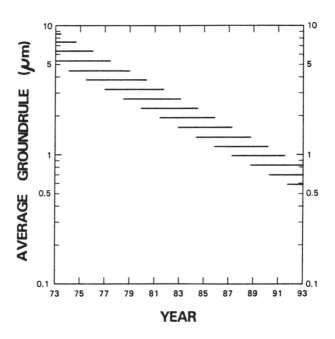

Fig. 2. Past and projected future trends in worldwide, average lithographic capability in manufacturing.

stepper, and e-beam exposure tools. X-ray lithography is best thought of as an extension of optical lithography and will not play a large role before the latter part of the coming decade.

It should be noted that, although we often talk as if resolution were the single appropriate measure of lithographic practice, it is often as important to specify the line-width control and level-to-level registration that are required if a given resolution is to be fully exploited.

The only one of the four technologies under consideration, which is gated by lithographic evolution, is silicon VLSI. Developments occur there first and appear in the high-performance bipolar technology somewhat later. Lithography is not a major issue for either GaAs or JJ technologies at this time.

Process Complexity and Control

Process development and process complexity are major issues for GaAs and JJ, as well as for continued progress in silicon. Even in silicon technology, unexpected difficulties arise despite our sophistication in solid-state physics and our accumulated process learning.

Similarly, control of process-induced defects (due to, for example, ion implantation, reactive ion etching of pattern, or hot processing) continues to be an uphill battle. In many cases, the mechanism for defect generation is imperfectly understood, and progress is made by costly, empirically defined procedures. There is a fertile field here for more and better-focused work on the materials and process science that underlie processes of known importance. This work can be done in university and government labs, as well as in industry.

Finally, thin-film metallurgy is another very important area of materials science, full of surprises for the process developer, but also a fertile source of scientifically attractive problems.

To conclude this section on process complexity and control, it is perhaps of interest to list some of the materials and process science issues of particular relevance to progress in JJ and GaAs.

In the case of JJ technology, it is necessary to control the average tunnel barrier thickness to an atom's width; insulator defect counts that rival the best achieved in silicon technology are required for memory, and new thin-film metallurgy must be developed, understood, and controlled. Finally, process tolerances are generally more stringent than in silicon, because threshold logic must be employed due to the lack of gain in JJ devices.

In GaAs, substrate electrical quality and reproducibility are still unsolved problems: epitaxial growth techniques must be perfected and scaled up; stability of activated dopant concentrations and profiles under hot processing must be achieved; satisfactory contact metallurgy must be perfected; and control of interface charge must be achieved. All of these problems come together in determining the root mean square spread in FET threshold voltages, which in turn determines the level of integration for which an acceptable design-limited yield can be obtained.

There has been substantial progress over the past several years in GaAs and JJ technologies. But whereas the materials and process problems that are being attacked are intrinsically more difficult than those of silicon technology, only a fraction of the accumulated learning in silicon may be effectively brought to bear on either GaAs or JJ. The development methodology transfers and some (but by no means all) of the tooling transfers, but little of the learning and art in the process development and control can be used. In view of the differences in level of effort on silicon and on the new technologies, the inescapable conclusion is that it will be much longer than supercomputer users would like before GaAs or JJ are at a stage comparable with where silicon is *now*. One should not underestimate the difficulty of what is being undertaken.

Packaging

The third of the generic issues I wish to discuss is the development of a package technology that is matched to the chip technology. By matched, I mean that the packaging technology should allow communication between chips with a delay short enough so as not to drastically dilute the performance represented by on-chip logic speed. Despite its great importance in high-performance systems, packaging is widely regarded in the university community and the popular press (to the extent that it is regarded at all) as less important and certainly as less glamorous than chip technology. There is certainly less work in university and government labs on packaging than on chips, even though university groups have occasionally made important contributions to packaging. This lack of attention to packaging is an important issue in technology for supercomputing.

Present day high-performance bipolar technology places great demands on packaging; there are many approaches being practiced, and packaging technology is much less uniform across the spectrum of manufacturers than is silicon technology. In all cases, improvements are needed to handle ever-larger heat loads, to support substantial increases in input/output (I/O) connections, and to increase the chip packing density. The article by A. Blodgett in the July 1983 *Scientific American*[1] gives a good description of sophisticated high-performance packaging for bipolar silicon.

A proposed route to high-performance computing is the concurrent use of a large number of VLSI microprocessors. I suggest that the packaging issues involved here have only begun to be faced. The delay introduced by off-chip drivers in today's technology is roughly three times that of the loaded on-chip delay. As the chip technology advances over the next decade, the ratio of off-chip driver to on-chip delay may well increase. This suggests an increasing disparity between chip and package performance. In concurrent VLSI, with large numbers of micro-processors, it will be very difficult to keep the various parts of the total delay matched. Wafer level integration schemes may conceivably help here.

In the case of JJ devices, the packaging technology is entirely new. Silicon is used as a substrate, with deposited superconducting ground plans, superconducting transmission lines, and—very impor-tant—ultralow-inductance connections between chip and package.

In the case of high-performance GaAs systems, I do not believe the packaging issues have been faced seriously as yet. It will be possible to build adequate drivers, but there will again be a substantial disparity between driver delay and on-chip delay.

Status and Trends (High-Performance Silicon Bipolars)

Figure 3 gives a representative set of points, based on public information from a variety of manufacturers, describing high-performance bipolar logic chips. The solid points show the loaded delay vs number of gates per chip for chips in manufacturing; the open circles are chips that have been described in the literature but are still in the development stage. The most advanced of these[2] has loaded delays of about 300 ps at an integration level of 2500 gates. The short arrow is meant to suggest the direction of progress that is likely to take place over the next years. How far and how fast this will proceed is not clear; for example, we do not know how long it may take to reach the 100-ps level in practical circuits or whether it will be possible to obtain substantial levels of integration at delays below 100 ps. As pointed out in the Generic Technology Issues

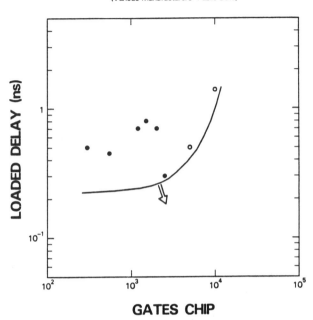

Fig. 3. Bipolar logic performance summarized from the
literature. Solid circles are chips in manufacturing, open circles are laboratory results.

section, it is becoming increasingly complex and difficult to extend this
technology.

Figure 4 shows the status, again in both manufacturing and development stages, of fast bipolar array chips that are key components of high-
performance systems. Again, the data came from many manufacturers
and are available to the public. The most advanced part is an experimental four-kilobyte (kB) chip[3] at about 3.2-ns access time. The progress we
expect in logic technology will be reflected in the arrays as well, along
with essentially the same uncertainty about how far this progress will
continue; certainly progress will continue over the next decade.

Figure 5 charts the development of high-performance silicon VLSI, as
measured by the total number of transistors per microprocessor chip.

SILICON BIPOLAR MEMORY ARRAYS

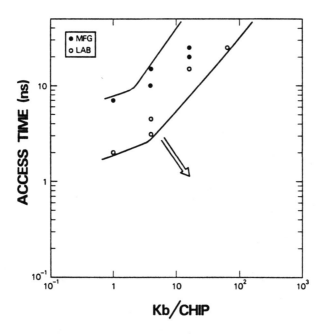

Fig. 4. Bipolar memory-array performance summarized
from the literature.

The points again are based on delivered or announced products. There is
no single trend line that describes all the data; the band corresponds to a
transistor count that increases roughly 40% per year; it suggests there will
be microprocessor chips with a million transistors before the end of the
decade and perhaps two million by 1993. This trend will make possible
remarkably powerful single-chip microprocessors—
undoubtedly with several-million-instructions-per-second (mips) performance (regardless of the lack of standardized measure of performance). Incidentally, the trend industry-wide is clearly to move from
NMOS into CMOS technology. If architectures and software are developed to allow genuine and efficient concurrency, and if packaging
technology is developed that does not seriously compromise the individual microprocessor performance when large numbers are aggregated,

FET EVOLUTION

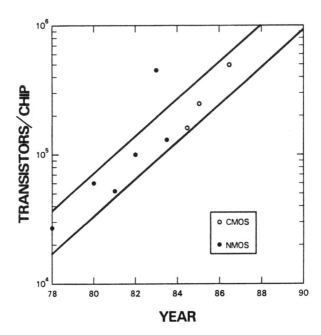

Fig. 5. Evolution of silicon VLSI summarized from the literature.

then there is a technology here of interest to supercomputing. The forces driving this microprocessor evolution are very powerful and will go forward quite independently of supercomputer applications. However, I mention again that packaging particularly suited to the aggregation of large numbers of microprocessors will have to be developed if the potential is to be realized. Again the moral: *packages are as important as chips.*

There has not been extensive enough work on either GaAs or JJ to present separate figures that show trends in actual loaded on-chip performance of functional large-scale integration (LSI) chips. There are many ring oscillator experiments, but few functional chips. Figure 6 is an attempt to bring all the technologies we have been discussing together using a power-delay graph and using on-chip loaded numbers. Except for

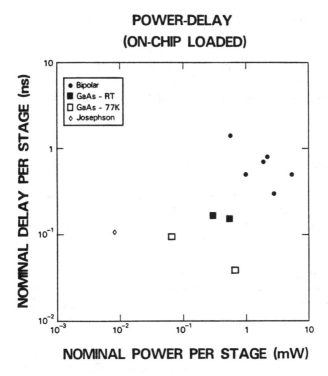

Fig. 6. Technology comparison based on loaded power-
delay performance.

the bipolar case, where there are plentiful data, there are very few publications from which on-chip loaded performance and per-stage power can be deduced. In fact, in the case of the low-temperature GaAs devices, I have violated my own rule and have been forced to use ring-oscillator numbers multiplied by engineering estimates of the factor that accounts for driving typical wiring capacitances encountered in practice. In assessing the implications of this graph, bear in mind that all the bipolar numbers represent chips in manufacturing, or close to that stage, whereas none of the other points represent anything like that level of development.

Figure 6 clearly shows the potential performance improvements that motivate those who are wrestling with GaAs and with JJ. There are substantially shorter switching delays to be obtained, along with decreases in power per stage, which would make very dense packaging possible. The JJ point, based on recent results at IBM,* corresponds to 105-ps delay per gate at 8 μW/gate dissipation. The integration level corresponds to 600 gates/chip. The room temperature GaAs points are for a 16 by 16 bit multiplier chip described by Nakayama et al.[4] (160 ps/gate at 300 μW/gate) and a gate array described by Texas Instruments[5] (150 ps/gate at 550 μW/gate).

Summary

I summarize some of the key issues in the production of fast components for future high-performance computers.

There is need for substantially more materials and process science to be focused on problems of long-term relevance to the silicon, GaAs, and JJ technologies. Much more of this could be done in university and government laboratories, as well as in industry. The materials and process sciences, as well as the design and electrical modeling of packaging technology, do not receive sufficiently broad and diverse attention from university departments of materials science and electrical engineering.

Finally, there is the question as to whether systems constructed from either JJ or GaAs technology would show sufficient advantage over silicon to justify the effort required for their introduction.

References

1. Blodgett, A. J., Jr.. *Scientific American* **249** (July 1983):86.

2. Lee, S. C., and Bass, A. S. "A 2500-Gate Bipolar Macrocell Array with 250-ps Gate Delay," *IEEE Journal of Solid State Circuits* **SC17**, No. 5 (October 1982):913.

3. Ooami, K., Tanaka, M., Sugo, Y., Abe, R., and Takada,T. "A 3.5-ns 4-kB ECL Ram." *ISSCC Digest of Technical Papers*. IEEE Cat. No. 83CH1854-9 (1983):114-115.

*D. Heidel. "Buffered Symmetric Current Injection Logic." Paper presented at the Workshop on Josephson Digital Devices, Circuits, and Systems, September 26-29, 1983, in Fallen Leaf Lake, California.

4. Nakayama, Y., Suyama, K., Shimizu, H., Yolcoyama, N., Shibatomi, A., and Ishikawa, H., "A GaAs 16 x 16b Parallel Multiplier Using Self-Alignment Technology." *ISSCC Digest of Technical Papers.* IEEE Cat. No. 83CH1854-9 (1983):48-49.

5. Namordi, M. R., and White, W. A. "GaAs E/D Logic Circuits." *ISSCC Digest of Technical Papers.* IEEE Cat. No. 83CH1854-9 (1983):38-39.

3

Great Gigaflops and Giddy Guarantees

N. R. Lincoln
ETA Systems, Incorporated
St. Paul, Minnesota

Introduction

The year 1983 began with *Time* magazine designating the computer as the "Machine of the Year" for 1982[1] instead of the usual "Man of the Year." Public attention was focused on the digital computer by media, manufacturers, and retailers to an extent never seen before. The somewhat invisible arena of computing called "supercomputers" was discussed at length in popular, nontechnical publications such as *Newsweek*[2] and *Business Week*,[3] while at the same time various commissions, committees, and agencies of the federal government were reviewing this country's large-scale computing future.[4-6] Given the high cost of supercomputers relative to the generally established computer market place, and given the fact that such computers tend to be at the leading edge of software and hardware technologies with all attendant risks, it is reasonable to question the premises on which both performance requirements and claims are being evaluated.

Requirements

A somewhat simplistic relationship between needs, goals, and probable outcome for supercomputing over a period spanning 1945 to the year 2000 is depicted in Fig. 1. The topmost curve (user demand) is meant to illustrate the perceived requirements of supercomputer users at that point in time. Obviously, the milieu of "supercomputer user" has changed significantly since 1945, when a handful of scientists sought solutions to artillery ballistic equations and when the need for extensive computations in support of this country's nuclear program was just becoming visible. In the 1980s, a vast and varied consuming community

16

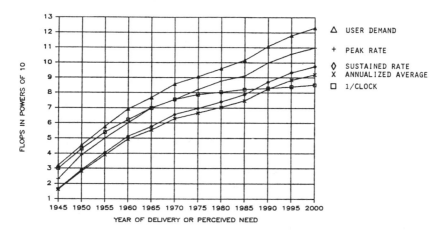

Fig. 1. Supercomputer performance—demand, potential, and reality.

encompasses petroleum exploration, research, and management; weather studies and forecasting; aircraft and automobile design and crash analysis; energy systems research and development; as well as the ever-present military and intelligence users. This plot is indicative of a growth in the perceived needs of this community in terms of each of their respective applications. Thus, in 1964 when the Control Data 6600 supercomputer was just being delivered to U.S. weapons laboratories, those same facilities were aware of computing requirements for some of their problems that exceeded that new and "fastest" computer by a factor greater than ten.[7,8]

Future projections for the users of the 1980s and 1990s indicate that the rate of delivery of supercomputer power continues to be exceeded by the growth in computing requirements. A number of major facilities in the U.S. have published studies of future needs that show that the degree of refinement and detail needed for new research and new designs of high-technology products—from air transport to windmills—will entail incredible numbers of computations performed repetitively and incessantly over years of development. The Ames Research Center of the National Aeronautics and Space Administration (NASA) has conducted studies and published illuminating data[11] on one aspect of future requirements: the simulation of full-scale aerodynamics to support the research and design of the next generation of aircraft. In these studies, Ames scientists concluded that for the Numerical Aerodynamic Simulator (NAS) to be effective, it must return its results to aerodynamicists within a few minutes. This requirement led to the specification of a computer capable of producing one thousand million (or one billion) floating point operations per second. This speed (which is also called a "gigaflop") is not a peak rate but, in fact, must be the sustained rate at which the computations are performed throughout a working day. Putting this into the context of today's supercomputers, the Cray 1 and Cyber 205 possess peak rates of execution three to four times their actual effective rate. Further, these machines now perform about one hundred million floating point operations per second at a sustained rate, or about one-tenth the performance demanded for the initial version of the NASA simulator.

An interesting quality of this "demand" curve should be noted in that it is not uniformly smooth but, rather, it possesses some bumps and nodes that conform somewhat to the corresponding "dents" in the second trace (peak rate—described below). This is due mainly to the fact that users who have made documented and thoroughly reviewed demands for computer power were not aware of the limitations of the industry. It is obvious that, if gigaflop performance was available in 1950, it would have been needed and utilized, although many methodologies have evolved as a result of new generations of computer power. The interaction of available power and applications technologies, plus the realistic expectations of thoughtful consumers, leads the demand curve to move spasmodically through the 1960s, 1970s, and 1980s.

Technology Trend

Another trace (1/Clock) is presented here to illustrate the limitations foreseen for exclusively technology-limited performance improvements. It assumes that a basic "clock" cycle in a computer represents a quantum of work, such as a two's complement, 48-bit, add operation, and that the speed of the clock is a function of gate density and speed. On this semilog graph, the performance of supercomputers can be seen to rise asymptotically over the years since 1945, reaching a theoretical threshold between 500 and 1000 megaflops by the year 2000. The performance rate in megaflops presumes that some form of processor could produce, at best, one floating point result per given clock cycle.

This curve represents projections of standard silicon technology; however, it appears that even the most exotic new technologies would only improve its asymptote by a factor of 2 to 4. The peak performance of a supercomputer, in years subsequent to the "knee" of the technology curve, had to be achieved through architectural innovations and design techniques rather than by relying on raw technology horsepower.

Peak Goals

The second curve (peak rate) in Fig. 1 is intended to demonstrate the peak performance delivered by supercomputers since 1945, where the Electronic Numerical Integrator and Computer (ENIAC) and successor machines, such as the Engineers Research Associates (ERA) 1101 (the fastest machines in their time), are loosely included in that genre. The power of basic Single Instruction Stream machines was chosen to plot this line. The trace in the 1970s and 1980s does include multiple data stream machine performance, however, as represented by the vector processors. From the mid-1980s onward, an assumption is made as to the presence of commercially viable multiprocessors. It should be noted that this line represents a growth in computing power, due to a combination of factors—technology, architecture, and design. As each architectural development reaches maturity and hence begins to taper off in the degree of improvements seen, it is replaced with a new innovation. This process can be seen historically to work as single-address scientific machines gave way to two- and three-address machines, thence to complex, multifunctional units (CDC 6600) and pipeline computers (CDC 7600), followed by the vector processors of the 1970-1980 period, and inevitably by the multiprocessors that are emerging in the latter half of this decade.

It is significant that with even the inclusion of vector processing in the peak power of machines in the past 10 years, the rate of supercomputer power increase is tapering off. Further, this tapering is happening at a much greater rate than the requirements curve, thus increasing the disparity between needs and available power. At the extreme, this difference could be on the order of 200 times by 1990. When one includes the possible effects of new, exotic technologies that could improve the peak rate curve in the 1990s, it can be seen that the difference will still be greater than 100 times between requirements and available computations.

More sobering still, when these curves are examined in detail, is that even the introduction of multiprocessing in the form of either classical MIMD (Multiple Instruction Stream, Multiple Data Stream) or data flow does not improve the peak rate sufficiently to close the computational gap. It is true, however, that multiprocessing must be incorporated in the upcoming generations of supercomputers to sustain the demand for computing, which the top trace illustrates. Regardless of its source or form, supercomputing in the next 10 years must attain gigaflop rates, and must provide this power at a reasonable cost to the wider audience that is rapidly making itself known to computer manufacturers and the federal government.

Readers of current technical literature and perusers of polytechnical propaganda will find that the peak rate, as shown here, seems substantially inferior to some predictions and claims based on technological breakthroughs and architectural innovations. It is to those "giddy guarantees" that some comments are addressed here.

Computing power derives from an assemblage of technologies, which includes memory, registers, and "gates." The basic speeds of these devices and the number of devices incorporated, to a large measure, determine the computational performance of the resulting processor. A set of costs attendant to generating this computer power exists for any given generation of technology. There is, of course, the actual cost of components, which are necessarily at the leading edge of the state-of-the-art, and, therefore, are usually quite expensive at the outset. There are the costs for electrical power and cooling, which tend to be high, because it takes a specific amount of energy to move "carriers" and "holes" around a large-scale machine. Because essentially "nothing is for free" in this world, it is reasonable to expect that promises of (in Carl Sagan's words) "billions and billions . . ." of floating point operations must be analyzed in terms of reality. If cost were no object, one can see that a simple multiplying of the peak rate curve in Fig. 1 by 200 would escalate the delivered compute power in 1990 to somewhere close to the apparent requirements. It must be remembered, however, that the peak curve represents the best (and by far the most expensive) single processor available at the time. Because these single supercomputers traditionally have been sold at prices of $5 million to $10 million, it is obvious that an outlay by a single customer of $1 billion to $2 billion would be required to achieve this goal. This cost presumes that somehow the 200-machine ensemble could be made to harmonize effectively for the customer's main problem solutions, not a very simple problem in itself.

Clearly, even the U.S. government could little afford such expenditures for each of its vital laboratories. The answer to this dilemma is offered by some who believe that 16 thousand, very cheap processors could attain the requisite performance at a wee fraction of the cost of the first method just described. One must hark back to the fundamental premise though, which is that the computing power can be measured somewhat as the product of gate speed and gate quantity. In addition, it must be reiterated that machine costs for supercomputers are generally dominated by memory costs. Because each generation of supercomputing has led to concomitant demands for increased memory capacity, it is asserted that there can be no "cheap" solution to the acquisition of massive computational capability.

More "giddy guarantees" can be found in the world of technology than in architecture or design. The spendid promise of Josephson junction hyperspeed of the past several years always ignored the problems of manufacturability, input/output (I/O) interconnect, and maintenance methodologies. These aspects are critical to the commercial success of any machine, even the low-quantity varieties of supercomputers. Without commercial viability, few systems of such grand scale would be available to the broad range of consumers that makes up the coming generation. A similar caution must be heeded when examining the more probable technology families of high electron mobility transistor and gallium arsenide devices. As yet, they suffer from poor component densities and a lack of proven high-volume manufacturability.

Probable Achievements

The third plot (sustained rate) on the graph in Fig. 1 represents the expected level of actual sustained performance on major computational jobs. That is, each supercomputer is usually acquired on the basis of a need to solve one or a set of critical problems completely and/or as fast as possible. For that type of occupation, it is expected that supercomputers will, over time, be well "tuned" to take maximum advantage of the machine structure and design. This curve requires a bit of explanation, for it represents a time lag between when a particular computer power is delivered and when the system and applications software can bring the power to bear on the target computations. Obviously, this trace will be lower than the peak capability, and certainly it will rise more slowly than the theoretical hardware curve. In actual fact, what is presented in this chart is a smooth version of what one could see with a historical microscope. As one generation of supercomputer matures, the software begins to catch up to its architectural properties. At that moment, a new and different architecture emerges, with a consequently new software interface between man and machine. The new machines are sufficiently powerful to overcome the inevitable drop in performance percentage, and the cycle starts once again with the software catching up to the machine's potential.

The important notion in this curve is that real performance is achieved on actual production computations with the combination of hardware and software tools provided, and that these achievements can, at best, be well below that peak performance claimed in curve 2. The sustained rate curve not only has a slope that is shallower than that of curve 2, but it appears that it will approach a horizontal asymptote earlier than the peak rate curve. This implies that there could be a point of no real improvement in the computational situation within this century, without some unforeseen "breakthroughs" in methodology.

Real Expectations

To further confound the issue, yet one more curve (annualized average) has been included to indicate the actual utility of the system (as seen in effective megaflops delivered by the supercomputer, averaged over a year or more of experience). As expected, this curve illustrates a lower scale of expectations than curves 2 and 3. A major influence on the shape and height of this plot is the fact that few installations have the resources to adapt all problems in their facility effectively to new generations of supercomputers, one upon another. This adaption can take many forms: conversion, kernel optimization, language-based reconstruction, or wholesale algorithm redevelopment. In many cases, rethinking of physics, mathematics, and algorithms has yielded enormous improvements in computational solutions by reducing the number of gigaflops required, or by making it possible to bring to bear all the gigaflops possible on a given machine. In total, though, an installation performs many more tasks than the highly visible, budget-justifying, "stupendous" jobs that can justifiably be renovated and recoded to optimize computational speed. The degree to which onerous programming and debugging tasks are not improved in speed can seriously impact an installation's overall megaflop profile.

Because this curve is a function of its predecessor, it too will always have shallower and more level characteristics than the peak rate curve, and its potential to approach the "no appreciable" progress asymptote is thus considerably greater than that of its ancestors. The prospects for the future, if these curves are even remotely close to reality, could be tremendously gloomy, except for the existence of a growing number of multiprocessing computing systems and the very real possibility that applications and systems software development may be able to make some "quantum leap" in realizing performance in the next decade.

The utilization of multiprocessing systems to their maximum potential is seen by most forecasters as a difficult and long-term task. For that reason, the two curves representing the effects of software and algorithms do not grow as fast as many "great gigaflop" salespersons would hope to propound. Perhaps not until the next century will the computing industry have available truly general-purpose compilers and operating systems that can wring the best out of an array of high-performance processors.

A Final Note

The curves in Fig. 1 were introduced in this discussion to make some philosophical points. They seem to represent historical experience to a degree, and future projections are consistent with known technology and architectural trends. In spite of their spurious microscopical accuracy, they do present a message. The choice was to compare user demand for computational power with a mathematically projected line. A hypothetical "peak" demand curve was used so that the plotted traces would be reasonably spread out. This was derived from the sustained or "actual" computational requirements that are projected for a variety of industries and researchers. There are some potential supercomputer customers who will argue that this "peak" demand curve reflects the true sustained performance that they need to conduct their research and engineering projects in the next 15 years. In that case, the user demand curve must be compared against the sustained rate curve, if one wants to see the worst-case scenario confronting the supercomputer user of 1999. It can be argued that things are not now, and will not be, all that bad; but it must be remembered that the power represented here is on a logarithmic scale, and therefore, absolute growth in capability could appear to be worse in the future. Man's technology has been able to transcend similar stumbling blocks, and in the future, with the aid of sufficient computing power, a solution, a methodology, a new future for supercomputing will be realized.

References

1. "The Machine of the Year." *Time* (January 3, 1983):12.

2. "The Race to Build a Supercomputer." *Newsweek* (July 4, 1983):58.

3. "The Battle of the Supercomputer: Japan's All-Out Challenge to the U.S." *Business Week* (October 17, 1983):156.

4. Lax, P. D. "Report of the Panel on Large-Scale Computing in Science and Engineering." National Technical Information Service, Springfield, Virginia, order number DE83902818 (1982).

5. Decker, J. F. et al. "Report to The Federal Coordinating Council on Science, Engineering, and Technology Supercomputer Panel on Recommended Government Actions to Retain U.S. Leadership in Supercomputers," U.S. Department of Energy report (1983).

6. Decker, J. F. et al. "Report to The Federal Coordinating Council on Science, Engineering, and Technology Supercomputer Panel on Recommended Government Actions to Provide Access to Supercomputers." U.S. Department of Energy report (1983).

7. Worlton, W. J. "SIVA: A System Design for Vector Arithmetic." Los Alamos Scientific Laboratory report LADC 7890 (1965).

8. Carlson, B. G. "Some Suggestions and Requirements for a More Effective General-Purpose Computer." Los Alamos Scientific Laboratory internal document T-1-448 (July 14, 1965).

9. "Future Computer Requirements for Computational Aerodynamics." National Aeronautics and Space Administration report CP-2032 (1977).

4

Advanced Computer Projects

L. T. Davis
Cray Research, Inc.
Chippewa Falls, Wisconsin

Introduction

Thank you for this opportunity to speak at the "Frontiers of Supercomputing." Cray Research is a leader in the development and production of fast scientific computers and is committed to the continued development of the fastest scientific computers.

Cray Research's strategy is to design, *build*, and deliver very fast processors with very large memories, and to develop efficient software for the new design.

Overview

As background information, Figs. 1-7 indicate the installed Cray systems, the research and development expenditure level at Cray Research, and the performance levels of present and future systems.

Fig. 1 shows the cumulative installations. Foreign installations include the United Kingdom, West Germany, France, the Netherlands, and Japan. The 1983 figures will include eight X-MP systems. There is significant foreign demand for large scientific computers, as indicated by the foreign installed base. In Fig. 2, the research and development expenditures represent approximately 15 to 20% of revenue and do not include capital expenditures. Approximately $20 million in capital expenditures will be made over a 3-year period for integrated circuit (IC) development. In Fig. 3, the performance figures are based on FORTRAN code and reflect useful work performed vs simple performance tests.

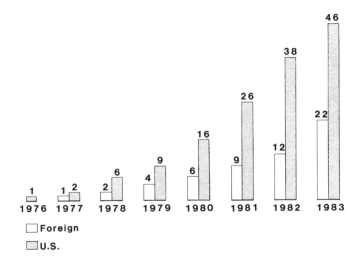

Fig. 1. Cumulative Cray system installations.

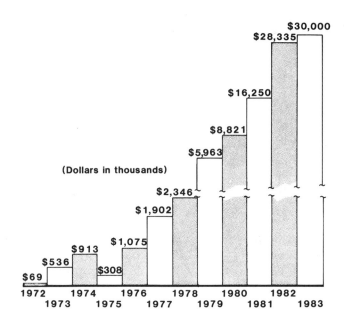

Fig. 2. Engineering and development expenditures.

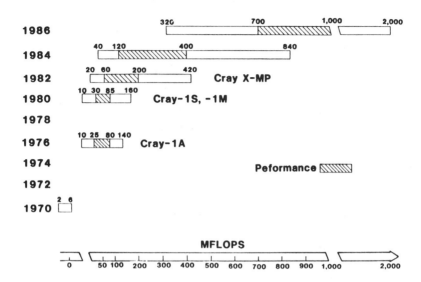

Fig. 3. Performance based on FORTRAN code.

- Multitasking is running on the X–MP.
- For two processors the speedup is 1.8–1.9 over one processor.
- Parallelism is at a high level – program modification is minimal.
- Multitasking overhead with the X-MP hardware/software is negligible.
- Multitasking has been demonstrated with PIC code, SPECTRAL code, and a seismic three-dimensional migration model.

Fig. 4. Multiprocessing performance.

— A particle-in-cell simulation program for electro/magneto static interaction between collisionless beams of plasma.

— Particle tracking and charge distribution accounts for 96% of the execution time of a model experiment involving 37,000 particles and 50 time steps.

— 1-CPU execution time = 22.5 seconds on an X–MP.

— By multitasking the tracking and charge distribution portion of the code, the execution time is reduced to 12.1 seconds.

— Actual 2–CPU speedup = 1.86 over 1–CPU.

Fig. 5. X-MP multiprocessing performance, PIC.

— This is a benchmark code for short-term weather forecast work with a global grid composed of 160 latitude by 192 longitude points and 200 time steps.

— Parallel processing is possible on the latitude level, i.e., the outermost loop inside each time step, which is 98% of the execution time.

— 1–CPU run time = 380.8 seconds on an X–MP.

— Actual 2–CPU speedup = 1.89 over 1–CPU.

Fig. 6. X-MP multiprocessing performance, SPECTRAL.

- This model handles 200 x 200 traces, with 1024 time samples each trace.

- For 1000 depth level, the number of floating point operations is 1.5×10^{12}. The total I/O performed is 40 billion words.

- 1—CPU run time 3.58 hours on X—MP.

- Actual 2—CPU speedup = 1.89 over 1—CPU.

Fig. 7. X-MP multiprocessing peformance, a new numeric seismic three-dimensional model.

Development Programs

There are two major development programs within Cray Research, the Cray-2 program and the X-MP program. Each has significant hardware and software development projects. The major goals within each program are improved system architecture, compiler and operating system development, and IC component development.

System Design

The demand for increased system performance will not be matched by improvements in component speeds in the coming years. As a result, system designers must resort to increased parallelism. Multiple processor systems with improved vector and scalar capability will be designed. The uncertainty is how many processors will be developed. Software development will be a key factor in determining this issue.

The availability of very high density memory chips—256,000 bits/chip and greater—although slower than desired, provides the system designer with a new and challenging tool. Memories that are orders of magnitude larger than today's will be possible. The design challenge in using the larger memory chips will be to avoid performance degradation of scalar-oriented codes.

Cray Research is currently delivering the Cray-1M, a uniprocessor system with 4 million words of main memory and 32 million words of fast secondary storage; and the Cray X-MP, a two-processor system with 4 million words of main memory and 32 million words of fast secondary storage. In development, the Cray-2 has four processors and up to 128 million words of memory. Demonstration is scheduled for late 1984. In the design phase, for demonstration in 1986, is an 8- to 16-processor system with memories of 500-1000 million words.

Software Development

Software development has unlimited challenge. Software design for systems with very large memories, multiple processors, and increased input/output (I/O) bandwidth and software design that is compatible, reliable, user-friendly, and economical will challenge our best software designers.

Cray's software development continues to grow in dollar expenditure and more ambitious software goals. Today Cray can demonstrate and deliver to customers efficient multiprocessor software that allows the two central processing units (CPUs) in the X-MP to operate on one job. Figures 4-7 illustrate our current limited but significant multiprocessor capability.

In 1984 Cray will demonstrate a four-processor system, and in 1986 an even larger multiprocessor system will be demonstrated. These are very ambitious goals, but the confidence gained in designing a compiler and operating system for the two-processor X-MP gives us hope that our goals can be realized. Loftier aims of many more processors in a system have been entertained. However, challenging but more realistic goals were chosen.

A significant improvement in system performance can be achieved with enhanced software. The development of new algorithms for compilers and multiprocessor operating systems is essential if increased system performance is to be realized. It is crucial for Cray to continue the interchange of software information with government labs in the Department of Energy (DOE) and the National Security Agency (NSA). These laboratories and other scientific users have been the dominant force driving the development of large scientific computers. Universities can play a more active role in the development of software for scientific problem solving. However, to do this, they need more tools and cooperation from industry. We hope Cray can help to improve this situation.

IC Component Development

To build the faster logic circuits and the larger memories required for new computers, significant IC development is required.

The choice of technologies for logic circuits, although not large, is difficult. Silicon is the current leading technology; production capability and capacity provide momentum for silicon. Improvements in large-scale IC speeds less than 500 ps and power reduction are extending the life span of silicon circuits. Gallium arsenide (GaAs), high electron mobility transistor (HEMT), and Josephson junction (JJ) all have potentially significant speed and power advantages over silicon. The production and reliability of circuits using the newer technologies are uncertain. Cray is investing substantial capital dollars in IC facilities and personnel to explore the silicon and the GaAs technologies. Joint development efforts have been negotiated with U.S. semiconductor suppliers to facilitate this technology exploration.

Development of large, fast memories is essential for the design and development of computers to solve very large scientific problems. The availability of fast bipolar memory circuits will continue to be important for main memory development. The rapid advances that have been made in metal oxide semiconductor (MOS) memory speed and density have provided computer designers with a powerful new design tool. Memory circuits with 256,000 bits allow the design of very fast secondary memories of 1/4-billion words and larger.

The lack of availability of state-of-the-art memory circuits from U.S. IC suppliers is the most serious problem Cray Research has in the development of new computers. It is a well-known fact that the Japanese have dominated the 64K MOS memory market and have the lead in the 256K MOS memory development. However, it is more disturbing to watch the advances the Japanese are making in the development of fast, large bipolar memory circuits and fast, large static MOS memory circuits. Since the introduction of the 1K bipolar memory chip in 1973 by U.S. IC suppliers, there has been a steady decline in U.S. IC suppliers' ability or desire to deliver newer memory circuits. Dependence on Japanese IC suppliers is not desirable; however, the alternative is to delay or cancel development projects. Unlike logic devices, the resources to build competitive memory circuits are beyond the reach of most companies. Current government-sponsored programs do not address the issue of fast memory circuits, and U.S. industry is lagging. Consequently, we face a serious dilemma. During the past 20 years there have been only two major U.S. semiconductor companies dedicating resources to the unique memory circuits required for the very fastest computers. If these resources or comparable U.S. resources are not available to us, we will be dependent upon Japanese suppliers and subject to their price and availability decisions.

Peripheral Equipment

Cray's immediate concern is the on-line disk used with the very large computing systems. The need for disk files with higher transfer rates, greater storage densities, and reliability improvements is well recognized. Cray has development programs that are addressing the disk file requirements. The achievement of the disk file development goals is impeded by the limited number of suppliers willing to undertake the development of high-performance equipment.

Summary

The task to retain leadership in supercomputers is significant but achievable. To do so, we must be able to sell our products in the market place within the same set of ground rules our foreign competitiors can. We cannot cope with import restrictions by foreign governments and export restrictions by our government.

We must have a favorable business climate to encourage capital expenditures for equipment that faces rapid obsolescence and to provide a favorable investment climate for high-technology companies. U.S. industry must compete at the production level, as well as the design level. System reliability is becoming an increasingly important requirement for successful large computing systems. U.S. production must match overseas competition in reliability and cost effectiveness.

The export of technology is not at the finished-product level but at the design level. The Japanese and others have open access to design information through conferences, U.S. graduate schools, and other U.S.

information exchanges, including vendor relations with our government agencies. There is no counterpart in Japan for U.S. companies.

Our segment of the industry is very delicate. Size and money do not in themselves produce results. The emphasis must be on technological development at the architectural, component, and software levels. The development of the fastest scientific computers has occurred during the past 20 years, not in a vacuum, but in cooperation with government labs and other scientific users. It is important that this relationship continue.

5

The Cyber 2XX Design Process

L. M. Thorndyke
Control Data Corporation
Minneapolis, Minnesota

Introduction

My subject today is the Cyber 2XX, the follow-on supercomputer to the Cyber 205. In my discussions about the Cyber 2XX, the data I am citing are objectives rather than specifications.

As with all supercomputer development projects, there are multiple areas of technological risk, and this one is no different. Instead of dwelling on details of the Cyber 2XX, it is my intent to provide you with insights, at least from my point of view, into the significant historical milestones of supercomputers. This will be followed by an examination of the requirements for the next generation, some potential solutions, some of the constraints imposed on the selection of the most appropriate solution, and the rationale we have used in reaching our key decisions. Finally, I will describe the Cyber 2XX in terms of the objectives that we believe can be achieved.

History

There are a lot of definitions given to supercomputers. The simplest, for my purposes today, is that a supercomputer is the fastest machine available at any point in time. That makes the definition transitory relative to any particular machine.

In the quest for higher performance, supercomputer designers must always be at the frontiers of the relevant technologies. Among them are components, packaging, architecture, engineering design tools and methodology, manufacturing processes, peripherals, and operating and maintenance software.

In the early days of computing, the improvement in components was the major factor in computer performance, particularly as the logic technology evolved from vacuum tubes to discrete components and then to integrated circuits. Similarly, memories moved from drums to cores and then to chips. These advances themselves certainly made significant contributions. Just so you won't be lulled into a sense of false confidence, it is interesting that the Control Data Corporation's CDC 7600 was designed over 15 years ago using transistors, and with its 27.5-ns clock, it is still a respectable processor today.

In my mind, supercomputers got their start at the Los Alamos National Laboratory with STRETCH. The 6600 was, in my opinion, also a true supercomputer. Not only was it basically fast, but it also implemented some major architectural improvements in areas of parallelism. Its derivative, the 7600, was very similar in design, offering refinements in parallel operations and an almost fourfold improvement in speed.

These machines and their predecessors operated almost exclusively in scalar mode. The next major step was incorporation of vector processing into the supercomputer. This is where we are today, with systems that can operate at peak rates exceeding 100 megaflops for properly structured problems. The Cyber 200 models, the Cray offerings, and the new Japanese systems all fall into this area.

Statement of Problem

As we, the designers and builders of supercomputers, look to advance the frontiers, we first have to decide on the problems we need to address. The first of these is performance. In meetings in Washington with the Department of Energy and the National Aeronautics and Space Administration, we received input that these agencies, which represent major government users, are looking for two orders of magnitude improvement in performance in the next generation. To put things in perspective, we have rarely seen one order of magnitude of system improvement as we move from generation to generation.

In addition to performance as measured by megaflops, we designers must more adequately address parameters such as reliability, availability, and maintainability—or RAM. From the vendor point of view, we are experiencing strong pressures from users via their contracting officers to guarantee ever higher levels of availability. We are fully cognizant of the need for improvements in this area, but I have to point out that this complicates the tradeoffs with performance.

I think we all recognize that there are inadequacies and deficiencies in the current software that must be remedied to take advantage of the new hardware. At the same time that we make improvements in hardware, it is also incumbent upon us to recognize that even greater investments are required in the software. We are just now learning how to realize the potential of vector processing.

The most difficult financial problem a vendor faces is derived from the limited market that exists for supercomputers. There are today something fewer than 100 supercomputers installed, and even the most optimistic forecasts keep the base below 1000. Every supercomputer sale is a sizable effort, and not all efforts are successful. The way a normal U.S. business enterprise works tends to militate against supercomputer projects because of the need to show favorable financial results in relatively short time. Clearly, with a limited market and long development cycles, supercomputers do not appeal to the typical "bean counter." To pursue the supercomputer market really requires entrepreneurial champions of supercomputers that convince the "bean counters" and the financial community that the rewards are worth the risk.

The limited market leads to financial risks. We also have major technological risks. It is extremely difficult, if not impossible, to apply proven technology successfully to products that are supposed to advance the state of the art. To achieve supercomputer goals, one must take risks in circuits, packaging, peripherals, design tools, process tooling, etc., to advance the machine on all fronts simultaneously to attain a balanced system.

Potential Solutions

There is a wide range of potential solutions to the kinds of requirements that I have just described, and I shall treat them in order. In a given situation, one is constrained in the selection of suitable options. As I proceed through the choices, I will discard those that violate the constraints.

In supercomputers, sheer speed is the dominating consideration. In trying to improve the speed, one can use several methods. Generally, a speedup in the circuits will be reflected in the speed of the processor, although not necessarily in a linear way. As we have surveyed the available circuits technology, a twofold improvement over the ECL circuits used in the Cyber 205 appears to be the state of the art in switching speeds. Clearly, this alone cannot meet our goals, so we must look for improvements in other areas.

One can consider modifications to existing architectures or even a totally new architecture. The major constraint on a radical departure from an existing one is the compatibility issue affecting both the vendor and the user. I am sure that you have had some experience with what compatibility and incompatibility cost the user. On the vendor's side, the costs of redeveloping software strongly deter severe departures from existing architectures. On the other hand, one can certainly entertain architectural modifications that allow a system to evolve over time while maintaining strong threads of compatibility. The sequence of the CDC 6000, Cyber 70, Cyber 170, and the new 170/800 models is a relevant example of a long-running architectural evolution.

One approach to increasing performance is to replicate the entire processor and develop a multiprocessor system. There are two crucial issues here. The first is the development of software that can work effectively in a multiprocessing environment. Time does not permit me to explore this issue any further. The second is a technology issue that deals with the need to develop physically small processors so that they can communicate effectively with each other and their memories in a high-performance system.

The RAM area deserves an entire session by itself. I am going to touch on only a few of the highlights. Redundancy at the circuit level can improve reliability, but this increases the manufacturing costs sharply, raises the parts count, and in my mind, results in a dubious tradeoff. A multiprocessor environment can provide a level of redundancy under the right set of conditions, albeit at a reduced level, if we can solve the software problems.

One can improve the RAM as seen by the user by being more tolerant of system errors. Memory SECDED is a good hardware example of error tolerance and transparency to the user. Obviously, we must make many more improvements of this type. As circuit densities increase, the opportunity to utilize part of the circuit for self-checking and self-diagnosis is one that we will capitalize on.

The user requirements for software features are certainly worthy of extended discussion. I will leave this issue to others, but I will offer the comment that it is more productive to enhance an existing base of software than to go through an entirely new development. Not only the expense but, more important, the allocation of scarce programming resources and schedule impacts persuasively argues against reinvention of the wheel.

The problem posed by a limited market cannot be solved by a single company nor by any group of companies. However, one thing that can be done is to develop software technology to make supercomputers easier to use, more efficient, and applicable to a wider range of applications. This would help expand the market to less sophisticated users. We also need to get more user involvement, particularly from the government, in the early development phases when funding is so critical.

Before I get into a description of the Cyber 2XX, it is necessary to provide explanations for the rationale in choosing the technology paths we are pursuing for the new machine.

The first decision we had to make in the design process was the architecture of the new machine. From its name, Cyber 2XX, it is easy to deduce that it is a member of the Cyber 200 family. It was, in fact, a straightforward decision to make the new system upward compatible with Cyber 205. This decision was heavily driven by software compatibility and the importance of that to RAM, the users, and schedules. Another important factor was the virtual memory feature of the Cyber 200 that provides a flexible and expansible memory structure.

Because it became obvious very quickly that we could not achieve the performance goals we had set simply from progress in electronic circuit technology, we have decided the Cyber 2XX will utilize multiple processors to increase performance. This has the significant additional benefit of improving the availability.

For the first time, supercomputer designers have a selection of circuit technologies to choose from. I cannot emphasize strongly enough the impact that this choice has upon the designer and the system itself. There is no single correct choice for all design situations. Only history will tell us whether the choice made by a particular designer was appropriate.

In addition to the traditional silicon semiconductor technologies, we have examined Josephson junction and gallium arsenide as technology candidates for the Cyber 2XX. The last two were rejected in favor of a very dense silicon technology that exhibits favorable operating characteristics over a wide range of conditions. Silicon technology is highly favored because it is a mainstream technology that enjoys broad semiconductor vendor support.

Increasing the circuit density (or degree of integration) offers many significant benefits to a designer. First, it reduces the parts count. This not only aids in reduction of the size of the system but also increases the reliability. As circuit density increases and parts count goes down, the distances separating the functional units decrease. This serves to increase the speed of the system and contributes to a reduction in the physical size of the machine. All these factors lead to improved packaging, lower cost, and higher reliability.

Description of the Cyber 2XX

I now want to describe the Cyber 2XX in terms of the general objectives we have established.

First, the Cyber 2XX will be upward compatible with the Cyber 205, with some new features added to support multiprocessing configurations. The compatibility will facilitate the migration of installed Cyber 200 customers to this new machine. The VSOS operating system used on the Cyber 2XX will support all of the Cyber 205 VSOS user interfaces. In addition, we will augment the VSOS interface with an industry standard transportable user environment such as UNIX.

Once the key attribute of Cyber 205 compatibility was established, many of the remaining technical attributes were defined. For those of you not familiar with the Cyber 200, some key characteristics are worthy of mention. The data structures include both 32- and 64-bit floating-point formats. The 32-bit values are stored two per word and processed at twice the rate of 64-bit numbers in the vector pipelines. As I mentioned earlier, the system uses a virtual memory structure with 48-bit addressing that encompasses an address space that is clearly adequate for the rest of this century. The Cyber 200 central processing unit (CPU) contains a scalar processor, which is a complete computer in its own right, and a vector processor with multiple pipelines.

The Cyber 2XX will be a multiprocessor configuration with two to eight identical processors. Each processor will offer three to five times the performance of the Cyber 205. The single processor is capable of reaching speeds of 1.6 gigaflops using 32-bit formats or peak rates of 3.2 gigaflops for the minimum dual processor configuration. The peak performance rate in a 64-bit mode for a maximum system configuration will be in excess of 12 gigaflops, with a sustained rate of 5 gigaflops on vectorized codes.

Each processor has a scalar unit and a vector unit that operate concurrently with input/output (I/O) operations. The performance target for scalar operations is an instruction issue time of 5 ns, yielding a

200-mips peak-scalar rate. The vector processor will contain two vector pipelines with an aggregate peak rate of 1600 megaflops running 32-bit vector/scalar triad operations, with 64-bit triad operations running at half that rate.

A hierarchy of memories will be configured on the Cyber 2XX. Each processor will have a dedicated high-speed local memory of 4 million words with 102-gigabits/second bandwidth. The local memories will interface to a shared main memory that ranges in capacity from 32 to 256 million words. The memories will be interconnected for interprocessor communications via a special link. All memories will use SECDED for reliability.

The I/O structure of the Cyber 2XX will be very similar to that of the Cyber 205. However, the total bandwidth available for I/O will be doubled by increasing the number of I/O ports from 16 to 32. The I/O interfaces for the Cyber 2XX will be compatible with the Cyber 205, allowing connection of the loosely coupled network used for Cyber 205 I/O, as well as directly attached devices.

I want to conclude my remarks by summarizing the key attributes of the Cyber 2XX. First, it is upward compatible with the Cyber 205 but has new performance and maintainability features that make it a significant technology advance. Second, it will offer a performance improvement over the Cyber 205 ranging from 5 to 50 times; this, of course, depends upon configurations of CPUs and types of problems addressed. Third, it will use dense silicon circuits as the base technology. Fourth, it will achieve a significant size and power reduction and excellent availability characteristics through the use of dense silicon technology.

I do not want to leave you with the impression that we are not interested or concerned about the competition from Japan; indeed we are, and the Cyber 2XX system will help our country retain the leadership in supercomputers.

6

Latency and the Heterogeneous Element Processor (HEP)

B. J. Smith
Denelcor, Incorporated
Aurora, Colorado

Introduction

The Heterogeneous Element Processor (HEP) parallel computer system[1,2] is able to overcome most of the undesirable effects of latency by pipelining without the usual consequences. For example, a vector-pipelined architecture must have a short pipeline (low latency) to have good performance on short vectors, but the HEP achieves excellent performance even on scalar codes using a typical data memory pipeline length of about 20 instruction segments. To cite another example, the register operation pipeline in HEP is eight segments long, significantly longer than most of the pipelines in a Cray-1, but the HEP closely approaches its peak processing rate on a much broader class of problems than just those considered "vectorizable."[3,4]

The reasons for HEP's latency tolerance may be found in a few unusual features of the HEP architecture, one of which seems contradictory: the HEP has very low latency process synchronization and communication facilities compared with other multiple instruction/multiple data (MIMD) machines. The HEP is closer architecturally to data-flow computers than to conventional MIMD computers in the way it exploits relatively high-latency instruction execution.

Latency and Pipelining

One way to explain why latency is so harmful in single-instruction-stream (SI) computers is to say that dependencies in the programs prevent sufficient concurrency to keep the processor busy. Unfortunately, many of the dependencies in typical SI programs result from the need to transform the algorithm into SI-executable form and not from data dependencies present in the algorithm. While an SI computer may have fully pipelined or parallel functional units and plenty of registers to avoid dependencies due to conflicts for those resources, the single program counter is an unavoidable bottleneck. The dependencies resulting from the program counter include not just the traditional conditional branch problems, but a broader class of dependencies that result merely from the fact that the SI model of computation requires that any side effect of an instruction must be able to affect subsequent instructions. Perhaps the most important and obvious dependency of this kind might be called the memory dependency: data writes and reads at a given memory location must occur in the order issued.

When vector instructions are incorporated in an SI architecture, the effects of latency can be reduced to some extent through the use of pipelining. It is not an accident that the two most highly successful vector architectures, the Cray-1 and the Cyber 205, use pipelined rather than parallel processing elements to accomplish vector operations. Pipelined vector SI computers partially solve the latency problems caused by memory dependencies; this is primarily because the components of the vectors are loaded and stored at disjoint memory locations. Unfortunately, the presence of short vector and scalar operations in an algorithm reduces the effectiveness of pipelining as a way of concealing latency effects. In addition, the larger the memory of such a computer becomes, the longer the pipelines must be to access it and the worse the performance becomes on short vectors.

In a multiple-instruction-stream (MI) computer, latency effects due to memory dependencies still exist but are for the most part only local to a particular instruction stream. In a sense, the memory dependency situation for MI computers is very similar to that for vector SI computers; as long as the memory locations are disjoint, there are no memory dependencies between instruction streams any more than there are between components of a vector. This property allows the memory references of the HEP system, a scalar MI computer, to be pipelined in the same way that the components of a vector are pipelined.

It is also possible to dynamically vary the number of instruction streams in a pipelined MI design like HEP, just as one can easily vary the lengths of vectors in a pipelined vector SI computer. The effects are analogous. The more instruction streams (the longer the vectors), the more latency can be hidden and, therefore, the longer the pipeline can be. Unlike the pipelined vector SI case, however, the applicability and usefulness of pipelined MI parallelism is not directly determined by vector length but by another factor applicable to MI computers generally, namely, how many instructions a stream can execute before it must communicate with another stream. Put another way, the key performance-limiting factor for MI computers is this: How much performance is lost implementing interstream memory dependencies?

Interstream Dependencies

Ideally, the only MI interstream memory dependencies that should occur in a program correspond to data dependencies present in the original algorithm. Memory organization and size constraints, programmer decisions, compiler implementation decisions, and other factors typically add additional memory dependencies, but these will be ignored; we will assume that all memory dependencies are due to data dependencies. The implementation of an algorithm on MI hardware requires the (usually heuristic) scheduling of the algorithm on the instruction streams available. If the number of instruction streams is variable, this may be exploited to improve the schedule. The scheduling may be accomplished by a compiler, by the programmer, or by a combination of the two; however, the objective is obviously to reduce the total execution time of the program. If the parallelism available in the computer is sufficiently high, there will be an optimum number of instruction streams for that algorithm on that computer, and attempts to further increase speed through parallelism will be more than offset by the increased cost of implementing the additional interstream data dependencies.

There are two kinds of prices that may be paid when exchanging an intrastream for an interstream data dependency: increased latency and reduced parallelism. The increased latency price is paid in proportion to the required number of additional instructions needed by either the sending or the receiving instruction stream (this overhead also has the effect of reducing parallelism slightly), and in proportion to any pure (pipelined) delay between one instruction stream and another for either communication or synchronization. The reduced parallelism price is paid especially when a critical section is employed either to manage a scarce resource used in the implementation of the data dependencies (for example, the ability to interrupt another processor) or to actually implement the dependencies, but in a naive way (for example, controlling all acceses to mesh points in an iterative algorithm with a single monitor).

The effect of increased latency is not to directly increase the execution time of every algorithm, but to restrict the amount of parallelism that can be obtained on some algorithms before waiting (and, therefore, reduced parallelism) occurs. For example, an interstream data dependency implementation having a sufficiently high bandwidth, but a latency of several hundred instruction times, is not particularly suitable for the execution of parallel back substitution against a small upper triangular matrix; the net effect would be manifested as reduced parallelism simply because the data dependency graph of the back substitution algorithm exhibits high connectivity. However, high latency would not dramatically influence the degree of parallelism that could be obtained for a time-independent, complex geometry Monte Carlo simulation whose data dependency graph resembles a number of simple chains joined at their terminal ends. To summarize, the effect of high latency for interstream data dependencies in an MI computer architecture is only to restrict its applicability to a narrow class of algorithms.

Reduced parallelism, unlike increased latency, has an undesirable effect on the execution rate of essentially all algorithms, and an architecture that must significantly reduce parallelism to implement each interstream data dependency is really not much of an MI computer. One probably should use its instruction streams to run independent user programs rather than try to use it as a parallel processor.

The way in which the HEP implements interstream data dependencies is by using a distributed shared memory equipped with a "full/empty" bit at each memory word. This bit can be used to enforce alternation of reads and writes, among other things. Unlike most schemes, there is no overhead whatsoever for single-producer, single-consumer interstream dependencies. The latency is quite low—just two instruction times (one load plus one store)—and the only reduction in parallelism that occurs is due to memory bank conflicts. Given these properties, one would anticipate that the HEP is effective on a very broad class of algorithms, and this has indeed proved to be true. It is usually not a good idea to create and destroy HEP processes to enforce the synchronization of an interstream dependency, but rather to let the processes that are busy wait for "full" or "empty." Even though the additional overhead required to destroy and then recreate a process can be quite small, the condition in which there is no actual waiting for "full" or "empty" occurs so often in reasonably well-designed programs that a net reduction in performance will usually result if a "fork/join" approach is taken.

Conclusions

The use of pipelining to avoid the undesirable effects of latency is possible in MIMD as well as in data-flow computers. To accomplish this, sufficient parallelism is necessary; the key ingredient required to achieve this parallelism is an effective and economical way of implementing interstream dependencies. The HEP system is a good example of how this can be done.

References

1. Grit, D. H., and McGraw, J. R. "Programming Divide and Conquer on a Multiprocessor." Lawrence Livermore National Laboratory report UCRL-88710 (May 12, 1983).

2. Jordan, H. F. "Performance Measurements on HEP—A Pipelined MIMD Computer." *Conference Proceedings: The 10th Annual International Symposium on Computer Architecture,* IEEE Computer Society Press (1983).

3. Smith, B. J. "A Pipelined, Shared Memory MIMD Computer." *Proceedings of the 1978 International Conference on Parallel Processing,* IEEE Computer Society, Association for Computing Machinery and Wayne State University (1978):6-8.

4. Smith, B. J. "Architecture and Applications of the HEP Multiprocessor Computer System." *Proceedings of the Society of Photo-Optical Instrumentation Engineers* **298**, edited by T. F. Tao, 241-248. Bellingham, Washington: Society of Optical Engineering, 1981.

7

Japanese Supercomputer Initiatives: Challenge and Response*

W. J. Worlton
Los Alamos National Laboratory
Los Alamos, New Mexico

Introduction

A Lesson from the Greeks

In 331 B.C., a Greek army led by Alexander the Great met a Persian army led by Darius the Third in a battle at a place called Gaugemela. Although the Persian army outnumbered the Greek army by five to one, the Greeks won an overwhelming victory and drove the Persians from the battlefield with great losses.[1]

The relevance of this to the subject of this conference is that the Japanese have adopted as a stategy in world trade the military tactic used by Alexander the Great in winning the battle of Gaugemela. It is a tactic based on what is called "the principle of local superiority." For what Alexander did was to mass a very large force of his troops on his right wing and, before the Persians could react, he attacked a numerically inferior force on the Persian left. Because Alexander had numerical superiority in that local area, he was able to penetrate their line, attack them from both front and rear, and cause great panic and a general retreat.

Similarly, the Japanese face a numerically superior competitor in the United States. Their land mass would fit nicely into the state of Montana; their population and their gross national product are both about half as large as that of the United States; and their computing industry is about a factor of 7 smaller than that of the United States. But they have targeted a particular portion of the computing industry—the

---

*This work was performed under the auspices of the U.S. Department of Energy.

supercomputer area—and brought to bear more resources than the American supercomputer vendors have available. This, then, is a classical example of the application of the principle of local superiority. Japan has formed the Superspeed Computer Research Association (SCRA), which consists of their six largest computer companies [Fujitsu, Hitachi, Nippon Electric Corporation (NEC), Mitsubishi, Oki Electric, and Toshiba] and the Electro-Technical Laboratory (a national laboratory). Furthermore, the Ministry of International Trade and Industry (MITI) has provided $100 million for this project.

If Japan were competing with the full American computer industry, it would be facing numerically superior resources. However, in this project the Japanese are competing with only the supercomputer portion of the American computer industry; the computing revenues of the six Japanese companies are a factor of 2 larger than that of the American supercomputer companies, and the total revenues of these Japanese companies are a factor of 8 larger than the revenues of the American companies. If we include the contributions of Electro-Technical Laboratory (ETL) and MITI, then there are approximately an order of magnitude more resources available to the Japanese competitors than those available to the American supercomputer companies. (Note: Since the formation of ETA Systems, Control Data Corporation is no longer a supercomputer competitor; hence, the disparity is even greater than indicated above because most of the American revenue in the above comparison came from Control Data.)

Professor Richard Hamming wrote a paper years ago on order-of-magnitude effects in computing, and he pointed out that when a fundamental parameter of a technology or of a system changes by an order of magnitude or more, then not only quantitative effects but also unexpected qualitative effects often occur. So the order of magnitude more resources that are available to the Japanese companies might have qualitative effects on this competition. For example, Hitachi, NEC, and Fujitsu are ranked number three, number four, and number eight, respectively, in semiconductor sales in the world. Thus, the Japanese supercomputer companies are vertically integrated and the American supercomputer companies are not; this may allow the Japanese companies to more rapidly develop the new high-speed components needed for supercomputers, and thereby bring out new generations of supercomputers more quickly than the American companies. American companies can counteract this advantage, but they will have to take new initiatives in semiconductor development to do so.

Understanding Japan as a Competitor

There have been many explanations for Japan's success in rebuilding their economy from a state of utter prostration after the Second World War to where it is now the third largest in the world, following only after the United States and the Soviet Union. There is a whole literature explaining Japan's success, and it behooves those concerned with supercomputing to understand some of these driving forces. Some popular explanations are half myth and half truth.

Management consultants have written extensively on the management style of the Japanese as a major contributing factor for Japan's success, and indeed there are many well-run Japanese firms. But there are also poorly run Japanese firms; there are some 18 000 business failures in Japan each year. Management techniques—such as consensus decision making, management-labor consultation, and the use of quality circles—no doubt contribute, but these alone do not account for all of Japan's successes. The most important management strategy used by successful Japanese firms is "quality first."

Japan's "three sacred treasures" are sometimes cited as explanations of Japan's economic success: lifetime employment; the "nenko" reward system, which is based on length of service rather than on merit; and enterprise unionism (a union serves the employees of only a single company).[2] But each of these has some element of myth in it. For example, lifetime employment applies to only 25 to 30% of the Japanese work force, and even in the large companies, where it does apply, the employees are required to retire at age 55 to 60. The Japanese retirees do not have enough money to live on at that age, and they have to take jobs at a much lower pay rate. So, although there are some influences from the three treasures, these are probably not decisive.

The term "Japan, Incorporated" or "Japan, Inc." is often used to explain Japan's successes. This refers to the collaboration between government and industry, the role of MITI, and the government support of national projects. This indeed has had a strong influence in the past, but the role of MITI has been changing in important ways from the 1950s to the present time, and it is now much less influential than it has been in the past. However, MITI still plays the role of "harmonizer" for Japanese industry.[3] You can read in the literature that "Japan, Inc." no longer exists,[4,5] but that's inaccurate. "Japan, Inc." does exist, although it has changed its targets from the basic industries that were supported soon after World War II to increasingly sophisticated industries such as supercomputing and the fifth-generation computers. The government of

Japan does not directly manage industry, but through national projects and funding support it still has a major influence on the development of the Japanese economy in general and supercomputers in particular. This is not to say that government/industry collaboration exists in Japan and not in the United States or other nations; all nations, including the United States, support their industries in many ways. What is different about the Japanese style is that it is not just a hodge-podge of historical pork-barrel policies typical of most other nations, but is the result of a systematic attempt to "rationalize" Japanese industry by phasing out declining and noncompetitive industries and supporting those that have high growth potential.[6]

Another reason often cited for the economic success of Japan is the free ride Japan has been getting in a number of areas. In the military area, for example, Japan spends only about 1% of its gross national product on defense.[7] The Western European nations spend 3 to 5%, the U.S. spends 6 to 7%, and the Soviet Union spends over 10%. If you integrate American and Japanese defense expenditures over the past 20 years, you find that the U.S. has spent about a trillion dollars more on defense than has Japan. For foreign aid and defense, the U.S. spends about $800 for every man, woman, and child in our country, whereas Japan spends only about $135. By avoiding large defense expenditures, Japan has been able to avoid high taxes on their individuals and industry; corporations can invest these funds, which would otherwise go to taxes, in plans and equipment to achieve higher productivity.

Japan has been given a free ride by its people by delaying social investments, such as highways, housing, sewers, and social security. For example, Japan has not had to invest as much in social security as other nations because the Japanese population is, relatively speaking, younger: there are fewer people over the age of 65 in Japan than in any other major industrial nation.[8] However, that's changing quite rapidly. The average lifetime of a person in Japan is about 3 years longer than it is in other major nations, so the Japanese population over 65 is growing very rapidly. In the future—say, by the 1990s—Japan will be spending more for social security than will other nations.

Japan has been getting a free ride on the technology of other nations. It has been estimated that since the Second World War, Japan has invested only about $9 billion in buying foreign technology, and that includes investments in technology for steel, automobiles, textiles, machine tools, and electronics. That has been one of history's greatest bargains. However, this is changing in important ways. Japan's goal was to quickly catch up with the Western nations, and they have done that now; they will have to get off the technological trails blazed by other people and do some bushwacking on their own. Technology development will be more expensive for Japan than technology acquisition has been in the past, not only in terms of money, but in terms of time and manpower.

Finally, there are strong ethnic reasons for Japan's successes. They have probably the world's strongest work ethic; they believe strongly in will power, and they have a penchant for group action in the national interest. And most important of all, the Japanese believe devoutly in education. The growth of the educational level of their people since the Second World War has been nothing short of spectacular. In 1950, 86% of Japan's population had only middle school education, 14% had a high school education, and Japan's pool of university level personnel was less than 1% of their population. Today the figures are dramatically different: only 6% have only middle school training, 55% have a high school education, and 39% have university level education.[9] Perhaps all other explanations for Japan's success pale in significance compared to this dramatic change.

Some Historical Perspectives

No subject can be properly understood apart from its history; however, a full treatment of that subject is beyond the scope of this paper, so I will mention only a few highlights. In 1957 the Japanese Diet (legislature) passed the Electronic Industries Act; that act provided financial assistance to computer and electronics manufacturers through subsidies and loans of various kinds.[10] They developed a very innovative kind of loan called a "conditional loan." A conditional loan works in the following way: the government and an industry agree that a project should be undertaken in the national interest, but the project may have a greater risk than the commercial firms are willing to accept. The government then provides industry with a loan that has to be repaid only if the project leads to commercially viable products; then the profits are used to repay the loan. If there are no profits, the loan does not have to be repaid. This is a way for the government and industry to share the risks of innovative projects.

Another provision of the Electronic Industries Act was to give MITI the authority to selectively exempt firms in their computing and electronics industries from antitrust action. The United States Congress is now reviewing the American antitrust laws that were written in very different environments from the modern environment of international competition, but Japan has been operating in a very liberal antitrust environment for more than 25 years.

The success of these policies can be seen by the trend in the early production of Japanese computers. In 1960, they had essentially no electronic computer industry at all. They restricted imports even though they needed computers because they were waiting for their domestic production to meet these needs. Japan's computing industry began growing rapidly in the 1960s and 1970s; by the early 1970s they were making over a thousand computers a year. Imports were still growing, but at a much lower rate—only about a third of the rate of the domestic production—and they had already begun exporting computers.

In 1964, International Business Machines (IBM) announced the System 360. This caused consternation both in the Japanese government and in industry because they realized they were never going to be able to sucessfully compete as individual companies against a company as powerful as IBM. To meet this powerful competition, Japan formed a collaborative high-speed computer project that set a pattern that has been followed for other national projects. The participants in the earlier project and in the supercomputer project are the same, except Fujitsu has been added for the current project. The ETL has led both projects; the government contributed $35 million to the earlier project and $100 million to the current one. The deliverable system from the earlier project was the Hitac 8800, which competed with the IBM 370-165.

In 1970, IBM announced the System 370, and in response Japan formed another national project. They referred to the IBM 370 as a "3.50-generation computer," and Japan wanted to have something better, so they planned to develop a "3.75-generation computer." MITI orchestrated three marriages: between Fujitsu and Hitachi, between NEC and Toshiba, and between Mitsubishi and Oki. The Fujitsu-Hitachi marriage didn't work out very well—these companies essentially got a divorce. They were supposed to develop a single computer line, the M-series of computers, but Fujitsu and Hitachi are vicious competitors, and they developed their own versions of the M-series of computers, rather than the unified series envisioned by MITI. This is but one of many examples that makes it clear that MITI works more by persuasion and informal agreements than by legal or formal authority.

In 1976 Japan initiated the very large-scale integration (VLSI) project, which is very instructive of Japanese industrial policy methods.[11] In one sense, you can say that project utterly failed, because it missed its goal of the development of a dynamic RAM chip with a capacity of one million bits by a factor of 16 (Ref. 3). But in the process, Japan became the world leaders in the 64K chip market, and they now have 70% of that market. This illustrates their methodology in these national projects. They have what they call a MITI vision: they pick an objective far ahead of the state-of-the-art, and they let that vision drive them and focus their energies to achieve as much as is possible. But they don't want to be constrained by some near-term objective. A lot of people have taken the fifth-generation project as being too visionary and impractical. But the merits of having a strong vision are illustrated by the success of Japan's VLSI project.

Summary

Trends in Japanese industrial policies include the following. MITI was formed in 1949 and during the 1950s it provided guidance, protection, and financial assistance for industry in general and the computing industry in particular. It is in this period of time that the term "Japan, Incorporated" is most relevant. Japan continues their industrial policies of antitrust exemption, government subsidies, special loans, national projects, and MITI guidance, although at a lower level than in previous decades. One of Japan's current goals is to increase their investment in research and development from about 2.5 to 3% of their gross national product. If Japan is able to follow through on this, they will be the nation with the highest percent of their gross national product invested in research and development.

Japan's Strategic Plan for Supercomputing

Now let me describe Japan's plans for supercomputers in the format of a strategic plan. I don't mean to imply that they actually have a formal strategic plan that covers everything I'll discuss, but I will use the usual outline of a strategic planning exercise to explain the Japanese initiatives.

Mission Statement

Their mission appears to be to become the world leader in supercomputer technology, marketing, and applications. They are evidently interested in the technology because there is quite often fallout from this high-performance technology down to other product lines that have larger markets. They are interested in marketing, both in Japan itself and in other nations. There are various estimates of how many supercomputers Japan itself will need during the 1980s, ranging from 30 to 100. One hundred of this class of machines would cost approximately a billion dollars, so just the Japanese market alone drives them to undertake the development of supercomputers to avoid importing on such a large scale. Various Japanese commentators have expressed the opinion that the supercomputer market will expand, and they hope to share in that market. Japan is also intensely interested in supercomputer applications. Even if the supercomputer market turns out to be not very large, Japan will still gain from their supercomputer initiatives because supercomputers are the key technology to becoming a world leader in other areas. In 1981 a meeting on supercomputer applications was held, and the journal *Joho Shori* published the list of subjects they discussed. Nine lectures were given on the following topics:

1. Atomic energy
2. Aerospace engineering
3. Meteorology
4. Seismic exploration for underground resources
5. Structural analysis
6. Electrical power problems
7. Image analysis
8. Molecular science
9. VLSI design.

It is in these areas that the Japanese hope to use supercomputers to strengthen their economy.

Situation Audit

Another requirement of strategic planning is a situation audit to assess strengths, weaknesses, and opportunities.

Strengths

One of Japan's strengths as a supercomputer competitor is their semiconductor industry, and especially the fact that it has a vertically integrated capability for their supercomputer manufacturers. Hitachi, NEC, and Fujitsu are not just supercomputer manufacturers; rather, they are world-class semiconductor manufacturers who have also become interested in supercomputers. These companies don't have the problem that has been described by American supercomputer vendors: having to go hat-in-hand to other companies such as Motorola and Fairchild and ask them to build some high-performance circuits, and then wait many months for each turnaround. The Japanese companies can more readily control the pace at which this happens than can their American competitors, and that is a very great strength.

Another strength is the fact that Fujitsu and Hitachi are developing IBM-compatible supercomputers. Let me try to evaluate the impact of that on the supercomputer market. The impact here will be not only on the supercomputer market but on the high-end computer market as well—where by "high-end" computers I mean computers such as the IBM 308X and the Amdahl 580 series, computers that are very fast but not quite as fast as the supercomputers. For more than a decade, there have been no IBM-compatible supercomputers, so the customers doing scientific or engineering calculations have had to choose between buying IBM- or non-IBM-compatible high-end computers or non-IBM-compatible supercomputers. But there has been no option of buying an IBM-compatible supercomputer—that has been a marketing vacuum. However, the Japanese are about to fill that vacuum. The effect of these new marketing initiatives is shown in the eight-way classification in Fig. 1. Fujitsu and Hitachi will both be offering IBM-compatible supercomputers in late 1983. It seems to me this threatens not only the supercomputer market but the high-end market as well. The high-end computers are reportedly about a $20 billion market, and 15 to 20% of these computers are used for science and engineering applications. So you might think of the high-end IBM-compatible market as being about a $3 billion to $4 billion market. The customers who have acquired high-end computers for scientific and engineering applications have done so because they wanted access to a $200 billion base of IBM-compatible software. They have chosen the software-rich but moderate-speed high-end computers over the software-poor but higher speed supercomputers. Customers will no longer have to make that choice once Japan begins deliveries of the Fujitsu VP and the Hitachi S810 computers. Customers can have software richness and high speed at the same time. So this Japanese initiative especially threatens the $4 billion science and engineering portion of the high-end market, and even giant IBM can't ignore that kind of a threat. It also threatens the non-IBM-compatible supercomputer market because some of the expansion in this market may be diverted into IBM-compatible sales.

What responses are appropriate to this marketing threat? First, IBM, Amdahl, and Trilogy—the American firms that make IBM-compatible

TYPE	IBM COMPATIBLE	NON-IBM-COMPATIBLE		
HIGH-END COMPUTERS	IBM 308X AMDAHL 580	CDC CYBER 180 UNIVAC 1100/90		USA
	FUJITSU M380 HITACHI M280H	NEC ACOS 1000	J A P A N	
SUPERCOMPUTERS	FUJITSU VP HITACHI S810	NEC SX-2		
	(NONE)	CDC CYBER 205 CRI CRAY X-MP DENELCOR HEP		USA

Fig. 1. IBM compatibility and supercomputers.

high-end computers—must offer faster products for the high-end market, as well as products for the supercomputer market, or they will be viewed as having an incomplete product line.

Second, how do the traditional supercomputer vendors—the non-IBM-compatible vendors—respond? In two ways. First, they must respond the same way as NEC is planning to do—by offering a machine that is faster than the Fujitsu and Hitachi machines. The NEC machine (the SX-2) is about twice as fast as the Fujitsu and the Hitachi supercomputers, and the American supercomputer firms must offer supercomputers that are a factor of 2 or 4 faster than the IBM-compatible Japanese supercomputers. A factor of 2 is, in my mind, marginal. The other thing that the American firms must do is to enrich their software environment to minimize the advantage of the IBM-compatible offerings. Finally, the American firms could offer systems with an IBM-compatible front end.

Weaknesses

The Japanese firms lack the extensive experience with vector processor design enjoyed by the American firms, although both Fujitsu and

Hitachi have had some relevant experience. For example, the Fujitsu FACOM F230-75, a vector processor, was produced in 1977.[12] Although only two of these vector processors were made, Fujitsu gained valuable experience in the effort. Hitachi offers the Integrated Array Processor (IAP) with their M200 and M280 computers.

Japan lacks an innovative tradition, and they are now competing in an area of technology that will require fundamental innovation in parallel processor architecture, software, algorithms, and applications. Japan has been buying, borrowing, copying, and licensing technology for three decades. Indeed, importing of external ideas has a long historical tradition in the Japanese culture. There was extensive borrowing of cultural ideas from the Chinese in the sixth to the eighth centuries AD.[13] A second period of major borrowing of foreign ideas occurred after the Meiji Restoration in 1868, when Japan imported Western technology to catch up with the advances that had been made during their self-imposed isolation during the Tokugawa Shogunate of over 200 years. A third major borrowing has occurred since World War II. In each of these periods, Japan borrowed many foreign ideas but made them uniquely Japanese in order to preserve the unique elements of the Japanese culture: Japan has become modernized but not "Westernized." Other nations must not take too much comfort in this lack of an innovative tradition in Japan, however, because Japan is very quick to incorporate new ideas into new generations of their products.

A third weakness cited by some authors is Japan's higher education system. Japanese students go through very difficult qualifying examinations, but after entry to the university, there are very few pressures for achievement. Further, whereas about 75% of the university students in the United States attend institutions funded by some government entity, in Japan only 20% of the students are able to qualify for entry into the better quality state-supported schools, and the rest of the students attend poorly funded private institutions.[13] The other side of this coin, however, is the fact that Japan graduates more engineers than does the United States and uses the American university system for their graduate students.

The Japanese firms lack the extensive supercomputer application and system software of the American firms, but they counterbalance that to some extent by IBM compatibility. They lack a supercomputer marketing base, and by that I mean the sales force, the analysts, and the maintenance personnel that support these machines.

Opportunities

Finally in our situation audit, we note that Japan sees several opportunities in the supercomputer field. There is minimal competition; the IBM-compatible supercomputer market is a vacuum; the supercomputer market is projected to expand, and they need to satisfy their own needs to avoid expensive imports.

Supercomputer Projects

The Japanese have both national and commercial supercomputer projects. There are three relevant national projects: superspeed computers, high-speed components, and the fifth-generation computers. The national projects can be summarized briefly as follows.

• The superspeed computer project was begun in late 1981 and will continue through 1989, with funding of $100 million from MITI. The participants include Japan's "Big Six" (Fujitsu, Hitachi, NEC, Mitsubishi, Oki, and Toshiba), with leadership from ETL. The general objectives include an execution rate of 10 billion floating-point operations per second and a main memory of a billion bytes. The schedule for this project calls for the prototype to be built in Japan's fiscal year 1987 (April 1987 to April 1988).

• The Next-Generation Industries project is much broader than is of interest to supercomputing, but will include new component technology for high-speed components, three-dimensional structures, and components to work in hostile environments. This project will run from 1981 to 1990 and is funded at $470 million.

• The fifth-generation computer project began in April 1982 and will run for 10 years. The funding for this project is still somewhat uncertain, although it will be at least several hundred million dollars. The participants will be led by a new institute called The Institute for New Generation Computer Technology (ICOT); the participants include the "Big Six," Sharp, and Matsushita, as well as two national laboratories, ETL and Nippon Telephone and Telegraph (NTT), which is Japan's equivalent of Bell Labs. This project is essentially working on things that might fall into the category of artificial intelligence—intelligent interfaces, knowledge-base management, and problem-solving and inference mechanisms.

Japan's commercial projects come from Fujitsu, Hitachi, and NEC; each of these firms is making both a high-speed and a low-cost version of their machines. The announcements from the commercial companies include the following:

- Fujitsu is offering the VP-200 and the VP-100, with peak performance rates of about 500 and 250 million floating-point operations (mflops), respectively. Initial deliveries will occur in Japan in 1983; foreign marketing will take place in 1984. Memory capacities will be up to 32 million 64-bit words.

- Hitachi is offering the S810-20 and S810-10, with peak performance rates of about 600 and 300 mflops, respectively. Deliveries and memory capacities are roughly the same as for the Fujitsu machines.

- NEC is planning to offer the SX-2 and SX-1, with peak performance rates of about 1300 and 570 mflops, respectively. Initial deliveries are scheduled for first quarter of 1985, and the memory capacity offered will be 32 million 64-bit words.

The architectures of these machines are remarkably similar and are obvious descendants of their American competitors. Each is a vector machine, each uses register-to-register vector operations, each has a separate scalar unit, and each has a separate mask unit. They differ from each other in the number of memory channels, the number of vector pipelines, and whether or not they include extended memory.

Table 1 provides a detailed comparison of the Japanese supercomputers with the Cray X-MP; I am using the X-MP for comparison because it is a register-to-register machine and its first delivery occurs in the same year as the Fujitsu and Hitachi computers. Although there are many similarities, note the following differences:

- The Cray X-MP is a dual processor, whereas the Japanese machines are single processors.

- The level of integration of the logic chips is much higher for the Japanese machines than for the X-MP.

- Larger memory capacities are being offered in the Japanese machines than in the X-MP, although this is expected to be increased for future X-MP offerings.

- The Japanese machines use slower memories but a larger number of memory banks than the X-MP; memory elements are static RAMs in the Japanese machines but bipolar in the X-MP.

TABLE I
COMPARISON OF JAPANESE SUPERCOMPUTERS

	FUJITSU VP-200	HITACHI S810-20	NEC SX-2	[CRAY X-MP]
First Installation Date	4Q 1983	4Q 1983	1Q 1985	3Q 1982 (INTERNAL) 2Q 1983 (EXTERNAL)
Performance				
• Cycle Time (NS)	15/7.5	15	6	9.5
• Peak Vector (MFLOPS)	500	500	1300	420
• Ave. Scalar (MFLOPS)	6	6	20	18
• No. PEs	1	1	1	2
Logic Elements				
• Technology	BIPOLAR	BIPOLAR	N.A.	BIPOLAR
• Gates/Chip	400/1300	550/1500	N.A.	16
• Circuit Delay (NS)	.35/.35	.35/.45	N.A.	.35-.50
Main Storage				
• Capacity (MWORDS)	8-32	4-32	16-32	4
• Banks	128/256	N.A.	256/512	32
• Element	64K SRAM	16K SRAM	64K SRAM	4K BIPOLAR
• Access Time (NS)	55	40	40	30
Vector Registers				
• Capacity (WORDS)	8192	8192	10,000	512
• No. x Length	(8-128)x(1024-32)	32x256	40x256	8x64
Extended Memory				
• Capacity (MWORDS)	N.A.	32-128	16-256	32
• TX Rate (Bits/S)	N.A.	$8x19^9$	$10x10^9$	$8x10^9$
Rental ("STARTING")	$276K/MO	$280K/MO	$375K/MO	

- The Japanese machines provide larger vector register capacities than in the X-MP. Also, the Fujitsu vector registers can be reconfigured by altering the number of registers and their length.

Responses

Government

There have been a number of responses in both the United States and Europe to the Japanese initiatives. The Office of Science and Technology Policy in the Executive Office of the President, headed by Dr. George A. Keyworth II, has formed the Federal Coordinating Council for Science, Engineering, and Technology (FCCSET), which in turn has formed three working groups on supercomputers. Two of these are headed by the Department of Energy (DOE) to study supercomputer acquisition and access, and the Defense Advanced Research Projects Agency (DARPA) has been assigned to stimulate exchange of information.[14] The National Science Foundation (NSF)-sponsored LAX committee and its report have been instrumental in spreading awareness of this problem.[15] The Department of Defense (DoD) is planning a Strategic Computing and Survivability Project.[16] The Justice Department has become more flexible in enforcing antitrust laws, and both the Administration and Congress are proposing bills to modify these laws to allow collaboration on basic research.[17,18] Congress has been holding hearings on supercomputers and related subjects. And there is even talk of forming a Department of Trade that looks something like MITI.[19]

Industry

There is a growing number of business relationships in the U.S., some of which were probably triggered by the need to compete with foreign companies that have industrial and governmental collaboration in research and development. The most notable of these American collaborative efforts are the Microelectronics and Computer Technology Corporation (MCC),[20] and the Semiconductor Research Corporation (SRC).[21] MCC will provide a vehicle for shared basic research, with the objective of producing patentable technology and giving first access to this technology to MCC members. SRC is a collaborative effort to channel funds to American universities to promote semiconductor research and development.

European Interests

Japan's initiatives threaten not only American interests but European interests as well, and the strongest responses so far have come from Europe. The European Economic Community (EEC) has formed a project called "ESPRIT," which stands for European Strategic Plan for Research in Information Technology. This project is to be funded at the $1.5 billion level, with the funding to be shared by the EEC member governments and the participating firms.[22] The project will provide a vehicle for multinational collaboration on "precompetitive" research and development. The scope of the ESPRIT project is very broad, as shown in Fig. 2.

Britain has formed the "Alvey Project," named after John Alvey who headed the committee that recommended this action.[23] This project will be in addition to Britain's participation in the ESPRIT project. It is to run for 5 years and be funded at about $525 million, with the costs to be shared by the British government and the participating commercial

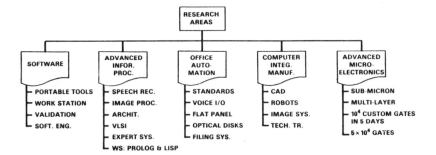

ESPRIT

- SPONSOR: E.E.C.
- FUNDING/DURATION: $1.5B/5 YEARS

Fig. 2. The ESPRIT project.

firms. Areas of research include software engineering, man-machine communication, artificial intelligence, and VLSI.

France has in progress a supercomputer project, the "Mariane Project," to design and build a supercomputer.[24] France has also passed the "Science Program Law" that provides for the increase of national investment in research and development from the current level of 1.8 to 2.5% over a 5-year period. These funds will support increased funding and staffing at national research centers, as well as provide grants, loans, and tax exemptions for industry. France will also participate in the ESPRIT project.

West Germany has several research efforts under way to study parallel processors and recently increased the funding for such studies. Germany will participate in the ESPRIT project as well.

East Germany recently reported on the MAMO project, an array processor that is attached to the EC1055,[25] and the Soviet Union has a supercomputer project under way called "Hypertron."[26]

Conclusions

It is not yet possible to foresee which firms will be successful in the supercomputing market, but some of the key factors for success are summarized in Table 2 ("X" denotes potential advantage). Speed is perhaps the most important single factor, but this is left as a question because there are no available benchmark data on the speed of the Japanese computers. The length of the design cycle may favor Japanese firms because they are vertically integrated. This implies that the American firms must counter this Japanese advantage, and both Cray Research (CRI) and Engineering Technology Associates (ETA) Systems are taking steps to do this. CRI is developing an in-house gallium arsenide development capability, and ETA is planning to use CMOS technology, which, although not an in-house capability for ETA, is expected to be available on the time scale needed. The reliability factor has been noted as a Japanese advantage just on general grounds of the well-known reliability of Japanese electronics.

TABLE 2
KEY FACTORS FOR SUCCESS

Key Factors	U.S.	Japan
Hardware		
• Speed	?	?
• Design cycle		X
• Reliability		X
• MIMD	X	
Software		
• Applications	X	
• System	X	
• Algorithms	X	
• IBM compatibility		X
Marketing		
• Market share	X	
• Infrastructure	X	
• Cost and pricing		X
• Financial support		X

The MIMD factor is shown as an advantage to the U.S. firms because all three of them (CRI, ETA, and Denelcor) have either experience in this kind of architecture or commercial products under development using it. Japanese firms are still developing single-instruction-stream computers.

Software advantages are shown for the American firms, with the exception of IBM compatibility, which will favor Fujitsu and Hitachi until IBM, Amdahl, and Trilogy make their responses.

Marketing position favors the American firms at the moment for both market share and the marketing infrastructure. However, I have noted cost and pricing as a potential advantage for Japan on the assumption that they will be as aggressive in their supercomputer pricing as they have been in other markets they have attempted to penetrate. Their market penetration philosophy can be summarized as, "We cannot afford profits when we are attempting to penetrate a new market."

It is inherent in the nature of the future that it contains both dangers and opportunities. The danger for other nations in Japan's supercomputer and fifth-generation initiatives lies in the possibility that this coordinated and concentrated effort by Japan's government and industry might give Japanese firms a competitive advantage that will be difficult for individual firms in these other nations to counter effectively. However, the growing awareness of Japan's initiatives, both in the United States and elsewhere, has triggered the opportunity to make some long-needed changes in industry, government, and academia that will increase the effectiveness and reduce the cost of basic research.

It will not become clear for at least 5 years which firms will survive this competition. I think the American firms will retain their customer base, in part because it is very costly to convert supercomputer codes to an incompatible architecture. It is in the expansion of the supercomputer market that Japan will succeed or fail. The present market size is only about $100 to $200 million per year, and that supports just two firms. With half a dozen firms attempting sales, there must be either a very large expansion of this market or there will surely be fallout among the competitors.

The survival of the American supercomputer industry is an issue not just for the firms involved but for the nation as a whole. The Japanese have correctly identified supercomputers as a key technology that promotes technological strength in other areas, many of which are crucial to America's economic and security interests.

References

1. "Tactics." *Encyclopedia Brittanica* **21** (1968):604.

2. Shimada, H. "Japan's Success Story: Looking Behind the Legend." *Technology Review* (May-June 1983):47-52.

3. Hoard, B. "MITI Director Cites 'Harmonizing' as Factor in Japan's Industrial Success." *Computerworld* (May 9, 1983):75-76.

4. "Japan, Inc. Goes International." *Business Week* (December 14, 1981):40-49.

5. Tsuruta, T. "The Myth of Japan, Inc." *Technology Review* (July 1983):43-48.

6. Asao, S. "Myths and Realities of Japan's Industrial Policies." *Wall Street Journal* (October 24, 1983):31.

7. Solarz, S. J. "A Search for Balance." *Foreign Policy* **49** (Winter 1982-83):75-92.

8. "The Aging of Japanese Social Security." *The Economist* (May 14, 1984):94-95.

9. Abegglen, J. C., and Otori, A. "Japanese Technology Today." *Scientific American* **247**, no. 5 (1982):J1-J30.

10. Lindamood, G. E. "The Rise of the Japanese Computer Industry." *ONR Far East Scientific Bulletin* **7**, no. 4 (1982):55-72.

11. Galinshi, C. "VLSI in Japan." *Computer* (March 1983):14-21.

12. Uchida, K., Seta, Y., and Tanakura, Y. "The FACOM 230-75 Array Processor System." *Proceedings of the 3rd USA-Japan Computer Conference*, AFIPS (1978):369-373.

13. Reischauer, E. O. *The Japanese.* Cambridge: Harvard University Press, 1977.

14. "Science Advisor Sets Up Oversight Groups for Supercomputers." Press Release of the Office of Science and Technology Policy, Washington, D.C. (May 4, 1983).

15. Lax, P. D. "Report of the Panel on Large-Scale Computing in Science and Engineering." National Science Foundation report NSF 82-13 (1982).

16. Roth, H. "Reagan to Request $40 million for Supercomputer Thrust." *Electronic Engineering Times* (January 31, 1983):12.

17. Curran, L. J. "Meeting the Japanese Challenge." *Mini-Micro Systems* (July 1982):107-108.

18. "Antitrust Immunity for Joint Research is Studied by Agency." *Wall Street Journal* (June 29, 1983):10.

19. Madison, C. "MITI Anyone?" *National Journal* (March 26, 1983):665.

20. Bartimo, J. "Inman Defines Goals of Fledgling MCC Venture." *Computerworld* (February 14, 1983):120-122.

21. Baker, S. "Semi-Group to Fight Japan with Joint Research Plan." *Electronic Times* (December 21, 1982):1, 4.

22. See, for example, Marsh, P., and Lloyd, A. "Europe Pools Its Resources on R&D." *New Scientist* (June 23, 1983):850-851. Malik, R. "ESPRIT to Pool European Research Resources." *Computerworld* (June 27, 1983):87. "Science and Technology: Invented in Europe, Patented in America, and Made in Japan?" *The Economist* (April 2, 1983):93-94.

23. Dickson, D. "Britain Rises to Japan's Computer Challenge." *Science* **220**, no. 20 (1983):799-800.

24. Adelantado, M., Comte, D., Siron, P., and Syre, J. C. "A MIMD Supercomputer System for Large-Scale Numerical Applications." *Proceedings of the IFIP 9th World Computer Congress*, IFIP (September 19-23, 1983):821-826.

25. Krause, G. "Architectural and Functional Features of Matrix Model (MAMO)." *Proceedings of the IFIP 9th World Computer Congress*, IFIP (September 19-23, 1983):827-832.

26. Worlton, W. J. "Foreign Travel Trip Report." Los Alamos National Laboratory C-Division trip report (October 30, 1983).

8

The New York University Ultracomputer*

A. Gottlieb
New York University
New York City, New York

Introduction

Continuing advances in very large scale integration (VLSI) technology promise to provide fast floating-point processors and megabit memory chips within the present decade. By assembling 10^4-10^5 such components (roughly the same parts count as found in present and past large computers), one obtains a configuration having the potential for extremely high computation rates. However, it is not immediately clear how to ensure that this potential is realized in practice, that is, how to achieve effective cooperation among the individual processors.

The New York University (NYU) "Ultracomputer Group" has been studying how such ensembles can be constructed and has produced a design that includes novel hardware and software components. A pervasive consideration for this design is that it be free of serial sections (that is, hardware or software modules to which each processor requires exclusive access), because even small serial sections become a bottleneck bounding the maximum possible speedup. This paper outlines the proposed hardware design and describes its relation to other research in parallel processing.

Machine Model

In this section we review the paracomputer model, upon which our machine design is based, and the fetch-and-add operation, which we use for interprocessor synchronization, and illustrate the power of this

*This work was supported by U.S. Department of Energy grant DE-AC02-76ER03077 and by National Science Foundation grant NSF-MCS79-21258.

model. Although the paracomputer is not physically realizable, we shall see in the Machine Design section that close approximations can be built.

Paracomputers

An idealized parallel processor, dubbed a "paracomputer" by Schwartz[1] and classified as a WRAM by Borodin and Hopcroft,[2] consists of autonomous processing elements (PEs) sharing a central memory. The model permits every PE to read or write a shared memory cell in one cycle. Flynn[3] has classified such machines as MIMD, because they support multiple instruction streams acting on multiple data streams.

The Fetch-and-Add Operation

We augment the paracomputer model with the "fetch-and-add" operation, a simple yet very effective interprocessor synchronization operation that permits highly concurrent execution of operating system primitives and application programs. The format of this operation is F & A(V,e), where V is an integer variable and e is an integer expression. This indivisible operation is defined to return the (old) value of V and to replace V by the sum V + e. Moreover, concurrent fetch-and-adds are required to satisfy the following serialization principle: if V is a shared variable and many fetch-and-add operations simultaneously address V, the effect of these operations is exactly what it would be if they occurred in some (unspecified) serial order. That is, V is modified by the appropriate total increment and each operation yields the intermediate value of V corresponding to its position in this order. The following example illustrates the semantics of fetch-and-add: Assume V is a shared variable, if PE_i executes

$ANS_i \leftarrow F$ and $A(V,e_i)$,

and if PEj simultaneously executes

$ANS_j \leftarrow F$ and $A(V,e_j)$,

and if V is not simultaneously updated by yet another processor, then either

$ANS_i \leftarrow V$ or $ANS_i \leftarrow V + e_j$

$ANS_j \leftarrow V + e_i$ or $ANS_j \leftarrow V$.

In either case, the value of V becomes $V + e_i + e_j$.

For another example, consider several PEs concurrently applying fetch-and-add, with an increment of one, to a shared array index. Each PE obtains an index to a distinct array element (although one cannot say which element will be assigned to which PE). Futhermore, the shared index receives the appropriate total increment.

The Machine Design section presents a hardware design that realizes fetch-and-add without significantly increasing the time required to access shared memory and that realizes simultaneous fetch-and-adds updating the same variable in a particularly efficient manner.

The Power of Fetch-and-Add

If the fetch-and-add operation is available, we can perform many important algorithms in a completely parallel manner, that is, without using any critical sections. For example, as indicated above, concurrent executions of F & A(I,1) yield consecutive values that may be used to index an array. If this array is interpreted as a (sequentially stored) queue, the values returned many be used to perform concurrent inserts; analogously, F & A(D,1) may be used for concurrent deletes. An implementation may be found in Gottlieb, Lubachevsky, and Rudolph,[4] who also indicate how such techniques can be used to implement a totally decentralized operating system scheduler.* We are unaware of any other completely parallel solution to this problem. To illustrate the nonserial behavior obtained, we note that, given a single queue that is neither empty nor full, the concurrent execution of thousands of inserts and thousands of deletes can all be accomplished in the time required for just one such operation. Other highly parallel fetch-and-add-based algorithms appear in Kalos,[5] Kruskal,[6] and Rudolph.[7]

Machine Design

In this section we discuss the design of the NYU Ultracomputer, a machine that appears to the user as a paracomputer. A more detailed hardware description, as well as a justification of various design decisions and a performance analysis of the communication network, can be found in Gottlieb, Grishman, and others.[9] The Ultracomputer uses a message switching network with the topology of Lawrie's Ω-network[10] to connect $N = 2^D$ autonomous PEs to a central shared memory composed of N memory modules (MMs). Thus, the direct single cycle access to

---

*As explained in Gottlieb and Kruskal,[8] the replace-add primitive defined in Gottlieb, Lubachevsky, and Rudolph[4] and used in several of our earlier reports is essentially equivalent to fetch-and-add.

shared memory characteristics of paracomputers is approximated by an indirect access via a multicycle connection work.

Network Design

For machines with thousands of PEs, the communication network is likely to be the dominant component with respect to both cost and performance. The design to be presented achieves the following objectives, and we are unaware of any significantly different design that also attains these goals:

1. Bandwidth linear in N, the number of PEs.

2. Latency, that is, memory access time, logarithmic in N.

3. Only O(N log N) identical components.

4. Routing decisions local to each switch; thus routing is not a serial bottleneck and is efficient for short messages.

5. Concurrent access by multiple PEs to the same memory cell suffers no performance penalty; thus interprocessor coordination is not serialized.

Ω-Network Enhancements

The manner in which an Ω-network can be used to implement memory loads and stores is well known and is based on the existence of a (unique) path connecting each PE-MM pair. We enhance the basic Ω-network design as follows:

1. The network is pipelined, that is, the delay between messages equals the switch cycle time, not the network transit time. (Because the latter grows logarithmically, nonpipelined networks can have bandwidth at most N/log N.)

2. The network is message switched, that is, the switch settings are not maintained while a reply is awaited. (The alternative, circuit switching, is incompatible with pipelining.)

3. Queues are associated with each switch to enable concurrent processing of requests for the same port. (The alternative adopted by Burroughs[11] of killing one of the two conflicting requests limits bandwidth to O(N/log N); see Kruskal and Snir.[12]

When concurrent loads and stores are directed at the same memory location and meet at a switch, they can be combined without introducing any delay (see Klappholtz[13] and Gottlieb, Grishman, and others[9]). Combining requests reduces communication traffic and thus decreases the lengths of the queues mentioned above, leading to lower network latency (that is, reduced memory access time). Because combined requests can themselves be combined, the network satisfies the key property that any number of concurrent memory references to the same location can be satisfied in the time required for one central memory access. It is this property, when extended to include fetch-and-add operations, that permits the bottleneck-free implementation of many coordination protocols.

Implementing Fetch-and-Add

By including adders in the MMs, the fetch-and-add operation can be easily implemented as follows: When F & A(X,e) reaches the MM containing X, the value of X and the transmitted e are brought to the MM adder, the sum is stored in X, and the old value of X is returned through the network to the requesting PE. Because fetch-and-add is our sole synchronization primitive (and is also a key ingredient in many algorithms), concurrent fetch-and-add operations will often be directed at the same location. Thus, as indicated above, it is crucial in a design supporting large numbers of processors not to serialize this activity.

Local Memory at Each PE

The negative impact of the network latency can be partially mitigated by providing each PE with a local memory in which private variables reside and into which read-only shared data (in particular, program text) may be copied. One common design for parallel machines is to implement a separately addressable local memory at each PE, imposing upon compilers and loaders the onus of managing the two-level store.

The alternative approach, which we intend to adopt, is to implement the local memory as a cache. Experience with uniprocessor systems shows that a large cache can capture up to 95% of the references to cacheable variables.[14] Moreover, a cache-based system supports dynamic location of segments and thus permits shared read-write segments to be cached during periods of exclusive read-only access.[9]

Machine Packaging

We conservatively estimate that a machine built in 1990 would require four chips for each PE, nine chips for each 1-megabyte MM, and two chips for each 4-input/4-output switch. Thus, a 4096 processor machine would require roughly 65,000 chips, not counting the input/output (I/O) interfaces. Note that the chip count is still dominated, as in present day machines, by the memory chips and that only 19% of the chips are used for network. Nevertheless, most of the machine volume will be occupied by the network, and its assembly will be the dominant system cost, due to the nonlocal wiring required. Our preliminary estimate is that the PEs, network, and MMs would occupy a 5- by 5- by 10-ft (air-cooled) enclosure.[15]

Other Research

In this section we show how our work relates to other research in parallel processing.

Alternate Machine Models

Gottlieb, Grishman, and others[9] discuss systolic processors, vector machines, data-flow architectures, and message passing designs, and explain the choice of an MMID shared-memory machine. We summarize their remarks as follows.

Systolic processor designs[16] have a significant and growing impact on signal processing but are less well suited for computations having complex control and data flow. We expect to use VLSI systolic systems for subcomponents of the NYU Ultracomputer that have regular control and data flow, specifically for the combining queues found in the network switches.

Current vector supercomputers may be roughly classified as SIMD shared-memory machines (compare with Stone[17]) that achieve their full power only on algorithms dominated by vector operations. However, some problems (especially those with many data-dependent decisions, for example particle tracking) appear to resist effective vectorization.[18] Our simulation studies have shown that the NYU Ultracomputer is effective for particle tracking,[19] as well as for the vectorizable fluid-type problems[20] also mentioned by Rodrigue et al.[18]

Data-flow researchers, joined by advocates of functional programming, have stressed the advantages of an applicative programming language. We discuss the language issue below and note that Gottlieb and Schwartz[21] have shown how a paracomputer can execute a data-flow language with maximal parallelism.

We subdivide message-passing architectures based on whether or not the interconnection topology is visible to the programmer. If it is visible, then by tailoring algorithms to the topology, very high performance can be obtained, as in the Homogeneous machine[22] and the original Ultracomputer design.[1] However, we found such a machine to be more difficult to program than one in which the entire memory is available to each PE. If the topology is hidden by having the routing performed automatically, a loosely coupled design emerges that is well suited for distributed computing but is less effective when the PEs are to cooperate on a single problem.

Languages

Our applications have been programmed in essentially trivial extensions of Pascal, C, and FORTRAN (primarily the last). One should not conclude that we view these languages as near optimal or even satisfactory. Indeed, we view the progress we have achieved using FORTRAN as a worst case bound on the results obtainable. We do, however, consider it a strength of the paracomputer design, in that it imposes few requirements on the language. Even simple extensions of old serial languages permit useful work to be accomplished. Of course, more useful work can be accomplished when better language vehicles are available, and we expect our language-related research efforts to increase as we study a broader range of applications.

Granularity of Parallelism

The NYU Ultracomputer emphasizes a relatively coarse grain of parallelism in which the units to be executed concurrently consist of several high-level language statements. This should be compared with the fine-grained data-flow approach, in which the corresponding units are individual machine operations, and with the extremely coarse-grained approach taken by current multiprocessor operating systems, in which the units are entire processes.

Processor Count and Performance

The few thousand PEs specified for the Ultracomputer represent an intermediate value for this parameter. On one end of the scale, we find architectures that support only a few dozen PEs; on the other end sit designs specifying millions of PEs. When the PE count is modest, as in the S1,[23] a full crossbar interconnection network is possible as is the use of high-speed, high-power, low-density logic. When the PE count is massive, as in NON-VON,[24] many PEs must share a single chip. This restricts the interconnection pattern chosen due to the I/O limitation inherent in VLSI. Often the tree network is chosen, because for any k, 2^k PEs can be packaged together with only four external lines. Moreover, there is not likely to be sufficient chip area for each PE to store its own program or to contain instruction decoding logic. Thus, a SIMD design seems natural.

When the PE count lies between these extremes, as in the Ultracomputer, high-density logic is required and a crossbar is not feasible. However, an Ω-network (which avoids the tree's bottleneck near the root) is possible, as is a MIMD design.

Networks

As indicated in the section on Machine Design, the Ω-network permits several important objectives to be achieved and thus appears to be a favorable choice. However, more general Banyan networks also share these favorable characteristics and remove the restriction that the PEs and MMs be equal in number. In essence we have tentatively selected the simplest Banyan and also have not pursued the possibility of dynamically reconfiguring the network. This last possibility has been studied by the PASSM, TRAC (Sejnowsky and others[25]), and Blue Chip (Snyder[26]) projects.

Compilers and Local Memory

By specifying a cache rather than a (separately addressed) local memory, we have removed from the compiler the task of managing a two-level address space.* However, for some problems, advanced compiler optimization techniques can improve the results obtained by caching.

---

*Strictly speaking, this is false, because the PE registers constitute a second level.

More significantly, local memory can be used in addition to caching. Kuck and his colleagues at the University of Illinois have studied the compiler issues for several years,[27] and the Cedar project[28] intends to use this expertise to effectively manage a sophisticated multilevel memory hierarchy.

Conclusion

Until now, high-performance machines have been constructed from increasingly complex hardware structures and ever more exotic technology. It is our belief that the NYU Ultracomputer approach offers a simpler alternative, which is better suited to advanced VLSI technology. High performance is obtained by assembling large quantities of identical computing components in a particularly effective manner. The 4096 PE Ultracomputer that we envision has roughly the same component count as found in today's large machines. The number of different component types, however, is much smaller; each component is a sophisticated one-chip VLSI system. Such machines would be three orders of magnitude faster and would have a main storage three orders of magnitude larger than present-day machines.

Our instruction-level simulations indicate that the NYU Ultracomputer would be an extremely powerful computing engine for large applications. The low coordination overhead and the large memory enable us to use efficiently the high degree of parallelism available. Finally, our programming experience using simulators indicates that the manual translation of serial codes into parallel Ultracomputer codes is a manageable task.

We have not emphasized language issues, reconfigurability, or sophisticated memory management. Advances in these areas will doubtless lead to even greater performance.

To demonstrate further the feasibility of the hardware and software design, we intend to construct a 64-PE prototype that will use commercial microprocessors and memories together with custom-built VLSI components for the network.

References

1. Schwartz, J. T. "Ultracomputers." *ACM TOPLAS* (1980):484-521.

2. Borodin, A., and Hopcroft, J. E. "Merging on Parallel Models of Computation." Unpublished manuscript (1982).

3. Flynn, M. J. "Very High-Speed Computing Systems." *IEEE Trans.* **C-54** (1966):1901-1909.

4. Gottlieb, A., Lubachevsky, B., and Rudolph, L. "Basic Techniques for the Efficient Coordination of Large Numbers of Cooperating Sequential Processors." *ACM TOPLAS* (April 1983).

5. Kalos, M. H. "Scientific Calculation on the Ultracomputer." Ultracomputer Note 30, Courant Institute, New York University, New York (1981).

6. Kruskal, C. P. "Upper and Lower Bounds on the Performance of Parallel Algorithms." Ph.D. Thesis, Courant Institute, New York University, New York (1981).

7. Rudolph, L. "Software Structures for Ultraparallel Computing." Ph.D. Thesis, Courant Institute, New York University, New York (1982).

8. Gottlieb, A., and Kruskal, C. P. "Coordinating Parallel Processors: A Partial Unification." *Computer Architecture News* (October 1981):16-24.

9. Gottlieb, A., Grishman, R., Kruskal, C. P., McAuliffe, K. P., Rudolph, L., and Snir, M. "The NYU Ultracomputer—Designing a MIMD Shared Memory Parallel Computer." *IEEE Trans.* **C-32** (1983):175-189.

10. Lawrie, D., "Access and Alignment of Data in an Array Processor." *IEEE Trans.* **C-24** (1975):1145-1155.

11. "Numerical Aerodynamic Simulation Facility Feasibility Study." Burroughs Corp. report NAS2-9897 (March 1979).

12. Kruskal, C. P., and Snir, M. "Some Results on Interconnection Networks for Multiprocessors." *Proceedings of the 1982 Conference on Information Sciences and Systems*, Princeton University (March 1982).

13. Klappholtz, D. "Stochastically Conflict-Free Data-Base Memory Systems." *Proceedings of the 1980 International Conference on Parallel Processing*, New York:IEEE (1980):283-289.

14. Kaplan, K. R., and Winder, R. V. "Cache-Based Computer Systems." *Computer* 6 (1973):30-36.

15. Bianchini, R., and Bianchini, R., Jr. "Wireability of an Ultracomputer." Courant Institute Note 43, New York University, New York (1982).

16. Kung, H. T. "The Structure of Parallel Algorithms." In *Advances in Computers 19*, edited by M. C. Jovits, 65-112. New York:Academic Press, 1980.

17. Stone, H. S. "Parallel Computers." In *Introduction to Computer Architecture*, edited by H. S. Stone, 318-374. Chicago:Science Research Associates, 1980.

18. Rodrigue, G., Giroux, E. D., and Pratt, M. "Perspectives on Large-Scale Scientific Computing." *Computer* 13, (October 1980):65-80.

19. Kalos, M. H., Leshem, G., and Lubachevsky, B. D. "Molecular Simulations of Equilibrium Properties." Ultracomputer Note 27, Courant Institute, New York University, New York (1981).

20. Rushfield, N. "Atmospheric Computations on Highly Parallel MMD Computers." Ultracomputer Note 22, Courant Institute, New York University, New York (1981).

21. Gottlieb, A., and Schwartz, J. T. "Networks and Algorithms for Very Large-Scale Parrallel Computation." *Computer* 15 (January 1982):27-36.

22. Seitz, C. L. "Ensemble Architectures for VLSI—A Survey and Taxonomy." *Proceedings Conference on Advanced Research in VLSI*, Cambridge: Massachusetts Institute of Technology (1982):130-135.

23. "S-1 Project, Vol. 1, Architecture." Lawrence Livermore Laboratory report UCID-18619, Vol. 1 (August 1980).

24. Shaw, D. E. "The NON-VON Supercomputer." Department of Computer Science, Columbia University technical report (August 1982).

25. Sejnowski, M-C., Upchurch, E. T., Kapur, R. N., Charlu, D. S., and Lipowsky, G. J. "An Overview of the Texas Reconfigurable Array Computer." *National Computer Conference Proceedings*, AFIPS Press, Montvale, New Jersey (1980):631-641.

26. Snyder, L. "Introduction to the Configurable, Highly Parallel Computer." *Computer* **15** (1982):47-56.

27. Kuck, D. J., and Padua, D. A. "High-Speed Multiprocessors and Their Compilers." *Proceedings of the 1979 International Conference on Parallel Processing*, IEEE, New York (1979):5-16.

28. Gajski, D., Kuck, D., Lawrie, D., and Samah, A. "Construction of a Large-Scale Multiprocessor." Cedar document 5, University of Illinois, Urbana (1983).

9

Data-Flow Ideas and Future Supercomputers

J. B. Dennis
Massachusetts Institute of Technology
Cambridge, Massachusetts

Introduction

Recent discussions of supercomputer research programs have concerned two major areas of development: supercomputers for scientific computation, which will be able to perform the same sorts of computations as existing supercomputers but with substantially increased performance, and supercomputers for "knowledge-based" pattern recognition and problem solving—areas that are not application areas for contemporary supercomputers.

In both areas, parallelism is the key to achieving significant advances in cost/performance. Enough work has been completed in the first area that highly parallel forms of many important algorithms are known, programming languages exist in which these algorithms can be expressed for highly parallel execution, and machine architectures have been proposed that can perform them effectively. In contrast, the area of knowledge-based applications calls for development of a new conceptual basis for computation before successful parallel system architectures will evolve.

Data-flow concepts are applicable to both areas. In scientific computation, research at the Massachusetts Institute of Technology (MIT) has shown that data-flow architectures for supercomputers and programming with functional/applicative languages can achieve high performance for practical computer applications. For knowledge-based systems, the corresponding work is at a relatively primitive stage. There is at present no sound and accepted conceptual model for the massively parallel execution of "artificial intelligence" computations. There have been no studies or research results that show how supercomputer levels of performance can be achieved. Yet data-flow concepts show promise of providing a sound semantic foundation for computer systems applicable to a broad range of applications[1] including knowledge-based systems.

Some Predictions

My subject is very different from the kind of computer architecture the manufacturers have told you about in this conference. Although the American supercomputer builders now recognize that parallelism is essential to meaningfully increased performance in the next generation of machines, they have taken only the first small step. Moreover, they have adopted a conservative approach—not merely retaining the basic mechanism of conventional computer architecture, but maintaining upward compatibility from current products as well. This path simply cannot exploit the potential of massive parallelism and fails to recognize the very different style of programming that will be needed to effectively employ large-scale parallel computers. I believe that supercomputers of the 1990s will be very different from those in immediate prospect from the American and Japanese manufacturers, for the conceptual basis is in hand for a genuine revolution in the way problems are formulated, programs are developed, and computations are carried out.

> First Prediction: Supercomputers in the 1990s will support massive parallelism, thousandfold parallelism, exploited by the hardware.

In this way they will gain high performance—not through use of fast circuits, but by means of high-density devices with many thousands of gates. Four-, eight-, or sixteenfold parallelism is not enough. There is so much to be gained in going to massive parallelism that the problems of building and programming such machines will be addressed and solved. Data-flow concepts provide one conceptual approach for such computers. Advanced multiprocessor systems such as the New York University Ultracomputer may provide another.

> Second Prediction: The supercomputers of the 1990s will use high-density custom chips containing many thousands of gates apiece.

We have seen an example of a trend in this direction in the announcement that the Cyber 2XX will employ CMOS technology on the scale of 20,000 to 30,000 gates per device. From bipolar technology there is a valid move toward technology that has somewhat more gate delay but many times greater density of gates on a chip and, therefore, better performance in return for the space and power consumed. It may well be that further investment in improving the performance of bipolar devices for faster computation is not warranted.

The massively parallel architectures will perform best using program structures radically different from those tailored to conventional concepts of program execution. Very different approaches to program development and to translating (compiling) programs into efficient machine code structures will be used.

Third Prediction: In the 1990s, programs for supercomputers will be written in functional programming languages.

The massive parallelism present in most large-scale scientific computations is very evident when the program is expressed in a functional language. While it is true that one can discover parallelism in FOR-TRAN programs through data-flow analysis and that many FORTRAN programs can be successfully vectorized, I question whether these techniques can succeed for ordinary programs when the degree of parallelism needed is many thousandfold.

My final prediction concerns the difficulties we will encounter in making large, parallel computer systems work reliably. With high logic densities and many parts operating concurrently, it may be exceedingly difficult to understand what is happening in these machines if they are not working right. Their design must include provisions for recognizing and dealing with problems.

Fourth Prediction: The supercomputers of the 1990s will embody full-coverage fault detection for single, independent hardware failures.

In such a computer, whenever a program runs to termination without detected fault, the user is guaranteed that the results are not invalid due to hardware failure. Moreover, fault detection will provide substantial assistance in locating failures. In current designs for supercomputers, this quality would be expensive to achieve and would lead to degraded performance. Yet in the supercomputers I foresee in the 1990s, full fault coverage will not only be achievable but will involve straightforward and inexpensive mechanisms.

Data-Flow Models for Computation

In thinking about computer systems and how they will be programmed, it is very important to have a *model of computation* to guide the mind. For conventional computers one does not usually think of there being an abstract model—the abstraction is so familiar and implicit. Yet the model of the store (or address space) and the program counter selecting successive instructions for execution is at the heart of all conventional computers and the languages used to prepare programs to run on them. Even in the case of machines that embody substantial augmentation of conventional architecture, such as today's supercomputers, one can always fall back on the conventional subset of the machine (its scalar instruction set) and use ordinary compiling techniques to get the old FORTRAN programs working.

For highly parallel machines, new models of computation are required, and little guidance can be had from past experience with programming for conventional machines. Conventional ideas about machine program structure and the compilation of efficient codes will be replaced with ideas appropriate to the new architectures. Data-flow models of computation can provide this guidance for a class of machines capable of supporting massively parallel computation.[2]

Two major approaches to the architecture of data-flow computers are currently being pursued. They are based on similar but different computational models: the *static data-flow model* and the *tagged-token model*.

The Static Data-Flow Model

In the static model,[3] a computation is represented by a directed graph as shown by a simple example in Fig. 1a. The arcs hold tokens that carry data values from one operator node to another. An operator may "fire" if there are tokens on each of its input arcs. In the static model we insist that only one token occupy an arc; so once the addition operator has fired, we cannot fire it again until the previous result has been consumed by the target (multiplication) operator.

In a computer based on static data-flow principles,[4] a program, as stored in the computer's memory, consists of instructions linked together, as shown in Fig. 1b. Each instruction has an operation code, space for holding operand values as they arrive, and destination fields (represented by the links) that indicate what is to be done with the results of instruction execution.

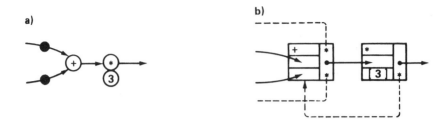

Fig. 1. The static data-flow model.

Each instruction is activated by the presence of its operand values; its execution consists of performing the indicated operation and delivering copies of the result value as specified by the destination fields. Instructions are prevented from executing before their target instructions are ready to receive new data by requiring that acknowledge signals arrive before an instruction can be activated again. This mechanism is implemented by destination fields tagged to indicate that an acknowledge signal is to be sent instead of the instruction's result (the dashed links in the figure). The complete condition for an instruction to be activated is that its operand fields must be filled and it must have received a specified number of acknowledge signals. The acknowledge links add a little complexity to static data-flow programs, but the processing element required to do this, as you will see, is simple and straightforward.

The Tagged-Token Model

The other popular data-flow model is the tagged token model.[5] In this model, many tokens may be present simultaneously on an arc of a data-flow graph. Tokens on the same arc are distinguished by a tag carried by each token, as illustrated in Fig. 2a. The tags correspond to different instantiations of the data-flow program graph, for example, the separate activations of a data-flow program graph by a procedure call mechanism. The rules of behavior require that an operator needing two operands consume tokens having identical tags. A realization of the tagged-token architecture (illustrated schematically in Fig. 2b) must sort out which tokens belong together. The scheme used employs a *matching store*, a form of associative memory.[6] Tokens arriving at a processing element of the machine are held in the matching store until they can be paired with a second token bearing the same tag. Once a matched pair is formed, the

a)   b)

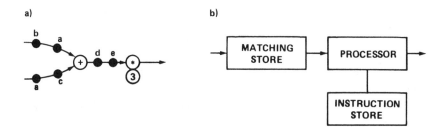

Fig. 2. The tagged-token model.

target instruction is fetched and the specified operation is performed by a functional unit. The use of the matching store makes the tagged-token architecture more complicated than the static architecture, but it has the advantage that certain additional instances of parallelism can be exploited by the machine. Also, the tagged-token architecture offers a more direct implementation of some high-level language features—procedure calls, for example.

Data-Flow Projects

Work on data-flow concepts is being pursued in many universities and institutions, primarily in the United States, Great Britain, and Japan. A couple of exploratory machines using static data-flow architecture have been built or planned. Texas Instruments built an experimental four-processor data-flow machine, which ran FORTRAN programs translated by an augmented version of the compiler for the Texas Instruments Advanced Scientific Computer (ASC).[7] An interesting and carefully developed paper design of a data-flow machine for signal processing applications was sponsored by ESL Incorporated.[8]

Developing a practical static data-flow supercomputer is the primary goal of my MIT research group. We have built an engineering model of a data-flow multiprocessor with eight processing elements, which we are using to study machine code structures suitable for building efficient data-flow programs and to develop techniques for transforming programs and generating good machine code.

My MIT colleague, Professor Arvind, is evaluating program behavior for the tagged-token architecture by building a multiprocessor emulation facility that will permit experimental execution of significantly sized data-flow programs on a large configuration of emulated tagged-token processors. At the University of Manchester, an experimental tagged-token machine has been built by Watson and Gurd.[9]

In my judgment, these are the most exciting developments in data-flow architecture. There are, nevertheless, several very interesting projects that also have the objective of developing machine proposals to support functional programming languages: work at the University of North Carolina by Mago, at the University of Utah by Keller, and in England by Turner at the University of Kent. In my judgment these proposed machines, which are being based on the reduction principle of program execution, do not have the same potential for high performance as the static architecture or the tagged-token architecture and, therefore, are not serious candidates for high-performance scientific computation.

Chuck Style Data Flow

In several projects, the data-flow program execution mechanism is being applied to larger chunks of program than single scalar operations. This proposal may make good sense in some areas—signal processing, for example—where specific chunks or computational modules are used often. In a more general framework, including supercomputers for scientific computation, I believe it would be difficult to design a compiler to do an effective job of partitioning a large program into such chunks, and it seems to me that the data-driven activation mechanism for a chunk style machine would be more complex and less efficient than the simple and elegant mechanism of the static architecture.

The Static Architecture

The organization of a computer based on the static data-flow model is shown in Fig. 3 and consists of *processing elements* interconnected by a *routing network*; it is a kind of *data-flow multiprocessor*. The instructions making up a data-flow machine-level program are partitioned among the processing elements. Each processing element identifies which of the instructions it holds are ready for execution; it executes these as fast as it can, generating result packets containing operand values for other instructions. The routing network provides the pathways needed to send

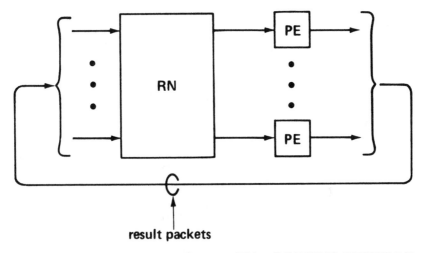

result packets

PE = PROCESSING ELEMENT   RN = ROUTING NETWORK

Fig. 3. Data-flow multiprocessor.

result packets to instructions residing in other processing elements. This machine organization carries further the idea used in the Denelcor machine and discussed by Burton Smith: if a processor has many independent activities waiting for its attention, then delay can be tolerated in the interconnection network. The more important quality of the network is its throughput, how many packets per second it can handle.

It is true that the amount of concurrency required of an application code to make this architecture effective is very large. If a data-flow computer has 100 processing elements and each must have at least 10 independent activities to maintain its limit of performance, then at least a thousandfold concurrency must be present in the application code. Our analyses of benchmark programs have shown that this degree of concurrency is indeed available.

The Data-Flow Processing Element

A data-flow processing element (Fig. 4) consists of mechanisms to recognize when instructions are enabled and to carry out their execution.

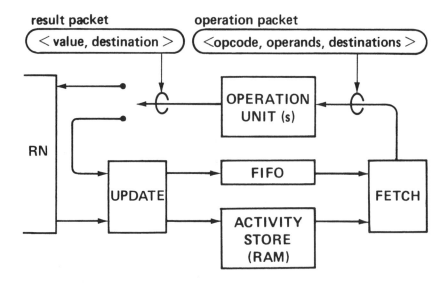

Fig. 4. Data-flow processing element.

The data-flow instructions assigned to a processing element are held in its *activity store*. A simple FIFO queue holds the addresses of those instructions that are enabled. The *fetch unit* picks the address of some enabled instruction from the queue, fetches that instruction (with its operands) from the activity store, and delivers it to an operation unit. Execution of the instruction creates one or more *result packets*, which are sent on to the *update unit*. The update unit places the result value in the operand field of the target instruction and decides whether the instruction has become enabled. If the instruction is enabled, its address is entered in the FIFO queue. If the target instruction of a result packet resides in some other processing element of the machine, the packet is sent off through the network. Thus the processing element has a simple and straightforward function.

Pipelining

We have found that pipelining is a very effective way of organizing computations on the static data-flow machine. Here we mean pipelining successive operands through the instructions of a program, not through the stages of a processing unit. In Fig. 5 we show four data-flow instructions operating as three stages of a pipeline. Once the multiply instruction in stage 1 has fired, the add and substract instructions of stage 2 are enabled and can fire. This provides operands to enable the stage 3 instruction and acknowledge signals to the multiply instruction of stage 1, indicating that it may fire again. If successive data are supplied from the left, stages 1 and 3 will fire alternately with stage 2, yielding a very effective utilization of the data-flow instructions. In a typical large-scale scientific computation, the data-flow machine program may contain a principal pipeline that is many hundreds of instructions long and perhaps hundreds of instructions wide, offering many thousands of instructions for concurrent execution.

By *pipeline headway* we mean the time interval between successive executions of any stage of a pipeline. In a pipelined data-flow program on the static architecture, it is the time that passes from the moment an instruction is enabled to the time the instruction is enabled again. It includes the time required to send a result packet through the routing network to a successor instruction, plus the time for that instruction to send an acknowledge packet through the routing network to permit the first instruction to be re-enabled. The pipeline headway may be as much as 10 µs or so. Because the pipeline consists of a large number of instructions operating concurrently, the machine will achieve high performance in spite of the large pipeline headway.

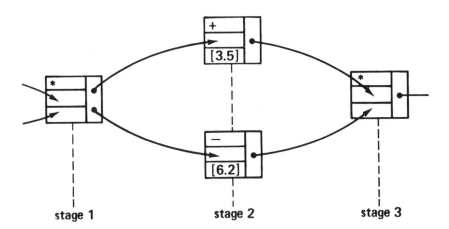

Fig. 5. Pipelining of data-flow instructions.

Array Memories

As I have described the static architecture so far, the only place data values are stored is as operands in data-flow instructions. This is certainly unsatisfactory, because we expect that the problems to be solved will involve very large amounts of data, much larger than the number of instructions in a program.

To hold this information in the data base of a large-scale computation, we include in the architecture separate units called *array memories*. Thus the form of a static data-flow supercomputer suitable for practical application would be that shown in Fig. 6. The functions of processing

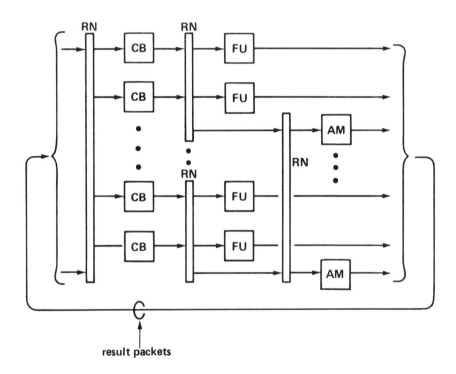

CB = CELL BLOCK   FU = FUNCTIONAL UNIT
AM = ARRAY MEMORY   RN = ROUTING NETWORK

Fig. 6. Data-flow supercomputer.

elements are performed by two separate kinds of units: *cell blocks* and *functional units*. The cell blocks hold the data-flow instructions and perform the basic function of recognizing which instructions are ready for execution. The machine has three classes of instructions: those instructions that call for floating-point arithmetic to be done are sent off to functional units; those that require simple operations, such as duplicating values and performing tests, are executed in the cell blocks that will contain a simple arithmetic logical element; and those instructions that build arrays or access elements of arrays are sent to the array memory units where data organized as arrays are held.

The general pattern of machine operation is that most of the computation takes place within just the cell blocks and functional units. Instructions are identified for execution in cell blocks; they are sent off to the functional units for execution; and result packets are generated and sent through a routing network to enable other instructions. Information is brought in from the array memories on an as-needed basis to participate in the computation, and the main results of the computation are dumped into the array memories and held for later use. This is why the number of array memory modules provided is less than the number of processing elements. For the applications that we have studied, the packet traffic to the array memories turns out to be a small fraction of the traffic needed among processing elements of the machine.

Pipelining of Array Processing

A typical block of code from a scientific application is shown in Fig. 7. As in this case, much of scientific computing is the construction of array values from arrays of data computed earlier. Thus the treatment of arrays is critically important to efficient computation. In the static data-flow machine there are two fundamental ways of dealing with arrays, neither of which corresponds directly to the way arrays are usually handled in a conventional computer. One way is to represent an array as a set of scalars. In data-flow terms, this means the array elements are carried by tokens on separate arcs of a data-flow graph. This allows the elements of the array to be handled simultaneously by independent data-flow instructions. The second way is to represent the array as a sequence of values, spreading out the array in time, so the array elements can be fed through a succession of data-flow instructions in pipeline fashion.

```
D: ARRAY [ARRAY [REAL] ] : =
   FORALL i IN [i, m] , j IN [i, n]
      im: INTEGER: = IF i = 1 THEN m ELSE i − 1 ENDIF;
      jm: INTEGER: = IF j = 1 THEN i ELSE j − 1 ENDIF;

      G: REAL: =
         (A [i, jm] + a [im, jm] + B [i, jm] + B [i, j] )
            * (C [i, j] + C [im, jm] )
      H: REAL: =
         (A [i, j] + A [i, jm] + A [im, j] + A [im, jm] )
            * (C [i, j] + C [im, j] )
   CONSTRUCT G + H
   ENDALL
```

Fig. 7. Typical "scientific" code block.

We have found that many application codes can be organized as a collection of code blocks where each code block takes in some array values and generates an array as its result. The arrays passed between code blocks may be represented by streams of tokens so each pair of connected code blocks is essentially a producer/consumer relationship. When many code blocks are joined in this style, the result (Fig. 8) is called a *pipe-structured program*.[10] To balance this kind of pipeline computation, it is necessary to introduce FIFO buffers to make things come out even, as illustrated in the figure.

Benchmarks

To evaluate what structure of data-flow supercomputer is best matched to important applications, we have analyzed five different benchmark problems. The steps we have followed are to (1) rewrite the code in the functional programming language Val, developed by my group at MIT;

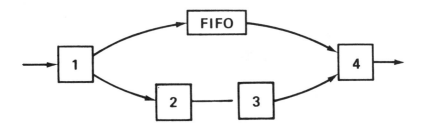

Fig. 8. Pipe-structured programs.

(2) design (by hand) machine-level program structures to match a proposed data-flow machine configuration; and (3) check that the data constraints of the program do not prevent achievement of full performance by the chosen hardware configuration. We have applied this scheme of analysis to a weather model,[11] to the three-dimensional Navier-Stokes problem, to the simple code supplied by the Lawrence Livermore National Laboratory, and to an object detection image processing problem obtained from the MIT Lincoln Laboratory, and we have sketched out how we would implement a particle-in-cell-type plasma simulation. In each case, we have shown how to construct machine-level data-flow programs that would support operation at a billion floating-point operations per second.

The Proposed Machine

The proposed 1-gigaflop data-flow supercomputer has the configuration shown in Fig. 6. My estimate of the number of devices required to build such a machine is shown in Fig. 9. We assume that each cell block can recognize and process enabled instructions at a rate of one-million per second; thus, 1024 cell blocks and a similar number of functional units will be required. The number of array modules is 32, about one-eighth the number of processing elements because the data rates required are much less.

Memory is required in the cell blocks to hold data-flow instructions and in array memory units to hold the data base of the problem. Each cell block will consist of some control hardware and random access memory, as will the array memory modules. For the array memories, I have chosen 64 million 32-bit words using 64-kilobit chips. For the cell

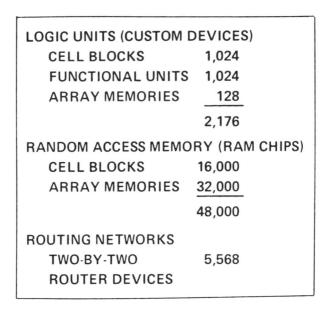

Fig. 9. Estimated parts count for a 1000-megaflop machine.

blocks, I have chosen 16 million words built of 16-kilobit chips for greater speed.

In this architecture, if the cell block control, the functional units, and the array memory control can each be built using one to three custom chips, then the chip count is dominated by memory. The next largest population of units is the communication units, the two-by-two routers. But note that the router requirement does not really dominate. By using packet communication and trading off latency for throughput, the hardware requirement for the routing networks is modest compared to the rest of the machine.

Fault Tolerance

Within the framework of the static data-flow architecture, it seems very attractive to implement some very strong form of fault detection or fault masking. Standard techniques are available for fault detection, even fault masking, for memories and for communication channels. The place where fault detection or fault masking is most difficult is in random logic, the part of the machine which is not so orderly in its construction. In the data-flow computer, these parts would be the cell block control modules, the functional units, and the array memory control modules. However, the number of devices used in the machine to implement these functions is relatively small. One could use redundant units of these types in the machine to gain full fault masking or fault detection, without inordinate extra cost. This is very different from the situation for computers of conventional architecture.

I don't know anyone who has debugged or run a large program on a 1000-processor machine. I imagine it would be an extremely trying proposition if the path were not carefully prepared by building in specific features to aid the process. Thus I expect that future highly parallel supercomputers will be structured to provide full fault detection, or perhaps fault masking. This will be essential for maintaining correct operation of the machines and the computations to be run on them.

Language-Based Architecture

The data-flow computers I have been discussing are *language-based machines*. This means that the hardware architecture of the machine is carefully chosen to behave precisely according to a well-defined model of computation. For the static data-flow architecture, the computational model is data-flow program graphs; this conceptual model makes very clear what the architecture must accomplish. The chosen computational model also defines the target program representation for a compiler from the user programming language. The task for the compiler writer is to map user programs (expressed, for example, in Val) onto the computational model (data-flow graphs).

To demonstrate the validity of an architecture, one must establish that the computational model and its implementation can support efficient execution of real computations. This we have done for scientific computation and the static data-flow model through the analysis of benchmark programs.

The Fifth Generation

The Japanese fifth-generation project has the goal of achieving massive parallelism in "knowledge-oriented" computers. To quote Dr. Tanaka,[12] "[We want] to meet the challenge of formulating human intellectual activities . . . and of embodying them in computers." Of course, this project involves very different ideas about computation than those familiar to us in supercomputers for scientific computation. In particular, the Japanese are searching for a suitable computational model based on logic programming.

In Fig. 10 I show our favorite example, the factorial function, written as a logic program. Here we are defining X to be the factorial of N, and we are representing this function as a relation that has value true or false: if X is the factorial of N, then factorial (N, X) is true. The body of the program is a set of assertions of properties of the factorial function. The first line of the body follows from the fact that factorial (0, 1) is true without any hypothesis. The remainder of the body expresses the fact that, in general, for X to be the factorial of N, certain assertions about N and X must hold.

This is the style of progamming proposed for the fifth-generation computer. It is an interesting proposal because the language of logic programming is more general than the language of functional programming that is increasingly being discussed as a desirable direction for advances in programming. Now, if you write functional programs in the logic programming language, it is possible in many cases for a compiler and a machine, working together, to figure out how to do the computa-

```
FACTORIAL (N, X):

FACTORIAL (0, 1): −.

FACTORIAL (N, X): −
    X = N*Y,
    FACTORIAL (N − i, Y).
```

Fig. 10. Example of logic programming.

tion efficiently. Beyond that, logic programming allows one to express other functions like pattern matching in semantic data bases. The extended expressive power of logic programming will likely make ordinary computations more difficult to express, and it is not clear that the pattern matching and semantic search cannot be done at least as effectively in the functional programming style.

Thus a big issue for "fifth-generation computing" is the following: What is the appropriate computational model? Is it functional programming or logic programming? The Japanese project is a concentrated exploration of one avenue toward such machines—the road of logic programming. Others, including my MIT group, are following the path of functional programming, but at a slow pace. Still other projects, which pursue ad hoc designs not guided by an adequate model of computation, are unlikely to have nearly as effective products.

Now what does this have to do with supercomputers for scientific computation? The potential of hardware advances to make high-performance computation cheap is so great that the programming advantages of computers based on fifth-generation concepts will eventually prevail, even for high-performance scientific computation. If we wish to stay ahead in areas of computation important to our national interest, we must put effort into fifth-generation computer technology as well as advance high-performance computer technology along more conventional lines. At the moment, the Japanese are doing very interesting work, but there is little comparable work being done in the United States.

References

1. Dennis, J. B. "Data Should Not Change: A Model for a Computer System." Submitted for publication in *ACM Transactions on Programming Languages and Systems.*

2. Agerwala, T., and Arvind, editors. Special Issue on Data-Flow Systems. *Computer* **15**, no. 2 (1982).

3. Dennis, J. B. "First Version of a Data Flow Procedure Language." In *Lecture Notes in Computer Science*, vol. 19, edited by B. Robinet, 396-376. New York:Springer-Verlag, 1974.

4. Dennis, J. B. "Data Flow Supercomputers." *Computer* **13**, no. 11 (1980):48-56.

5. Arvind, and Gostelow, K. P. "The U-interpreter." *Computer* **15**, no. 2 (1982):42-49.

6. Arvind, and Iannucci. R. A. "A Critique of Multiprocessing von Neumann Style." *Proceedings of the 10th International Symposium on Computer Architecture.* New York:ACM, 1983.

7. Cornish, M. "The TI Data Flow Architectures: The Power of Concurrency for Avionics." *Proceedings of the Third Digital Avionics Systems Conference,* IEEE, New York (1979):19-25.

8. Hogenauer, E. B., Newbold, R. F., and Inn, Y. J. "DDSP—A Data Flow Computer for Signal Processing." *Proceedings of the 1982 International Conference on Parallel Processing.* IEEE, New York (1982):126-133.

9. Watson, I., and Gurd, J. "A Practical Data Flow Computer." *Computer* **15**, no. 2 (1982):51-57.

10. Dennis, J. B., and Gao, G. R. "Maximum Pipelining of Array Operations on Static Data Flow Machine." *Proceedings of the 1983 International Conference on Parallel Processing.* New York:IEEE Computer Society (August 1983).

11. Dennis, J. B. "Data Flow Computer Architecture." Massachusetts Institute of Technology, Cambridge (1982).

12. Tanaka, K. "Artificial Intelligence and Computers—Toward Use-Friendly, Intelligent Computers." *ICOT Journal* (June 1983):3-7.

10

Cedar Project

D. J. Kuck, D. Lawrie, R. Cytron, A. Sameh, and Daniel Gajski
University of Illinois at Urbana-Champaign
Urbana, Illinois

Introduction

The primary goal of the Cedar Project is to demonstrate that supercomputers of the future can exhibit general purpose behavior and be easy to use. The Cedar Project is based on five key developments that have reached fruition recently and, taken together, offer a comprehensive solution to these problems.

1. The development of very large scale integration (VLSI) components makes large memories and small, fast processors available at low cost. Thus, basic hardware building blocks will be available off the shelf in the next few years.

2. Based on many years of work at Illinois and elsewhere, we now have a shared memory and a switch design that will provide high bandwidth over a wide range of computations and applications areas.

3. The Parafrase Project at Illinois has for more than 10 years been aimed at developing software for restructuring ordinary programs to exploit these supercomputer architectures effectively. The success of the work has now been demonstrated by achieving high speedups on hypothetical machines, as well as on most of the existing commercial supercomputers.

4. The control of a highly parallel system is probably the most controversial of the five topics listed here, mainly because it seems to be the least amenable to rigorous analysis. By using a hierarchy of control, we have found that data-flow principles can be used at a high level, thus avoiding some of the problems with traditional data-flow methods.

5. Recent work in numerical algorithms seems to indicate great promise in exploiting multiprocessors without the penalty of high synchronization overheads, which have proved fatal in some earlier studies. These can generally use a multiprocessor more efficiently than a vector machine, particularly in cases where the data are less well structured.

The first phase of the Cedar Project will demonstrate a working prototype system, complete with software and algorithms. The second phase will include the participation of an industrial partner (one or more) to produce a large-scale version of the prototype system called the production system. Thus, the prototype design must include details of scaling the prototype up to a larger, faster production system.

Our goal for the prototype is to achieve Cray-1 speeds for programs written in high-level languages and automatically restructured via a preprocessing compiler. We would expect to achieve 10 to 20 megaflops for a much wider class of computations than can be handled by the Cray-1 or Cyber 205. This assumes a 32-processor prototype, where each processor delivers somewhat more than 1 megaflop.

The production system might use processors that deliver 10 megaflops, so a 1024-processor system should realistically deliver (through a compiler) several gigaflops by the late 1980s. Actual speeds might be higher if (as we expect) our ideas scale up to perhaps 4096 processors, if high-speed VLSI processors are available, and if better algorithms and compilers emerge to exploit the system.

An integral part of the design for the prototype and final system is to allow multiprogramming. Thus, the machine may be subdivided and used to run a number of jobs, with clusters of eight processors, or even a single processor being used for the smallest jobs.

The Cedar Architecture

Figure 1 shows the structure of the Cedar system.[1]

Processor Cluster

A processor cluster is the smallest execution unit in the Cedar machine. A chunk of program called a compound function can be assigned to one or more processor clusters. Each processor consists of a floating-point arithmetic unit, integer arithmetic unit, and processor control unit, with

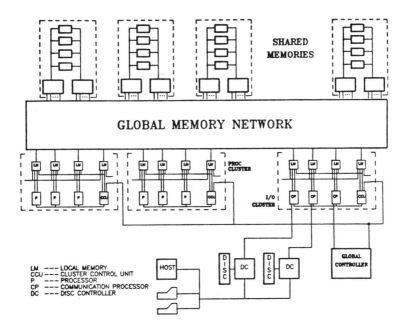

Fig. 1. Overall system diagram.

program memory. The entire processor cluster is supervised by the cluster control unit, which mostly serves as a synchronization unit that starts all processors when the data are moved from global memory to local memory and signals the global control unit when a compound function execution is finished.

Global Memory Network

The global memory network provides processor access to the shared memories and the processor-to-processor communications. The design is based on omega networks with extensions for fault tolerance.[2]

Global Control Unit

The global control unit is designed to adapt to the granularity of the data structure. We treat large structures (arrays) as one object. We reduce scheduling overhead by combining together as many scalar operations as possible and executing them as one object. In our machine, each processor cluster can be considered as an execution unit of a macro-data-flow machine. Each processor cluster executes a chunk of the original program called a compound function.

From the global control unit point of view, a program is a directed graph called a flow graph. The nodes of this graph are compound functions, and the arcs define the execution order for the compound functions of a program. The graph may have cycles. The nodes in our graph can be divided into two groups: computational functions and control functions. All control functions are executed in the global control unit, and all the computational functions are done by processor clusters. All computational functions have one predecessor and one successor. Control functions are used to specify multiple control paths, conditional or unconditional, and can have many predecessors and successors. The compound function graph is executed by the global control unit. When the number of compound functions executable in parallel is smaller than the number of processor clusters available, the global control unit assigns one compound function to several processor clusters.

There are several well-recognized difficulties in providing data storage on a multiprocessor. The first is providing rapid data access at the rate required by the processors, while at the same time providing a common, shared memory. Access to a common memory shared by thousands of processors implies short delay, high-bandwidth communication facilities. Pin limitations and speed-of-light limitations make it unlikely that a satisfactory solution will ever be provided for fast, common memory access. One way around this problem is to use processor caches to improve the apparent speed of shared memory. However, this leads to the cache coherency problem,[3,4] that is, making sure the potentially many copies of the data stored in each cache are kept up to date. This requires even more communication hardware for more than a few processors. Finally, the structure of many computations requires that certain data be used and updated in a specified order by many processors. Some type of synchronization primitives must be provided to ensure this use/update ordering.

Our solution to these problems involves a mixture of compilation and hardware techniques designed to avoid those problems when possible and to solve them with reasonable efficiency when avoidance is not possible.

The Cedar memory system has a great deal of structure to it, but the user need not be concerned with anything but the global shared memory. However, the fast local memories present in the design can be used to mask the approximately 2- to ?-second access time to global memory. Each cluster of eight processors contains eight local memories (16K of 50-ns access each).

User transparent access to these local memories will be provided in several ways. First, the program code can be moved from global to local memories in large blocks by the cluster and global control units. Time required for these transfers will be masked by computation. Second, the optimizing compiler will generate a code to cause movement of blocks of certain data between global and local memory. Third, automatic caching hardware (using the local memories) will be available for certain data where the compiler cannot determine a priori the details of the access patterns, but where freedom from cache coherency problems can be certified by the compiler.

Three Basic Memory Types

Cedar provides three separate address spaces, each of which can be segmented and each with different properties of access time and sharability: local, partially shared, and fully shared. The remainder of this section will discuss these from a logical or programmer's point of view. Private memory is intended for local (unshared) variable storage and storage of active program segments. It provides the fastest access from processors and is implemented by using the memory modules, which are local to and directly accessible by each processor.

Fully shared memory is implemented using global memory, and access is provided via a large global switching network. This memory must be used to store read-write data shared by all processors. However, the compiler (or user) can frequently determine that even though certain data might be read-write shared, there exist epochs in the program when the data are read-only, and during those epochs the data can be stored in private or partially shared memory, thereby improving access time.

In the middle, between fully shared and private memory, lies partially shared memory, which is implemented in an area of the private memories (that is, cluster memory), and access is provided via a communication facility within each cluster of processors. Partially shared memory was motivated by the discovery that in many algorithms, which require shared, read-write data, the amount of sharing can be limited to small clusters of processors, at least for significant epochs, thus saving global switch bandwidth. It also provides certain economies of storage for fully shared read-only data, which might otherwise be stored more redundantly in private segments.

The average user of Cedar will normally be concerned only with private and fully shared memory and, in fact, need worry only about the latter. Compilers and advanced users may use the other adressing modes for optimization of memory access time. The remainder of this section deals with other addressing modes currently under consideration for Cedar.[5]

Virtual Memory

Each of the three logical types of memory can also be accessed virtually. Thus, private virtual memory uses global memory as a physical backing store for private memory, which serves as the fast access physical temporary store. Similarly, partially shared virtual memory uses global memory as a physical backing store for cluster memory, which serves as the fast access storage. Fully shared virtual memory uses disks as backing storage for global memory, which is the fast access store. This gives us six types of memory mapping.

Cache Memory

The fully shared memory can be cached using either the private memory or cluster memory as a physical cache. Note that locally cached, fully shared memory is a dual of private virtual memory in that they use the same physical memories and address mapping hardware. However, locally cached, fully shared memory allows distinct processors to generate common addresses in global memory. Thus, it can generally be used only in read-only situations.

The other pair of duals are partially shared, virtual memory and cluster-cached, fully shared memory. Again, they use common memory and address mapping hardware, but cluster-cached fully shared memory allows all processors to address common segments of global memory and hence can generally be used only for read-only access.

Program Development System

The following goals are regarded as essential to the Cedar program development system:

- The compiled code should yield good execution speed (high efficiency) when run on the Cedar system.

- Source languages should be convenient for the Cedar user community.

- The program development system should be easy to use interactively.

Although these goals may seem quite old fashioned for users of some systems, they are seldom met by operational supercomputer system software. We believe they will all be met for the Cedar system and will now explain how and why this is so.

Execution Efficiency

When typical programs are run through compilers and executed on the Cray-1 (and its derivatives) or the Cyber 205, users can expect only 10 to 20% efficiency. The relatively simple (only a few statements/kernel) Lawrence Livermore National Laboratory (LLNL) kernels generate an average of only 30-35 megaflops on these machines that are rated at more than 100 megaflops. When more realistic programs are run, much worse performances are typical, and there is no reason to expect the forthcoming Japanese machines to do any better. There are two reasons for this: the architectures of the machines are not well-matched to the computations being run and the compilers are unable to restructure programs sufficiently to match the machines. This has led to a great deal of manual program restructuring and rewriting to get programs in a form that is reasonably well matched to the architectures.

In the Cedar system we have solutions to both of these problems. First, the multiprocessor architecture is more flexible in achieving high efficiencies over a wide range of computations. This has been demonstrated by a number of benchmarking efforts in the Denelcor Heterogeneous Element Processor (HEP),[6] and the Cedar solution for a number of program examples will be shown in this paper. Second, we are developing a supercompiler that can restructure programs drastically in order to match their structure to the Cedar System. Evidence for our ability to do this is available in a very preliminary manner through related work done using the Cyber 205.[7] This work demonstrated an average speedup improvement of 20% for the LLNL benchmarks. Additionally, we have a broad set of new multiprocessor algorithms under development.

Although on the one hand it is clearly impossible to solve the "dusty deck" problem optimally in a fully automatic way, the amount of human interaction needed with a properly designed system can be very small indeed. This point will be discussed in more detail below. On the other hand, it is extremely important to realize that a powerful restructuring compiler can do a better job than most humans can when working from "dusty decks." The complexity of restructuring programs with nested loops, conditional branching, subroutine calls, and so on can easily become very difficult.

Source Language

Given that one can effectively restructure sequential source programs (almost) automatically and given that we have a major interest in scientific computation, FORTRAN (in its many dialects) is a language with which we must deal. In fact, given our long involvement with automatic FORTRAN restructuring, we are sometimes accused of being FORTRAN advocates or even FORTRAN diehards. On the contrary, we are planning a number of extensions to FORTRAN for scientific users. Nevertheless, we expect to attract a number of initial users via the automatic restructuring route.

Later in this paper we will present a number of Cedar programs and discuss their compilation for Cedar. In this way we will outline some of the language extensions planned. It should be noted that we do not believe that language extensions can totally replace automatic program restructuring. It is fairly clear that, in the long run, both ideas will be used.[8]

While FORTRAN is the most widely used and most transportable scientific language, it is based on array data structures that are inadequate in many applications. When trees, linked lists, and so on are required, we must turn to other languages. Because the Cedar system is intended to be useful over a wide range of applications, we are working on hardware and software methods for handling data structures other than arrays and the concomitant program structures. Preliminary studies of LISP-like[9] and Prolog-like[10] languages have been undertaken and appear to be quite promising, but it is too early to say exactly what will be implemented in this regard for Cedar.

It is important to realize that our approach to automatic program restructuring is general enough so that it can be applied to many program constructs and data structures and, hence, many types of languages.

Interactive System

We envision a software system like that shown in Fig. 2 as the ultimate programming environment for Cedar. A user might approach the system with serial programs. An initial source-to-source restructuring attempt may lead to certain unknowns about a program, the resolution of which could allow much faster program execution. The system will, in such cases, prompt the user to make assertions about the original program. These assertions will then be taken into account in restructuring the program.

The assertions may be regarded as language extensions, and thus users may be expected to spontaneously add them to new or old programs (as aids to the compiler). However, it will be necessary to provide run-time checking of some assertions so that users can feel confident to take full advantage of them (as executable parts of the language). The failure of some assertions at run time will lead to nonoptimal but correctly executed codes. An example of this is the assertion that an inner-loop limit is greater than an outer-loop limit in guiding the system for loop interchanging. Failure of other assertions to be valid at run time would lead to incorrect execution and would be fatal to a run. An example of this is a computed subscript (subscripted subscript) that was asserted to be monotonically increasing in guiding the system to build a good

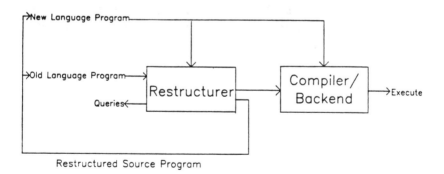

Fig. 2. Restructuring-compiler system.

dependence graph. If the subscript index set actually repeated a value, incorrect results could be computed.

The use of an interactive system would be important to new and naive users, particularly remote users or those who seldom interacted with other users. Thus, a user who approached the machine with a program written in a sequential language would greatly benefit from system-generated queries about the program. This would lead to assertions about the program by the user, which in turn would allow the system to generate a restructured program that is much more Cedar compatible.

We plan to have levels of restructuring that will allow the user to control the degree to which his source program is changed. There are serious questions about how this should be handled, as certain restructuring steps make the program more easily understandable (for example, the replacement of a sequential loop by a well-known array operation), but other steps may make it harder to understand (for example, blocking a loop to manage data flow from global to local memory). The user will probably choose a certain restructuring level initially, and when he feels that his program is in a form that will give good performance, he will use the maximum restructuring level and run the program. This will lead to the best performance, and he will not need to look at the intricately restructured program actually executed.

Thus, our goal is to make the interactive system one that teaches the user what good Cedar programs look like but does not force him to write overly complex details into his programs. By allowing levels of restructuring and by having the Cedar restructurer accept all of the language constructs it generates, we feel that the user can have maximum flexibility in this regard.

Sample Programs

In this section we discuss Cedar programming and present illustrative program examples. These examples contain a number of programming language extensions to FORTRAN, the semantics of which we feel are crucial for efficient Cedar programming, although the syntax is only a preliminary specification. All of these contructs will be generated by our own restructurer from ordinary serial FORTRAN, and all will be accepted as language extensions for the expert programmer to use.

Each programming example is presented in ordinary FORTRAN and in a highly optimized form using the extensions. In some cases, an intermediate, restructured form is also given. The restructuring level and, hence, the restructured source code form with which individual users wish to operate will depend on personal taste, expertise, and so on.

We also use the examples to illustrate a number of Cedar hardware features that are difficult to appreciate by studying only a block diagram of the system. This discussion also makes some comparisons between the Cedar and traditional vector supercomputers.

Table Lookups

Many applications involve table lookups via computed addresses. Consider the serial program of Fig. 3 that steps through the array CUBE, which contains pressure values in some physical region. These values are used via the index pressure to obtain a corresponding temperature value from TEMPTAB. In real applications, such a program would be more complex, but we can illustrate the use of the memory system and the compiler's role with this simple program. It should be noted that existing vector machines typically have difficulties with such programs, although the Cyber 205 is much better suited to them than is the Cray series.

```
      INTEGER CUBE (100, 100, 100)
      REAL TEMPTAB (20000)
      REAL ANSWER (100, 100, 100)
C
      INTEGER PRESSURE
      INTEGER I,J,K
C
      DO 10 I=1,100
        DO 20 J=1,100
          DO 30 K=1,100
            PRESSURE = CUBE (I, J, K)
            ANSWER (I, J, K) = TEMPTAB (PRESSURE)
30          CONTINUE
20        CONTINUE
10      CONTINUE
```

Fig. 3. Serial program for table lookup.

Because the CUBE and TEMPTAB arrays are read-only, they can be cached in cluster memory with no intercluster cache coherence problems. In this addressing mode, eight work blocks are fetched at once so that normal cache advantages can be expected. For arrays that may be accessed by many processors, PARTIALLY-SHARED storage is appropriate, so that the eight-word block is stored *across* the cluster memory, allowing multiple simultaneous accesses to the array.

The programmer of Fig. 3 could be prompted for an assertion in this regard, and the compiler could thus be informed that TEMPTAB has this characteristic. If adjacent processors mostly access nearby locations in TEMPTAB (that is, pressure does not vary much locally), then most accesses will not have to access fully shared memory. Because ANSWER is a shared output variable, it is declared FULLY-SHARED because otherwise this could lead to local memory coherency problems.

Blocked loops can be used to represent data that are moved in blocks to and from global memory. In most cases, loop blocking can be compiler generated.[11] Figure 4 shows an example where the compiler-generated temporary row (k) (declared PRIVATE because it need not exist in fully shared memory) is used to buffer a row of data. The WRITE copies the private row back to shared storage in ANSWER. Although READ and WRITE normally transfer data between external storage and main memory, they will be used here to denote block transfers of data in the Cedar memory system. The file descriptor of the READ and WRITE will represent the source and target of a block transfer, respectively.

By comparing the programs of Figs. 3 and 4, we can conclude that a compiler can preprocess the source program to yield substantial memory optimizations. Note that all of the declarations of Fig. 4 can be compiler generated from Fig. 3, with the help of only one user assertion.

Matrix Multiplication

Consider the program of Fig. 5 that performs matrix multiplication. The matrix A is assigned the product of matrices B and C. The program performs the multiplication by forming the dot products of the rows of B with columns of C. Every memory access in the program of Fig. 5 is to the fully shared memory. The program can be restructured to take advantage of the faster private memory by fetching and storing entire rows and columns of the three matrices. The overhead of the memory transfer is thus amortized over the computations performed on the columns and rows. Consider the restructured version of Fig. 5 as shown

```
        LOCAL-CACHED FULLY-SHARED INTEGER CUBE (100, 100, 100)
        CLUSTER-CACHED FULLY-SHARED REAL TEMPTAB (20000)
        FULLY-SHARED REAL ANSWER (100, 100, 100)
C
        PRIVATE INTEGER pressure
        PRIVATE INTEGER i,j,k
        PRIVATE REAL row (100)
C
        DOALL 10 i=1,100
          DOALL 20 j=1,100
            DO 30 k=1,100
              pressure = CUBE (i,j,k)
              row (k) = TEMPTAB (pressure)
30          CONTINUE
C
          WRITE (ANSWER (i,j,*)) row (*)
C
20        CONTINUE
10      CONTINUE
```

Fig. 4. Cedar version of a table lookup.

```
        REAL A(N,N),B(N,N),C(N,N)
        INTEGER I,J,K
C
        DO 10 I=1,N
          DO 20 J=1,N
C
C         Compute the dot product of B(I,*) with C(*,J)
C
            A(I,J) = 0.0
            DO 30 K=1,N
              A(I,J) = A(I,J) + B(I,K) * C(K,J)
30          CONTINUE
20        CONTINUE
10      CONTINUE
```

Fig. 5. Matrix multiplication.

in Fig. 6. The outer DOALL loop is executed in parallel, with each iteration supervising the calculation of a row of the A matrix. For each row of the A matrix, an entire row of the B matrix is transferred from the shared to the private memory via the READ statement, as described earlier. The READ statement transfers a row of data [B(I,*)] to the private vector b(*). Once a row of B has been moved to private memory, each column of C is then formed and stored in the a vector. This vector is then moved to shared memory via the WRITE statement, which takes its input list [a(*)] and moves it to A(I,*).

Note that the dot product has been replaced by the Vdot intrinsic; this representation is clearer than in the inner loop, as shown in Fig. 5. Even if processors are not available for improving the performance of the dot product, the intrinsic form is still preferred due to its clarity. Restructuring a program for execution on a high-performance architecture can improve the clarity of programs by translating low-level constructs into their high-level representations.

The analogy of block data transfers and FORTRAN READ and WRITE statements can be carried one step further; input/output (I/O) transactions are normally buffered to overlap processor and I/O activity. In the program of Fig. 6, the explicit data movements can be buffered such that the next column or row is moved to local memory while the computational portion of the program segment (the dot product) is active. The optimal case for this buffering technique will ensure that processors never wait for data movement, although space is consumed in local memory due to the extra buffers.

Conditional Loop Exits

Many programs contain loops with conditional exits. Because such loops can terminate before the entire index set is executed, the iterations cannot be executed independently. Consider the program of Fig. 7. The first portion of the loop computes a sum of A(I,*) in SUM(I). If that sum is not zero, then the sum of B(I,*) is added to the accumulated sum in SUM (I).

The inner loops of Fig. 7 are calculating a special form of a first-order linear recurrence: the vector sum. If the language is extended to allow recurrence intrinsics, an optimizing compiler can recognize vector sums and translate the program of Fig. 7 into the program of Fig. 8. The program of Fig. 8 has been improved through the translation, or restructuring, of its inner loops into Vsum intrinsic function references. The improvement is reflected in the enhanced readability of the program and

```
        FULLY-SHARED REAL A(N,N),B(N,N),C(N,N)
        PRIVATE REAL a(N), b(N), c(N)
        INTEGER i,j,N
C
        DOALL 10 i=1,N
          READ (B(i,*)) b(*)
C
          DO 20 j=1,N
            READ (C(*,j)) c(*)
C
            a(j) = Vdot (b(*),c(*),N)
C
20          CONTINUE
C
          WRITE (A(i,*)) a(*)
10        CONTINUE
```

Fig. 6. Restructured matrix multiply.

```
        DO 10 I=1,N
C
        SUM(I) = 0.0
        DO 20 J=1,N
          SUM (I) = SUM (I) + A (I,J)
20        CONTINUE
C
        IF (SUM(I) .EQ. 0) GO TO 100
C
        DO 30 J=1,N
          SUM (I) = SUM(I) + B (I,J)
30        CONTINUE
C
10        CONTINUE
C
C  Loop exits to here
C
100  CONTINUE
```

Fig. 7. Serial program with loop exit.

```
        DO 10 I=1,N
C
            SUM (I) = Vsum (A(I,*),N)
C
            IF (SUM(I) .EQ. 0) GO TO 100
C
            SUM (I) = SUM(I) +  Vsum (B(I,*),N)
C
10          CONTINUE
C
C   Loop exits to here
C
100    CONTINUE
```

Fig. 8. Restructured program.

the restructuring of the serial inner loops into a more parallel form. The Vsum routine can be implemented by a summation tree that will reduce the program's execution time to time proportional to log (N) (using N processors) or $\frac{N}{P}+ \log(p)$ (using p processors).

An array machine must be content with the program, as shown in Fig. 8. The outer loop cannot be executed in parallel because the loop exit condition depends upon values calculated in the loop itself [that is, SUM(I) is computed and tested in the loop].

The architecture of a multiprocessor can allow the first and second vector sums of consecutive iterations to execute in parallel, once the decision has been made to continue execution of the outer loop. Specifically, once iteration i has decided that SUM(i) is not zero, then iteration i + 1 can begin execution. The resulting program, as shown in Fig. 9, takes approximately half the time of the program in Fig. 8.

The first loop is a DOALL loop that initiates the SIGNAL vector. Once the next loop starts executing, each iteration waits on its SIGNAL element before beginning the body of the loop. The loop is called a DOACR (rather than a DOALL) loop because a delay is observed at the start of each iteration. In a DOALL, all iterations can start simultaneously; the iterations of a DOACR are staggered in time to satisfy dependences. A DOALL is really just a special case of a DOACR loop that requires no delay between iterations. The SIGNAL element can be set in two ways. Once an iteration has decided that the loop exit is not

```
        DOALL 1 I=2,N
        CALL EMPTY (SIGNAL(I))
1       CONTINUE
C
        CALL FULL (SIGNAL(1))
        OKAY = .TRUE.
C
        DOACR 10 I=1,N
C
        CALL WAIT (SIGNAL(I))
        IF (.NOT. OKAY) GO TO 100
C
        SUM (I) = Vsum (A(I,*),N)
C
        IF (SUM(I) .EQ. 0) GO TO 100
        CALL FULL (SIGNAL(I+ 1))
C
        SUM (I) = SUM(I) + Vsum (B(I,*),N)
C
10      CONTINUE
C
C  Loop exits to here
C
100     CONTINUE
C
        OKAY = .FALSE.
        DOALL 101 I=1,N
        CALL FULL (SIGNAL(I))
101     CONTINUE
```

Fig. 9. Multiprocessor version of a loop exit.

taken, then the next iteration can be signalled to start its loop body. If the exit is taken, then the processors must be signalled to abort the loop. The logical OKAY variable records whether processors are to continue executing the loop or exit the loop.

In practice, the CALL WAIT may involve spinning on a signal (that is, a busy-wait). Because we know the approximate time the vector sum intrinsic will take, an iteration could wisely choose to delay that long before spinning on its signal. This delay avoids unnecessary traffic to memory, thus increasing the performance of other memory transactions. Our language extensions will include a delay intrinsic.

Pattern Matching with Output Dependences

Programs often contain loops that update a location; the semantics of such loops, when executed serially, are that a common location is repeatedly updated. The value retained in a location, after the loop has completed, is the value computed in the last iteration that performed a store to the location. For example, consider the program segment of Fig. 10. A string T is searched for occurrences of n different patterns. The search is to return the last occurrence of each pattern in T.

An array machine must be satisfied with executing only the inner loop in parallel. If just the inner loop is executed in parallel, then the searches occur in parallel for a given location in T. However, the outer loop can be executed in parallel if the output dependence on LASTFOUND can be solved. Because the output dependence can only be solved at run time, the architecture must provide hardware to deal with the multiple updates of LASTFOUND.

Consider the program of Fig. 11 that computes the same result as Fig. 10. The language has been extended to include an intrinsic WLTR that synchronizes updates for the store to LASTFOUND(J). Associated with each data field of memory is a key field that will (in this case) hold the value for the highest iteration that is stored to the data field. When another iteration wants to store to a data field, it checks the key field to make sure that the previous update of the data field had an earlier iteration number than the current iteration number. A store to the data field replaces the key field with the current iteration number.[12]

```
      DO 10 I=1,LENGTH(T)
  C
         DO 20 J=1,N
            IF (MATCH(T,I,PATTERN(J),LENGTH(PATTERN(J)))
      X        LASTFOUND (J) = I
  20        CONTINUE
  10     CONTINUE
```

Fig. 10. Serial program with output dependences.

```
        DOALL 10 I=1,LENGTH(T)
        DOALL 20 J=1,N
           IF (MATCH(T,I,PATTERN(J),LENGTH(PATTERN(J)))
    X          CALL WLTR (LASTFOUND(J),I,I,I)
20         CONTINUE
10      CONTINUE
```

Fig. 11. Parallel version of pattern matching.

Wavefronts

Some programs contain loops that can be executed in parallel, only if the index set of such loops is shifted. Consider the program of Fig. 12 that computes elements of a two-dimensional array. The program is a finite-difference method, whereby an element is computed as the average of its four (North, South, East, and West) neighbors. Although the program of Fig. 12 appears to form a recurrence around both loops, there are elements of the array that can be computed in parallel. For example, once A(1,1) is computed, A(2,1) and A(1,2) can both be computed concurrently; then, elements A(3,1), A(2,2), and A(1,3) can be computed. The program of Fig. 13 shows how the index set of Fig. 12 can be shifted, such that all elements lying along NW to SE can be computed in parallel.

```
        REAL A(N,N)
        INTEGER I,J
C
        DO 10 I=1,N
         DO 20 J=1,N
          A(I,J) = (A(I-1,J)+ A(I+ 1,J)+ A(I,J-1)+ A(I,J+ 1))/4.0
20        CONTINUE
30        CONTINUE
```

Fig. 12. A wavefront loop.

```
        DO 10 I=2,2*N
            Compute A(q,r), such that q+ r=I, in parallel
   10       CONTINUE
```

Fig. 13. Shifted index set of a wavefront.

The program of Fig. 13 generates, for each iteration of the I loop, the elements of A that can be computed in parallel. Each iteration of I generates a different number of parallel elements; the first and last iterations generate only one element each (A(1,1) and A(N,N)); when I=N + 1, there are N elements that can be computed simultaneously. For an array machine, the program of Fig. 13 generates 2N vectors of varying sizes. Because the resources of an array machine are all commited to executing a single vector instruction, the wavefront computation of Fig. 12 cannot be executed efficiently on such a machine; a multiprocessor can be more flexible with its resource allocation. Consider the program of Fig. 14; it performs the wavefront computation of Fig. 12, but without the need to shift the index set. The body of the loop has been restructured to wait on the elements that were previously computed by the loop (that is, the elements that participate in the recurrence). Note that the setting of A(I,J) has the additional effect of setting the full status of A(I,J). For programs that follow a single-assignment philosophy, the implicit setting of the full status is semantically sound.

```
        DO 10 I=1,N
            DO 20 J=1,N
                IF (I .GT. 1) CALL WAIT(A(I-1,J ))
                IF (J .GT. 1) CALL WAIT(A(I ,J-1))
                A(I,J) = (A(I-1,J)+ A(I+ 1,J)+ A(I,J-1)+ A(I,J+ 1))/4.0
   20           CONTINUE
   10       CONTINUE
```

Fig. 14. Multiprocessor wavefront.

A Graph Algorithm

Figure 15 shows the algorithm that is traditionally used to compute the transitive closure of an adjacency matrix.[13] For each pair of nodes, node$_i$ and node$_j$, if there is a connection from node$_j$ to node$_i$, then node$_j$ can reach all nodes that node$_i$ can reach. The outer two loops consider the pairs of nodes and the inner loop establishes the transitive connections.

The algorithm is column-oriented because it processes all the edges incident into a vertex before it begins to process the next vertex. Consider the restructured form of Warshall's algorithm, as shown in Fig. 16. The cached variables ROW1 and ROW2 are equivalenced to the fully shared adjacency matrix to obtain two cachings of the A array, since two rows are referenced in the innermost DOALL loop.

Symbolic Differentiation

Supercomputers and their associated software have been developed around the FORTRAN language because large scientific programs are usually posed in FORTRAN. The academic environment, notably the field of artificial intelligence, has emphasized languages that allow a more flexible form of data structures. As mentioned earlier, we are

```
      LOGICAL A(N,N)
      INTEGER I,J,K,N
C
      DO 10 I=1,N
        DO 20 J=1,N
C
        IF (.NOT. A(J,I)) GO TO 20
C
        DO 30 K=1,N
          A(J,K) = A(J,K) .OR. A(I,K)
30        CONTINUE
C
20      CONTINUE
10    CONTINUE
```

Fig. 15. Serial transitive closure algorithm.

```
      FULLY-SHARED LOGICAL A(N,N)
      PRIVATE INTEGER i,j,k,N
C
      CLUSTER-CACHED FULLY-SHARED LOGICAL ROW1(N,N)
      CLUSTER-CACHED FULLY-SHARED LOGICAL ROW2(N,N)
C
      EQUIVALENCE (A(1,1),ROW1(1,1))
      EQUIVALENCE (A(1,1),ROW2(1,1))
C
      DO 10 i=1,N
        DO 20 j=1,N
C
        IF (.NOT. A(j,i)) GO TO 20
C
        DOALL 30 k=1,N
          ROW1(j,k) = ROW1(j,k) .OR. ROW2(i,k)
30        CONTINUE
C
20        CONTINUE
10      CONTINUE
```

Fig. 16. Restructured transitive closure algorithm.

currently studying various approaches to this subject. Here we sketch one such approach. Consider the program of Fig. 17 that performs symbolic differentation over expressions containing variable names, constants, sums, and products.[14] LISP was chosen for the representation of this problem due to the ease with which expression trees can be processed. The form of each expression is first examined for its arithmetic structure, and then the rules of differentation are applied. The CAR of an expression yields either the operator of a binary expression or a single variable or constant. If the expression is a binary expression, the first and second operands are represented by the CADR and CADDR of the expression, respectively. The program of Fig. 17 has a purely functional form because the function DYDX does not have any side effects; argument evaluation can therefore proceed in parallel.

For an infinite number of processors, a balanced tree could be symbolically differentiated in time proportional to log (/EXPR/), where /EXPR/ is the length of the expression. A processor executing an instance of the program in Fig. 17 must wait for any recursive calls to

```
(DEFUN DYDX (EXPR X)
  (COND
      ((ATOM EXPR)
       (COND
           ((EQUAL EXPR X) 1)
           (T 0)))

      ((OR
        (EQUAL (CAR EXPR) 'PLUS)
        (EQUAL (CAR EXPR) 'DIFFERENCE))
       (LIST
         (CAR EXPR)
         (DYDX (CADR EXPR) X)
         (DYDX (CADDR EXPR) X)))

      (EQUAL (CAR EXPR) 'TIMES)
       (LIST
         'PLUS
         (LIST
            'TIMES
            (CADR EXPR)
            (DYDX (CADDR EXPR) X))
         (LIST
            'TIMES
            (CADDR EXPR)
            (DYDX (CADR EXPR) X)))) ))
```

Fig. 17. Symbolic differentiation in LISP.

DYDX to complete before it can construct the differentiated list expression. The processor is therefore idle while any subtrees are differentiated. The efficiency of the parallel schedule (that is, a limited processor schedule) can be improved by deallocating processors from invocations of DYDX when the processes block; this deallocation necessitates a synthetic stack structure to retain the state and ordering of the incomplete blocked processes. The order of the processes must be maintained because the LIST operator is nonassociative, and, therefore, the order in which the blocked processes are resumed is crucial.

Another approach to a limited processor schedule is to create a list according to the rules of differentiation and then spawn processes to differentiate expressions that should participate in that list. Because the list is created before any sons are differentiated by DYDX, an invocation of DYDX can be instructed where to place its result. The invocations of DYDX are self-scheduled by maintaining a queue of items awaiting differentiation. Each entry in the queue represents a packet of work that must be performed; the entry contains an expression that requires differentiation and a location to store (a pointer to) the result. Processors remove an item from the queue, perform the DYDX routine of Fig. 17, and perhaps place more items on the queue. Processing continues until the queue is empty. The algorithm of Fig. 18 outlines this self-scheduled approach to parallel function evaluation. The tree is represented by the scheduled approach to parallel function evaluation. The tree is represented by the TREE array, such that the CAR, CADR, and CADDR of node TREE(e) are located at nodes TREE(3*e+2) and TREE(3*e+3), respectively. Alternatively, hashing may be used to speed up data access over indirect addressing. The FORK intrinsic calls the routine that is specified as its first parameter, passing the other parameters to that routine. Execution of the called routine is concurrent with the caller.

A new version of DYDX must be written to examine the structure of the expression as reflected in its first argument (a single atom or the

```
      PARTIALLY-SHARED INTEGER TREE(*)
      PARTIALLY-SHARED INTEGER QUEUE(*)
      INTEGER e
C
10    CONTINUE
C
C     Indivisibly dequeue an item into the variable "e"
C
      CALL FORK (DYDX, TREE(3*e+ 1), TREE(3*e+ 2), TREE(3*e+ 3),
               TREE(e), QUEUE)
C
C     Wait for something to be added to the queue or for all
C        processors to terminate.
C     If they all terminate and the queue is empty,
C        RETURN
C     Otherwise
C        GO TO 10
C
```

Fig. 18. Self-scheduled symbolic differentiation.

operator of a binary expression) and between terminal atoms and continued lists. The atoms can be represented by pointers to a symbol table.

Conclusions

Cedar software will emphasize an easy-to-use code development system. To this end, we plan an interactive source program restructurer. This will also lead programmers to use the language extensions that make parallelism explicit in new programs. We have presented a number of simple example programs that illustrate what Cedar programs will look like and have used them to illustrate what automatic restructuring will do. Also, we have focused on performance improvements of Cedar over traditional vector supercomputers.

Acknowledgment

We thank Clyde Kruskal and G. H. Lee for their help with the graph algorithm in the Sample Programs section.

References

1. Gajski, D., Kuck, D., Lawrie, D., and Sameh, A. "CEDAR—A Large-Scale Multiprocessor." *Proceedings of the International Conference on Parallel Processing,* IEEE Computer Society Press, order no. 479 (1983).

2. Padmanabhan, K., and Lawrie, D. H. "A Class of Redundant Path Multistage Interconnection Networks." Accepted by *IEEE Trans. on Computers* (1983).

3. Censier, L. M., and Feautrier, P. "A New Solution to Coherence Problems in Multicache Systems." *IEEE Trans. on Computers* **C-27** (1978):1112-1118.

4. Tang, C. K. "Cache System Design in the Tightly Coupled Multiprocessor System." *National Computer Conference Proceedings* **45** (1976):749-753.

5. Lawrie, D. H. "Address Segment Access Attributes and Primitive Memory Operations in Cedar." Cedar document 20, Department of Computer Science, University of Illinois, Urbana-Champaign (1983).

6. Smith, B. J. "A Pipelined, Shared Resource MIMD Computer." *Proceedings of the International Conference on Parallel Processing,* IEEE Computer Science Society, publication no. CH1321-9-C (1978):6-8.

7. Arnold, C. N. "Performance Evaluation of Three Automatic Vectorizer Packages." *Proceedings of the International Conference on Parallel Processing,* IEEE Computer Society Press, order no. 421 (1982):235-242.

8. Kuck, D., Padua, D., Sameh, A., and Wolfe, M. "Languages and High-Performance Computations." In *Proceedings of the IFIP Working Conference on the Relationship Between Numerical Computation and Programming Languages,* edited by J. Reid, 205-221. Boulder: North-Holland Press, 1982.

9. Kuck, D. "Fast Pure LISP Evaluation." Cedar document 13. Department of Computer Science, University of Illinois, Urbana-Champaign (1983).

10. Kuhn, R. "Prospects for Theorem Proving and Programmed Logic on a Supercomputer." Unpublished manuscript. Department of Computer Science, University of Illinois, Urbana-Champaign.

11. Abu-Sufah, W., Kuck, D. J., and Lawrie, D. H. "On the Performance Enhancement of Paging Systems Through Program Analysis and Transformations." *IEEE Trans. on Computers* **C-30** (1981):341-356.

12. Zhu, C. Q., and Yew, P. C. "Cedar Synchronization Primitives." Cedar document 18, Department of Computer Science, University of Illinois, Urbana-Champaign (1983).

13. Warshall, S. "A Theorem on Boolean Matrices." *J. Amer. Chem. Soc.* **9** (1962):11-12.

14. Winston, P. H., and Horn, B. K. P. *LISP*. Philippines: Addison-Wesley Publishing Co., Inc., 1981.

11

Supercomputer Trends and Needs: A Government Perspective

J. T. Pinkston
National Security Agency
Ft. George G. Meade, Maryland

Introduction

Nobody has to tell this group about the importance of very high performance computing to many different and very important government activities. My own agency has survived in the past and will continue to survive in the future because of our capabilities in this area. And we are not alone in this respect.

The needs for computing power continue to grow unabated, and one of the reasons we are all here is the concern that the computing capabilities that will come just in the natural course of events will not keep up with these needs.

A Supercomputer Definition

Now just what are these capabilities that I am talking about, which are generally provided by machines that have come to be called supercomputers? I'll bet everybody in this room would have an answer to this question. But I would also bet that there would be some significant differences among those answers. The term "supercomputer" is widely taken to refer to the largest scientific general-purpose machines commercially available. These machines all have three necessary characteristics. They have a fast processor capable of floating-point operation. They have a large primary memory—in fact, the numbers in Fig. 1 are probably too small already. They have a large word size for numerical resolution.

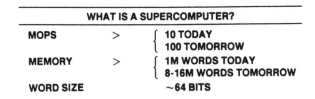

Fig. 1. Characteristics of a supercomputer.

Although these machines have been designed primarily with partial differential equations applications like those of the national laboratories in mind, my agency has historically made very good use of these products. Many of the computations we do are quite different from the floating-point numerical ones that most supercomputer users perform, and yet the combination of speed, memory size, and word size has served well for us.

For this talk, though, I would like to broaden the definition of "supercomputer" to include any computing system that operates at a high compute to input/output (I/O) ratio, and that delivers a very large number of effective computing cycles per second for the solution of some large problem.

Supercomputer Usage

When we talk about what developments we would like to see nationally in this supercomputer area, we must keep in mind not only what class of machines we are talking about, but also what we collectively want these machines to do for us and how they are typically going to be used (Fig. 2).

First, the supercomputer today is not used as just more of the same kind of resource as its lower performance brothers. The kinds of jobs run on it tend to be longer running jobs and tend to operate compute bound. There are classes of problems that require a very large number of cycles and that the scientist or designer wants solved in an accepable time—usually measured in hours (rather than days).

At a conference here in Los Alamos 2 years ago, Lowell Wood of Lawrence Livermore National Laboratory made the statement that "a moderately fortunate and serious physical modeling researcher presently gets use of about 3% of a Cray-1 on the time average." And, of course,

---

**SUPERCOMPUTER USAGE
(AS COMPARED WITH "BIG" COMPUTERS)**

- HIGHER COMPUTE TO I/O RATIO

- LONGER RUNNING JOBS

- FEWER USERS

- USERS TEND TO BE MORE SOPHISTICATED

- FEWER JOBS SIMULTANEOUSLY ACTIVE

- LESS EXECUTION OF VENDOR-SUPPLIED CODE

- DEBUGGED CODE TENDS TO BE RUN MANY TIMES

- OTHER MACHINES EXIST IN THE COMPLEX

Fig. 2. Uses of supercomputers.

such users tend to be substantially more sophisticated than the average user.

Another characteristic of supercomputer usage is that fewer jobs tend to be simultaneously active. Again, these are substantially larger jobs than would be running on the lesser machines. As a result of this and because much of the running is compute-bound, the time slices are set longer and there is less of a premium on the ability to swap jobs in a highly efficient manner.

There tends to be less execution of vendor-supplied software and more generation by the owner of application codes that will be run extensively. The typical state of affairs is that the programmer/scientist is willing to spend a lot of time and effort optimizing his software, once he decides that the algorithm he has is indeed the one he wants to run. This extends into the systems software area also, with the National Security Agency and the Department of Energy laboratories all running operating systems of their own making.

Finally, another characteristic that supercomputers have is that they tend not to be the only machine in the complex. Virtually every supercomputer owner I know has other machines around and available for general usage. This implies that the supercomputer need not do all things for all people.

So already we see the supercomputer used as a not fully general-purpose machine. You could, if you wanted, do your payroll and word processing on them, but it is pretty universally accepted that you are better off putting this kind of job on lesser machines. The supercomputer is general purpose, and yet it is specialized also. The recognition of this fact is important because the more a design strives for complete generality, the less well (both in raw speed and cost effectiveness) it is going to perform the very compute intensive calculations that the high-end machine is really needed for.

The message here is that, while most computers aim to maximize some mix of speed and ease of use, the balance is shifted for the supercomputer toward getting the ultimate in speed. The users are sophisticated—even writing their own operating systems, as mentioned earlier—and are both able and willing to go to a fair amount of effort to get the highest possible compute power.

Supercomputer Spectrum

Indeed, as the demand for computing power grows, I think we should not be surprised to see the machines becoming even more specialized in order to concentrate on the problems that they are really being acquired to solve.

One example of such an architecture is the Control Data Corporation (CDC) Advanced Flexible Processor (AFP). In the AFP (Fig. 3), all of the memories and processing units can operate on every clock cycle, with outputs of these units being routed to inputs of other units through the big crossbar switch. Microcode sets up the paths in the switch, and these paths can change on every clock cycle. The result is that the programmer can configure specialized pipelines as he needs them.

By no stretch of the imagination can this machine be called friendly and easy to program. Writing a 160-bit-wide microcode where different pipelines may be involved in the same word and the same pipeline may span several words is not a job for timid souls. But when working on problems that are well suited to it, the AFP achieves a significant speedup over the best general-purpose machines around. In fact, an eight-processor AFP outperforms a Cray-1 by about an order of magnitude on such applications. And while nobody is going to write any million-line software package for the AFP, there are serious users who are willing to go to a lot of work to pick up this kind of order of magnitude performance improvement.

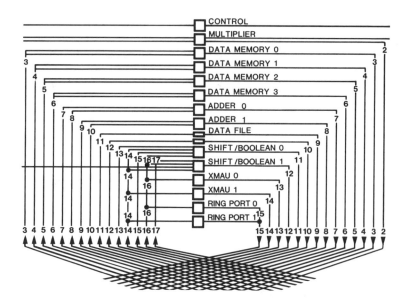

Fig. 3. AFP crossbar configuration.

Array processors are another example where significant improvements in cost performance over general-purpose machines can be obtained (Fig. 4). This figure is a Floating-Point Systems architecture and is typical. In this case, the specialization is for repetitive floating-point adds and multiples. We've all seen the advertisements and headlines in technical publications for these systems: "Array processor hits 62 Mflops—breaking the $2000/Mflop barrier" (Electronics, July 14, 1983); or "Create a 10 to 100 Mflop supercomputer for your VAX" (an advertisement in the same issue); or a recent news release, "First 100 Mflop array processors shipped."

You don't have to believe these numbers. In fact, you are well advised not to take them too seriously. But even allowing for the hyperbole, it is clear that these systems do provide quite a respectable cost-performance ratio when doing their speciality. After all, $2000/Mflop is pretty impressive compared to a $10 million machine running at 100 Mflops, which divides out to $100,000/Mflop.

Further specialization can lead to even greater performance increases for yet smaller problem classes. Gene Shapiro and colleagues at International Business Machines (IBM) have reported on an experimental

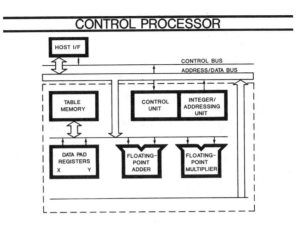

Fig. 4. Array processor.

physical design machine they built to do wire routing for gate array, custom-integrated circuit design. It has 64 Z-80 processors in an 8 by 8 array, wired and coded solely for this application (Fig. 5). Now, while you might conceivably be able to do your payroll on an AFP if you really wanted to (and were willing to stand the cries of anguish and other verbal abuse from your programmer), it is absolutely impossible on this machine.

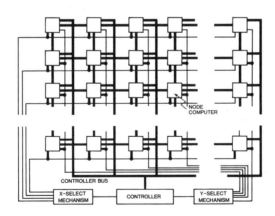

Fig. 5. Gate array, custom-integrated circuit design.

This special-purpose machine is faster by a factor of 40 than an IBM 3033. In wiring a 300-circuit chip, the cost-performance ratio must be even larger. Furthermore, no heroics are needed to achieve this kind of speedup over a general-purpose machine—it comes naturally when the designer can concentrate the machine on only one problem.

Figure 6 shows a spectrum of computing systems—of supercomputers, as I have broadened the definition. They all deliver very large compute power for the solution of big, highly compute-intensive problems. This spectrum starts at the largest general-purpose scientific machines and ranges upward from there in performance, while simultaneously downward in generality.

We, of course, would like performance to be increased all across this supercomputer spectrum, from the fully general-purpose machines on into the more specialized limited-purpose ones. When we look at trends, which is supposed to be one of the subjects of this talk, we need to consider both the commercial general-purpose machines that are going to come as successors to the Cray-1 and Cyber 205 and the technology that could be used for designing and building the more specialized, probably more powerful, and probably smaller production quantity machines; and we need to do this in an economical and rapid way.

Trends: Past Decade

During the early history of general-purpose computers, there was an exponential growth in compute power. Over the past decade, progress

INDUSTRY GROWTH - CPU POWER 35 YEARS				
TIME PERIOD	"SUPER" COMPUTER	POWER FACTOR	COST FACTOR	P/C RATIO
LATE 50s	CDC-1604	1	1	1
EARLY 60s	CDC-3600	4.5	3	1.5
LATE 60s	CDC-6600	25	5	5
EARLY 70s	CDC-7600	125	7.5	16.7
LATE 70s	CRAY 1A	500	9	55.5
EARLY 80s	CRAY X-MP	2000	15	133.3
LATE 80s	YYYY	8000	22.5	355.5
EARLY 90s	ZZZZ	32000	32	1000

Fig. 6. Spectrum of computing systems.

continued in the industry, but a slowing trend was evident. In particular, the speeds of the logic devices themselves barely doubled over this time, from somewhat below 1-ns gate delays 10 years ago, to around 400 ps in today's fastest systems.

The system speeds have not done that well (Fig. 7). CDC's fastest technology today is about a 20-ns clock, compared to 25 for the 7600 in 1970. IBM stayed in the 50- to 60-ns range from the 360/91 in the mid 1960s through the 3033 and just recently moved to 26 ns with the 3081 and its new packaging techniques. Cray, the fastest, had the Cray-1 running at a 12.5-ns clock in 1976 and is now preparing to deliver the XMP at 9.5 ns. The meaningful comparisons here are the numbers within a given company. Different architectural philosophies lead to different amounts of computing in a clock cycle and, therefore, substantial differences in the number of gates in critical paths. But the numbers from each of these manufacturers make one message clear: things are getting harder because of some very fundamental physical limitations.

For machines to get much faster than they are today, they are going to have to become physically smaller. The speed of light is about 1 ft/ns in free space and somewhat slower as electrical signals propagate down conductors.

Figure 8 shows a Cray-1 with the covers removed. The circuit boards are plugged into a cylindrical arrangement from the outside in order to have the interconnect wiring in the center of the cylinder, where lengths of wire can be minimized.

Controlled lengths of twisted pair cables are used—all connected by hand (Fig. 9). Yet in a Cray-1, about half of the 12.5-ns cycle time is taken up by time of flight in the interconnect wiring. That says that if you were to magically replace all of the logic gates by infinitely fast ones, you would only double the overall speed of that system.

The circuits in these machines have all been based on silicon. Silicon technology is firmly entrenched as the in-place technology today, and

CDC 6600	100 ns	1965
CDC 7600	25 ns	1970
CDC CYBER 205	20 ns	1978
IBM 3033	54 ns	1975
IBM 3081	26 ns	1980
CRAY 1	12.5 ns	1976
CRAY X-MP	9.5 ns	1983

Fig. 7. System clocks.

Fig. 8. A Cray-1 with the covers removed.

Fig. 9. Twisted cables in the Cray-1.

steady improvements have come. But as the technology matures, advances are slowing.

The device speed itself is not really the main worry of the designer today; rather, it is the packaging of these devices in ways that get them close together and with connections that do not slow down the very fast signals. The biggest obstacle in doing this is the heat. The circuits generate heat and have to be cooled, and as they are crowded closer and closer together, the cooling problem becomes very difficult.

In the Cray-1, again, the cooling is accomplished by bonding the circuit boards to copper plates to conduct the heat from the chips out to the edges, which are in contact with a chilled liquid coolant that circulates throughout the cabinet. About 100 kW, which all has to be extracted as heat by the cooling system, is drawn by the circuitry.

Ten years ago, most of the large machines were air cooled—they just had fans blowing chilled air from under a false floor up through the cabinet. Today, virtually all high-performance systems have a circulating liquid coolant.

The scheme that CDC uses in the Cyber 205 involves a cold bar snaking back and forth across every board (Fig. 10). Each chip is mounted in a socket stradling the cold bar, with the chip held in good

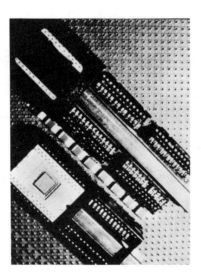

Fig. 10. Silicon Circuits on a cold bar.

thermal contact with the bar by a spring clip. Here, the chip technology is a 168-gate gate array (vs two gates per chip used in the Cray-1 logic).

IBM developed a complete new set of packaging technologies and the thermal conduction module (TCM) was the result (Fig. 11); it was used first in their 3081. Some of the numbers for this package illustrate the magnitude of the problem and the lengths that people will go (and have to go) to get performance at the system level.

The 90-mm^2 ceramic substrate has sites for up to 118 chips, depending on the logic/memory mix, with each logic chip being about a 700-gate complexity and averaging about 1.5 W per chip. The multilayer ceramic has 33 levels of wiring to connect about 30 000 logic circuits on a module.

Each chip has a spring-loaded piston pressed against its back to make good thermal contact to carry the heat away (Fig. 12). Chilled water flows through the cold plate on top, and the entire package is filled with helium gas to increase the thermal conductivity, so that a module can handle up to 300 W, or up to 4 W on any individual chip. There are 1800 pins on a module—1200 signal pins, 500 for power and ground, and 100 spares.

Even with all of this effort to get the logic parts close together, the circuit delay of 1.15 ns turns into an average packaged gate delay of 2.5 ns, with a system cycle time of 26 ns. An entire 3081 processor with two central processing units (CPUs) fits on four boards, each holding about eight TCMs.

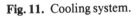

Fig. 11. Cooling system.   **Fig. 12.** Close-up of the IBM module.

The message ought to be clear that packaging and cooling are difficult and are getting more exotic. These are currently the limiting factors in large system performance.

Trends: Past

To summarize the trends we have seen over the last 10 years or so, device speeds have continued to increase, but at slower rates compared with previous decades (Fig. 13). The system speeds were further limited in their rate of growth by the problem of cooling ever denser packages.

And even 10 years ago, parallelism was entering the picture as people realized that device speeds alone were not going to be enough. There are various ways of getting concurrency of operation, including instruction pipelining, multiprocessing, and vector streaming. The vector architectures have been dominant over the past decade, with the Cray-1 and Cyber 205 both in this class.

Trends: Future

As we look ahead, what developments are coming? Silicon technology is still firmly entrenched and device speeds will continue to push up (Fig. 14). Not before the latter part of this decade will any serious challenge from other technologies such as gallium arsenide or Josephson junction appear.

TRENDS - PAST DECADE

- SPEED: ADVANCES SLOWING
- TECHNOLOGY: SILICON INTEGRATED CIRCUITS
- COOLING: DEMANDS GREATLY INCREASED
- VECTOR ARCHITECTURES

Fig. 13. Trends seen during the past 10 years.

TRENDS - FUTURE

- SPEED: FASTER BUT NOT ENOUGH
- LSI AND VLSI
- COOLING: EVEN MORE EXOTIC
- MULTIPROCESSOR ARCHITECTURES
- VERY LARGE MEMORIES

Fig. 14. Future supercomputer developments.

All manufacturers are pushing to higher levels of integration. This permits more compact packaging and somewhat lower power dissipation per gate. But as performance demands increase, more and more gates will be designed into these systems, and the cooling techniques will get even more exotic.

For example, the Cray-2 is designed to be totally immersed in a bath of liquid fluorocarbon coolant circulated over the chips. It is physically smaller than the Cray-1 and uses modules that have eight boards, each 4 by 8 in., stacked into a 1-in. thickness.

The Cray-2 will have a 4-ns clock time, which will be obtained partly by reducing the number of gates in any path between registers—from eight in the Cray-1 to at most four in the Cray-2 (and it is four only when the physical path length is short—two if it is long).

At four processors, people are still reasonably comfortable about being able to effectively use the parallelism on a single problem and, after all, this is really what is desired; we want to solve more complex problems rather than just more problems of the same complexity.

But as the degree of parallelism goes much higher, nobody really knows what will happen. Nobody seems comfortable about this, but then nobody knows what else to do.

As for the memory, the drive is the partial differential equations. The manufacturers perceive their best customers wanting to go to three-dimensional calculations and finer mesh sizes, which demand the large primary memories. Sixteen million words seem about the smallest amount anyone is considering, and it goes up from there. Also, making big memories is something that the manufacturers know how to do. It is a lot easier to double the size of main memory than it is to double the system clock rate or make a large number of processors work in concert.

Finally, a trend I do not see yet but would like to see is one toward some kind of customizable product. There is no question that a few special, carefully selected instructions can greatly increase performance. Is it necessary that computers be like Model Ts, that is, all identical? Why not permit custom operations to be available as options for individual customers? I think this might be an interesting area of research.

A National Supercomputer Program

After we have looked at some of the trends in the industry (and here I make no claims of completeness), it is logical to ask what we think we will get if we do nothing extraordinary and simply let nature take its course. Do we like what we see? If not, then some action is called for to stimulate or modify the direction of development.

The arguments in favor of some kind of support are well known—the costs of doing a major development and the uncertainly of volume sales seem to be combining to deter industry from pursuing the supercomputer market. And this market may get thinner if the private sector does not perceive the same needs for compute power as the government perceives (Fig. 15).

There are several relatively independent directions that should be followed in advancing supercomputing capabilities, including component speed, advanced architectures (probably parallel), and design and fabrication tools (Fig. 16).

IS A GOVERNMENT PROGRAM NEEDED?

- HISTORICALLY, WE HAVE WAITED AND PURCHASED

- HIGH DEVELOPMENT COSTS, THIN MARKET

- GOVERNMENT NEEDS DIVERGING FROM PRIVATE SECTOR(?)

- THE JAPANESE

Fig. 15. Arguments in favor of national support for supercomputers.

WHAT SHOULD A PROGRAM CONTAIN?

- ARCHITECTURES

- FASTER SYSTEM HARDWARE

- TECHNOLOGY TO SHORTEN DEVELOPMENT TIME

- SOFTWARE - LESS IMPORTANT HERE

Fig. 16. Directions to advance supercomputing capabilities.

Component speed can always be used independently of whatever architecture is implemented. Work in this area should include device and circuit work including silicon, gallium arsenide, and Josephson junction technologies (Fig. 17). There is no need to make a decision among these possibilities yet, and so nationally we should keep the options open and not put all the eggs in one basket.

Packaging is also an absolutely necessary component of any effort to improve system speeds. In fact, with today's packaging and interconnect technologies, it makes little sense to work on faster devices—the reduced logic time would simply be swamped by the package delays.

As for architecture, it is clear that any national program must include a lot of investigation of ways to effectively increase the number of computing circuits working simultaneously (Fig. 18). Nobody is projecting that even the most exotic device technologies are going to give by themselves the performance that is demanded for future systems. New ideas are needed, but even more, techniques for evaluating proposed new architectures are needed. It is easy to come up with parallel designs, but difficult to definitively say how well they would work, what problem classes they could work well for, and what difficulties would be associated with their use.

Yet another element of a comprehensive national program should be design and fabrication tools and technologies that permit rapid and efficient mapping from ideas into working hardware. This is particularly important for the development of machines at the high performance, limited-generality end of spectrum, where the design cost cannot be spread over a large production run.

Finally, there must be a technology transfer scenario. If work being done in research laboratories or universities does not somehow change the way some computer maker does his job, then it is for naught. To accomplish a transfer, some kind of demonstration or experiment is

- PACKAGING
- DEVICES
- CAD/CAM WHERE NECESSARY
- JOSEPHSON JUNCTION TECHNOLOGY

Fig. 17. Hardware technologies.

- METHODOLOGY AND TOOLS FOR EVALUATING AND CHARACTERIZING
- IDENTIFY PROBLEM CLASSES WITH ARCHITECTURES
- HARDWARE DEMONSTRATION
  - AFTER SIMULATION
  - AFTER DESIGN OF EXPERIMENT

Fig. 18. Architectures.

almost always needed. These demonstrations may, but need not, be complete machines. They may be test vehicles, but they absolutely must address the concerns of whatever group is going to take over the ideas and make machines. These test vehicles must be agreed upon in advance by the builders, so that if they are successful, they do indeed demonstrate the feasibility of the development. And there must be advance agreement on what constitutes success.

Summary

In summary, there is really no limit in sight to the amount of compute power that can profitably be used. From what I've seen, this is equally true for the national laboratories and others.

Now we, the users, will take anything we can get. And I believe that, if left alone, industry will produce good machines that are better than today's machines. But they could be even better and arrive sooner with added stimulation. The question, then, is whether or not the improvements are worth the expense. I believe they are, although it is very hard to quantify this.

A superspeed program should address high-performance computing technology across the board. The intent is not to design one ultimate computer; rather, the intent is to advance the tools and technology for designers and builders to use to make more powerful machines for each user.

This program should explore more than one option for achieving these ends: circuit and system speed, concurrent architectures, and possibly customization for individual users. There should be more than one option considered within each of these areas: silicon, gallium arsenide, HEMT, and Josephson device technologies all need to be pursued for speed; and techniques for evaluating and characterizing the many extant architectural ideas are needed.

We should not assume that all of these advances will show up in the next generation of machines; in fact, we really should assume that most won't, and maybe not even in the generation after that, depending on how you define a generation. Silicon is firmly set for a few more years for circuits, and architectures seem to be fixing on multiple CPUs. It is the following generation that any program stated now really wants to try to impact with the more exotic technologies entering at that time.

Finally, I believe that there exists an opportunity for achieving greatly improved performance in yet another way different from any of the above. By trading off generality with performance, new architectural options open up. When the problem class is restricted, it becomes straightforward to configure an architecture with all the right numbers of the right kinds of processing elements, all able to function in concert.

The problems may lie in economics, but the performance is clearly there for the taking; with the new design automation, manufacturing, and software tools coming along, it is time to take a look at this option.

12

Computation: The Nexus of Nuclear Weapon Development

D. B. Henderson
Los Alamos National Laboratory
Los Alamos, New Mexico

The real questions behind what I was asked to discuss are, "Why do we want all these computers, and why don't we ever have enough of them?" The answer is that computation is the center of the program, the nexus where everything is joined.

The development of nuclear weapons is qualitatively unlike any other engineering enterprise in that a broad collection of phenomena from generally distinct fields of science is exploited in a tight interdisciplinary fashion. Many of the parameters are at the limits of both our practice and our (accurate) knowledge base. Moreover, and most importantly, the exploited phenomena are deliberately nonlinear. In contrast, almost all other engineering practices are linear or are at least linearized. If we build a bridge, we don't want to go beyond linear limits. If we build an airplane, the aerodynamics may be nonlinear but are usually linearized when we carry out design calculations. Nuclear weaponry deliberately uses a $1 + 2 = 10$ logic in making things work.

The nonlinear processes are often nonlocal and are often in non-equilibrium. How things work depends on unobserved and, in general, unobservable phenomena. Numerical simulation through computer codes is, therefore, central to the design process. Simulation is the only place in which all of the nonlinear complex phenomena are integrated. The only place, that is, other than integrated system testing. Those tests—each is really a whole set of exquisite experiments and measurements—are also dependent upon numerical simulation, not only for design, but also for interpretation. Often parameters of direct design interest have no direct observable or measurable signal. We must settle for those external signals that we can get. The crucial linkage among these signals, the physical processes, and the device design parameters are available only through simulation.

Simulation is beyond mere modeling of things. I characterize modeling as an *ad hoc* treatment; designers do it—they talk about "knobs," arbitrary parameters that they adjust. Modeling is certainly useful because we can achieve fits to observed data; modeling allows interpolations. We can design devices between those we have done before. But, by simulation I mean the inclusion of a priori correct physics throughout, including the unobserved and unobservable phenomena. If we don't do this, then we can't get to what we need, which is the ability to extrapolate and to develop the useful exploitation of new phenomena.

A code is a compendium of lots of stuff, mostly physics. I look at it as books on a shelf: textbooks on chemical kinetics, detonations, fluid mechanics (we usually call them hydro codes because of this textbook), equations of state, radiation processes (emission, absorption, transport, and opacity), heat transfer by means other than radiation, and particle transport. Because we are building a nuclear device, nuclear processes and cross sections are needed. Finally, we include electricity, magnetism, and plasma physics. We collect all these things together with numerical analysis and some *ad hoc* rules—and that makes a code.

It is a big collection, this whole library of stuff, and a consequence of its size and variety, which I think we don't realize as often as we should, is that people tend to think in terms of codes. They do this because the codes are the only integrated compendium of this complex set of stuff. In pursuing applications, the confusion is an advantage. Designers, if you listen to them, really know their codes, and that means they can do their job very well. But that the two are confused is a handicap sometimes, at least, if we don't understand the distinction or fail to remember it. The distinction certainly has important implications when we think about qualitatively new applications, bringing in new physics methods, or adapting the codes to new computers.

Computer codes are not quite the only compendium of all we do; there is also nuclear testing, which provides the only other integration of the complicated nonlinear phenomena. Tests aren't just tests where we see whether it goes or fizzles. They are tightly knit sets of dynamic experiments, which together address issues of system reliability (did it work), design issues (did some part of the device work as expected, or did it work but some other way), and constituent physics. We may also measure a basic physics parameter such as some cross section that has nothing to do with weapons; occasionally, we take advantage of a unique physics opportunity and exploit it for the general good of science. A consequence of having done these experiments together in a single package is that the experiment interferes with itself. Avoiding interference between different experiments within a test package often requires the most of our design codes. As mentioned, typically we are looking at indirect observables, and numerical simulation is required just to get the data and understand what they mean. That is to say, we have to model the experiment as well as the design of it. That goes around a circle—we design an experiment, engineer the experiment, conduct the experiment, and then extract and interpret the data; then we go back to design. Each of these involves simulation on the large computers using the whole shelf of "textbooks."

I've been a little vague in these remarks, and I would like to excuse that by putting in an aside about classification. Computer codes are special because they are central—they have it all together. It's obvious that we deny outsiders access to our design information and test data; perhaps it is less obvious that for the same reasons we have to restrict what is said about the codes. Let me explain why that is and the kinds of questions an outside party, if he knew the evolution of our codes, would look at and exploit. He could ask, "What are they working on now?" Or, "What do they plan to develop?" He would infer that by which parts of the codes are markedly better than they were previously and which parts are the same. "Which physics topics are being improved and where is something being modeled not quite correctly and being improved?" This is important information to the other side, from which he might anticipate improvements in our weaponry. Finally, "Which things are they not doing correctly, and what does that imply in terms of design weaknesses of their weaponry that they may not even appreciate?" There are substantial reasons, to which I subscribe, that force me not to list all my examples here.

Back to the subject. How big are the codes? They're sizable, typically 50 000 to a quarter million lines of FORTRAN, and they run up the memory limits of the Cray-1; we routinely do problems using 3 million words of memory, and in so doing use up lots of cycles and central processing unit (CPU) hours. Why? Let's consider a typical problem and, as a useful analog, imagine an automobile engine. In doing an automobile simulation, I can talk about the parts. First, we want to draw it up on a mesh, so let's imagine an axisymmetric automobile engine on a large two-dimensional mesh. In the tally in Table 1, we have a 100 by 100 mesh or 10 000 mesh points. That sounds like a lot, but there is a fan, a

TABLE 1
SIMPLIFIED CALCULATION OF THE RUNNING TIME
OF A TYPICAL PROBLEM[a]

Structure of a Typical Problem	
Number of mesh points (100×100)	10^4
Number of variables per point	100
Number of operations per variable per point per time step	30
Number of time steps	4×10^3
Number of operations	1.2×10^{11}
Running time at 20×10^6 flops	

$$\frac{1.2 \times 10^{11}}{2 \times 10^7} = 6000 \text{ seconds} = 1\frac{2}{3} \text{ hours}$$

[a]As noted in the text, overnight turnaround is really a requirement that constrains the data.

timing belt, cylinders and spark plugs, and finally a fly wheel filling up the mesh. Our mesh is not large; it's really rather coarse. How many variables do we have? Well, let's see. We have two positions; velocities are two more; and temperature and density. The variables do not count up rapidly. Wait a minute! A functioning weapon is pretty hot, so we will have to talk about the different material constituencies, each having several states of ionization. When we begin to count ionization states, we add many variables. We are also doing nuclear physics. We have many particles fluxing through the devices, and they can have many energy bins—100 is rather a small number. How many operations per variable? Per point? Per step? Roughly 30, at least. The number of time steps depends upon these things, and in typical problems constructed this way, about 4 000 time steps are needed. Multiplying these things together, we get 1.2×10^{11} floating-point operations. What we really achieve isn't 160 megaflops, it's 20. Why this is so is an interesting question, but that's accepted and that's what we get. If we divide, we calculate that the problem runs in 1 hour and 40 minutes, which allows everyone overnight turnaround. That is nice because people who are pursuing an orderly design process, trying to get something done, need overnight turnaround for most of their problems; otherwise, they can never get the job done. The exercise also works the other way: we start by recognizing that we really need overnight turnaround for almost every designer in order to get the work done, and computers only go so fast, so this constrains the amount of arithmetic to be done and compromises the physics models.

Codes are constructed basically from standard FORTRAN with some extensions because of the size of the problem or because we must use the hardware efficiently. Codes are modular; again, think of them as volumes on the shelf. We can take one off the shelf, look at it, examine it, write a new and better one, and put it back. Each volume or chapter has its own module in a well-structured code. Codes are generally interactive; that is, people work from terminals, look at intermediate results, sometimes change what's going on, and are part of the system. Although inside a volume or a chapter we use second-order accurate implicit methods, the whole shelf is one large first-order explicit serial loop. I think we don't really understand all the implications of this.

Our resources have grown nearly exponentially. Fortunately, computer power per dollar has grown almost exponentially as well. I think everyone at the conference knows that. It's less obvious that each qualitative jump in the technology has explicit dividends. We have certain new features in our products because we had new classes of computers with which to pursue designs or with which to understand the physics. We have classified lists of specific improvements that we have achieved with the Class VI machines, the Cray machines, which simply would not be there or be available to the military today, if we had not had these machines over the last few years. Physics issues are understood better and the design envelope is correspondingly enlarged. In a similar way, we have rather specific lists of dividends that we can already anticipate from the Class VII machines. Although we do not know which vendor will produce them or exactly what they will be like, we do know what they're going to do for us. Finally, in emphasizing the importance of evolving computer technology, we must remember that exploiting each qualitative jump in the hardware requires new code technology and sometimes new terminal technology.

The exponential growth of our computer resource is shown in Fig. 1, and because it's almost a straight line on a semilog plot, it's almost exponential. But the growth is slowing down; 30 years ago we had a doubling time in our installed capacity of less than a year and a half, whereas now it's more than 4 years. This is hurting what we can do. It is also evident from the figure that the real gains come from the new classes of what we now call supercomputers. Adding additional units of a given

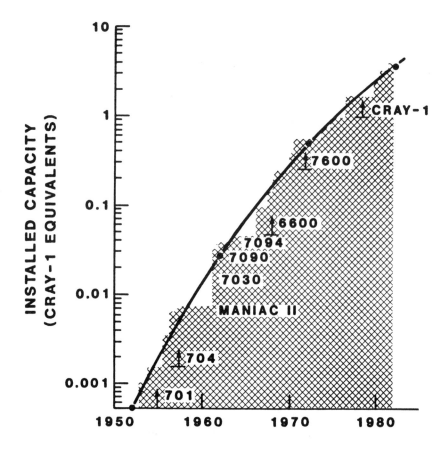

Fig. 1. Almost exponential growth in the installed computational resource at Los Alamos over three decades. The doubling times have lengthened notably from 1.45 years in 1952, to 2.06 years in 1962, to 2.93 years in 1972, and to 4.17 years in 1982.

supercomputer becomes relatively insignificant when we have acquired several units. There is a diminishing return. Typically, we get the latest supercomputer, and then we get several more, but not many. That is the way we have exploited the resources in the past and the way we expect to in the future.

This huge computer resource is used by many people at Los Alamos, but most of it is used in the weapons program. In round numbers, 20% of the people use 80% of the resources. Because both weapon and nonweapon communities are important, this poses some hardware, procedural, sociological, and management problems that the next speaker will tell you about. All I will say is that he solves them very well, and that it is possible to keep these very different communities happy and happy with each other, sharing a common stable of supercomputers.

"Why do you have so many codes?" That's the question we are usually asked after we are asked, "Why do you have so many computers?" "Why don't you just have one, or two, or three?" Computer codes are a technology that has many dimensions, as sketched in Fig. 2. For instance, we can talk about the parameter of device parts. Like the automobile engine, we can have a code that includes the fan, the belts, the spark plugs, the cylinder liners, the fly wheel, or what-not. We include or exclude various parts of the hardware. Similarly, we can look at a parameter of physical processes: do we include high-explosive (HE) ignition, or equations of state (EOS), or thermonuclear (TN) burn, or something else? We can talk about a parameter of physics methods and approximations that we apply to those; for instance, do we assume local thermodynamic equilibrium (LTE), or do we integrate line rates, or do we look at a parameter of mathematical and numerical methods. Do we solve by successive over-relaxation (SOR), ICCG, diffusion, or something else? We can categorize our code by its logical structure, the data structure, or the machine structure for which it is intended. Is it serial? Is it vector? Is it parallel? The last parameter includes things that matter to

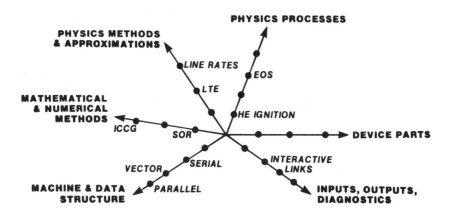

Fig. 2. Representation of the many dimensions of computer code technology. Each code covers many points on this matrix; no code covers it all.

the people using a code. What are the inputs? What are the outputs? What diagnostics are provided? Is it an interactive code? Does it link to another? Each code covers many points on this multidimensional matrix. No code covers all of it; if it did, we could neither debug it nor afford to run it. Because we have different things that are important to different problems, each code is different. Because the space is so broad, we have many code projects.

How are the code improvements made? They are not made by magic—they're made by hard-working people who may do several things. For example, they may put in more complete physical models or more accurate models that cover the same physics. They may use faster algorithms to solve the same models. They may use more accurate algorithms on the same models. Or they may put the code up on a more capable computer that can deliver more megaflops or that has a larger memory. These improvements go on all the time. Our investment in software is larger than our investment in hardware by several fold. The codes have to be tested and verified while maintaining a stable production capability because the person who is busy in some design process doesn't want the code changing out from under him; he must be able to do the same problem and get the same answer. Small changes must be due only to his changes in the input.

Our codes cannot be ideal. Mother Nature, I contend, works with integral equations and communicates through interfaces. Physicists don't do that; they are schooled in differential equations and think in terms of gradients. Real codes don't do either of these. They build finite representations on a grid, with attendant difficulties in centering. Time centering is a problem because things that need to be simultaneous cannot be. The text volumes must be covered one at a time, even when in some way the insides of a single book can be covered simultaneously. Spatial centering is a problem because the representation is discrete. This brings up serious issues; usually we put extensive variables on the mesh and intensive variables in between, but there are difficulties and serious problems to be addressed.

We foresee no computer that's big enough. Why not? First, the real world is in three dimensions, not two, while most of our codes are really two dimensional. Second, we need a lot more variables per point. The numbers in Table 1 allow just an approximation or a set of approximations. Third, more variables per point tend to imply more operations per point as each variable is linked to each of the others. Finally, finer resolution drives us to smaller time steps. We need many more floating-point operations per job than we have now, and we also must work with a lot more data. Remembering that people still need overnight turn-around for most problems, we conclude that "big enough" or a state of diminishing return is not foreseen.

There is progress. Vectorization has been a success. Parallel machines are coming. Data-flow architecture is being studied. Artificial intelligence is being explored. Are there methods from the artificial intelligence community to make our codes more efficient? We believe there may be and we are exploring the possibility. We are evaluating scientific work stations to replace dumb terminals.

Our effort in vectorization has paid off. A certain hydrodynamics and diffusion code is 5 to 10 times faster than its nonvectorized version. The particle-in-cell hydrodynamics method is three to five times faster. Using an equation of state, which implies table lookup, it is 10 to 12 times faster. A collisionless plasma physics code is 10 times as fast. An S_n neutronics transport treatment is three times as fast. Monte Carlo photon transport treatment is five times as fast. As stated several times in this conference, we have to beware of the scalar residuals. We have to have a balanced scalar speed, we need reasonably low vector startup time, and we need good speed on short vectors. These are messages to the hardware community. A good optimizing compiler is needed; that's a software requirement. We also need to apply analysis to look at algorithms; it's hard work, so patience is needed.

Some questions are obvious when we look at parallel processors. Are they split up by process (is each volume taken off the shelf put on a different machine), or are they split by region (is one processor the cooling fan and another the spark plug)? Both of these lead to bottlenecks where we don't really get anything like n times as fast for n processors. Instead, we will have to split dynamically, that is, also look at the machine state (which parts of the computer system are working at the moment). We will look at the problem dependencies (optimum processor allocation is not simply something that can be done once and for all in a code). How best to allocate the many processors will vary during the execution of the problem. Fortunately, our problems are lopsided; they're not equally balanced. Therefore, we can see a quick payoff to parallelism. Figure 3 indicates that for a typical job about 10% of the code is using 90% of the cycles. We can imagine reasonably early success with the parallel processors, when they're available to us, by simply paralleling that part of the code that dominates the CPU time. Otherwise, we will execute separate job streams on the several CPUs. We will thereby get a significant speedup with relatively little work.

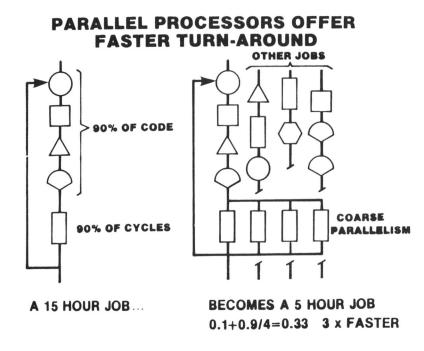

PARALLEL PROCESSORS OFFER FASTER TURN-AROUND

OTHER JOBS

90% OF CODE

90% OF CYCLES

COARSE PARALLELISM

A 15 HOUR JOB...   BECOMES A 5 HOUR JOB
                                $0.1+0.9/4=0.33$ 3 x FASTER

Fig. 3. Representation of appreciable gain from coarse-grained parallelism expected to be realized with Class VII supercomputers.

We actively await the Class VII supercomputer. And while we wait, many things are going forward. We have in progress some parallel code development. We're experimenting and maintaining close contact with the vendors (those of you in the hardware business know we track what you're doing). We run benchmarks and emulators. We're studying new algorithms and we pay attention to the proposals for new machine architecture. Finally, we have conferences like this.

Even though our computational resources have grown in power some 6000-fold in 3 decades, they are far short of the need. Our detailed understanding of the physical phenomena is limited by the complexity of the models which our computers can handle. Our design envelope is similarly limited to those circumstances and configurations which we can model. The implied inverses are also historically demonstrated as follows: each increase in computer power (and in accompanying software) has resulted in improvement in our physics understanding, in broadening our useful design envelope, and in qualitatively improved products delivered to the military. These last improvements have been in military values—yield, weight, and size—and in more social values—yield selections, weapon security, and weapon safety.

The limits imposed by our computers are still all-encompassing; future increases in computational power will result in continued system improvements without approaching a diminishing return. When will we have a big enough computer? The only foreseeable answer is "never."

13

An Overview of Computing at Los Alamos*

R. H. Ewald
Los Alamos National Laboratory
Los Alamos, New Mexico

The Los Alamos National Laboratory is operated by the University of California for the United States Department of Energy (DOE). The Laboratory employs about 7000 people, and its mission is to perform research and development activities related to national security and energy programs.

To support its own and other national programs, the Laboratory has developed a state-of-the-art scientific computing network that supports about 4500 users (about 3500 are Laboratory employees and about 1000 are users at other installations throughout the United States). The network, called the Integrated Computing Network (ICN), is shown in Fig. 1. About 100 computers are connected to the ICN, and it is separated physically or logically into three security partitions: Secure for classified computing, Open for unclassified computing, and Administrative for administrative computing.

At the center of the network are the large "worker" computers that today include five Cray Research, Inc., Cray-1s, five Control Data Corporation (CDC) 7600/176s, three CDC Cyber 825s, and several Digital Equipment Corporation (DEC) VAX-11/780 computers. All of these computers run interactive timesharing operating systems, and a common set of software is supported on all workers to allow users to move easily from one computer to another. The operating systems in use on the computers are the following:

CTSS (Cray-1s). Cray Timesharing System developed by the Magnetic Fusion Energy Computing Center, Livermore, California, for the Cray-1. CTSS is the successor to LTSS.

*This work performed under the auspices of the U.S. Department of Energy.

152

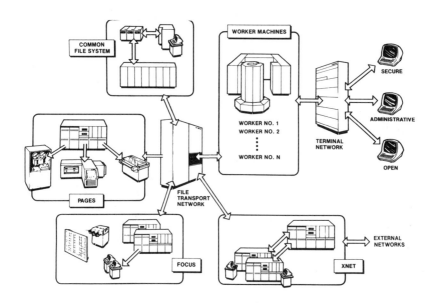

Fig. 1. ICN functional configuration.

LTSS (CDC 7600s). Livermore Timesharing System developed at Lawrence Livermore National Laboratory.

NOS (CDC Cyber 825s and 176s). Network Operating System developed by CDC.

VMS (DEC VAX-11/780s). Virtual Memory System developed by DEC for the VAX family of computers.

UNIX (DEC VAX-11/780s). Operating system developed by Bell Laboratories.

The common software available on all worker computers includes FORTRAN 77 compilers; three graphics libraries—our own Common Graphics System (CGS), the National Center for Atmospheric Research (NCAR) library, and DISSPLA; our standard mathematics library (called the SLATEC library, which was developed jointly with other DOE and Department of Defense laboratories); and common utilities to perform such functions as file shipping, graphics file processing, inter-machine process-to-process communication, and production job submission.

To provide additional computing for users at remote locations or users who have a need for some local computing capacity, the Laboratory selected the DEC VAX as its standard distributed processor. There are currently about 20 VAX distributed processors in the Laboratory connected to the ICN through 3 other VAXs that act as gateways into the network. All of the common software available on the workers is also available on the distributed processors, and a "terminal passthrough" capability has also been added to allow VAX local terminals to access the worker computers.

Most users typically access the network through terminals in their offices, which are connected to about 25 DEC PDP/11 minicomputers that act as concentrators and switches to allow any user to access any worker computer, provided the user has authorization to do so. Once a user selects a computer and has provided the proper security and accounting information, this part of the network becomes transparent, and it appears that the user is logged on directly to a worker computer. Most terminals operate between 300 and 9600 bit/s, with about 25 graphics terminals running at speeds up to 300 kbit/s. Intelligent workstations are also being supported for terminal traffic and file shipping by this part of the network.

So that large blocks of information could be transmitted between worker computers and service nodes, the file transport network was constructed with five System Engineering Laboratory (SEL) 32/55 computers. Using Los Alamos-designed interfaces and communication software, this portion of the network allows files to be shipped at up to 50 Mbit/s.

A centralized node called the Common File System (CFS) is provided for long-term file storage. The system is accessible from any worker computer or distributed processor in the network and appears as an extension of a computer's local file storage system. It is an International Business Machines (IBM) system with two 4341s as controllers, numerous 3350 and 3380 disks, and a 3850 mass storage system. Online capacity is about 2.7×10^{12} bits, although the users currently have stored about 800,000 active files with a total volume of about 10^{13} bits. Three storage hierarchies are supported: disk, online tape cartridge, and offline tape cartridge. The system runs Los Alamos-developed software and automatically migrates user files between the three tiers of storage. Files that are expected to be accessed frequently are stored on disk and infrequently accessed files are stored off line. Because of this balancing, response is excellent, as indicated in Table 1.

TABLE 1
CFS STORAGE HIERARCHY

Type of Storage	Total Information Stored (%)	Total Files Accessed (%)	Response Time
Disk	1	83	5 seconds
Mass Storage System	24	16	1 minute
Offline	75	1	5 minutes

Printed and graphical output is handled centrally by the PAGES system. PAGES is a network node to which any worker or distributed processor may ship text or graphical files for processing. PAGES is controlled by two DEC VAX-11/780s that drive two Xerox 9700 laser printers (10,000 lines/min each), three FR-80 COM recorders (16-mm, 35-mm, and 105-mm film formats), a Dicomed D48 COM recorder (35-mm film), and two Versatec hardcopy plotters. PAGES currently processes more than 2×10^9 bytes of information daily, which contributes to a total output of 2-4 million pages of print per month, 4-6 million frames of microfiche per month, and about 250 000 frames of 16- and 35-mm film each month.

A new network node called FOCUS was implemented last year to control portions of the network, provide a unified operator interface, and gather utilization statistics. The FOCUS system consists of two VAX-11/780s, which operate the production computing environments on the Cray-1s and the CDC 7600s. Production (long-running) jobs are submitted to FOCUS, which schedules and monitors the execution of the jobs and the machine status. FOCUS also provides a single operator station for all of the computers under its control, so that typically only one to two operators are required to operate the entire set of Cray-1s and CDC 7600s.

The major computing network resources available at Los Alamos are summarized in Table 2.

TABLE 2.
MAJOR COMPUTING RESOURCES

Qty	Description	Operating System	Total Power (CDC 6600 = 1)
5	Cray-1	CTSS	80
4	CDC 7600	LTSS	16
1	CDC Cyber 176	NOS	4
3	CDC Cyber 825	NOS	3
20	DEC VAX-11/780 (DPs)	VMS	10
1	Common File System (CFS)	MVS	
1	Output Station (PAGES)	VMS	
1	Production Controller (FOCUS)	VMS	

14

Operating Systems and Basic Software for High-Performance Parallel Architecture*

J. C. Browne
University of Texas
Austin, Texas

Introduction

It is well established that future generations of supercomputers will be based on parallel architectures. It is critical to recognize that parallel computing is a systems problem, not just an architecture problem or a component problem. Development of basic software, including operating systems and programming languages for parallel architecture, is intrinsically more difficult than development of basic software systems for sequentially structured architectures. This added degree of difficulty results from the greater dimensionality and complexity of models of parallel computation over models of sequential computation. This paper will explore the sources of complexity and the development of efficient basic software systems for parallel architectures. One approach to the two problems of management of many resources and the complexity of parallel architectures will be defined and discussed in detail. This is the approach built upon reconfigurable architectures and partitioning rather than sharing of resources. The structure of the TRACOS operating system for the Texas Reconfigurable Array Computer (TRAC) will be used as an example.

*This work was supported by the U.S. Department of Energy, grant number DE-AS05-81ER10987, and by the U.S. Air Force Office of Scientific Research, contract number F49620-83-C-0049.

Premises and Theses

It is the basic premise of this talk that future supercomputers will have parallel architectures. Therefore, an entire new generation of software systems and application programs will be required to utilize the super-computer systems of the future. Thus, the applications of future (parallel) supercomputers represent systems problems, not merely architecture and component problems.

It is a further premise of this talk that algorithms and software systems for parallel architectures, particularly architectures involving very many processors, will be much more difficult to design, develop, and evaluate than algorithms and software systems for sequentially architectured computer systems. Therefore, the availability of algorithms and software systems will actually be the rate determining step in the use of future supercomputers. The sources of this difficulty will be discussed in a subsequent section of this paper.

An example of this can be seen in the case of the vector architecture supercomputers of the current day. It is commonly accepted that, as of this date, there are no higher level language compilers that deliver the dominant fraction of vectorization that is attainable from a given program. Typically, the degree of vectorization attained for codes, even at laboratories that have been running vector computers for a decade or more, is far less than the potential vectorization. Even the concepts of vectorization are still not well developed 15 years after their initiation. For example, it was a widely accepted traditional viewpoint that vec-torization of discrete event simulation was not possible. Yet Brown, Callahan, and Martin[1] recently demonstrated vectorizability of Monte Carlo codes, and a general theory of vectorization of discrete event simulation has just been developed by Chandak and Browne.[2] Software, algorithms, and application should receive at least equal emphasis in the development of future supercomputers with that of architecture and components if parallel architectured supercomputers are to be effec-tively utilized without an extended delay after hardware is available.

It is a further premise of this paper that the dominant economic benefits of future supercomputers will be derived from new applications that are more demanding with respect to software and that will integrate numeric, symbolic, and signal processing modes of computation. The key element will be to drive down the cost of very powerful computing so that these applications, which will involve interfacing of computer systems to the real world in both control and decision support roles, will be cost effective. The economic benefits of supercomputers will come from leadership in applications. Therefore, we stress that the United States program for development of supercomputers should stress software, algorithms, and applications and architectures that integrate capabilities for numeric, symbolic, and signal processing applications.

Models of Computation and the Complexity of Algorithms and Software for Parallel Computing

The essential element in the understanding of the development of algorithms, software, and applications for parallel supercomputer systems is an understanding of the models of computation required by significant problems specified in higher level languages and realized on hardware architectures. A model of computation for sequential computing includes the following elements:

- Primitive units of computation.

- Composition rules for composing the primitive units of computation into executable and schedulable units.

- Definition of address spaces that control the data to which the computation is applied.

Models of parallel computation add to the elements of sequential computation requirements for the following:

- Modes and topology of communication between units of computation that are executing in parallel.

- Modes and types of synchronization mechanisms.

The typical situation is illustrated by Fig. 1. Each application is typically made up of algorithms, steps, and phases within algorithms, each of which may be characterized by some model of computation. Units of computation and the modes and topology of communication are often disjointed between phases of an algorithm. These algorithms and applications must be mapped to a hardware architecture that also realizes one or more models of parallel computation, including the specification of one or more modes of synchronization and/or topologies and modes of communication. More commonly, however, the algorithms of an application are programmed in a higher level language that offers the ability to represent programs in some model of computation not necessarily identical to or completely overlapping with that of either

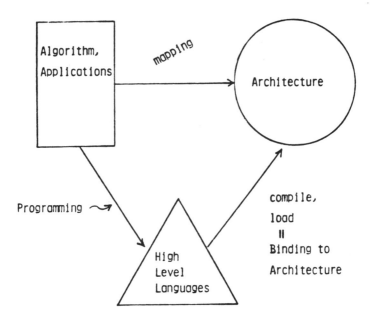

Fig. 1. Models of computation and their relationships.

the algorithms and applications or the architecture. In the three figures representing algorithms and applications (Fig. 1), higher level languages and architectures are drawn as square, triangular, and circular to emphasize that it is often the case that they do not necessarily mesh easily. The act of programming is the act of mapping an algorithm to a higher level programming language, while compiling and loading are the acts of mapping and binding an expression of a computation in a model of computation (that given by some programming language) to a realization in another model of computation (that realized by a hardware architecture).

It is our thesis that all computations have some natural structure that can be used to define possible mappings between models of computation. Figure 2 displays a simple computation. The natural structure of this computation is a tree structure. Figure 3 shows the mapping of this simple computation structure to a sequential architecture and then to a two-processor parallel architecture. Note that mapping to a parallel

ALL COMPUTATIONS HAVE SOME NATURAL STRUCTURE

A := (B/C) + (D*E)

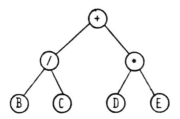

EXECUTION OF THE COMPUTATION REQUIRES <u>MAPPING</u>
UPON SOME ARCHITECTURE

Fig. 2. Structure of a simple computation.

architecture introduces the concept of data movement between processors (because T1 must be moved to processor 2 before execution can continue) and synchronization (because processor 2 must wait for the arrival of T1 before it can complete the computation).

Another example is given in Fig. 4, which illustrates the computations and data flow for a bisection algorithm for parallel structuring of polynomial root finding. The ith and $(i+1)^{st}$ instantiations of the program for evaluating the polynominal must communicate with the ith instance of the program for comparing the two values to determine if a zero occurred between the two points of evaluation.

An algorithm for determining a histogram of the grey level values of the pixels of an image is another slightly more complex example that illustrates mapping between algorithms and architectures. Let us assume that we are dealing with a fixed interconnection geometry architecture where each processor in an array of processors is connected to its four

MAP TO A SEQUENTIAL ARCHITECTURE

$$T1 := B/C$$
$$T2 := D*E$$
$$A := T1 + T2$$

MAP TO A PARALLEL ARCHITECTURE

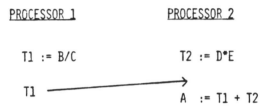

Fig. 3. Mapping of a simple computation to a
        sequential architecture.

nearest neighbors. Figure 5 is an example of such a mesh. Let us assume that we begin by assigning the pixels of one column of an image to a given processor. Figures 6, 7, and 8 illustrate this concept for eight processors and eight columns. The histogramming algorithm used is the recursive doubling algorithm of Stone.[3] It is illustrated in Fig. 7. The histogram for the image is accumulated in Fig. 7. The histogram for the image is accumulated as a series of partial histograms. Step one computes the histogram for each column of pixels. Then the values for two columns are combined, then the values for each of four columns, etc. Thus, it is the case that communication must be implemented between processors 1 and 2, 3 and 4, 5 and 6, and 7 and 8 in step 1, and between the processors that have the pairs 1 and 2, 3 and 4, 5 and 6, and 7 and 8 at step 2, etc. The data elements to be moved between processors are vectors of length 2^k, where k is the number of bits determining the grey level of pixels. Figure 8 shows two possible assignments of columns to processors. In Fig. 8, a communication between the first and second steps of the algorithm is between nearest neighbors; between the second and third steps of the algorithm it is one neighbor removed, and it is also

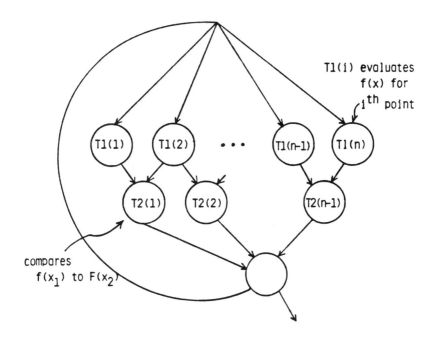

Fig. 4. Data flow for rootfinding algorithms.

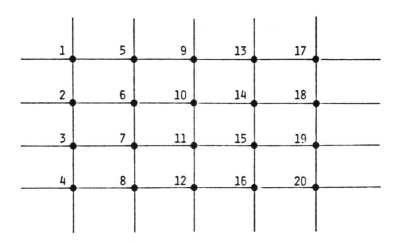

Fig. 5. A segment of a mesh of processors.

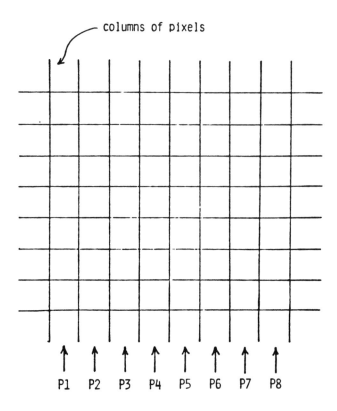

Fig. 6. Assignment of columns of pixels to processors.

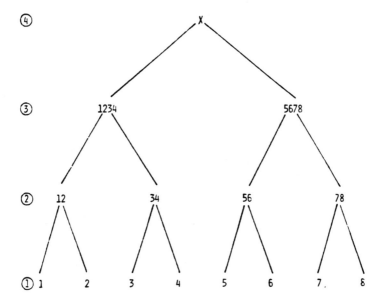

Fig. 7. Recursive doubling histogramming algorithm.

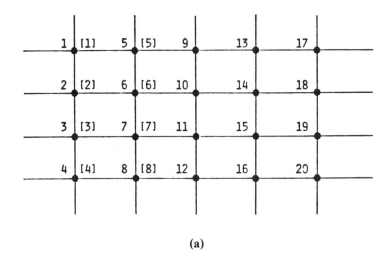

(a)

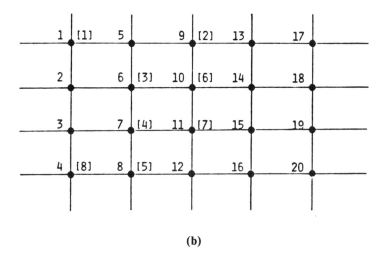

(b)

Fig. 8. (a) Localized assignment of columns to processors. (b) Nonlocalized assignment of columns to processors. The numbers in brackets represent columns of the image.

one neighbor removed between the third and fourth steps of the algorithm. The second assignment, however, which might be caused either by the assignment of processors to other processes or by faulty processors, etc., creates a far more complex communication problem. The difficulty for the software system arises from the fact that the program must work correctly no matter what the assignment of columns to processors. It is clear that the algorithm for mapping will be complex if a near-optimal solution is to be implemented across any spectrum of cases.

It is not that any particular solution is difficult. The difficulty is that all possible models of computation and algorithms must be mapped to all possible programming languages and ultimately to all possible architectures. This is a problem of substantial conceptual difficulty that we have not yet explored.

There are special circumstances with certain types of architectures that give specific character to the solutions for mapping of synchronization and communication requirements to parallel architectures. A full shared memory machine, such as the New York University Ultracomputer,[4] has no communication topology problem. All processors share the same address space. All communication requirements are mapped to the requirements for synchronization between processors to guarantee data consistency. Synchronization and communication are bound at run time.

A purely functional data-flow architecture eliminates all synchronization problems in favor of communication between specific computations. The communication requirements of algorithms are bound to the architecture at run time.

A reconfigurable architecture, such as TRAC,[5] PASM,[6] or CHIP,[7] constructs an architecture that reflects the synchronization and/or communication requirements of the algorithm or application. This configuration process is normally done at load time in response to decisions taken at compile time. Thus, the binding of synchronization and communication aspects of an algorithm are done at load time.

Fixed topology architectures normally do compile-time or load-time binding and minimize run-time binding. The difficulty here is that one may be forced to do extra communication work due to mismatches in topology between the algorithms and the architectures.

The time when binding, which is the accomplishment of a mapping, is executed has a strong impact on efficiency. Compile-time binding is the most efficient (provided a "natural" mapping can be used) because then the interpretation of the map is done only once. Load-time binding is probably the next most efficient. Run-time binding requires interpretation of the map at each step of the computation.

It is worth asking why communication and synchronization are significant research issues. These two issues have, after all, been major subjects of research in the data base and operating system areas for decades. The answer to this conundrum is to be found by considering the characteristics of the problems to be solved in the operating system and data base areas and contrasting them with the problems of explicit parallel structuring of algorithms and applications. In the operating system and data base problem area, the problem to be solved is normally that of maintaining consistency of data and establishing atomicity of computation steps. Order properties of the computations are not usually considered. It is also the case that only a very small number of active processes are present in any given system at a given time. The methods for synchronization and communication for operating systems and data base systems have been designed for implementation of multiprogramming and not multiprocessing. Generally, the topology of communication is not considered. In explicit parallel computations there will often be explicit sequencing requirements built into a given algorithm. There will be many active processes executed on the many processors. Topology of communication is a major efficiency-determining factor.

Those considerations lead to the following research requirements for development of a base of knowledge for implementation of applications and software for parallel architectures:

- Applied theory—we need to thoroughly understand parallel models of computation as they are reflected in algorithms, applications, languages, and architectures.

- An integrated approach to algorithms and application studies of software—we need a great many more analytical and experimental studies of algorithms and real applications.

- Integrated studies of software—it is important to develop and evaluate software systems, languages, and operating systems for parallel computation structures.

The Trac and Its Operating System: An Example of Software Design for a Reconfigurable Many-Processor Architecture

The TRAC[5] is a system that establishes models of computation appropriate for all forms of computing, including numeric computing, symbolic computing, and signal processing. This capability is based upon two concepts: reconfigurable parallel structuring and varistructured operations. Each of these concepts will be explained in the following paragraphs. The basic paradigm for general-purpose parallel computing, which TRAC implements, is that problem structure and not computer architecture should determine the structure of the programs that execute on the machine. TRAC implements multitype multiphase parallel structuring.[8] The means by which these capabilities are realized will be discussed subsequently.

The basic concept is that a complex computation structure may have many types of parallelism, many degrees of parallelism, and perhaps multiple communication geometries in the course of the computations leading to the complete solution of a complex problem. Any attempt to map complex structures onto an architecture representing a single model of computation, unless it is a very general one such as a paracomputer, must frequently lead to poor algorithms and/or use of excess storage. TRAC establishes the ability to generate communication and synchronization architectures reflecting all types of parallel computing, including multiple instruction/multiple data (MIMD), single instruction/multiple data (SIMD), pipeline, and data flow.

The historical justification for multitype multiphase parallel structuring includes the difficulties in utilizing such machines as fixed topology arrays (ILIAC-IV) and vector processing architectures. It is also founded on recent application studies. These studies, analyzing for natural computation structures of significant problems, include those of Kapur and Browne[8] on the natural parallel structuring of odd-even elimination and odd-even reduction, the work by Grosch[9] on mapping of Poisson equation solution methods to processor arrays with different interconnection geometries, and the similar but extended work of Gannon[10] on the mapping of partial differential equation (PDE) algorithms. Agerwala and Lint[11] have established communication geometry for several different algorithms.

It is the thesis of this talk that many important new applications of very high performance computing will require all three types of computation: numeric, symbolic, and signal processing. We argue that of the principal elements in a model of computation for each of these classes of computing, only the basic primitive units of operation differ. The requirements for communication and synchronization and for address space and composition rules remain essentially the same across all classes of parallel computation.

TRAC implements a virtual architecture concept.[12] The virtual architecture concept is built upon a reconfigurable network architecture. The reconfigurable network used in TRAC is a banyan network.[13] A banyan is a multilevel switching network. Figure 9 shows a 4 × 9 TRAC model that has four processors at the apex of the network and nine memory units at the base of the network.

The configuration process for constructing an architecture to match a problem goes as follows. One first constructs logical processors, defining the precision of the arithmetic and the number of processors to be assigned to the process. A single TRAC processor can execute operations with a precision of from 1 to 256 bytes. Any number of processors from one to the number in the system can be mapped upon the execution of

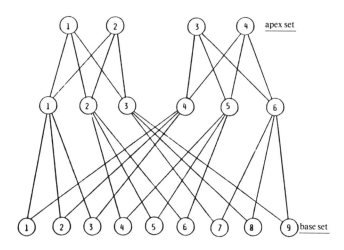

Fig. 9. A banyan network architecture with each switch
node having a fanout of 2 and a spread of 3.

arithmetic of any precision. The more processors, the faster the execution of an operation (up to where the number of processors equals the byte width of the arithmetic). The number of processors mapped to a task is determined through establishment of carry-linkage circuits in the reconfigurable network. Logical computers are established with either an SIMD mode of execution or an MIMD mode of execution by establishing circuits in the network for broadcasting instructions. Address spaces are constructed by creating network circuits that connect memories to processing elements. This completes the definition of a complete logical computer. The network is then used to establish communication between logical computer systems.

All of these structures can be realized with two types of tree circuits in the network. Trees can be formed that have their roots at the apex on a processor and connect a processor to from 1 to N memories. This is illustrated by Fig. 10. The second type of tree has its root in the base and its leaves at the processors. This type of tree implements connection of one memory to many processors (Fig. 11). Figure 12 shows the establishment of four logical computers, each of which consists of one processor and one memory from the set of resources connected by the 4 × 9 network. Figure 13 shows the establishment of a single configuration

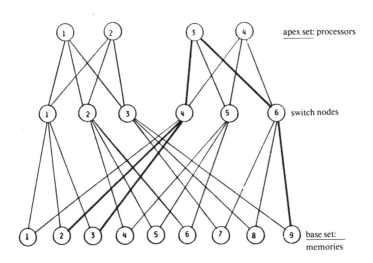

Fig. 10. Trees formed that have their roots at the apex on a
processor and connect a processor to the memories.

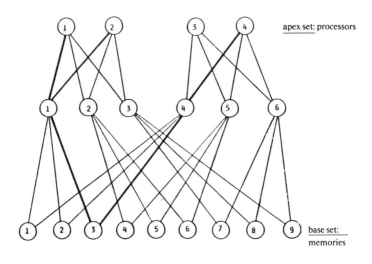

Fig. 11. This type of tree connects one memory to many processors.

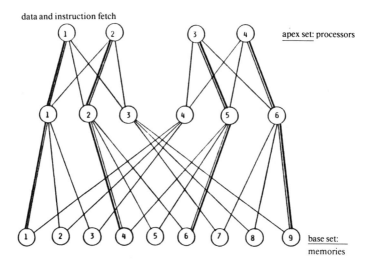

Fig. 12. A four-MIMD configuration.

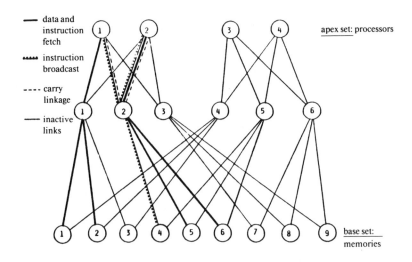

Fig. 13. Two physical processors coupled to form a logical computer system.

that has two physical processors coupled to form a logical computer to execute arithmetic of some fixed precision with a carry linkage between the two processors and the establishment of instruction broadcast between the two processors.

Intercomputer communication is attained by the use of switchable memories and packets. Switchable memories are constructed from base rooted trees. In a given tree, there will be a single *active* link from the root to a given leaf. A given processor can be attached to as many memories as there are "colors" in a tree.[14] The current implementation of TRAC has eight colors.

Figure 14 illustrates a configuration of the 4 × 9 that has two two-processor logical computer configurations connected by a single shared memory. The shared-memory unit may be switched between the two logical computer configurations by a two-instruction sequence. The network also implements packet routing. Any memory can send packets to any processor. This communication mechanism supplements and extends the communications capabilities provided by the switchable memories.

The circuits established *partition* the resources of the system among individual logical computers that interact only in specified ways through

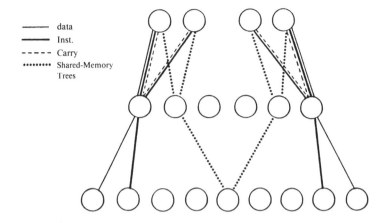

Fig. 14. A two-processor logical computer configuration with a single switchable memory unit.

switchable memories or through sending packets. Thus, the network circuits partition and configure resources into problem-specific architectures.

Partitioning simplifies the basic operating system software. Synchronization is accomplished at configuration time. Construction of configurations specifically reflecting a given problem structure minimizes data movement and maximizes parallelism. The ability to switch memories between logical computers results in a very high bandwidth mechanism for the movement of data. Control information can be sent by the packet routing system.

A job in TRAC consists of a set of tasks and a control process. This is illustrated in Fig. 15. Each job executes on a partition of resources. Each task has a subset of the resources allocated to a job. The structure of a job may change as the system develops.

The overall structure of the system is then shown in Fig. 16. The system scheduler has only the functions of setting up the circuits that partition the resources into configurations and initiating the job monitors. The job monitor programs may either be written in the Computation Structures Language (CSL)[15] or may be the initiator/terminator procedures of a data-flow formulation of a parallel problem.[16] Each task has a particular structure that is configured to the computation unit it is executing. The communication between the tasks

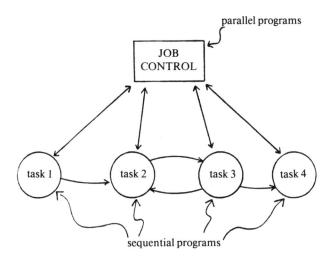

Fig. 15. Job structure. Each job consists of tasks or processes each executing on a specifically structured architecture.

is configured to represent the structure of the problem that is being executed by the job.

Each processor has a resident monitor that virtualizes and integrates each processor into the architecture to make the software execute consistently, no matter how large or how small the set of resources assigned to the task.

Notice the following properties of this operating system design. It is hierarchically structured. The functionality of the system is distributed by *job* and indeed specifically tailored to a *job* with replication where essential.

This type of structure keeps all of the high-volume communication local. High-volume communication will always be between tasks of a particular job. The communication required for control of the system is between the tasks and the job monitor and the job monitor and the system scheduler. The latter class of communication typically has very small data volume.

We have carefully implemented hardware support for the potential bottlenecks. The only potential serialization bottleneck is the system scheduler, which has the task of establishing configurations. The system

SOFTWARE SYSTEM STRUCTURE

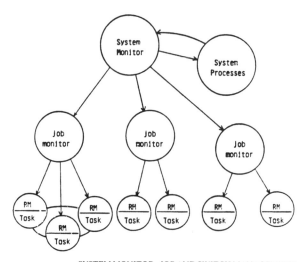

SYSTEM MONITOR - JOB AND SWITCH MANAGEMENT
JOB MONITOR - TASK MANAGEMENT
RESIDENT MONITOR (RM) - PAGE FAULTS
TRAPS, ETC.

Fig. 16. Overall structure of TRACOS.

monitor has a network controller[17] to which it can give high-level commands to establish configurations.

The system does not maintain state over the entire network. If a snapshot of the condition of the network of resource assignment is needed, it can be gained through executing the patterns of assignment resources.

The properties of the resulting system are that the complexity growth in the system is linear—not in the number of resources, but in the number of *jobs*. Communication is mostly local. Each actual unit of execution is small. This structure can support SIMD, MIMD, pipeline, and data-flow models of computation. The design principles are such as to define consistent hardware/software architectures that can be extended to perhaps thousands of processors without explosion of overhead.

References

1. Brown, F. B., Callahan, D. A., and Martin, W. R. "Investigation of Vectorized Monte Carlo Algorithms." Working paper, Department of Nuclear Engineering, The University of Michigan, Ann Arbor, 1981.

2. Chandak, A., and Browne, J. C. "Vectorization of Discrete Event Simulation." *Proceedings of the 1983 International Conference on Parallel Processing,* IEEE Computer Society Press, order no. 479 (1983):359-361.

3. Stone, H. *Introduction to Computer Architectures.* Chicago: Science Research Associates, Inc., 1975.

4. Schwartz, J. T. "Ultracomputers." *ACM TOPLAS* **1** (1980):484-521.

5. Sejnowski, M. C., Upchurch, E. T., Kapur, R. N., Charlu, D. P. S., and Lipovski, G. J. "An Overview of the Texas Reconfigurable Array Processor." *Proc. AFIPS NCC* (1980):631-641.

6. Siegel, H. J., Siegel, L. J., Kemmerer, F. C., Mueller, P. T., Jr., Smalley, H. E., Jr., and Smith, S. D. "PASM: A Partitionable SIMD/MIMD System for Image Processing and Pattern Recognition." *IEEE Trans. on Computers* **C30**, no. 12 (1981):934-947.

7. Snyder, L. "An Introduction to the Configurable Highly Parallel Computer." *Computer* **15** (1982):47-56.

8. Kapur, R. N., and Browne, J.C. "Block Tridiagonal System Solution on Reconfigurable Array Computers." *Proceedings of the 10th International Conference on Parallel Processing,* IEEE Computer Society, publication no. 81CH1634-5 (1981):92-99.

9. Grosch, C. E. "Performance Analysis of Poisson Solvers on Array Computers." In *Supercomputers: Vol. 2,* edited by C. R. Jesshope and R. W. Hockney, 147-181. London: Infotech, 1979.

10. Gannon, D. "On Mapping Non-Uniform PDE Structures and Algorithms Onto Uniform Array Architectures." *Proceedings of the 10th International Conference on Parallel Processing,* IEEE Computer Society, publication no. 81CH1634-5 (1981):100-105.

11. Agerwala, T. K., and Lint, B. J. "Communication Issues in the Design and Analysis of Parallel Algorithms." *IEEE Trans.* 7 (1981):174-188.

12. Browne, J. C., Tripathi, A., Fedek, S., Adiga, A., and Kapur, R. "A Language for Specification and Programming of Reconfigurable Parallel Computation Structures." *Proceedings of the 1982 International Conference on Parallel Processing,* IEEE Computer Society Press, order no. 421 (1982):142-150.

13. Goke, L. R., and Lipovski, G. J. "A Banyan Network for Partitioning Multiprocessor Systems." *Proceedings of the First Annual Symposium on Computer Architectures,* IEEE Computer Society, publication no. 82CH1754 (1973):21-28.

14. Kapur, R. N., Premkumar, U. V., and Lipovski, G. J. "Organization of the TRAC Processor-Memory Subsystem." *Proc. AFIPS NCC* **49** (1980):623-630.

15. Han, S. Y. "A Language for the Specification and Representation of Programs in a Data Flow Model of Computation." Ph.D. Dissertation, Department of Computer Sciences, University of Texas, Austin (1983).

16. Jenevein, R., and Browne, J. C. "A Control Processor for a Reconfigurable Array Computer." *Proceedings of the 9th Symposium on Computer Architectures,* IEEE Computer Society, catalog no. 82CH1754 (1982):81-89.

15

General-Purpose Languages for the 1990s

M. B. Wells
New Mexico State University
Las Cruces, New Mexico

Introduction

A "general-purpose" language is defined here to be a language capable not only of conveniently expressing algorithms from varied professions but also of providing bases for complete programming environments. ADA will be an important general-purpose language for the 1980s (the second half, at least) and likely into the 1990s. However, ADA is big. Also, it is perhaps too "imperative" for both concise algorithmic expression and/or efficient realization in some instances. Current research on applicative (or functional), equational, and object-oriented programming will surely lead to improved general-purpose languages for the 1990s. Thoughts on this technical evolution and its impact on future supercomputing are presented.

The Importance of General-Purpose Languages

This paper is concerned with the evolution of high-level, general-purpose programming languages. The adjective "high-level" implies that the languages are primarily for communication among people. The adjective "general-purpose" basically implies that algorithms from many and varied professions can be conveniently expressed in the language and can be easily translated for efficient execution on most machines. I intend this adjective also to imply that the language can be used effectively to "integrate" rather disparate programs to accomplish rather large interactive tasks. Actually, such program integration is still viewed as programming, but at a different level.

Furthermore, I presume that, at the level of general-purpose language, "supercomputing" is little different from any other kind of computing. I would hope that a satisfactory notation for specifying vector operations or more general concurrency would be essentially machine independent.

Before the emergence of the concept of abstract data types in the 1970s, commonly used languages were not particularly for general purpose. For instance, FORTRAN was (and is) primarily a numerical manipulation language, LISP primarily a language for artificial intelligence and symbol manipulation, and SNOBOL primarily a text-processing language. In fact, many people felt (and many still do) that it is not realistic to expect a single language to do everything. This attitude was particularly strong in the late 1960s when it was realized just how big and complicated the "general-purpose" language Pl/1 really is. However, the unifying idea of abstract data types—originating (perhaps) from the language SIMULA 67 and carrying through today in ADA—greatly mitigates that feeling. Organization of a program using data abstraction allows varied-application algorithms to be combined easily and naturally. This approach promotes the design of very sophisticated and efficient algorithms—see, for instance, the work of Kahaner and Wells[1] in which an advanced algorithm for n-dimensional quadrature that relies on combining number and symbol manipulation was designed.

In my opinion, general-purpose languages are important even at a level above algorithm design, at the level where complete programs are combined to form interactive applications-oriented packages or systems. It seems obvious that problems of communication between the individual programs are minimized. The limiting case in which all programs are written in a single (general-purpose) source language is ideal. Then, combining the programs is as easy as compiling procedures from a library—parameter passing (or general data transfer) is handled uniformly across the programs. Even though I do not consider C to be an ideal general-purpose language, its use in developing UNIX and UNIX-based systems is a good example of the power of language/system unification.

Of course, a truly ideal situation is difficult to obtain; it certainly cannot be obtained today. Vast libraries of reliable and efficent programs exist today in FORTRAN, LISP, C, and many other not-so-general-purpose languages. We certainly do not want to throw these away, at least not until they are supplanted by better programs developed through natural evolution of machines and techniques. Thus, our future general-purpose languages should contain mechanisms to allow integration of programs written in various source languages.[2] ADA has such a mechanism (conceptually, at least). Research on the basic relevant problem on translating abstract data from one representation to another is exemplified directly by the work of Herlihy and Liskov[3] and indirectly by the work of Schonberg, et al.,[4] for instance.

I wish to emphasize, however, that this latter approach to integration, though pragmatic, is not ideal. We should not give up our quest for a general-purpose language just because we develop implementable techniques for integrating programs using existing languages. A truly general-purpose language will always be simpler than the disjoint union of several special-purpose languages because common concepts will be unified.

Also, I believe we should resist the temptation of creating, for reasons of vested interest, essentially upward-compatible extensions of old languages when useful new concepts arise (for example, data abstraction). The resulting extensions are almost surely more complicated than a new and unified language with up-to-date integration techniques.

ADA: Its Virtues and Faults

I should justify my advocacy of the near-term use of ADA. ADA is certainly a controversial language. It has its advocates and adversaries in both academia and industry. I myself have mixed feelings. I have debated it on the con side and have taught it as the wave of the future. My basic conclusion is that we can do much better, but that ADA is an extremely powerful, reasonably clean, and quite easy to use general-purpose language—certainly the best one existing today. Moreover, because of its backing by the Department of Defense (DoD), its use has a good chance of becoming widespread. The following are some of its important technical virtues:

It is *strongly typed*. Strong typing (that is, handling data types entirely at compile time) permits substantial compile time error detection and simplifies efficient code generation. More importantly, however, it imposes a programming discipline that has proved to be highly effective in producing truly reliable programs. Lack of strong typing is one of the primary faults of languages like LISP and C.

It has *packages*. These are legitimate program units "larger" than procedures and functions that may be separately compiled. Because packages may be split into visible and private parts, they provide (in conjunction with "overloading") the basic mechanism for *data abstraction*, the ability to view data at a level independent of its representation.

It has a (primitive) polymorphism mechanism. ADA's generic feature effectively allows parameters of type type. A generic function (or procedure or package) is thus polymorphic in the sense that it can give rise, at compile time, to many distinct functions, each operating on arguments of quite different type. This mechanism provides still more data abstraction possibilities.

It uses *rendezvous-based* tasking. That is, communication among concurrently evaluating sequential processes depends on rendezvous among the processes.[5] This is a very high-level form of synchronization with significant potential for expressiveness.

Other virtues are a simple and general looping mechanism, aggregates (array literal forms), and discriminated record types (parameterized types). However, these are far less crucial in my mind to a general-purpose language than true strong typing, sound data abstraction mechanisms, and high-level concurrency capabilities.

The primary fault of ADA is that it is big and complex. There are 62 key words and over 150 syntactic constructs. One compiler for ADA is estimated to contain about 100 000 lines of source (D. Ziesig, Martin Marietta Corp., private communication, 1983). Actually, in spite of this, it has a certain cleanliness that makes it surprisingly easy to learn, at least up to some reasonable level of competence. Students in my spring 1983 class were writing quite sophisticated 200- to 300-line codes involving tasking and generics toward the end of the semester.

Nevertheless, it is my contention, as well as that of others,[6] that some of ADA's complexity is a direct result of initial over-specification and can be reduced simply by elimination of unnecessary features and unification of others. The following two questions should be seriously considered in this regard by designers of future general-purpose languages.

Is an independent exception handling mechanism necessary or desirable? Actually, this question has been eloquently answered in the negative by Black.[7] One of Black's arguments is that many such mechanisms, including ADA's, are really just separate control structures with extremely complex semantics that cater to cases that should not be considered "exceptional." He also points out that the more general feature of having subprograms be "first-class" objects in the sense that they can be values of variables and passed as parameters would be useful and desirable for specifying control of this sort. Such a feature was specifically outlawed by the Steelman specifications that led to ADA.

I tend to agree with Black. Certainly ADA's exception-handling mechanism introduces language complexity all out of proportion to its usefulness. The interaction of this mechanism with tasking is mind-boggling.

Are five separate subprogram units—functions, procedures, packages, generics, and tasks—necessary and desirable? I say no, and am stating my case with development of the MODCAP language.[8] In it, "functions" that return zero or more values are the only subprogram units. I believe the separation of functions and procedures in PASCAL, ADA, and other languages is artificial, as well as complicating. Other modern-language designers seem to have arrived at this same conclusion—compare early Russell[9] with a later version,[10] for instance. It is nice to say that functions shall have no unwanted side effects, but it is extremely difficult for the compiler to detect "good" from "bad" side effects and to enforce such rules. (The question of whether or not any side effects belong in modern programming languages is far from being resolved today. I am hopeful that experience with MODCAP as a block-structured language with functions as first-class objects will shed some light on this question.)

Packages and generics provide three basic capabilities: the ability to make certain program parts invisible and inaccessible, the ability to parameterize subprograms with types, and the ability to precompile program segments once and for all for incorporation in programs written later.

How do functions supply these capabilities? Capability A, which concerns information hiding, is what block structuring is all about. This capability is automatic in a block-structured language with function as first-class objects, that is, in a language with activation-record retention.[11]

Not only should functions be first-class objects, but so should some form of data types themselves. This, plus "static instantiation," automatically gives capability B on parameterizing subprograms with types. In MODCAP, it is the sets of operations, called spaces, which are used to define (compile time) types that are the first-class objects. ADA's generics correspond in MODCAP to statically invoked functions parameterized with static (known at compile time) spaces.

Capability C, separate compilation, is actually independent of the exclusive use of functions as the subprogram modules. However, the basic ADA facility with its required order-of-package compilation is maintained when packages are replaced by function literals as blocks in a block-structured language, such as MODCAP. In fact, in such a system, a library is itself just a precompiled but incomplete function literal containing a number of nested functions within it.

Finally, is it realistic to use functions as tasks? Again, I believe so, but there are some questions that are best decided by actual experience. For instance, rendezvous-based communication requires output parameters, as well as input parameters. Is this necessary extension to the syntax of functions a confusing complication to the simple use of functions?

There are numerous questions relating to ADA's complexity that have to do with its typing scheme. Perhaps the most fundamental is, "Are type declarations really necessary in a strongly typed language?" I believe not, but it would carry me too far afield to pursue this issue in depth here. (ADA's loop variables, in fact, do not need declaration.) Let me just say that simplifications, such as (1) the elimination of declarations, (2) the removal of the necessity for identifier overloading, and (3) the removal of the need for specific "macro" notation in order to obtain efficiency of implementation, seem to follow naturally from a type inference scheme and a hierarchical classification of types. Our work in this area is unpublished.[12,13] Related work (most of it for a somewhat different purpose, however) has been done by Tenenbaum,[14] Milner,[15] Albano,[16] and others.

Imperative, Applicative, and Equational Programming

It is convenient to classify programming languages by the chief style of programming that their use promotes. Languages like ALGOL 60, PASCAL, and ADA are basically imperative because their statement orientation (especially with the assignment statement) fosters an algorithmic (*how*) approach to programming. LISP, APL, LUCID,[17] and Backus' functional language,[18] for instance, are more applicative in that their natural programming style depends on functional application (often embedded within mathematical expressions). One tends more to think *what* rather than *how* when using them. Programming in the relatively new language PROLOG (for Programming in Logic) involves listing a set of logical equations involving known and unknown quantities. Another essentially equational language is OBJ.[19] The style of these two languages also emphasizes *what* more than *how*; in fact, because of the ability to "solve" implicit equations, they are even more "nonprocedural" than the above-mentioned applicative languages.

There are both imperative and applicative elements in all these languages. Expressions of PASCAL and aggregates of ADA can be classed as applicative constructs. On the other hand, programs in applicative or equational languages of today are still algorithms in the sense that they represent one of many indications of *how* to produce desired results. It is largely a question of levels of abstraction. The *what* at one level must always be clarified with precisely *how* at a lower level. In the case of applicative and equational languages, these lower levels are handled by the compiler or even the machine itself.

I believe there is a natural evolution from imperative, to applicative, to equational programming. However, I don't believe that our languages can or should be purely equational or even purely applicative until we know much more about the "how to" of computing. Certainly, as we learn a better "how to," more can be accomplished by the compiler and the machine rather than by "lower levels" of a program. However, we should provide language to let users experiment with algorithmic "how to" during—in fact, to promote—this evolution.

Languages that have such expressive capabilities at various levels have been called "wide-spectrum" languages.[20] MODCAP and LUKKO[21] perhaps, besides the languages of the above-referenced Munich group,[20] can be classified as wide-spectrum languages. I believe that general-purpose languages of the 1990s will be wide spectrum.

There are two interesting features of MODCAP in this respect. First, as with other modern languages such as SMALLTALK, there is very little distinction between base-language spaces (the abstract typing modules) that contain built-in operations, and user-defined spaces whose operations are given entirely by source-language functions. Thus, when particular user-defined operations prove generally useful, they can easily be built in with no disruption to anyone, but possibly with improved efficiency for everyone. This would be done especially if new hardware such as an array processor was made available to improve the efficiency of vector operations, for instance. Such language capability provides an excellent way, of course, for users to detect the need for hardware improvements.

The second feature of MODCAP worthy of mention, one different from most languages, is its notational orientation. Because functions and spaces are first-class objects, it is possible to use identifiers only for names of "variables." (In practice, however, most functions and spaces do not actually vary.) With such a unification, function evaluation no longer has its own distinctive notation. Juxtaposition of a variable name and an argument indicates function evaluation if the variable happens to be a function, but it may indicate some other operation, say multiplication, if the operands have a different type. It is thus necessary to distinguish basically between the notations $\sqrt{\ }(x)$ and f(x), for instance. The first is a prefix operation applied to an argument x, while the second is the infix operation juxtaposition applied to two arguments f and x. The upshot of this is that "overloading" is restricted to operators only—it does not apply to functions as in ADA, for instance. However, MODCAP does have a large supply of operators that can be used as prefixes, infixes, or suffixes. Since the meaning of these operators can be assigned by the user (by defining appropriate spaces), various and quite different symbolisms and programming styles are possible. One can do LISP-like, APL-like, or even PROLOG-like programming within MOD-CAP. While some of the list, array, or logical equation manipulation might not be built in, the notational facilities are at least there.

The evolution to applicative and equational programming is not only important because of increased abstraction and expressiveness, but also because of the potential for significant gains in program efficiency and verifiability. The main gains in efficiency derive from implicit parallelism possible within data-flow[22] or reduction-machine[23] models of computation that may be used with certain applicative languages. The gains in verifiability derive from the ready analyzability of (true) functions and equations as mathematical objects.[18]

The impact of this research on general-purpose languages for the 1990s, while not totally clear today, will certainly be felt. However, I believe that our models of computation, like our languages, will evolve rather more slowly than some of this work suggests. First will come the increasing incorporation of applicative and equational ideas into languages that are modeled more or less classically. Then it will become obvious (partly because of the advanced research being done today) how the models and our machines should be modified to accommodate these ideas more efficiently.

Value- and Object-Oriented Data Organization

Closely associated with the applicative/imperative classification of programming styles and languages is the value/object classification of data organization. The difference between values and objects is well described by MacLennan.[24] Essentially, values are time independent while objects can change internally over time. Integers are best considered to be values and stacks to be objects, for instance. Values tend to be associated with applicative programming because the elements of the domain and codomain of mathematical functions have classically been thought of as internally unchangable, once defined. A purely applicative language without (re)assignment in fact has no mechanism for modifying data items short of their total reconstruction. Pure LISP, SETL,[25] and VAL[26] are value-oriented languages (although SETL in particular does let an implementation modify values for the sake of efficiency as long as the value semantics are not violated).

Object-oriented programming is associated foremost with the SMALLTALK language. In SMALLTALK, all data items are objects and receive messages from other objects, indicating modifications to be undertaken on themselves or associated objects. Actually, object-oriented programming is based at a lower level on the idea of pointer (or reference) semantics. In this brand of semantics, all data items are represented by references (pointers) to the actual values. Assignment does no copying; it only passes pointers. Complex data structures (objects) are easily set up and modified under such a regime. SNOBOL 4, MODCAP 6,[27] and CLU[28] are examples of languages using such semantics.

The chief contribution of SMALLTALK in this respect was raising the level of the user point of view. Rather than being concerned with low-level concepts, such as pointers and assignment statements, the user is concerned with high-level concepts such as objects, their naming, and their modification. A similar viewpoint has been adopted for MODCAP, although the spark that prompted it originated not from SMALLTALK but from an insightful paper by Hehner.[29] He believes, rightly so in my opinion, that we should "assign" names to data items and not vice-versa as we have done since the time of von Neumann's $X + 1 \rightarrow X$ notation. This forces us to consider data structure modification at a higher level than assignment.

Are value orientation and object orientation incompatible? I think not! Each has its place. It is probably more natural to view the product of two matrices as a new matrix value, and it is probably more natural to view a stack with a new top as a revised version of the same object. Note that it is not a matter of efficiency of implementation that we consider a stack an object. It is conceptually unappealing to think of reconstructing a new value for this naturally updated thing. Likewise, we do not (or at least should not) consider the possibility that both of the matrix factors might still be needed when we choose to imagine the product as a new matrix. It is, conceptually, a new thing.

Thus, I believe that general-purpose languages for the 1990s will accommodate both values and objects. I am not willing to predict whether there will be different mechanisms and notations for creating and manipulating values from those for objects. In MODCAP now, the mechanisms (which, as with many modern languages, are based on the construction of abstract data types) are essentially the same. While there are no enforced notational distinctions, it seems on one hand (the little we have) that value manipulation notation is mostly mathematically classical . . . f (M•N) . . . . On the other hand, object manipulation seems to follow the SMALLTALK mode with suffixed messages: . . .; S push X; . . . or perhaps . . .; S + X; . . . .

Conclusions

I organize my conclusions about general-purpose language evolution around the four theme questions posed by organizers of this conference.

What are the exciting technological opportunities? One will be the use of general-purpose languages implemented on high-performance machines to develop truly advanced and efficient algorithms. I believe that we have only begun to scratch the surface of the power of data abstraction. The easy mixing of numerical, symbolic, functional, or whatever data in a single algorithm presents exciting possibilities.

A second opportunity is the use of general-purpose languages to develop an environment of tools that will substantially automate the programming process. Here, the general-purpose languages are helping us tie together even more diverse algorithms (programs) for numerical computing, file manipulation, and graphics interaction.[30] I include in this category the consolidation of established and reliable programs written, for instance, in FORTRAN with those written in newer, more expressive, and versatile languages. This leads into my answer to the second question.

What are the major pitfalls to be avoided? The most important pitfall in my opinon would be to let our large vested interest in obsolete languages such as FORTRAN serve as rationale for not using modern and advanced software developmental tools and languages. Just because we (rightfully) do not wish to dispose of our large, reliable FORTRAN libraries and programs, we should not restrict ourselves to writing new programs in FORTRAN. As I have suggested, we would be much better off directing our attention to making use of the established libraries within the framework of a modern language. ADA is the language of choice today for this. By the early 1990s, we can begin to think seriously about the language to supplant ADA, and so forth—such is progress.[31]

I have implicitly suggested, and I now wish explicitly to suggest, that we are wasting our time trying to upgrade FORTRAN to a modern language. By the time "FORTRAN 8X" is ready, it will likely be fully as complex as ADA, yet still 10 years behind. The vested interest argument can be answered as above or perhaps more forcibly by considering the dramatically increasing software costs due mostly to new applications over the next few years.[32] It seems that the staggering amount of new programming anticipated clearly suggests using the most advanced tools we have at our disposal.

There is a third reason for not evolving FORTRAN, one that to me is the most convincing of the three: it is becoming increasingly difficult to get good people to do FORTRAN programming. The computer science employment market is such that the good, young graduates can easily pick their work. Last year, one of my best students went after, and was successful in getting, a job with Xerox in order to work with MESA, a modern language of the 1970s. A. Faustini (Arizona State University, private communication, 1983) suggested one reason why the University of Leeds was perhaps behind other English universities, such as the University of Manchester, in computer science research. Namely, they continued to use FORTRAN in their beginning programming classes long after most others had switched to PASCAL as a far superior pedagogic language. Promising young faculty shied away from Leeds because of this. (Of course, in time PASCAL will be replaced by better languages, perhaps even by ADA, if good compilers can be developed on small machines.)

The upshot of this is that the best work will be done where the best tools are available because that is the attraction to our best minds. The Japanese made a quantum jump in automobile manufacturing with their intensive use of robots. We must not fall behind in supercomputing because of our inertia with respect to programming tools.

What supercomputer performance parameters will be required? A general answer to this question is that supercomputers of the 1990s should closely match the general-purpose languages to be used on them. This means that there should be close cooperation between hardware designers and language designers, as well as between both groups and the all-important users.

I do not believe that there will be breakthroughs either in language design or in computer architecture that will radically alter our view of supercomputing for the 1990s. This is not to say that there will not be changes, but only that the evolution will be reasonably slow and steady. The most important language "innovation" of the 1970s—data abstraction—has yet to fully impact architecture. Likewise, the very significant hardware innovations of array processing and raster-scan graphics are still being assimilated by language designers.

It is encouraging to see at many conferences today relatively close cooperation among the various parties on the subject of parallel computing, perhaps the premier research area of the 1980s. Topics from parallel computing "in the small" (data flow), as suggested by functional programming, to parallel computing "in the large" (distributed computing), as perhaps suggested by object-oriented programming, are being considered.

Let me give one slightly more specific answer to the above question on performance parameters. The importance of "automatic" memory management, management that is invisible to the user, is becoming increasingly clear in the language design business. The functional language LISP was the first language to recognize the importance of relevant "garbage collection" techniques.[33] The increased use of complex data structures for representing various abstract data types and of search algorithms for artificial intelligence applications (and equational programming) make such techniques essential for general-purpose languages of the future. Work on LISP has culminated in a LISP machine.[34] Our supercomputers of the 1990s must accommodate our more general-purpose languages with no perceived loss of efficiency relative to memory management.

What action by governmental and private agencies would most facilitate progress? Three parties seem to be involved—national laboratories, who are the primary users of supercomputers; private industry, which builds the supercomputers; and universities, who teach and study the theory of languages. Therefore, any actions that facilitate interaction between these three parties will certainly promote progress. Specific actions might be to establish more joint seminars to discuss the latest in applications, hardware, and languages, and to make existing supercomputers more accessible to the academic community. These and other actions will surely foster the development of general-purpose languages for the 1990s that are simple, expressive, efficient, and allow ready integration of existing proven programs.

References

1. Kahaner, D. K., and Wells, M. B. "An Experimental Algorithm for N-Dimensional Adaptive Quadrative." *ACM Trans. on Math. Software* **5**, no. 1 (1979):86-89.

2. Fateman, R. "Symbolic Manipulation Languages and Numerical Computation: Trends." In *The Relationship Between Numerical Computation and Programming Languages*, edited by J. K. Reid. Amsterdam:North-Holland Publishing Company, 1982.

3. Herlihy, M., and Liskov, B. "A Value Transmission Scheme for Abstract Data Types." *ACM Trans. on Prog. Lang. and Sys.* **4**, no. 4 (1982):527-551.

4. Schonberg, E., Schwartz, J. T., and Sharir, M. "Automatic Data Selection in SETL." *Conf. Record of Sixth ACM Symposium on Principles of Programming Languages*, New York, Association for Computing Machinery (1979).

5. Hoare, C. A. R. "Communicating Sequential Processes." *CACM* **21**, no. 8 (1978):666-667.

6. Boute, R. T. "Simplifying ADA by Removing Limitations." *SIGPLAN Notices* **15**, no. 2 (1980):17-28.

7. Black, A. P. "Exception Handling: The Case Against." Department of Computer Science report TR 82-01-02, University of Washington, Seattle (1983).

8. Wells, M. D. "The Modcap Programming Language." Department of Computer Science, New Mexico State University, Las Cruces (1981).

9. Demers, A. J., and Donahue, J. E. "Data Types, Parameters, and Type Checking." *Conference Record of the Seventh ACM Symposium on Principles of Programming Language,* New York, Association for Computing Machinery (1980).

10. Boehm, H., Demers, A. J., and Donahue, J. E. "An Informal Description of Russel." Department of Computer Science report TR 80-430, Cornell University, Ithaca, New York (1980).

11. Wells, M. B. "Implementation and Application of a Function Data Type." *AFIPS Conf. Proc.,* NCC **46** (1977):389-395.

12. Hug, M. A. "Data Types in Modcap." Master's Thesis, Department of Computer Science, New Mexico State University, Las Cruces (1983).

13. Wells, M. B., Brockmeyer, J., Hug, M. A., and Silver, R. "The Modcap Reference Manual." Department of Computer Science, New Mexico State University, Las Cruces, New Mexico (in preparation).

14. Tenenbaum, A. M. "Type Determination for Very High-Level Languages." Courant Institute of Mathematical Sciences report 3, New York University, New York (1979).

15. Milner, R. "A Theory of Type Polymorphism in Programming." *J. of Comp. and Syst. Sciences* **17** (1978):348-375.

16. Albano, A. "Type Hierarchies and Semantic Data Models." *SIGPLAN Notices,* **18**, no. 6 (1983):178-186.

17. Faustini, A. A., Mathews, S. G., and Yaghi, A. A. "The Lucid Programming Manual." Department of Computer Science, Arizona State University, Tempe (1983).

18. Backus, J. "Can Programming be Liberated from the von Neumann Style? A Functional Style and Its Algebra of Programs." *Comm. ACM* **21**, no. 8 (1978):613-641.

19. Goguen, J. A., and Tardo, J. "OBJ-O Preliminary User's Manual." *Proc. Specification of Reliable Software,* IEEE Computer Society, (1979):170-189.

20. Bauer, F. L., Broy, M., Gnatz, R., Hesse, W., Krieg-Bruchner, B., Partsch, H., Pepper, P., and Wossner, H. "Towards a Wide-Spectrum Language to Support Program Specification and Program Development." *SIGPLAN Notices* **13**, no. 12 (1978):15-24.

21. Heinanen, J. "A Programmer-Controlled Approach to Data and Control Abstraction." *SIGPLAN Notices* **18**, no. 6 (1983):41-52.

22. Dennis, J. B. "Data-Flow Supercomputers." *Computer* **13**, no. 11 (1980):48-56.

23. Turner, D. A. "A New Implementation Technique for Applicative Languages." *Software: Practice and Experience* **9** (1979):31-49.

24. MacLennan, B. J. "Values and Objects in Programming Languages." *SIGPLAN Notices* **17**, no. 12 (1982):70-79.

25. Dewar, R. B. K., Schonberg, E., and Schwarty, J. T. "Higher Level Programming: Introduction to the Use of the Set-Theoretic Programming Language SETL." Courant Institute of Mathematical Sciences, New York University, New York (1981).

26. McGraw, J. R. "The VAL Language: Description and Analysis." *ACM Trans. on Prog. Lang.* **4**, no. 1 (1981):44-82.

27. Wells, M. B., and Morris, J. B., Jr. "The Unified Data Structure Capability in MODCAP 6." *Int'l. J. of Comp. and Inf. Sci.* **1**, no. 3 (1972):193-208.

28. Liskov, B., Synder, A., Atkinson, R. and Schaffert, C. "Abstraction Mechanisms in CLU." *CACM* **20**, no. 8 (1977):564-576.

29. Hehner, E. C. R. "On Removing the Machine from the Language." *Acta Informatica* **10** no. 9 (1978):229-243.

30. Smoliar, S. W., and Barstow, D. "Who Needs Languages and Why do We Need Them? or No Matter How High the Level, It's Still Programming." *SIGPLAN Notices* **18**, no. 6 (1983):149-157.

31. Wegner, P. "On the Unification of Data and Program Abstraction in ADA." *Conference Record of the Tenth ACM Symposium on Principles of Programming Languages,* ACM, New York (1983):256-264.

32. Stephan, D. G., Doris, D., Barbazette, B., Johnson, L., and Murthpy, B. "DoD Digital Data Processing Study: A Ten-Year Forecast." Electronics Industries Association, 1980. (See also, Booch, G., *Software Engineering with ADA*, Menlo Park, California:Benjamin Cummings, 1983: Figures 24-31).

33. Cohen, J. "Garbarge Collection of Linked Data Structures." *Computing Surveys* **13**, no. 3 (1981):341-367.

34. Weinreb, D., and Moon, D. *LISP Machine Manual.* Cambridge: Massachusetts Institute of Technology, 1981.

General-Language Bibliography

Descriptions of and references to well-known languages mentioned herein without specific references may be found in one or more of the following commonly available textbooks.

Bourne, S. R. *The Unix System.* Reading, Massachusetts: Addison-Wesley, 1982.

Horowitz, E. *Programming Languages: A Grand Tour.* Rockville, Maryland:Computer Science Press, 1983.

MacClennan, B. *Principles of Programming Languages: Design, Evaluation and Implementation.* New York:Holt, Rinehard and Winston, 1983.

Pratt, T. W. *Programming Languages: Design and Implementation.* Englewood Cliffs, New Jersey: Prentice-Hall, 1975.

16

Supercomputing in Aerodynamics

W. F. Ballhaus, Jr.

Ames Research Center, National Aeronautics and Space
Administration (NASA)
Moffett Field, California

Introduction

Computational aerodynamics has emerged in the last decade as an essential element in the design process for all types of aerospace vehicles. This revolution has been driven by advances in computer power that have led to advances in numerical solution techniques. The result is better computational simulations achieved more cost effectively. Further advances in computer power are required for this revolution to continue.

In fiscal year 1984, the National Aeronautics and Space Administration (NASA) initiated the Numerical Aerodynamic Simulation (NAS) Program to provide this needed capability and to ensure continued U.S. leadership in computational aerodynamics. The program has been structured to focus on the development of a complete, balanced computational system that can be upgraded periodically to take advantage of advances in technology.

This paper reviews some of the progress in computational aerodynamics over the last decade and describes what remains to be done in the years ahead. The discussion includes a description of the NAS Program objectives, computational goals, and implementation plans.

Aerodynamic Simulation

The two basic tools of the aircraft designer, the wind tunnel and the computer, are depicted in Fig. 1. Both are simulations, one analog and the other digital. In spite of the continuing rapid advancement in the

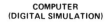

WIND TUNNEL
(ANALOG SIMULATION)

COMPUTER
(DIGITAL SIMULATION)

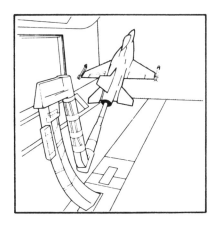 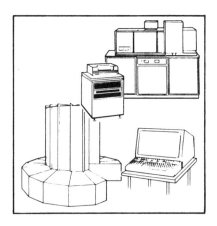

WIND TUNNELS AND COMPUTERS COMPLEMENT EACH OTHER

Fig. 1. Two basic tools for configuration design.

performance of supercomputers and numerical methods, it is not expected that computational simulations will completely replace wind-tunnel testing in the foreseeable future. Their roles instead are complementary. The wind tunnel is superior in providing detailed performance data once a final configuration is selected, especially for cases with complex geometry and complex aerodynamic phenomena. Computational simulations are especially useful for the following applications: (1) detailed fluid physics studies, such as simulations designed to shed light on the basic structure of turbulent flows; (2) the development of new design concepts, such as swept forward wings or jet flaps for lift augmentation; (3) sorting through many candidate configurations and eliminating all but the most promising before wind-tunnel testing; (4) assisting the aerodynamicist in instrumenting test models to improve resolution of the physical phenomena of interest; and (5) correcting wind-tunnel data for scaling and interference errors. Aircraft configuration design is an interactive process of trial and error. Computational simulations substantially reduce the time and cost involved in detecting and correcting design errors in much the same fashion that word processing reduces the time and cost involved in correcting errors in office correspondence.

Computational simulations can also provide data for conditions that are outside the operating range of existing experimental facilities. An example is a high-speed planetary probe entry condition, as in the case of the Galileo Probe, which is scheduled to enter the atmosphere of Jupiter in the late 1980s.

Inadequacies in testing are associated with limitations in operating range (such as Mach number, Reynolds number, gas composition, and enthalpy level) and the control of boundary conditions (such as flow nonuniformity, wall- and support-interference effects, and model fidelity). These factors must be properly controlled for the simulation to accurately represent the desired free-flight conditions.

The inadequacies in computational simulations are primarily associated with poor resolution of physical phenomena, and this is a direct result of insufficient computer power. Because of limited available computer power, aerodynamicists are forced to solve approximate forms of the Navier-Stokes equations. These approximations introduce phenomenological errors, with the consequence that certain aspects of the flow-field physics are not properly represented. Further discussion of these errors is deferred until the next section. For any given mathematical formulation, the approximating procedures used to solve the governing equations and boundary conditions introduce numerical errors. These errors are compounded by inadequate grid refinement or incomplete treatment of complex aerodynamic configurations, both of which result from inadequate computer power. The consequences are again that physical phenomena are not represented properly.

The penalties associated with inadequate simulation capability are illustrated in Fig. 2. This is a list of major aircraft development projects, which, in spite of the use of the best simulation tools available at the time, encountered major aerodynamic design problems that went undetected until flight test. The consequences were severe penalties in cost, schedule, and/or performance. Several of these problems could have been detected early in the design cycle, and the consequent severe penalties avoided, with the computational capability available today. The first, design of a military transport, is an example. Other examples would require a computational capability beyond that currently available. Specifically, these cases would require the capability to treat complex, three-dimensional viscous flow fields. This is beyond current capabilities but within reach in this decade. Successful design of next-generation aircraft will be even more difficult without further improvements in simulation capability.

INADEQUATE SIMULATION CAPABILITY IMPACTS AIRCRAFT COST AND RESULTS IN DELAYED OR REDUCED OPERATIONAL CAPABILITY

- BEST AVAILABLE METHODS WERE INADEQUATE TO UNCOVER DESIGN PROBLEMS BEFORE FLIGHT TEST

AIRCRAFT	PROBLEMS DISCOVERED IN FLIGHT TEST	CONSEQUENCE
MILITARY TRANSPORT · 1	INCORRECTLY PREDICTED WING FLOW	COMPROMISED PERFORMANCE, COSTLY MODIFICATIONS
MILITARY TRANSPORT · 2	INCORRECTLY PREDICTED DRAG-RISE MACH NUMBER	REDUCED WING FATIGUE LIFE
FIGHTER/ BOMBER	INCORRECTLY PREDICTED TRANSONIC AIRFRAME DRAG	COSTLY MODIFICATIONS
BOMBER · A BOMBER · B	INCORRECTLY PREDICTED TRANSONIC PERFORMANCE	REDUCED AIRCRAFT EFFECTIVENESS
FIGHTER · 1 FIGHTER · 2	INCORRECTLY PREDICTED TRANSONIC DRAG	REDUCED PERFORMANCE
2 CIVIL TRANSPORTS	INCORRECTLY PREDICTED NACELLE-WING INTERFERENCE	REDESIGN REQUIRED

- SOME PROBLEMS COULD HAVE BEEN AVOIDED USING TODAY'S COMPUTATIONAL CAPABILITY
- OTHERS WOULD REQUIRE NAS LEVEL CAPABILITY

Fig. 2. Problems associated with inadequate flight-test simulation capabilities.

Improvements in computational efficiency are illustrated in Fig. 3, which is an updated version of a figure in Ref. 1. The cost of a given computation has decreased at the rate of about two orders of magnitude over a 15-year period because of increases in computer power. There has been a similar two orders of magnitude decrease in the same time frame due to improvements in solution methods. The net effect is a reduction in cost for a given computation of about a factor of 10 000. For example, the two-dimensional viscous flow field about an airfoil can be computed today in about 15 minutes of computation time at a cost of about $1 000. Twenty-five years ago, such a simulation would have cost $10 million on an IBM 704 and would have required *30 years* of computer run time.

Until recently, the U.S. enjoyed a significant advantage in simulation capability over its military and commercial competitors. This was due primarily to an advantage in the availability of large-scale computers. Aerodynamicists in Europe and the U.S.S.R. were forced to shoehorn large problems into small computers. Today, the U.S. still maintains its advantage over the U.S.S.R. However, the U.S. advantage over Europe has eroded. For example, of the 16 orders for Cray machines in 1982, 10 were from Europe.

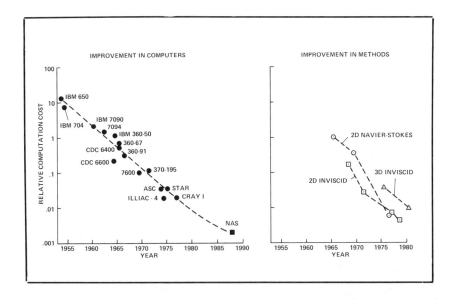

Fig. 3. Computation cost trends for computer flow simulation.

Mathematical Stages of Approximation

The coupled set of partial differential equations governing aerodynamic flow fields, the Navier-Stokes equations, have been known for over a century. Because of their complex form, closed-form solutions have been obtained for only a few simple cases. Even a numerical solution using advanced computers is generally unfeasible because current computer power is inadequate to resolve the wide range of length scales active in high-Reynolds-number turbulent flows of practical interest. Consequently, nearly all the simulations to date have involved solution of mathematical formulations that are approximations to the Navier-Stokes equations.

Figure 4 lists the four major stages of approximation in order of their evolution and complexity (updated from Ref. 1). Advances in computational aerodynamics have produced a variety of computer codes ranging from Stage I codes for complex aircraft configurations to Stage IV codes for very simple geometry. Each succeeding stage requires an increase in computer power for a given geometry but allows a new class of physical

STAGE	APPROXIMATION	CAPABILITY	GRID POINTS REQUIRED	COMPUTER REQUIREMENT
I	LINEARIZED INVISCID	SUBSONIC/SUPERSONIC PRESSURE LOADS VORTEX DRAG	3×10^3 PANELS	1/10 CLASS VI
II	NONLINEAR INVISCID	ABOVE PLUS: TRANSONIC PRESSURE LOADS WAVE DRAG	10^5	CLASS VI
III	REYNOLDS AVERAGED NAVIER-STOKES	ABOVE PLUS: SEPARATION/REATTACHMENT STALL/BUFFET/FLUTTER TOTAL DRAG	10^7	30 x CLASS VI
IV	LARGE EDDY SIMULATION	ABOVE PLUS: TURBULENCE STRUCTURE AERODYNAMIC NOISE	10^9	3000 x CLASS VI
	FULL NAVIER-STOKES	ABOVE PLUS: LAMINAR/TURBULENT TRANSITION TURBULENCE DISSIPATION	10^{12} TO 10^{15}	3 MILLION TO 3 BILLION CLASS VI

Fig. 4. Governing equation and computer requirements for computational aerodynamics.

phenomena to be simulated as follows: for example, subsonic lift distribution in Stage I, transonic wave drag in Stage II, airfoil drag and buffet in Stage III, and boundary-layer transition and aerodynamic noise in Stage IV. Computer codes based on Stages I and II are used now throughout the aircraft industry, while Stages III and IV are the bases for a number of pioneering research efforts.

Numerical computation methods for Stage I are called "panel methods" because complex aircraft geometries are modeled by a large number of contiguous surface panels. Whereas, the full Navier-Stokes equations representing conservation of mass, momentum, and energy contain altogether 60 partial-derivative terms when expressed in three Cartesian coordinates, the linearized inviscid (Stage I) approximation truncates these to only three terms: the Laplace equation for subsonic flows and the wave equation for supersonic flow. The principal advantage of this stage is that the governing three-term equation is linear and, hence, the forces on any panel are obtained by summing the influences from all the other panels. Thus, very complex geometries can be treated relatively simply. A major complication associated with approximations other than Stage I is that the entire flow field, instead of just the aircraft surface, must be divided into a very large number of small cells or grid points for which finite-difference approximations to the partial derivative terms can be expressed. This is a formidable task for treating general aerodynamic configurations because no straightforward, automated technique for grid generation has yet been devised. Considerable human effort working interactively on a computer graphics terminal is required.

The Stage I approximation, although crude, provides surprisingly useful simulations for purely subsonic or purely supersonic flows in which viscous effects are not dominant. An example situation where it is not applicable is flight near the speed of sound, that is, transonic flows, wherein there is mixed subsonic-supersonic flow and embedded shock waves. Another example is a fighter aircraft in a gross maneuver, for which viscous effects would be important. The effects of viscosity, which include boundary layers on surfaces, turbulence, and flow separation and reattachment, strongly affect aerodynamic performance, especially near the limits of performance.

Stage II, in its complete form, neglects only viscous terms and contains 27 of the 60 partial-derivative terms in the complete Navier-Stokes equations. There are subsets of the Stage II approximation that involve fewer than the 27 terms. This stage of approximation is applicable for subsonic, transonic, supersonic, and hypersonic flows as long as viscous effects do not dominate.

Stage III neglects none of the terms in the Navier-Stokes equations. However, the equations are time averaged over an interval that is long compared with turbulent eddy fluctuations, yet small compared with macroscopic aerodynamic flow changes. Such an averaging process introduces various new terms, which represent the time-averaged transport of turbulent momentum and energy, that must be modeled. No entirely suitable model for all flow types of engineering interest has yet been discovered. The current predominant thinking among researchers in the field is that no such universal turbulence model exists. Hence, attention is now focused on developing menus of turbulence models. The process consists of synergistic use of computation and experiment to develop and test models of various types of flows that are considered building blocks to more complete aerodynamic configurations. The primary merit of the Stage III approximation is that it provides realistic simulations of separated flows, of unsteady flows such as buffeting, and of total drag and the other aerodynamic forces. Prediction of these types of flows is fundamentally important in a wide range of aerodynamics problems of aircraft, missiles, helicopter rotors, and turbine and compressor blades. Generally, considerably more computer speed and storage are required for Stage III because of the large number of grid points needed to resolve viscous phenomena, even with the time averaging of turbulent fluctuations.

Stage IV, in its full complexity, involves the direct numerical simulation of large-scale turbulent eddies from the complete time-dependent Navier-Stokes equations. On the one hand, the main physical concepts are such that large eddies absorb energy from the mean flow, are highly anisotropic, vary from flow to flow, and transport the principal turbulent momentum and energy; on the other hand, small eddies dissipate energy, tend toward isotropy, are nearly universal in character, and transport relatively little turbulent energy or momentum. Thus, the large eddies are computed and the small subgrid-scale eddies are modeled. Such simulations can be extremely demanding on computer memory and speed. Given sufficient computer power, however, numerical simulations from essentially first principles could be made of phenomena such as laminar-turbulent transition, aerodynamic noise, surface pressure fluctuations, and all relevant quantities characterizing turbulence. This stage, although it is in a relatively primitive research phase, has already provided some information about the nature of turbulent flows that has long been intractable to experimental measurement.

Example Inviscid Computations

Stage I and II approximations, in their purest forms, are frequently referred to as "inviscid formulations." These approximations are applicable to cases for which viscous effects can be either neglected or accounted for by adding boundary-layer corrections. An example application is the cruise design point for a commerical transport.

Examples of current inviscid formulation capability are provided in Fig. 5 and 6. The first illustrates a panel method (Stage I) computation for the Space Shuttle Orbiter mounted on top of the B-747 carrier aircraft.[2] Accurate determinations were made of the lift characteristics for the combined configuration and for each vehicle during separation of the orbiter from the carrier. Configuration orientations selected from the computational design phase were tested in the wind tunnel for verification. Figure 6 illustrates the progress that has been made during the last decade in Stage II computations. In 1972, when the first three-dimensional nonlinear transonic computations were performed, about 18

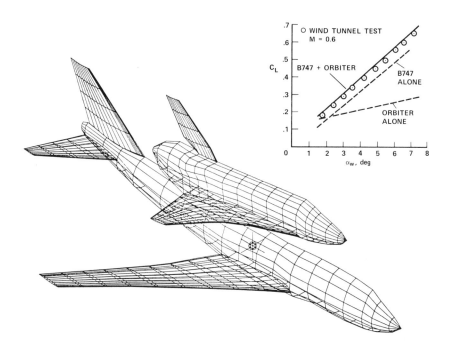

Fig. 5. Linearized inviscid panel method applied to Space Shuttle Orbiter/B-747 combination.

hours of computer time were required per case on the IBM 360-67. Now, more detailed simulations can be performed in substantially less time because of advances in numerical solution techniques and the availability of more powerful computers. Because design is normally a trial and error (iterative) process, such reductions in required computer run time can substantially reduce the time required for configuration optimization.

Inviscid computations have become an integral part of the design process in the aircraft industry today, and there are numerous examples of successful applications. One is the design of the European Airbus A-310. According to Ref. 3, the use of these methods was primarily

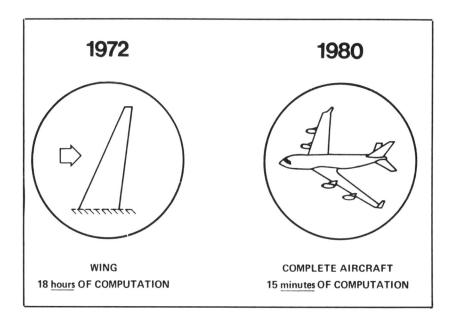

Fig. 6. Revolutionary advances in inviscid-flow technology during the 1970s. (Appropriate for analysis at design conditions.)

responsible for the claimed 20% improvement in fuel efficiency of the A-310 over the A-300, which was designed before these methods were widely available. Less wind-tunnel testing of wing designs was required, leaving more test time to address complex aerodynamic component interference problems. A simple back-of-the-envelope calculation, which assumes fuel costs of $1.30 per gallon for a 15-year life of a 400-airplane fleet, indicates a potential savings in fuel costs of $10 billion. (Incidentally, Airbus has captured a substantial percentage of the wide-body jet market from its American competitors in a very short period of operation.)

Example Viscous Computations

Examples of viscous-dominated aerodynamics problems, for which inviscid formulations generally are not applicable, are provided in Fig. 7.

- PREDICTION OF AERODYNAMIC FORCES

- INLET FLOWS

- COMPRESSOR STALL

- AIRFRAME/PROPULSION SYSTEM INTEGRATION

- STRAKE DESIGN

- STALL/BUFFET

- PERFORMANCE NEAR PERFORMANCE BOUNDARIES

Fig. 7. Examples of important viscous-dominated problems amenable to solution on NAS.

These problem areas can be addressed using the Stage III approximations, the Reynolds-averaged Navier-Stokes formulation. Currently, this stage is the basis for vigorous research focusing on the computation of complex flow-field phenomena. Thus far, investigations have been limited to simple geometries. Figure 8 illustrates some of the progress that was made during the 1970s. These building-block computations, verified by comparison with experiment, indicate that the basic physics of these flow fields can be computed, at least qualitatively. Good quantitative agreement will come in time as turbulence models (to reduce phenomenological errors) and solution-adaptive grid generation techniques (to reduce numerical errors) mature.

Currently, for three-dimensional cases such as the after-body drag computation for a fuselage with propulsive jet, shown in Fig. 8, as many as 20 hours of Class VI computer time are required. Clearly, for computations about complete aircraft, additional computer power is required. The specific requirements are quantified in Fig. 9, which is modified from Ref. 1 to include recent performance predictions. These requirements are also compared with the capabilities of existing machines, with the Cray-2, expected to be available in 1985, and with the Cyber 2XX and Cray-3, both expected to be available in the late 1980s. The requirements are stated in terms of computing speed and memory for a 15-minute computation based on solution algorithm efficiency

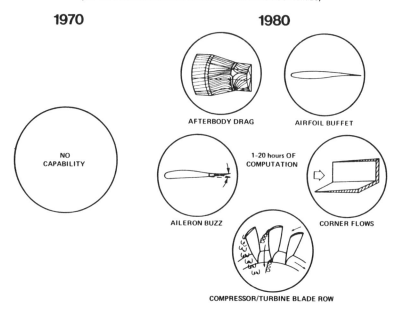

REVOLUTIONARY ADVANCES IN VISCOUS-FLOW
BUILDING BLOCK TECHNOLOGY DURING THE 1970'S
(APPROPRIATE FOR ANALYSIS NEAR PERFORMANCE BOUNDARIES)

Fig. 8. Revolutionary advances in viscous-flow building-block technology during the 1970s. (Appropriate for analysis near performance boundaries.)

anticipated for 1985. Experience indicates that 10-15 minutes of run time are typically required for adequate turnaround in an applications-oriented environment. Algorithm efficiency for 1985 is set by extrapolation, assuming the same rate of progress in algorithm development experienced during the 1970s. The computer speed requirements are stated in terms of *sustained* millions of floating-point operations per second, that is, the average speed expected for a typical flow-field computation. Note that two-dimensional airfoil computation requirements are well within the capabilities of the Cray-1S and Cyber 205 Class VI machines. Requirements for three-dimensional flow past a wing are beyond the capabilities of these machines, at the limits of the capability

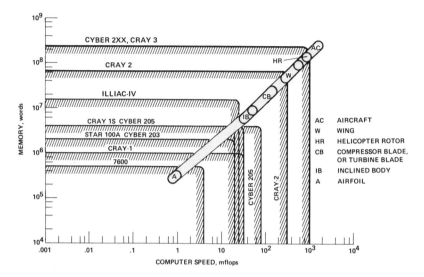

Fig. 9. Computer speed and memory requirements compared with computer capabilities.

of the Cray-2. Machine capability expected in 1988 will be sufficient to tackle the problem of a complete aircraft or a helicopter rotor with a 1 million-point computational grid system. This requires a computing speed of about 1 billion floating-point operations per second and a memory of 250 million words.

There are few examples of the Stage IV approximation, Large-Eddy Simulation (LES) computations, because of the enormous computing power required even for the simplest geometries. Figure 10 shows vorticity contours from a LES computation of a three-dimensional compressible jet.[4] The contours illustrate transition from laminar to turbulent flow.

PROVIDE INCREASED UNDERSTANDING OF FLUID FLOW PHYSICS

- EXAMPLE: TRANSITION TO TURBULENCE IN A JET (1979)
  VORTICITY CONTOURS M = 0.5, Re_D = 20,000

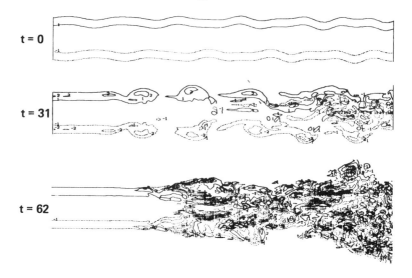

Fig. 10. Vorticity contours from a LES computation of a three-dimensional compressible jet.

The NAS System

The NAS Program is a fiscal year 1984 NASA aeronautics new start that will be an on-going, evolutionary, and pathfinding effort to provide a national computational capability available to NASA, the Department of Defense (DoD), industry, other government agencies, and universities. This program is a necessary element in insuring continuing leadership in computational fluid dynamics and related disciplines. For additional information on the NAS Program, including a summary of the 8-year evolution of the concept, see Ref. 5.

Specific performance goals of the NAS System are as follows:

1985
Speed—250 mflops, sustained
Memory—at least 64×10^6 64-bit words
Users—local and remote

1987
Speed—1 gflops, sustained
Memory—256×10^6 64-bit words
Users—support at least 100 simultaneously on a time-sharing interactive basis
Operating system and network—capable of accommodating a multivendor hardware environment

Beyond 1987
Continue to expand capability

The capability envisioned for the NAS System in 1987 will permit three-dimensional viscous flows, based on the Stage III approximation, about multiple-component (wings, fuselage, tail, nacelles, etc.) aircraft configurations. Furthermore, this capability will permit Stage IV computations in a research mode that will lead to a better understanding of turbulence and, hence, to better turbulence models essential to full realization of the Stage III approximation.

The planned NAS Processing System Network (NPSN) will be a large-scale, distributed resource computer network at Ames Research Center. This network will provide the full end-to-end capabilities needed to support computational aerodynamics, will span the performance range from supercomputers to microprocessor-based workstations, and will offer functional capabilities ranging from "number-crunching" interactive aerodynamic-flow-model solutions to real-time graphical-output-display manipulation. The NPSN resources will be made available to a nationwide community of users via interfaces to landline and satellite data communications links.

The NAS Program is structured to accommodate the continuing development of the NPSN as a leading-edge computer system resource for computational aerodynamics. This development process is dependent upon the acquisition and integration of the most advanced supercomputers industry can provide that are consistent with computational aerodynamics requirements. Figure 11 illustrates the continuing development of the NPSN functional and performance capabilities through

EVOLUTION OF NAS SYSTEM

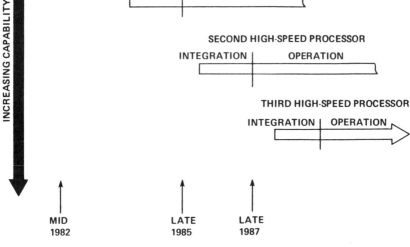

Fig. 11. Evolution of the NAS System.

successive introduction of advanced high-speed processors into the network. The introduction of each new high-speed processor involves an integration phase in which new software and interfaces are implemented and tested, followed by an operational phase. An important element in this evolutionary strategy is the early implementation and testing of a fully functional NPSN designed to accommodate new supercomputers from different vendors with a minimum impact on the existing network architecture and on operational use.

As shown in Fig. 12, the NPSN will consist of the following eight subsystems:

NUMERICAL AERODYNAMIC SIMULATION PROCESSING
SYSTEM NETWORK

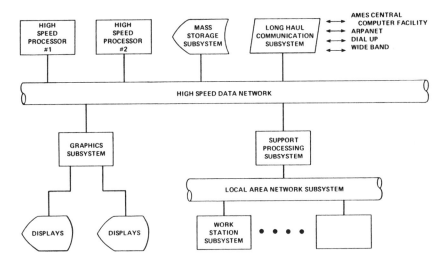

Fig. 12. The Numerical Aerodynamic Simulation Processing System Network (NPSN).

1. High-Speed Processor Subsystem (HSP)
2. Support Processing Subsystem (SPS)
3. Workstation Subsystem (WKS)
4. Graphics Subsystem (GRS)
5. Mass Storage Subsystem (MSS)
6. Long-Haul Communications Subsystem (LHCS)
7. High-Speed Data-Network Subsystem (HSDN)
8. Local-Area Network Subsystem (LANS)

Only the HSP, SPS, WKS, and GRS will be programmed by users. The MSS and LHCS will provide a mass storage facility and a remote data-communications interface, respectively. The HSDN and LANS will provide a data-transport function for the other subsystems.

The High-Speed Processor Subsystem (HSP) is the advanced scientific computing resource within the NPSN. This subsystem will provide the computational throughput and memory capacity to compute computational aerodynamics simulation models. In addition to batch processing, interactive time-sharing processing will be provided to aid in application debugging, result editing, and other activities that depend on close user-processing coupling to achieve optimum overall productivity.

Present plans call for two generations of HSP computers to be in the system at any one time. The first (HSP-1), planned for integration in 1985, will provide a capability to process optimally structured computational aerodynamics applications at a sustained rate of 250 mflops within a minimum 64×10^6 word memory capacity. The second (HSP-2), planned for integration in 1987, will increase these values to 1000 mflops and 256×10^6 word memory capacity.

Whereas the HSP is the ultra-high-speed, large-scale computer resource that will serve the global user community, the Workstation Subsystem (WKS) will be the microprocessor-based resource used by the individual researcher. The WKS will provide a "scientist's workbench" for local users to perform small-scale applications processing. Each individual workstation will have the appropriate memory, disk storage, and hard-copy resources to fit the local user's needs. Individual clusters of workstations will be networked together via the LANS for use within local user groups. In addition to local processing, the WKS will provide terminal access to other user-programmed systems and a file-transfer capability via the LANS and HSDN.

The Support Processing Subsystem (SPS) is a multi-, super-, minicomputer-based system that will provide a number of important functions. The SPS will provide general-purpose interactive processing for local and remote terminal-based users (that is, those without workstations) and provide an intermediate performance resource between the HSP and WKS performance as a WKS backup. The SPS will be a gateway between the HSDN and the LANS, the location for unit record input/output devices such as high-speed printers and microfilm, and the focal point for network monitoring and system operation.

The Graphics Subsystem (GRS) is a super minicomputer-based system that will provide a sophisticated, state-of-the-art, graphical-display capability for those applications requiring highly interactive, high-density graphics for input preparation and result analysis. The GRS will provide a level of performance and storage capability beyond that provided by workstations and will be shared by first-level user organizations.

The Mass Storage Subsystem (MSS) will provide the global on-line and archival file storage capability for the NPSN. This subsystem will validate and coordinate requests for files to be stored or retrieved within the NPSN and maintain a directory of all contained data. The MSS will act as a file server for other NPSN subsystems; control its own internal devices; and perform file duplication, media migration, storage allocation, accounting, and file management functions. Current requirements call for on-line storage of 200 gigabytes in 1985 and 800 gigabytes in 1987.

Users of the NPSN will create and use files on various subsystems, for example, HSP, SPS, GRS, or WKS. However, after the user has exited the NPSN, the main repository of these files will be the MSS. This subsystem will hold those very large files that will be used as input to, or generated as output from, the largest tasks that will be processed on the HSP and GRS. It will contain user source and object codes and parameter and data files that are kept for any significant length of time. The MSS will also contain the backup files that are created to improve the probability that long-lasting or high-value files are accessible when needed.

The Long-Haul Communication Subsystem (LHCS) will provide the data-communication interface between the NPSN and sites geographically remote from the Ames Research Center. This subsystem will provide the necessary hardware/software interfaces; modulation and demodulation devices; and recording, processing, data buffering, and management functions to support data transfers and job control by remote users.

In the sense that the MSS is a back-end resource for the entire NPSN, the LHCS is a front-end resource. It provides for access by remote users to the HSP, SPS, GRS, and WKS, but it is not specifically addressed or programmed by the user. The LHCS processor functions as a data-communications front-end by providing store and forward, protocol conversion, and data-concentrator service.

Current plans call for the LHCS to interface with data links capable of providing 9600 bits/second to over 1.5×10^6 bits/second transmission rates to interface with government-sponsored networks (for example, ARPANET and the proposed NASA Program Support Communication Network) and commercial tariffed services. Candidate data-communication protocols to be supported include ARPANET, IBM System Network Architecture (SNA), and Digital Equipment Corporation's network (DECnet).

The High-Speed Data-Network Subsystem (HSDN) will provide the medium over which data and control messages can be exchanged among the HSP, SPS, GRS, MSS, and LHCS. Major design emphasis will be placed on the ability to support large file transfers among these systems.

The HSDN will include high-speed (minimum 50 megabits/second) interface devices and driver-level network software to support NPSN internal data communications.

The Local-Area Network Subsystem (LANS) will provide the physical data transfer path between the SPS and WKS and between various workstations within a WKS cluster. The LANS will be designed to support up to 40 workstations and to provide a hardware data-communications rate of at least 10 megabits/second.

The LANS differs from the HSDN in data-communication bandwidth because of the smaller size of files transferred on the LANS and the lower cost per LANS network interface device. The HSDN and LANS will use the same network protocol.

The NPSN software will include a rich set of systems and utility software aimed at providing the most efficient and user-productive environment practical. Major software objectives are as follows:

1. a vendor-independent environment that allows the incorporation of new technologies without sacrificing existing software commitments,

2. common and consistent user environments across the NPSN,

3. the maximum transparency to the heterogeneous subsystem nature of the NPSN,

4. the optimal performance for critical resources, and

5. a rich set of user tools.

The strategy taken to satisfy these objectives is to use a UNIX™* or UNIX™ look-alike operating system on the user programmable subsystems (HSP, SPS, GRS, and WKS). This approach is the first attempt to achieve vendor independence and a common user environment and will be implemented by a combination of native UNIX™, vendor UNIX™ look-alikes, and virtual operating system approaches using software tools. The UNIX™ approach provides for the implementation of a rich set of user tools from text editors and compilers to graphics packages that are transportable among systems. This approach also provides a degree of transparency among subsystems. Vendor independence and high performance are aided by the implementation of

---

*The use of trade names of manufactures in this paper does not constitute an official endorsement of such products or manufactures, either expressed or implied, by NASA.

a highly functional and efficient network protocol, such as the Livermore Interactive Network Communication System protocol.

As the NPSN evolution continues, further gains in meeting these objectives in the areas of automatic-file and data-format conversion, common network directory, architecture-independent programming languages, and architecture-specific optimization from ANSI languages will be forthcoming.

Supporting Computer Science Research at NASA Ames

In mid 1983, the Research Institute for Advanced Computer Science (RIACS) was formed at NASA Ames and is operated under contract by the University Space Research Association. The intent was to bring additional computer science expertise to NASA and to initiate a number of research ventures involving personnel from NASA, RIACS, industry, and academia. The long-range research theme is to automate the process of scientific investigation from problem formulation to results dissemination. Principal areas of focus include concurrent processing, computer system networking, knowledge-based expert systems, and fault tolerant computing. It is envisioned that appropriate research advances from these ventures will lead to future upgrades in the NAS System in concert with the NAS Program pathfinding effort to provide a leading-edge system to a national community of aerodynamic and fluid dynamic users.

Conclusion

Remarkable progress was made during the 1970s in advancing the discipline of computational aerodynamics. This progress was sparked by increases in available computer power and was focused primarily on the development of inviscid flow-field simulation techniques. These techniques have been incorporated in computer codes that are now vital tools in the aerospace industry for design and analysis.

Today, research is focused primarily on extending simulation capability to the treatment of more complex aerodynamic configurations and more complete treatment of complex aerodynamic phenomena. A major goal is the simulation of the three-dimensional viscous flow field about a complete aircraft. Such a capability will substantially reduce the level of uncertainty in current simulations. This will permit early detection of design deficiencies, thereby avoiding severe penalties in cost, schedule, and performance in many aerospace system developments.

To achieve this objective, and for the rapid rate of progress in computational aerodynamics to continue, further substantial increases in available computer power will be required. The NAS Program, a NASA fiscal year 1984 new start in aeronautics, is designed to meet this challenge. The goal of this effort is to provide an advanced capability by the middle to late 1980s that will be available for use by government, industry, and academia. The NAS System will be continually upgraded as computer technology advances.

Acknowledgments

The author acknowledges the substantial contributions to the development of the NAS concept, as described here, by his friends and colleagues, F. R. Bailey and V. L. Peterson of NASA Ames, and D. R. Chapman of Stanford University.

References

1. Chapman, D. R. "Computational Aerodynamics Development and Outlook." *AIAA Journal* **17**, no. 12 (1979):1293-1313.

2. da Costa, A. L. "Application of Computational Aerodynamic Methods to the Design and Analysis of Transport Aircraft." *Eleventh Congress of the International Council of the Aeronautical Sciences*, Lisbon, Portugal, ICAS, Bonn, Germany (1978).

3. Jupp, J. A. "Wings of Success." *World Airnews* (December 1980):4-8.

4. Wray, A. A. "Study of Transitional Phenomena in a Flat Plate Boundary Layer and Effects of Small Scale Turbulence on Large Scale Motions." DCW Industries report DCW-R-22-01 (1978).

5. Peterson, V. L., Ballhaus, W. F., Jr., and Bailey, F. R. "Numerical Aerodynamics Simulation." NASA report TM 84386 (1983). To appear in the *Proceedings of the Conference on Large-Scale Scientific Computation*, Academic Press: New York.

17

The Role of Better Algorithms*

J. Glimm
New York University
New York, New York

Introduction

Computers will affect science and technology at least as profoundly as did the invention of calculus. The reasons are the same. As with calculus, computers have increased and will increase enormously the range of soluble problems. The full development of these events will occupy decades, and the rapid progress that we see currently is a strong sign that the impact of computers will be much greater in the future than it is today.

This rapid progress has been found in two areas: in the computers themselves and in the methods for using them, that is, in the hardware and in the software. In this paper we will focus on the second of these issues, which is the requirement of computational science for better algorithms. The needs for better algorithms have been recognized by others, and thoughtful people have projected comparable roles for hardware and software in overall computational progress.

It is important to start with the problem. The role of the computer is to give answers, but the questions are generated by the specific needs of science and technology. The problem may be a complex engineering problem, such as the design of an airplane wing, or it may be a complex scientific problem, such as the understanding of fluid instabilities. Generally, continuum problems are not amenable to today's computing technology without prior simplification and approximation. Equation-of-state problems, which define the nonlinear continuum response functions in terms of molecular or atomic physics, are in general even

---

*This work was supported in part by the National Science Foundation, grant MCS-8207965, and in part by the Department of Energy, grant DEA0276ER03077.

more difficult, and they involve 3^N dimensional integrals for the consideration of N molecular particles. In the same way, quantum chemistry generates problems with a high-dimensional phase space. In short, almost all interesting problems are undercomputed.

The Bad News and The Goods News

Problems will remain undercomputed for a considerable period of time. This is not only due to the human tendency to push at the frontiers of the possible. There is a simple mathematical reason, which is

$$3^4 = 81 .$$

To achieve an increase in resolution by a factor of 3 in a three-dimensional, time-dependent problem requires an increase in computing power by a factor of perhaps 81. This factor is greater than the scalar speed ratio between the VAX and the Cray. Thus, the cost of such an increase in resolution is also a factor in the same range. If cost is no object, which is seldom the case, it still may be necessary to wait several decades to achieve such a speedup. There is a similar problem with storage of data from the intermediate stages of the computation. Here the most optimistic figure is

$$3^3 = 27$$

as the amount of increased storage needed for an increase in resolution by a factor of 3.

To beat these negative projections, one needs better algorithms. Better hardware alone will not do the job. Typically one needs better resolution only in specific portions of a calculation, such as within a boundary layer, flame front, or region of large solution gradient. The extra degrees of freedom must be added preferentially within those portions of the calculation where they will be most critical to the quality of the solution. This can be accomplished in a variety of ways.

Adaptive or local mesh refinement methods carve up space time in a nonuniform fashion to place more computational degrees of freedom within the boundary layer, etc. Analytic information on the behavior of solution asymptotes or nonlinear wave structures in regions of singular behavior can be incorporated into a solution algorithm. Momentum or Fourier frequency space can also be carved up. Multigrid methods are based on a hierarchy of mesh scales and the efficient calculation of high-frequency modes on each mesh scale. The renormalization group is adapted to problems with important degrees of freedom on each length scale and with coupling to nearby length scales. For smooth or piecewise smooth solutions, a higher order method of degree k can improve convergence by a factor of 3^k, for a linear refinement by a factor of 3.

The goal of mathematical computations is first to find answers. An optimal goal is to develop robust methods that scientists and engineers, who are not specialists in computer algorithms, can use to obtain reliable answers. For ordinary differential equations that are not too singular, the second goal has been achieved; for partial differential equations, only the first goal has been obtained, and only in cases that are not too difficult. In summary, many practical problems are undercomputed. The goal is to have them overcomputed. To reach this goal will require improvements in both hardware and software.

Hardware Affects Software

It is widely recognized that changes in machine architecture affect the relative efficiency of algorithms. For example, regular grids and fast Fourier transforms perform well on modern vector machines. Logical operations cannot in general be vectorized and are penalized. Inexpensive and fast array processors change elliptic matrix inversion from a major cost-limiting factor in computations to a minor factor. Parallel architecture will favor algorithms with a large number of logically independent tasks, that is, ones whose order of execution is not prescribed.

Software Affects Hardware

It is equally important for the requirements of software to influence the design characteristics of machine architecture. For example, combined high-speed processing of logical and vector operations would be very helpful and in fact already exists on the Cyber 205. The rapid evolution of special chip technology should have implications for general- and special-purpose machines. There are many standardized collections of algorithms that are widely used in scientific computations, including the mathematics library functions, fast Fourier transforms, linear equation packages, and ordinary differential equation solvers. Presumably these will be and, in some cases, already have been implemented in hardware with an increase in speed as the payoff. There are also a number of problems that are dominated by small special-purpose code segments. Monte Carlo calculations are of this type. It would be desirable for the computer to allow for efficient user-added special-purpose chips having a standardized interface to the rest of the computer. Size constraints for the core memory remain a major limitation in machine utilization. For oversized problems, the speed of data transfer to and from the disk, as well as the complexity of data memory management, is a problem. Virtual memory addresses the complexity problem. Can it be provided for supercomputers? What about the speed of data transfer? The speed of computation is still a limitation, and some people feel that increased parallelism is the most promising route to achieve increased speed.

Front Tracking as an Example of Improved Algorithms

We will now illustrate some of the general ideas mentioned above by presenting some of the algorithm development work being done collaboratively at the Courant Institute, Los Alamos National Laboratory, and The Chevron Oil Field Research Organization in connection with front tracking.[1-7] We have been developing algorithms for the efficient handling of discontinuity fronts as they arise in fluid dynamics problems. To ensure a reasonable combination of generality and applicability, we are developing three specific application areas: oil reservoir simulation (where the discontinuities are the oil-water and oil-gas banks), material interfaces (subject to Rayleigh-Taylor and Kelvin-Helmholtz instabilities), and gas dynamics (with shock wave diffraction patterns as the discontinuities). In this work, three main types of difficulties have emerged, as follows:

1. Data structures. Elementary operations. Precomputed topological data with remaining data available in $O(1)$ time. Physical data defined at interface points. Modular programming.

2. Elliptic equations with discontinuous coefficients. Adaptive grids. Fast solution algorithms. Multigrid methods. Higher order and isoperimetric elements.

3. Hyperbolic equations with discontinuity interfaces. Nonlinear wave modes and their interactions. Coupling between the interface and the interior regions. Shock wave diffraction patterns.

Data Structures and Modular Programming

The basic data types for a front are POINT, BOND, NODE, CURVE, INTERFACE, and FRONT. An interface is the purely geometric part of a front; in addition, a front may contain physical state variables, boundary conditions, grid information, and algorithms concerning the propagation, remeshing, and untangling of an interface. An interface is a collection of nodes and curves. The curves are nonintersecting except at their endpoints, which are nodes. The curves are oriented and are composed of points and oriented bonds. The front-tracking code has been developed in the language C, which supports user-defined data types. To illustrate the idea, a point consists of two reals together with any other structure that a user might want to add. It is defined by the lines of C code

```
typedef struct {
        float x;
        float y;
        USER_POINT
}POINT
```

The entry USER_POINT above is set by some user to be any additional structure (for example, nothing), and it is then filled correctly in a prepass by the compiler. A bond consists of two points (start and end) and two bonds (next and previous). More precisely, a bond contains the addresses (pointers) for two points and two bonds. Thus we see that bonds are stored as a doubly linked list. For this reason, elementary operations such as insertion or deletion of a point or bond in a curve can be accomplished in $0(1)$ time. Continuing, a curve contains two nodes (start and end) and two bonds (first and last), while a node contains a point and a list of incoming and a list of outgoing curves. The curves also contain elementary topological information. Because an interface divides the plane into a union of connected components, each curve (which is oriented) has a left and a right component. A component is just an integer, used as a label, and the assignment of integers to label components is arbitrary. Several components can have the same label and will then not be distinguished by the code.

There are elementary routines to create, copy, print, and modify curves, nodes, and interfaces. It is frequently necessary to determine in which component a given point lies. This is usually done in $0(1)$ time on the basis of precomputed topological data. A rectangular grid of convenient size is chosen and the bonds, curves, and components meeting each grid block are then precomputed. The point (x,y) can be localized in a grid block in 0(1) time, and because usually only a small number of bonds, curves, and components meet this grid block, the computation of which component contains this point can also be done in 0(1) time. Here the left and right component information stored on the curve is useful. There are also routines to test and correct for intersecting curves, to remesh curves, to store physical state variables on the interface, and to interpolate state variables between the points of the curve where they are defined. For curves that run into the boundary and have interpolation at a higher than linear order, there are missing points in the interpolation stencil. If boundary data are supplied, it may be possible to fill in the missing data points in an intelligent fashion. Also a normal projection of a point onto the curve is available so that, in effect, normal and tangential coordinates are defined in a neighborhood of the curve.

There are many other data structures, as the C language makes this a natural device to employ. The code is modular and is organized into libraries. These libraries are shared by all applications. In addition, each application has its own library of physics-dependent routines. Thus there is a clear separation of code into physics-dependent and physics-independent parts. The physics-independent part is organized into portions dealing with equations of a similar mathematical structure, thus using a common set of methods. This separation of the code into independent libraries, each specialized to the consideration of a common class of methods and equations, is essential to our development effort. It increases both the scope and the reliability of the work, and without modularization of the code development, the work described here could not have been done.

Elliptic Equations With Discontinuous Coefficients

Material interfaces or phase boundaries typically generate discontinuous coefficients in elliptic differential equations. When the ratio of the coefficients on the two sides of the interface is greater than about 1.5:1, it is essential for the solution accuracy to remap the grid so that the discontinuity interface falls entirely on grid lines or finite element boundaries. Discontinuity ratios as large as 600:1 arise easily in practice (this is the density ratio of water to air), so an adaptive grid construction is the required first step in the solution algorithm. We use an algorithm that moves points of an originally regular rectangular grid.[8] This construction is thus based on grid alignment, not refinement, and results in a grid that is logically rectangular but locally distorted (quadrilateral) near the interface. In this construction the interface lies either on quadrilateral boundaries or on triangle boundaries formed by the bisection of a quadrilateral along one of its diagonals. More elaborate adaptive grid strategies, including curved bonds (isoperimetric elements) and local mesh refinement (not logically rectangular), are undergoing testing and development.

Given the grid, the equations are then discretized using linear, quadratic, or cubic elements on triangles and bilinear, biquadratic, or bicubic elements on rectangles. The discretized equations are solved by one of a variety of methods: direct (sparse matrix), preconditioned conjugate gradient based on a fast Fourier transform preconditioner, or multigrid. The choice among these methods depends on the size and singularity of the problem and on the hardware being used. We are currently getting very good results from a limited form of multigrid combined with conjugate gradient methods run on a vector machine (VAX with attached FPS or Cray). In this combination, the solution phase is a small portion of the overall problem.[9-11]

Hyperbolic Equations With Discontinuity Fronts

Material surfaces, phase boundaries, slip surfaces, contact discontinuities, and shock waves generate discontinuities in hyperbolic equations. The discontinuities may be present in the initial data, but they also occur spontaneously in the process of solving equations with initially smooth data. (This latter possibility is not supported in current versions of the front-tracking software.) For coupled elliptic-hyperbolic equations, the discontinuity fronts of the hyperbolic equation may give rise to discontinuous coefficients in the elliptic equation. The discontinuities may be thought of as moving internal boundaries; the remainder of space, that is, the part not lying on a boundary, is called the interior. There are then four issues to be resolved.

1. Interior motion. Any standard hyperbolic scheme, such as the Lax-Wendroff scheme, can be used in the interior.

2. Boundary motion. Locally near the front, the motion is predominantly one dimensional, and the leading term of the motion is described by the solution to a Riemann problem. Fix a boundary

point. If we approximate the solution locally on each side of the boundary by a constant, then these data define a Riemann problem. For a hyperbolic system,

$$U_t + F(U)_x = 0$$

in one space dimension. A Riemann problem is defined by the scale invariant Cauchy data

$$U(t = 0,x) = \begin{cases} u_l = \text{const}, x < 0 \\ u_r = \text{const}, x > 0. \end{cases}$$

The solution is known to consist of elementary rarefaction, contact, and shock waves, one of which will be the wave that the front is tracking. The Riemann problem solution then gives the wave speed of this tracked wave, and the wave speed is used to propagate the front to its new position at time $t + \delta t$. Also, the state variables on the interface, which must be double valued, can be given their correct time-incremented values for the time $t + \delta t$. Riemann problems can be solved by algebraic or functional equations and are more elementary than the hyperbolic partial differential equation that generates them.

3. Boundary-interior coupling. In general, interior waves will reach one of the moving discontinuity boundaries. When this happens, the interior wave can be partially reflected and partially transmitted. The interior wave can also be partially or completely absorbed at the boundary. In addition, a moving curved front can radiate waves into the interior. In particular, the boundary motion given by the above Riemann solution must be corrected. As necessary data, we must have linear rather than constant data given on each side of the interface. Then interior waves that reach the front within the time interval $[t,t + \delta t]$ are contained in the data. A corrected (higher order) Riemann solver gives (up to the desired order of accuracy in powers of δx) the solution of the hyperbolic equation with data of the form

$$U(t = 0,x) = \begin{cases} \alpha_l + x\beta_l, x < 0 \\ \alpha_r + x\beta_r, x > 0, \end{cases}$$

where α_l, α_r, β_l, and β_r are constants. It is assumed that these constants are bounded, so that the linear correction to the constant data contains a power of δx, if the solution is sought for a time interval of size $\delta t = O(\delta x)$. This higher order Riemann solver is then used as before to advance the front and to update state variables stored on it. This process accounts for the normal motion of the front and the states stored along it. It also allows for variation in the state variables in a direction normal to the front, that is, for normal waves coming from the interior. It does not account for variation of the state variables in directions tangential to the front. This tangential variation of state variables is responsible for surface waves and for the geometrical effects introduced by the curvature of the front. Both of these processes are dealt with by a tangential sweep, which updates the interface variables by a tangential differential equation. Thus we are using local, normal, and tangential coordinates within a mesh block of the front and a fractional step algorithm, with a normal and tangential operator splitting.

Finally, interior mesh points, which lie near a moving boundary, will not have a full stencil for their finite difference calculation. A modified difference method, of lower order, must then be used at such irregular points. Interior-boundary coupling of the type described above is slightly more advanced than that used in earlier tests[7] and is not yet fully tested.

4. Shock wave diffraction patterns. The intersection of two or more fronts creates a problem that is not locally one dimensional. Shock polars are used in place of Riemann problems to provide the elementary waves that arise in this fashion and to determine their speed of propagation. This problem has been studied extensively both experimentally and theoretically,[12,13] but it seems that a clear theoretical explanation of observed phenomena is not available in all cases. For scalar hyperbolic equations, Reference 14 is relevant to this question.

Results: The Rayleigh-Taylor and Kelvin-Helmholtz Instabilities

Our methods apply to both compressible and incompressible fluid flow, including multiple fluid components and material interfaces. The methods are general in the sense that they are compatible with the inclusion of detailed physics, including surface tension, viscosity, and heterogeneous driving forces. Such mechanisms must be modeled correctly if the calculations are to agree with experimental observations. These general features are not yet installed, and the present focus is on the validation of the code under idealized physical conditions. For such validation, there are very good special-purpose calculations available in the incompressible case. These comparison solutions are based on conformal mapping[15] or vortex and boundary integral methods.[16] We have done calculations with an air/water interface, initially at rest, with a sinusoidal disturbance, using incompressible Euler equations. Because of gravitational acceleration, the disturbance grows in time. We followed it up to a height-to-wavelength ratio of slightly more than one. At this point, the spike is into its asymptotic free-fall regime. This solution, obtained by the front-tracking method, was then compared to the infinite density ratio conformal mapping solution of Reference 15. The comparison included detailed diagnostics, as well as the comparison of interface position. The interface position comparison was good up to an amplitude of about one, while the detailed diagnostics started diverging earlier, depending on the number of derivatives they contained. Moderate density ratios were also studied both with and without heterogeneous driving force. We show in Fig. 1 the results for a density ratio 4 calculation without heterogeneity. The Rayleigh-Taylor results were obtained in collaboration with O. McBryan, R. Menikoff and D. Sharp and are discussed in References 9 and 17.

The Kelvin-Hemholtz calculations were done at low and moderate Mach numbers (0.1 and 0.5) using compressible Euler equations.[7]

Results: Shock Wave Diffraction Patterns

We show results for a bow shock interacting with a Prandtl-Meyer expansion fan (Fig. 2). For comparison in Fig. 2, we have solved this problem in steady state by the method of characteristics.[18] These data were then used to initialize the calculation to see whether the solution remained constant in time. In fact, this was the case, with the exception of a slight spreading of the sharp base of the rarefaction fan. Because this spreading is far from the shock, we conclude that in Fig. 2 the dominant errors are associated with the interior scheme. These results were obtained in collaboration with G. Marshall, O. McBryan, and B. Plohr of the Courant Institute.

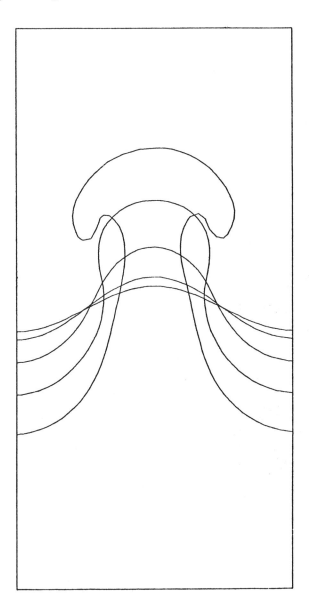

Fig. 1. A two-fluid interface subject to the Rayleigh-
Taylor instability. The initial and four subsequent interfaces are plotted.

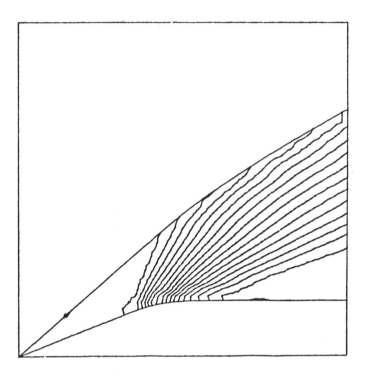

Fig. 2. Bow shock caused by wedge in a wind tunnel with supersonic flow. The wedge also gives rise to a Prandtl-Meyer expansion fan and this fan interacts with the bow shock. The calculation was started with data taken from a steady-state calculation based on a more exact method (the method of characteristics). The test was to see whether the steady-state data were then preserved in time. This was the case, except for some spreading of the rarefaction wave in time. The lines plotted are isopycnics.

References

1. Glimm, J. "Singularities in Fluid Dynamics." In *Mathematical Problems in Theoretical Physics*, edited by R. Schrader and D. A. Uhlenbrock. New York:Springer-Verlag, 1982.

2. Glimm, J., Isaacson, E., Marchesin D., and McBryan, O. "Front Tracking for Hyperbolic Systems." *Advances in Applied Mathematics* 2 (1981):91-119.

3. Glimm, J., Lindquist, B., McBryan, O., and Padmanabhan, L. "A Front Tracking Reservoir Simulator. 5-Spot Validation Studies and The Water Coning Problem." Unpublished manuscript.

4. Glimm, J., Lindquist, B., McBryan, O., Yaniv, S. "Statistical Fluid Dynamics II: The Influence of Geometry on Surface Instabilities." Unpublished manuscript.

5. Glimm, J., Marchesin, D., McBryan, O., and Isaacson, E. "A Shock Tracking Method for Hyperbolic Systems." Army Research Office report 80-3, Triangle Park, NC (1980).

6. Glimm, J., and McBryan, O. "Front Tracking for Hyperbolic Conservation Laws." *Proceedings of the 1981 Army Numerical Analysis and Computer Conference*, Army Research Office report 81-3, Triangle Park, NC (1981).

7. Glimm, J., McBryan, O., and Plohr, B. "Applications of Front Tracking to Two-Dimensional Gas Dynamics Calculations." *Lecture Notes in Engineering*, edited by J. Chandra and J. E. Flaherty. New York:Springer-Verlag, 1983.

8. McBryan, O. "Elliptic and Hyperbolic Interface Refinement." In *Boundary Layers and Interior Layers—Computational and Asymptotic Methods*, edited by J. Miller. Dublin:Boole Press, 1980.

9. McBryan, O. "Computing Discontinuous Flows." *Proceedings of the Meeting on Fronts, Patterns, and Interfaces*, Los Alamos, New Mexico:Amsterdam-North Holland, (1983).

10. McBryan, O. "Multigrid Methods for Discontinuous Equations." *Proceedings of International Multigrid Conference*, Copper Mountain, Colorado:Institute for Computational Studies at Colorado State University (1983).

11. McBryan, O. "Shock Tracking Methods in 2d Flows." *Proceedings of the 9th National Applied Mechanics Congress*, Cornell University:ASME, New York (1982).

12. Ben-Dor, G., and Glass, I. "Domains and Boundaries of Non-Stationary Oblique Shock Wave Reflections." *J. Fluid Mech.* **92** (1977):459-496 and **96** (1980):735-756.

13. Glass, I. "Nonstationary Oblique Shock-Wave Reflections: Actual Isopycnics and Numerical Experiments." *AAIAJ* **16** (1978):1146.

14. Wagner, D. "The Riemann Problem in Two-Space Dimensions for a Single Conservation Law." Unpublished manuscript.

15. Menikoff, R., and Zemack, C. "Rayleigh-Taylor Instability and the Use of Conformal Maps for Ideal Fluid." Unpublished manuscript.

16. Baker, G. R., Meiron, D. I., and Orszag, S. A. "Vortex Simulations of the Rayleigh-Taylor Instability." *Phys. Fluid* **23** (1980): 1485-1490.

17. Sharp, D. H. "An Overview of Rayleigh-Taylor Instability." *Physica* **12D** (1984):3-18.

18. Marshall, G., and Plohr, B. "The Random Choice Method for Two-Dimensional Steady Supersonic Shock-Wave Diffraction Problems. Unpublished manuscript.

18

Super Problems for Supercomputers

F. H. Harlow
Los Alamos National Laboratory
Los Alamos, New Mexico

Much of the focus in these discussions, and rightly so, has been on problems in engineering and the physical sciences. There are many people in this country and in the world who are asking, "Can modern technology have spinoff to other kinds of problems and other circumstances?" The questions they are asking pertain to society and to the future of civilization. It may sound far out, but nevertheless let us consider how we can extend our techniques of analysis from problems like the motion of molecules in a box, turbulence, and multiphase flow—the things that I have been familiar with for 30 years—to questions about the dynamics of mobs of people or thoughts in a human brain.

First, what do these things have in common? Basically, the common factor is that they are all problems involving numerous, discrete entities interacting with one another. By discrete entities, I mean the individual molecule or the person in a mob; but when we consider thoughts in a brain, it becomes a little more questionable exactly what is meant by discrete entities. Is it even remotely possible that we can tackle these and some of the other kinds of problems that I'm going to discuss? I think the answer is yes, and I would like to convince you that it is a resounding yes.

We shall talk about things like generalized Boltzmann's equations and flow in complex spaces. The mathematical problems get a little sticky here and there, and I am not going to get into the details. We have used some of these techniques for the study of problems in continuum mechanics and have become familiar with procedures that are available for their solution. I think that we can apply some of these same ideas to the most remarkable kinds of problems, with results that have a strong potential for being realistic. Indeed, one might go so far as to say that such investigations can be crucial to our understanding of where humanity is heading in future generations.

How should nations interact with one another? How should people think about things like nuclear disarmament? The number of questions seems endless. I'm certainly not going to get so far out on a limb as to offer you any solutions to some of these perplexing questions, but I would like to convince you that there are some exciting directions that I believe computers, supercomputers if you wish, are going to help us to go in the next years and decades.

To get started, let us talk about three different kinds of uses for computers. The first is for making predictions of purely deterministic circumstances. For example, suppose you have the equations for flow of water in a river and are furnished the data for rainstorms in the upstream areas. You want to predict the flood stages for the next 2 or 3 days. It is now possible to make very useful, effective, deterministic predictions using computer models. They work quite well, and the results are very useful, although once in a while you get surprised. We can think of computer predictions for all sorts of other deterministic circumstances, in numerous engineering and scientific applications.

The second use of computers is for the performance of experiments. Certainly the things we calculate have to be tied to physical reality. That means that you have to understand how nature works, and for that purpose, it is necessary to perform real laboratory experiments and to go out in the field to gather real data. But there are some kinds of circumstances that extend beyond the things you can do in the laboratory or in the field, for which you perform computer experiments. Mathematical experiments, for example, can examine the stochastic properties of nonlinear recursion relations, and some very interesting results are emerging with implications for turbulence and for all sorts of other interesting problems. You can also perform experiments for the entry of a vehicle into the atmosphere of Jupiter, or for circumstances in which the temperature is so high that you cannot conveniently do it in the laboratory. These are very useful things to do, provided you can trust the computer program. Performing a numerical experiment for some strange environment with a computer technique that is not very well checked out can lead to serious trouble.

The third use of computers is especially germane to what I would like to discuss today, and that is the testing of behavioral models. Newton's laws of motion furnish an example that has been around for years. They are behavioral models for the interaction of point particles colliding with one another or for describing what happens as the moon revolves around the earth. A classic expression of Newtonian behavior is that force equals mass times acceleration. This is a well-proven behavioral model, but many models that are required for our new directions of analysis are not nearly as well known, so that postulated forms require extensive testing for validation. You can test them by seeing their consequences on the computer. Interactions in physical systems can even require testing, for example, with reaction rates for a process in which there is uncertainty as to the dependence on species concentration. You can try different reaction rates and see what the consequences are in comparison with actual data. The greatest challenge, however, is to quantify sociological interactions among people, among groups of people, and among nations.

Let me say a little more about the business of predictions. There are two types of systems that we should keep in mind. The first is the system that's deterministic. The macroscopic initial and boundary conditions really do determine what happens, so that the chance effects of microscopic variations are not significant. The second is the system that exhibits what I like to call corporate capriciousness. As an example, I take a bucket of water and try to pour it carefully onto the very top of a symmetrical mound of concrete. That corporate body of water is capricious in its behavior. The exact pattern of flow depends upon minute details, and the water is likely to move in different ways each time the experiment is carefully repeated. The turbulence within a fluid can be said to demonstrate corporate capriciousness in the sense that turbulence in detail depends upon the fine-scale properties of the initial and boundary conditions.

For our discussion, a more relevant kind of corporate capriciousness is the question of what happens in a mob of people, a specific mob congregating on the street corner, yelling and getting excited. Will they go down the street and roll over police cars, or go around the corner and break windows, or parade back and forth before the governor's mansion? This uncertainty describes their corporate capriciousness. You are never going to be able to predict a priori exactly which direction they will go, but just as the capriciousness of water going over the mound doesn't prevent us from studying fluid dynamics, so also the uncertainty and capriciousness of predicting a specific mob should not prevent us from coming to grips with the interesting questions of mob dynamics.

Another example of corporate capriciousness is demonstrated by the train of thoughts in a human brain. A speaker may have a good idea of what he would like to be his specific train of thoughts, but as the talk progresses, there are numerous opportunities for digression that are triggered by minute flickers of memory; the mind departs from its prearranged patterns in a classic exhibition of corporate capriciousness. Nevertheless, the subjects of mental dynamics and the relationship of mental processes to certain integral properties are very interesting and are special kinds of things to study. The integral properties in this case are such traits as intelligence or the more transient moods and obsessions.

How do we even qualitatively analyze the kinds of things I am talking about? To see the answer, consider a circumstance for which we know very well how to proceed. Our essential tool will be a generalized Liouville Theory, which I consider to be one of the most beautiful creations of nature. Perhaps you have visited the Grand Canyon. When you first come up to the rim, the effect is dazzling, almost overwhelming. The same was true for me when I first began to understand the Liouville Theory and to see it as a product of the mental dynamics of superb human creativity. It's like first hearing a wonderful piece of music. How can the human brain accomplish these miracles? Perhaps the products of creativity will soon be used to discover the very processes by which human minds perceive thoughts in the first place.

To use the Liouville Theory, it is necessary to specify the variables for your system and to state the deterministic interactions amongst the variables. At that stage you might have a purely deterministic model, like describing the dynamics of molecules in a box. You can actually solve problems, some of them analytically and some of them with present-day computers. But even with 10 000 particles, you will not get some of the coherent properties you want, like sound waves, for example.

To proceed from this stage of the description to the full Liouville Theory generally requires some kind of a conservation principle. For example, the number of molecules in some subsection of phase space moving with the particles is a constant, and this principle is sufficient for derivation of the appropriate Liouville equation, describing variations of the probability distribution function for the number of molecules per unit phase-space volume. Finally, one can take moments of such an equation and get the gas-dynamics equations that describe just the main coherent properties of this extremely complex system.

For each molecule in a box, the appropriate variables are its position and its velocity as functions of time. The deterministic interactions are Newton's law: force equals mass times acceleration, plus the kinematic statement that the rate of change of position is equal to the velocity. For the Liouville equation, we introduce a distribution function together with the principle of conservation of particles in phase space. The resulting equation becomes more tractable with the introduction of stochastic assumptions, leading to the Boltzmann equation, or even simpler, a single-relaxation time equation.

With even further manipulations and appropriate moment calculations, we come to the last stage of the theory, the Navier-Stokes equations for gas dynamics, describing such mean properties as density, velocity, temperature, pressure, and internal energy. The detailed molecular trajectories are now irrelevant, and all that remains are the corporate or coherent properties of what we now call a fluid instead of a bunch of molecules.

I worked for years in these directions and applied this kind of approach to studies of turbulence, to multiphase flow, and to numerous other topics in continuum mechanics. I think these superb mathematical techniques can now be applied to new problems of the most remarkable nature, even including the interactions of nations with one another and the evolution of biological species. What about questions of social response to legislation or the business of staff morale and behavior in a large university? Even in these fields, I think there are things that can be done.

Let me try to make this more specific and, I hope, plausible. In order to do so, I would like to take the example of a mob of people. Our first step is to identify some variables. For each person there are a number of variables: how hungry he is, how tired, all kinds of things. But let's try to simplify this as much as possible to see if we can make a theory based upon just the smallest number of relevant variables that we can imagine. Consider the individual level of excitement. At first there is no mob at all. People are walking along the street, but then someone gets up on a platform and starts haranguing. The pedestrians are curious, and gradually they get closer. Excitement grows, but there is also a level of anxiety or fear, especially if there is a siren sounding in the distance. We postulate measures for excitement and fear, labeling them with the quantitative indices e and f. In addition, there is a level of sameness, s. To illustrate, suppose you have been doing something very exciting for 5 minutes, with exhilaration that is sustained by the novelty of what is happening. As time pases, however, the novelty wears off and a level of sameness grows in you, inducing a decay in the level of excitement. More easily defined are the coordinates, x, of each person's position, and his velocity, u. Even with only these five variables, three scalar and two vector, it is possible to build a very interesting and surprisingly realistic model for the deterministic interactions of each individual with his neighbors and with the mob as a whole. Nick Romero of the Los Alamos

National Laboratory and I have programmed this for a computer and have obtained some very strange and interesting results. The study has a long way to go but, nevertheless, indicates even at this stage the potential value for such investigations.

To illustrate qualitatively how we proceeded, consider the time rate of change of excitement for an individual, de/dt. One important source term comes directly from the excitement level of the close neighbors. Another is derived from the corporate excitement of the mob as a whole; when you hear a roar go through the crowd, you want to roar too. The effect of the speaker himself is also an important source term. But at the same time, we can't forget our feeling of sameness. Sameness is growing deep inside each person; he doesn't realize it, but the growth of that sameness is soon going to enhance the decay of excitement. What was fun for a little while becomes dull. Likewise, for fear we can identify source terms in a rate equation, for example in response to a mob member screaming out that the police are coming. Velocity in our model tends to propel each person principally either toward or away from the center of the crowd. If $e - f$ is positive, then you expect the person to be heading toward the center. If $e - f$ is negative, he is going to turn around and be heading the other way. Of course, there are some limitations. As the mean density of people around each individual increases, his mobility relative to the crowd is impeded. With sufficient crowding, his velocity becomes equal to the mean local velocity of the mob rather than to a magnitude that is determined by his own variables.

To investigate the properties of our model, we can look for several types of solutions to the equations. One of these works directly with the coupled equations, describing each person like following the individual molecules in a box. Another is to derive the equations for a distribution function and to look at moment equations for probable levels of excitement, fear, density of crowding, and numerous other effects. Predictions for a *specific* mob are not possible in detail, but a study of *probable* mob behavior resulting from various provocations can give us crucial insight into the avoidance of tragedy in mob-control techniques.

Several other investigators are also currently looking at similar problems regarding the interactions among people. An interesting paper by Hofstadter in *Scientific American* (May 1983) talks about Axelrod's tournament to study the so-called iterated prisoner's dilemma. He draws some interesting conclusions that seem surprisingly relevant to the relationships of nations to one another. If you were going to try to identify variables for the behavior of nations, you would consider, for example, gross national product, standard of living index, total population, index of nationalistic sentiment, and state of military preparedness. You can then postulate interactive equations among these variables. What Axelrod did was something far simpler, and even with this simplicity, he was able to reach fascinating conclusions. Specifically, his study of the iterated prisoner's dilemma was an investigation of the following problem. Suppose you and I decided to make an exchange of goods. I want to buy your peaches and you want my money. Each of us will take our sack of peaches or money to a preappointed place and then each of us will go over and pick up the other person's sack. We never meet in the process. You may think to yourself, if I put peaches in my sack then I will have lost my peaches, but if I just put rocks in there, and he gives me the money in his sack, I will have gotten something for nothing. Likewise I may think, I'll just put some dirt in my sack and get his peaches for free. But perhaps he will not have left any peaches. The obvious choice for both of us is to leave nothing of value; we may get something for nothing, but in any case there is nothing to lose. But suppose we plan to do this once a month, over and over again, for the next 30 years. In that case, what is the best way to proceed? What is the proper tactic whereby you maximize what you are going to get over the long haul? Axelrod submitted this question to many people who made algorithms of one sort or another, some very complicated ones, some of them very simple. After testing by computer runs, the one that won is a strategy called "Tit for Tat." The idea is simple. If you gave me peaches, then the next time I would give you money; if you defaulted and gave me rocks, then the next time I should default. In other words, I simply repeat exactly what you do. None of the other more complicated ideas fared nearly as well as Tit for Tat. This result supplies much food for thought regarding the dynamics of nations provoking one another, and Axelrod suggests some fascinating possibilities.

The next step is to incorporate simultaneous interactions among additional variables, and the complexity increases very rapidly, leading us to the stochastic analyses we have been discussing, and the use of supercomputers for testing the models and applying the results.

The last area I will mention is that of the human brain. There are two different kinds of problems with regard to the human brain: one biological and the other psychological. Biological means questions of memory storage and retrieval and the basic way in which the neurons and synapses work together within the brain to accomplish the patterns of mental activity. In this regard, there is some beautiful recent work by

J. Hopfield, of the California Institute of Technology, who studied in considerable detail the dynamics of content addressibility and formulated some marvelous implications with regard to how the brain actually can function.

Psychological questions address the changing patterns of activity of the human brain and the way in which thoughts interact with one another through coupling. We have actually written some computer programs for simple models of these processes and come up with some strange and interesting results.

One thing that has emerged from Hopfield's work is his postulate that a special kind of supercomputer could be designed to be content addressable. The user supplies a small fragment of information or an imprecise clue and the flow of patterns in memory space fills out to retrieve the full and correct memory. Hopfield believes that the hardware for such a machine could be designed and built. The result would be an entirely new and fascinating concept in computing.

Of the topics I've mentioned, we have already experimented with three—the dynamics of mobs, thoughts in a human brain, and the evolution of species. Only a beginning has been accomplished in each of these fields. Computer programs have been written and preliminary results are starting to come out. There is a lot more to do. I really believe that this is one of the major directions that future scientific research will go. We need bold and courageous postulates for interactions amongst things that we've never before thought about quantifying. We need Liouville techniques, flow techniques in complex spaces, and inevitably greater computing capacity for the testing and application of our results.

19

Supercomputers and Magnetic Fusion Energy

D. B. Nelson
U. S. Department of Energy
Washington, D.C. 20545

Introduction

Fusion research has its own fascination and its own complexity. In fact, development of controlled fusion energy has been called the most complex technical task ever undertaken by mankind. Statements of that sort are always debatable, but fusion certainly is complex, and it has a multiplicity of interactions similar to those that Frank Harlow discussed in "Super Problems for Supercomputers." There are short-range encounters, long-range encounters, multiple time scales, and multiple processes. There is, of course, a big distinction in that in fusion processes we think we know most of the single particle interaction laws, and assuming we are right, that means that all the fun is in the collective effects. I hope in this talk to give you some flavor of the fun and the complexity, and to help answer why the assistance of supercomputers is so beneficial.

Specifically, I will cover five topics: (1) what controlled fusion is, (2) why computing is important to fusion research, (3) contributions to fusion research from supercomputer use, (4) how we actually use supercomputers, and (5) remaining problems and opportunities and a glimpse into the future. Because of time limitations, some material will be covered at a somewhat superficial but, I hope, interesting level. A good reference for this talk is *Magnetic Fusion Energy and Computers*, DOE/ER0159, published by the Department of Energy in January 1983. I think it is a pretty good document. It was written by a committee, but the committee was a committee of experts, each of whom wrote his own section, and it gives a good overview of the role of computing in fusion.

Nuclear Fusion

It is worthwhile to begin by describing nuclear fusion, because the nature of the fusion process dictates the kind of computing we do. Fusion is one of the three known virtually inexhaustible energy sources—the others are fission and solar. (Solar energy is itself the result of fusion occurring in the sun.) The fusion reaction that is best known, with largest cross section and lower energy threshold, is the D-T reaction, which involves the hydrogen isotopes deuterium and tritium. This reaction produces an alpha particle, a neutron, and a lot of kinetic energy carried by the two reaction products:

$$D + T \rightarrow {}^4He + n + 17.6 \text{ MeV}.$$

Because of the electrostatic or Coulomb repulsion between the D and the T, they must be accelerated to high energy, greater than 10 keV, for the reaction to take place. (The reaction rate peaks at approximately 100 keV.) Hydrogen bombs reach these energies. They do it very fast and we call it uncontrolled fusion energy. It has been a lot harder to do it gently to create controlled fusion energy. The basic principle is to heat a sufficiently dense D-T gas to a high temperature by input of energy and then confine it long enough so that the energy produced by this reaction exceeds the energy input.

The chief problem is that this hot, high-pressure gas must be squeezed to keep it from expanding, and yet, it must be insulated from surrounding material or it will cool down too quickly. In the sun, gravity and the vacuum of space accomplish this. In inertial confinement, a D-T pellet is compressed very quickly by lasers or particle beams and confined briefly by its own inertial forces.

I will be discussing magnetic confinement, which uses externally applied magnetic fields to confine the fuel. This is possible because of the following process: if gas is heated to a high temperature, it ionizes; that is, the electrons are knocked free of the atoms. An ionized gas is electrically conducting. It interacts with magnetic fields, which, if artfully applied, can squeeze and confine the gas. Ionized gas is called a plasma. (The word plasma is ambiguous, because it is also a medical term.)

Unfortunately, plasma interacts with its own self-generated electromagnetic fields through collective effects that can lead to instabilities, expelling the plasma violently through the external magnetic field. Plasma instabilities have been studied exhaustively (often inadvertently) in laboratory experiments. They are thought to be the cause of solar flares as well.

The Importance of Supercomputers

Partly as a result of these collective interactions, there is a tremendous range of characteristic space and time scales for fusion processes, as shown below.

10^{-12} cm	— Nuclear Processes
10^{-8} cm	— Atomic Processes
10^{-3} cm	— Coulomb Collisions
10^0 cm	— Plasma Waves
10^2 cm	— Transport Processes
10^{-17} sec	— Nuclear Processes
10^{-11} sec	— Plasma Oscillations, Gyro-Motion
10^{-6} sec	— Alfvén Waves
10^{-3} sec	— Collisional Energy Relaxation
10^3 sec	— Resistive Magnetic Field Diffusion

It is not possible to conceive of a single computer code that could encompass all of these ranges. To arrive at computable models, we typically consider nuclear processes as being instantaneous and continuously in equilibrium. Atomic processes are often considered to be instantaneous; if so, we use what is called the coronal equilibrium model. Coulomb collisions, plasma wave, and transport processes are often modeled as time dependent. But you can imagine that, in order to make progress with this enormous span, you have to assume that the whole system is in near equilibrium. If it is not in near equilibrium, then you typically find out that it "blows up" on one time scale or another—terminating the experiment or the computer run. That is something you want to learn how to prevent.

The fusion experiments that we are now working on are very expensive and very large, and it takes a long time to build them and a long time to run them. Numerical modeling has saved us time and money; it has increased our effectiveness, and it has generated new ideas that have later proved correct or at least useful. As for the size, current leading fusion experiments cost about half a billion dollars each. The next generation, which we are starting to design, is on the order of a billion dollars each. Commercial reactors are probably going to range from $1 billion to $4 billion. So there is big money involved.

What do these experiments look like? Figure 1 shows a picture of our most advanced tokamak, a toroidal configuration originally invented by the Russians. This is the toroidal fusion test reactor (TFTR) at the Princeton Plasma Physics Laboratory. It started up on Christmas day of 1982, and it is working very well. It is roughly a $400 million device and uses about $60 million a year to operate it. The second example is shown in Fig. 2. This is the MFTF-B tandem mirror, under construction at the Lawrence Livermore National Laboratory and scheduled for operation in 1987. It will cost about the same to build and operate as the TFTR, but instead of being a toroidal configuration, it is a linear configuration. You get some idea of the size from the standard truck included in Fig. 2. (A standard man would probably not be visible.) Figure 3 is a photograph of one of the MFTF-B magnets, called a yin-yang because of the resemblance to the Chinese character. As you see, it is being rolled on logs to the construction site, as if it were an ancient Egyptian monolith. The magnet weighs approximately 300 tons, and it is the most complex and largest superconducting magnet ever built.

As I have said, it is advantageous to use computers to complement our experiments because the experiments are very expensive. Unfortunately, as you might surmise, the modeling of fusion processes far exceeds the capability of current supercomputers. We can write down realistic and predictive models of important processes. But we cannot run them on current-generation Class VI machines; we will not be able to on Class VII; we will not be able to on Class VIII. So it is a case of doing what we can when we can. Some examples of these processes are the plasma physics of the fuel in three-dimensional magnetic geometry; the atomic and surface physics of the interactions between the plasma and the first wall, and the contamination of the D-T plasma with heavier ions that radiate away energy; the interaction of fusion-produced neutrons with complex three-dimensional structures (like many others, we have encountered problems using Monte Carlo techniques on vector computers); and finally, the thermal hydraulics of heat removal. Computer requirements for each of these problems exceed present capability.

Engineering design of fusion experiments also requires, and in some cases exceeds, the capability of current supercomputers. Examples of large-scale engineering design problems include plasma simulation to optimize design performance; stress analysis of complex three-dimensional structures with transient magnetic and mechanical forces acting on them; neutron shielding analysis; and magnetic coil design to produce complex three-dimensional magnetic fields. Of course, there is a strong interaction among these design problems. A more specialized design

Fig. 1. Toroidal fusion test reactor.

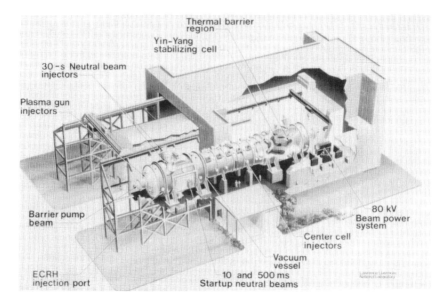

Fig. 2. MFTF-B tandem mirror facility.

problem is beam optics for particle-beam heating. I mentioned the necessity of heating the plasma. One of the ways to do it is to inject very fast, very energetic particles. But to do that right, especially with the small-beam divergence forced by the large stand-off distance, requires rather complex beam optics codes.

I believe we have made a lot of progress in controlling fusion. As I look back, I think it is attributable to two factors. First, starting in the 1970s, we began to develop detailed localized plasma diagnostics to understand what was going on in the experiments. Second, we began to use computers effectively to run numerical experiments and to solve complex equations. Then we began to iterate between the experiments and the computers—predicting experimental results, running the experiment, comparing the results, and improving the model. Now we are to the point that we have confidence that some of our computational models are correct. How do we know they are correct? Because when we turn on an experiment that we have predicted, it works in the same way as the prediction. In other cases, we know that our models are wrong; they may

Fig. 3. MFTF-B magnet.

be wrong by orders of magnitude. The areas where they are most wrong appear to be in the slower transport processors, where we know that turbulence and stochasticity, which we cannot model accurately, are enhancing the transport. Where the models are wrong we substitute empirical formulas, matched to experimental data, and use the disagreement as a spur to improve the quality of the model.

Contributions to Fusion Research from Supercomputer Use

Our present major use of supercomputers is for plasma physics modeling. Because of computer limitations, several simplified models are used, each of which is optimized for studying a particular class of phenomena. At the lowest level, we use fluid plasma models. They are related to the Navier-Stokes equation described in Bill Ballhaus' paper,

"Supercomputing in Aerodynamics." However, they are more complicated because the importance of electromagnetic fields requires the addition of Maxwell's equations (or a variant of them) and the inclusion of terms describing the interaction of fluid and fields. These models can be cast as elliptic, hyperbolic, and parabolic equation sets to study steady-state phenomena, waves and stability, or diffusive processes. Fluid plasma models are computational "work horses" for studying plasma behavior and comparing theory with experiments. Many extra modules can be added to the basic fluid equations—atomic physics, wall recycling, fusion heating, etc.

Unfortunately, many plasma processes cannot be accurately modeled by fluid equations, so to study these we turn to kinetic plasma models. These are derivable ultimately from the single-particle equations of motion and Liouville's theorem. The single particle equations are collapsed to a version of Boltzmann's equation, to which is added Maxwell's equations. This set of equations describes an intrinsically six-dimensional phase space problem, with multiple space scales. Current supercomputers do not have the capability to do six-dimensional problems. At best, they can handle simple three-dimensional problems, thus kinetic equations are useful only when symmetry and collisions reduce the number of important dimensions. Typically, kinetic equations are used to study velocity space instabilities and other nonthermal phenomena.

Obviously, the next step would be particle models, using Newton's law for individual particles, affected by forces resulting from applied and internal electromagnetic fields. Unfortunately, a typical experiment involves 10^{20} particles, and 10^6 particles is an upper bound to which we can handle on Class VI machines. Computer time limitations typically restrict particle models to not more than a few hundred thousand particles. The simplest explicit algorithms iterate between particle advance and field advance: given the fields, the particles are advanced with Newton's law; then the electromagnetic fields are updated using the new particle positions. The disadvantage of this algorithm is that for numerical stability the time step must be characteristic of fast plasma processes, making a simulation of slow processes prohibitively time consuming. Recent progress has been made in overcoming this problem by using implicit or time-averaged algorithms, as well as by analytic processing of the underlying equations.

Hybrid models of plasma behavior are also used, for example, a particle model for the ions and a fluid model for the electrons. Hybrid models allow different levels of description for different particle species, which may be appropriate for some plasma processes.

Although plasma physics accounts for our largest use of supercomputers, there are several other significant applications in fusion research. Transport of neutral particles—neutral atoms, neutrons, and photons—is modeled using Monte Carlo codes or various transport approximations. Atomic physics models are very important; not only does atomic physics enter into the global energy and particle balance, but it also yields spectroscopic diagnostic information obtained from very exact determination of excitation states and the intensity of radiation from those states. For example, we can add heavier ions, such as neon, to the plasma and observe the radiation intensity at different discrete wavelengths to determine the plasma temperature.

Finite element stress and thermal analyses are increasingly important. About 6 months ago, Nastran was installed on one of our Cray-1s, and we have other codes running on Control Data Corporation (CDC) 7600s. We use these not only to design but also to modify experiments. Sometimes we want to run an experiment in a way that it was not designed for, and we want to know whether it is going to be damaged mechanically. Magnetic field models are also important in designing experiments because of the very tight coupling between magnetic field characteristics and plasma behavior. Finally, systems analysis codes combine various submodels to simulate an entire experiment and reactor concept. These codes help to establish costs and overall feasibility.

Now to philosophize for just a minute. One of the problems that has resulted from the advent of good computers is that some of us have reduced the amount of thinking that we do. If you remember the days when all you had was a piece of paper and a pencil, you thought very carefully because that was the only way that you could determine even the qualitative behavior of complex physical systems. I think there is a temptation with computers to cut short that thinking. And to philosophize just a bit more, perhaps we have done ourselves some harm by making numerical computers so available and not making as available computational tools for analysis—algebra, calculus, and other mathematics that paper-and-pencil analysts use. There are computer codes to assist mathematical analysis, but they are still quite crude. The fusion program has made available two such codes to its users, REDUCE and MACSYMA. I think it would be very beneficial to develop improved codes of this sort to improve our analytical capability in step with our number crunching capability.

I would now like to describe some specific contributions of supercomputing to fusion research. The contributions are chosen for their importance and for the fact that, without supercomputers, they would probably not have been possible. My first example is the design of a new experiment, the ATF, now under construction at Oak Ridge National Laboratory. The experiment is a stellarator, which is a toroidal concept similar to a tokamak but with certain advantages. The problem with stellarators had been that they could contain only low-pressure plasma, hence they would not be attractive reactors. However, extensive three-dimensional calculations showed that this limitation could be overcome by a new magnetic field design, and this design was the basis for the ATF.

Even more recently, we have discovered that cross-section shaping in tokamaks may allow us to achieve better magnetic efficiency—that means holding a higher pressure plasma with a given field. An experiment to test this prediction is under construction at Princeton University.

I mentioned earlier the need to heat the plasma. The most successful technique has been neutral beam injection, in which ions are accelerated to high energy, neutralized, fired across the magnetic field, and then reionized by collisions with the resident plasma. To design injectors for TFTR, it is very important to know accurately how much beam power is needed, because the injectors are very expensive. Extensive kinetic and particle model simulations have confirmed that the heating is classical in existing beam heating experiments, that is, well modeled by simple physics. Armed with this knowledge, we have used these same codes to design the injectors for TFTR and have not had to build in a large safety margin of excess power.

My next example is the understanding of disruptive instabilities in tokamaks. These instabilities, which seemed to occur randomly, dumped all the hot plasma against the wall in an extremely short time. The occurrence of hot plasma in a reactor would be intolerable. Fortunately, extensive simulation with three-dimensional magnetohydrodynamics (MHD) models and careful measurements in experiments have revealed the likely cause of the disruption and have shown us how to avoid it.

My last example, also involving MHD models, is the discovery and demonstration of techniques for producing the magnetic fields of compact toroids. These configurations, as suggested by the name, might produce small, inexpensive fusion reactors. Unfortunately, we had no techniques for producing them that could be extrapolated to reactor conditions.

Simulation revealed several possibilities, some of which have already been demonstrated by experiment. By iterating between experiment and simulation, we have been able to optimize the formation process.

In each of these examples, and there are several others that I could have discussed, either we could not have achieved an important goal without supercomputers, or else, we would have had to pay more, take more time, and accept more risk to achieve that goal.

How Supercomputers Are Used in Fusion Research

The uses of supercomputers are closely integrated into the fusion program as a whole. The process is almost like a beneficial cancer that spreads throughout the ongoing activities. Most computing is provided through the Magnetic Fusion Energy (MFE) Computer Network, and all of the significant fusion contractors are nodes of this network. The hub of the network is at the National Magnetic Fusion Energy Computer Center (NMFECC) in Livermore, California. Our supercomputers are all at the NMFECC—a Cray-1S, a Cray-1, and a CDC 7600. Our philosophy is to move ahead as quickly as we can and to turn off older machines, so as not to retain a large stable of less cost-effective machines. There are a lot of users of the computer network, approximately 2000 at over 60 locations. This immediately presents us with a dilemma. How can we provide first-class supercomputing to remote users? Over 90% of the users are remote; the only ones who are not are the ones who are physically at Lawrence Livermore National Laboratory.

To maximize our cost effectiveness for remote computing, we have different levels of access capability at various nodes, depending on their size and needs. At our largest laboratories we have Users' Service Centers (USCs). These are based on the Digital Equipment Corporation (DEC) System-10 computers, with dual 56-kilobit satellite links to the NMFECC. At the next lower level, we provide a mini-USC that is based on a VAX computer, with a leased 9.6-kilobit line running to the nearest satellite node. The next level is a Remote User Service Station (RUSS), which is composed of a PDP-11-based terminal concentrator and a printer/plotter with a 4.8-kilobit line. Finally, we provide dialup access through ARPAnet, Tymnet, and other phone systems. We are also beginning to integrate personal computers into the network as intelligent terminals.

Figure 4 shows a map of the hard-wired nodes. Dialup users are not included. Figure 5 is a schematic of some of the network connections the

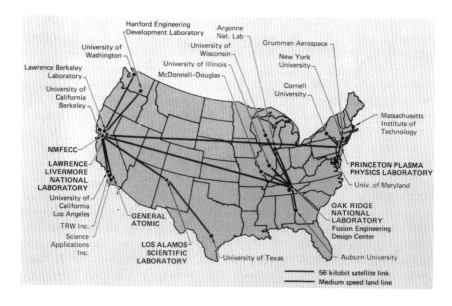

Fig. 4. National MFE Network, 1983.

users do not see. They log directly onto the supercomputers, all of which run in timesharing as well as batch modes. The operating system on the Cray computers is the Cray Timesharing System (CTSS), which was developed at the NMFECC and is now used at several laboratories; the CDC 7600 was the almost identical Livermore Timesharing System (LTSS).

Figure 6 shows the hardware configuration at the NMFECC. Our biggest current problem is file storage—we do not have enough. The storage system is hierarchical; files migrate automatically from a disk farm to a cartridge-based mass storage system to an automated library. Unfortunately, the hardware reliability is not perfect, the speed and capacity are limited, and 2000 users put a large strain on the system. Other speakers at this conference have reported similar problems with file storage.

Each one of the USCs is itself the hub of a local network, which includes data acquisition computers attached to the local experiments. So, in fact, we have networks of networks, with the capability of passing data from the experiments to the supercomputers and back to the

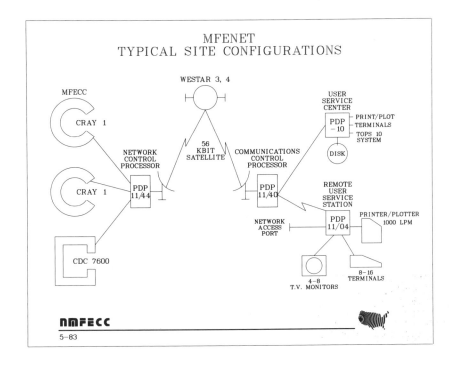

Fig. 5. MFENET typical site configurations.

experiments. The management and coordination of these networks is a big job. The management, like the computing, is distributed, which means it is sort of herd-like. Maybe some of Frank Harlow's models, as described in "Super Problems for Supercomputers," would be useful in determining which computer gets used for which functions by which people. In general, our philosophy is that massive data files stay near the experiment that generated them, and they are abstracted, integrated, and reduced as they move up the chain. So we do not push a whole lot of bits through the national network. Networks cannot take that—at least ours cannot.

Certain management aspects of the network appear to have improved its effectiveness. First, all usage of the MFE Computer Center and of the other nodes in the network is tied directly to Department of Energy (DOE) contracts. This is a single-purpose network. This concentrates decision-making and lets us move more effectively to meet perceived

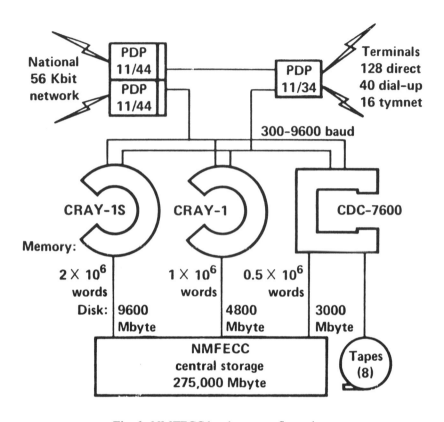

Fig. 6. NMFECC hardware configuration.

needs. Second, our contractors are heavily involved in the overall planning, allocating, and managing of computer resources. The Computer Users' Advisory Committee and the USC managers meet regularly with the DOE and NMFECC managers, and we also form ad hoc subcommittees to deal with specific issues. These activities tend to instill a spirit of community and break down the insularity of individual locations. Third, contractors do not pay for computer time; it is not cost-recovered. Contractors request and receive free computer time from the Office of Fusion Energy (OFE), just as they request and receive free dollars. It is commonly argued that computing should be cost-recovered; typically, this leads to fragmented local computing. We have found it advantageous to aggregate computing dollars because this allows us to acquire the supercomputers that no individual contractor could afford. Supercomputers are a unique resource for advanced scientific research, and our practice of allocating "free" computer time is analogous to that used for allocating time on particle accelerators, telescopes, and other large scientific facilities.

Most of the time is allocated yearly, and come October 1, our contractors will be very interested to know how much computer time they are getting. Each year they submit documentation, not voluminous but certainly adequate, to support their requests. Time allocations are determined by an OFE management committee. Besides regular time allocations, we reserve 5 to 10% for short-term requirements, and one can get a significant amount of time almost overnight if he can convince his program manager that it is urgently needed.

Our computing is not cheap; the computer center budget is $12 000 000. The rest of the network costs on the order of $2 million to $3 million, with some of those costs hidden in other program costs. The computer center has a staff of approximately 78 people, and we do not think we could satisfactorily operate the network with less money. The cost effectiveness of the network is quite good. Our cost per Cray-hour, including communications and file storage, is about $700 per delivered hour.

The supercomputers at the NMFECC are used all of the time. Our philosophy is that an idle computer does no one any good, and we work hard to ensure that idle time is held to a minimum. Figure 7 shows how one of our Cray computers performed over the last year and a half. We expect our machines to be available 24 hours a day, with no shutdown for weekends or holidays. Production, which is the time actually spent executing users' codes, averages over 90%, or 7900 hours per year. These machines are so reliable that we no longer perform scheduled maintenance; total maintenance is, therefore, kept to a few percent. Operations, including operating system overhead, accounting, and some file handling, are another few percent. Software development includes CTSS, the time and batch operating system developed for the Cray-1 by the NMFECC and now used on most DOE Cray computers.

The almost complete absence of idle time results partly from the auction scheme used to establish job priority. The allocated computer hours comprise a user's "bank account." He then bids the rate at which he wishes to use up his bank account in executing each job. (A bid of one debits 1 minute of bank account for each minute of execution. A bid of

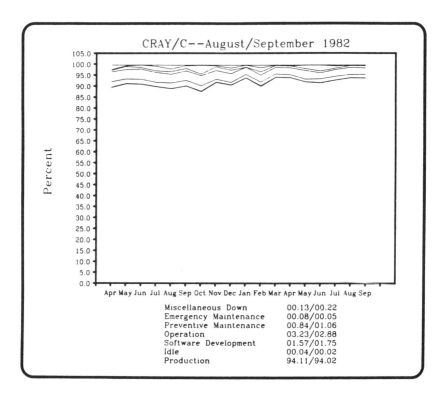

Fig. 7. Utilization percentage of the Cray 1C. The percentage of production time
is the first plot, and subsequent percentages (idle, system development,
etc.) are added to each other for a total of 100%. The values printed at the
bottom of the figure are the current month's percentages.

0.5 debits only 0.5 minutes, and so on.) The job scheduler generally picks
the highest bid job for next execution. Thus, a graduate student who has
maybe 20 Cray hours in a year can parlay that into 100 Cray hours by
working at 2:00 on Sunday morning. He does, and this results in
virtually no idle time.

We think that remote supercomputing has several benefits. First, by
concentrating the supercomputers in one location, we have benefited
from economy of scale. This has allowed us to afford state-of-the-art
supercomputers and to provide reasonably good software and services.
Second, by separating computer location from user location, we can
meet changing needs among our users. If, in the worst case, a contract is

terminated, the computer time associated with that contractor is available to be allocated to other contractors. In general, one makes much gentler changes than that, but changes do occur. Third, even the smallest of our contractors have access to the largest supercomputers if they need them. This has been especially important for university contractors, and it has allowed graduate students to learn supercomputing at the same time as they learn physics or engineering. Those who accept jobs in fusion research after completion of their studies are already adept at using our supercomputers and need no period of training.

Fourth, and something that we did not expect would be as important as it has turned out to be when we set up the network, is interinstitutional collaboration and code sharing. In some cases, people work almost on-line with one another. They may have a phone in one hand and a terminal in the other. They work on the same code, or else they use electronic mail to share messages. Furthermore, if somebody from Princeton comes out to Los Alamos for a summer, he has automatically carried all of his codes with him. We even find that some scientists, who go to a meeting at a particular laboratory, rush to the terminal to monitor their jobs and to keep their work going in the middle of the meeting. It is kind of fun to see, but it sometimes detracts from the meeting. We have encouraged this sense of community by providing electronic mail, computer bulletin boards for special interest groups, and general news service.

There are certainly special problems associated with remote super-computing. First, it is harder to learn the system and to keep up with changes; using a telephone to get help is not the same as walking to the next office. We have tried to minimize learning problems by having virtually all of the system documentation on-line and up to date, and to have the people at the computer center use the same documentation as the people out in the field. It costs money, it costs people, but we think it is important. There are telephone consultants available, and we have tried to maintain the ratio at approximately 1 consultant per 100 or 200 users. I do not hear complaints that the computer center is unresponsive to problems that the users have. We also have periodic training courses. Either users can come to the computer center to learn, or staff from the computer center can go out to user installations to conduct these courses. Some of the courses are also on video tape.

Second, you do not get communications for free, either in terms of cost or reliability. When we switched from landlines to satellites for our backbone links, the reliability went up a lot, and because of the vagaries of our national telecommunications policy, the cost went down a lot. But still we are paying the common carriers over $800 000 per year. When you add the in-house costs at the NMFECC and at the laboratories, communications cost almost $1 million per year. Third, remote graphics is a real problem because of limited network bandwidth. We have tried to be smart; engineers at the NMFECC designed a graphics user service station (GUSS) that uses some compression techniques to provide remote graphics service to users. We started deploying GUSSs about 6 months ago. Users like them; they are relatively cheap, they can use both vector and rastor format, and they overcome some of the problems of limited bandwidth. Fourth, the difficulty of transmitting large files through the network leads to more demand for central file storage. Our file system is saturated, and we do not expect any significant relief until optical disks and vertical magnetic techniques greatly increase storage density.

A Glimpse Into the Future

We need faster supercomputers with larger memories. Many important physics and engineering problems exceed the capability of present computers. Class VI machines (Cray-1 and Cyber 205) can handle simple three-dimensional problems but not complex ones. For example, a computer with 200 times the throughput of the Cray-1 and 500-1000 megawords of memory would allow us to begin studying MHD turbulence, which apears to be very important for plasma confinement. Such a machine appears feasible by 1990.

In the near term, we are budgeted to upgrade to a Class VII computer as soon as one is available, probably in the last quarter of 1984. The next generation of supercomputers will use multiple, parallel processors, and it will be a great challenge to learn how to "paralyze" codes (that is, distribute them among parallel processors). Class VII supercomputers will use four to eight processors; later designs may use hundreds. The move to parallel processors in Class VII machines will be as significant as was the move to vector processors in Class V and Class VI machines. It will probably take us several years to use these machines effectively.

Also, we will work on better graphics systems. I think the Achilles' heel of remote supercomputing, if there is one, is the ability to handle graphics information. We cannot afford multimegabit links to every user. So how does one provide adequate graphics? Yet graphics are very important for supercomputing. You cannot understand multi-dimensional computations in terms of numbers. I think the only way the human mind can comprehend such computations is in terms of lines or shapes. Eventually when you go into the details, you will use those numbers, but in debugging and in getting a sense of what is going on, I think the future is graphical. We have got to solve that, and we are working on that, but it is going to continue to be a problem.

We will be increasing the bandwidth of the network as traffic increases. Our present satellite links can go up to at least 256 kilobits per second, but the cost goes up as well. The major drive is for graphics requirements, but the addition of more users also pushes us to higher bandwidth. One inexorable problem with satellites is the roughly 0.5-second transmission delay. This is analogous to the start-up delay on a vector processor, and it limits the effective bandwidth for interactive graphics.

We are also installing a fusion, program-wide, distributed CAD-CAM system. It will be based on a local processor at the design station backed up by the supercomputers for engineering analysis. Compatibility and network access will allow exchange of design files, as well as multi-laboratory collaboration on designs of experiments. We have already seen the power of supercomputers for engineering analysis. Our networked CAD-CAM system should increase this.

We also hope to obtain and use better analysis codes, such as follow-ons to MACSYMA and REDUCE with expert systems to improve user friendliness. It is an open question whether these are suitable for use on supercompters because of their high ratio of memory fetches to calculations. As a possible alternative, we shall be monitoring closely the development of processors for artificial intelligence.

Generally, we anticipate being able to use the favorable cost-performance curve of future supercomputers to substitute computing for increasingly expensive experiments where possible, and to optimize by computer design the experiments we do build. Development of economical controlled fusion energy will take at least another 20 years, and we expect to be heavy supercomputer users during this period.

20

Numerical Analysis for VLSI Simulation: Pointers and Reflections

D. J. Rose
Computing Science Research Center
AT&T Bell Laboratories
Murray Hill, New Jersey

Introduction

The near horizon of very large scale integration (VLSI) will provide microelectronic systems that will expand the computing revolution into the next century. In this paper I attempt to show that modern numerical analysis, in an appropriate computing environment, will continue to have a significant role in this high-tech drama.

In a digital circuit, the role of a semiconductor device is to act as a switch and hence to realize the intended binary logic of the circuit. The intrinsic physical behavior of such a device, however, is described by a coupled system of nonlinear partial differential equations (PDEs). VLSI device technology will attempt to provide almost ideal, very fast switches. The equations describing such switches will become increasingly difficult to solve and will test the limits of our algorithmic abilities and computing resources.

PDEs also model other aspects of VLSI technology. They describe the growth of pure silicon crystals as well as the insulating oxide that can be grown on the silicon wafer. PDEs model the impurity processing of the substrate, a diffusion process, and annealing processes needed after ion bombardment.

The electrical behavior of an integrated circuit is captured by solving a large system of sparse, nonlinear, algebraic-differential equations. In the VLSI era, the traditional equivalent circuit view of a transistor device will be augmented by numerical approximation techniques to model this circuit element using the PDE device simulations described above.

Researchers are also pursuing the notion of macromodeling to approximate the characteristics of larger circuit blocks, say logic gates or memory pieces.

The discretized PDE and circuit analysis problems ultimately lead to large systems of simultaneous algebraic equations, both nonlinear and linear. These sets of equations are solved on supercomputers of yesteryear (like our Cray-1) in order to design the supercomputers (or supercomputing elements, like large memories) of tomorrow.

Reference 1 is a current collection of papers on numerical VLSI simulation. Much of our work at Bell Laboratories is presented in it, along with work by other industry and university colleagues. Sze's two books[2,3] provide a healthy dose of the technology of VLSI devices and processes. Finally, the September 1977 issue of *Scientific American*[4] is a readable, although dated, presentation of integrated circuits.

Reflections and Opinions

Collaboration is Essential

I will summarize aspects of a collaborative effort by an informal Bell Laboratories team consisting of myself, Randy Bank, Bill Coughran, Wolfgang Fichtner, Eric Grosse, Larry Nagel, Reddy Penumalli, Wes Petersen, and Kent Smith. My relationship with Wolfgang goes back almost 5 years; Randy and I have worked together, on various endeavors, for a decade. Wolfgang, Reddy, and Kent are semiconductor device engineers while Randy, Bill, Eric, and I are numerical analysts. Wes contributes to both areas, partially in his role as Cray guru and vectorizer. Larry is an electrical engineer responsible for our circuit analysis capabilities; his 1975 Ph.D. thesis produced SPICE.

Collaboration is not easy. Collaborators are people with attendant foibles. Interdisciplinary projects require a common language for scientific discourse including mathematical notations, engineering terms and physical concepts, and (to some extent) programming compatibility. More important, successful collaboration requires the awareness and resolution of the inner-loop problem.

Numerical analysts devise clever algorithms and produce mathematical software for specific computational tasks, for example, to solve nonlinear equations or to integrate systems of ordinary differential equations. They begin to view device simulation or circuit analysis as the solution to a mathematical description of the problem written symbolically as an equation. They suggest a collection of algorithms, sometimes including software, which when glued together solves the equation. It is this intense concentration on the specific algorithmic detail that produces a computationally efficient solution methodology. Hence, analysts may tend to view the simulation tool, say a circuit analysis package, as the collection of its inner loops that they have produced. This is a conceptual error.

On the other hand, an engineering group tends to view VLSI simulation in a systems sense, that is, as a coherent collection of tools that can be applied routinely by a user group of circuit designers. The process simulator, device simulator, and circuit analyzer must be able to communicate between themselves and other tools. The user group must be shielded from the details (for example, parameter selection) of the simulators, and their needs (expressed in constant phone calls) must be addressed. In the engineering view, the simulator predicts the behavior of a real device or circuit as opposed to solving a mathematical equation that describes it. Hence, there is a tendency to view the group's efforts as simulation of production VLSI and a tendency to overlook or forget the importance of optimization in the inner-loop calculations. This, too, is a conceptual error.

Despite the difficulties, large-scale problems run on supercomputers, like VLSI simulation, will require collaboration to solve them effectively. Such problems are simply too complex to solve without careful attention to the science, engineering, and computational requirements inherent in their formulation. At Bell Laboratories, VLSI simulation plays an important role in advanced chip design, for example, the 256K dynamic memory chip now in production at Western Electric.

Access to a Supercomputer Can be Difficult

Owning a supercomputer can be a powerful asset (as well as a status symbol)—provided that it can be used effectively. By access I mean both physical access and programming access. Physical access is high-quality data communication from your local computing environment to your supercomputer, with communication rates that are compatible with the processing power of the supercomputer. If the local computer is the supercomputer with, say UNIX* time sharing, the data communication

---

*UNIX is a trademark of Bell Laboratories.

problem is simpler, although there may then be inefficiencies that degrade performance (caused by sending verbose electronic mail, using fancy screen editors, running word processing programs, and so on). At Bell Laboratories, my numerical colleagues and I are part of the Computing Science Research Center, as well as part of the Cray user community. Our local computer is a VAX* 11/750, and many of these 750s are networked together as a central computing resource. The numerical group here had to deal with the Cray access problem at a level of detail that surprised me.

Programming access to a supercomputer is a more subtle problem. I think of it as the party-giver's nightmare in which the host plans and prepares an elegant celebration for many but only a few attend. At this conference there was considerable discussion of achieving gigaflop speeds through the use of massive parallelism and vectorization. There seemed to be less discussion about who would, or even how to, write the corresponding superoptimizing compiler. With current compilers, it is difficult to vectorize many useful numerical techniques and general software packages, for example, sparse LU factorization and David Gay's nonlinear least-squares package. While Bill Buzbee's group at the Los Alamos National Laboratory and Linda Kaufman at Bell Laboratories have shown that certain numerical algorithms can be nicely tuned for the Cray (sometimes at considerable human expense), it is clear that we cannot simply redo numerical analysis overnight. It is also unclear when an inferior vectorized algorithm will run faster than an optimal serial algorithm. Again there is a need for considerable collaboration between architects and algorithmists to insure that the party will be well attended.

Numerical Analysis Works

There has been explosive activity and progress in numerical analysis over the past quarter century—as in other areas of computing. We have sophisticated equation solvers and mature, portable mathematical software packages. As a group our interests range into mathematics, the physical sciences, engineering, and neighboring areas of computer science. We have a tradition and a sense of history. The supercomputer era is a consequence of the need to address large-scale problems that stretch the imagination. We will continue to refine and extend our algorithms,

---

*VAX is a trademark of the Digital Equipment Corporation.

we will synthesize and apply them to help solve these problems, and in so doing, we will retain an influential position in the future of computer science and applied mathematics.

The role of supercomputers is to supercompute—to solve the most compelling technical problems of an advanced society.

References

1. *IEEE Transactions on Electron Devices* **30**, no. 9 (September 1983). See also the SIAM *Journal of Statistical Computing* **4** (September 1983).

2. Sze, S. M. *Physics of Semiconductor Devices*. New York: Wiley-Interscience, 1981.

3. Sze, S. M. *VLSI Technology*. New York:McGraw-Hill, 1983.

4. "Microelectronics." *Scientific American* (September 1977).

21

Mathematical Problems in Robotics

J. T. Schwartz
Courant Institute of Mathematical Sciences
New York University
New York, New York

In the context of a conference on supercomputers, I must confess that this talk has the flavor of a cultural interlude. The topic, robotics, is not only interesting, but also has significant relationships to the supercomputer developments that are the main subject of this conference. My principal aim is to comment on the overall goals of robotics. I will describe just three of the very many research areas with which workers in this very active field are presently concerned; unsurprisingly, these are all things we have been involved with at the Courant robotics laboratory. I will also comment on the nature of the training that research in robotics seems to call for.

The general aim of robotics is to create a small and relatively regular body of computer algorithms that capture basic, elementary knowledge concerning the manipulation of bodies in three-space, which all of us possess as a matter of instinct. This knowledge is reflected in all those simple manipulative activities that we carry out daily. However, recreation of these straightforward, everyday capabilities involves a surprisingly challenging mix of geometric and physical issues. For example, a moment's reflection shows that, for a robot to move objects in an industrial setting and to carry out any sustained intelligent sequence of actions, it will have to maintain an internal geometric model of its environment; it must keep track of which objects have been moved. It is clear that people do this; if they did not, their handling of objects would be very much more confused than it is. But to create a capability, which simply embodies one very basic kind of geometric intelligence, the whole art of geometric modeling will have to be advanced substantially and many new high-speed geometric algorithms will have to be created. For this reason, such an environment-modeling and real-time, object-tracking system has not yet been put in place as a regular part of robotic technology, though admittedly it doesn't lie far beyond our present capabilities.

Beyond these purely geometric capabilities, robots will require other more physical forms of programmed knowledge to deal with bodies moving in contact with each other and with robot parts. They will need to understand and react to the forces that arise when bodies move in contact, will need to manage force feedback to grasp, squeeze, hold, and feel, and will need to coordinate the activity of several arms, partly through force feedback. To illustrate the importance of force in everyday object manipulation as distinct from purely positional feedback, note that I can hand you a ball or a wrench, and you can successfully grasp it simply by adapting to the forces that you sense me to be applying to it. This allows the object to pass from my hand to your hand without us sharing a common brain. Robots need to achieve these same modest but significant and challenging levels of sophistication. Generally, we need to master sensor-assisted manipulation, so that robots can look at what they are doing and use visual information to guide the manipulation that they are attempting to carry out. Beyond this, sensors other than the most obvious visual, tactile, and proximity devices need to be integrated into the robot manipulation software. My own recent research encourages me to believe that these problems do not lie so far beyond the current state of the art to preclude very real progress over the next few years. Such progress will result in a new generation of robots considerably more sophisticated than the very primitive devices we now have.

After this cautiously optimistic prognostication, let me say a bit about the present situation. Robot technology is now very modest in the robotic equipment you can go out and buy and in the laboratory products that work reliably. We now basically have single-armed, six-degree-of-freedom robots that are able to position a gripping hand (typically equipped with very simple, pliers-like, two-finger grippers) in any position and orientation in three-dimensional space. These state-of-the-art manipulators have good precision, reasonable strength, moderate speed, and simple positional control. Control of this type allows manipulators to be moved accurately to a specified position and orientation; however, when they touch a body, unsolved control problems arise. For example, in all but the most advanced present experimental systems, it is not possible to command a robot arm to run its finger across a table top until it feels a hole. All that one can order the robot to do is to move through empty space until it feels something, and then to terminate its motion and branch to some specified statement in the program that it is following.

The sensory capabilities of present robots are few and limited. Standard libraries of peripheral tools are lacking. If you need a gripper of some slightly nonstandard kind, you must go to your machine shop and have it built. Robot locomotion is a subject of active research, but outside of a few laboratories, mobile robots are not available. Basically, today's mobile robots are simple robot carts that run on tracks in the floor to deliver packages.

A few additional comments on robot sensing will help to characterize the present situation. Technology for image acquisition has become well established for the crude decomposition of images into regions, for the fairly satisfactory calculation of global region parameters, and for detection and edge following. These latter techniques have taken on a certain sophistication. However, in spite of 15 years of work, we still have no reliable procedures for analyzing images into meaningful gestalts, and our ability to convert scenes into symbolic descriptions is still extremely primitive. We can break an image up into blobs, but we really can't tell very reliably what these blobs are.

Present tactile sensors generally consist of nothing more than a few strain gauges; however, a great deal of activity on finer, more skin-like tactile sensors is in progress. Proximity sensors are also under very active investigation.

Robot control languages used at present generally range from extremely primitive to primitive, though the most advanced languages of this type can be rated as modestly sophisticated. Internal world models of the kind described above are not maintained by any commercially available robot control language, so that once a robot puts an object down, it doesn't know where the object is anymore. To a robot with such a limited degree of spatial intelligence, the external world is really just a source of sensory interrupts.

Accuracies and repeatability of motion range down to a thousandth of an inch; payloads go up to 500 pounds in the biggest, strongest robots; speeds go up to 60 inches per second. In particular, robot speeds lie considerably below the speeds of special-purpose industrial automated equipment, but are still high enough to be economical in favorable applications. However, to compete better with special-purpose automated devices, considerably higher speeds would be desirable.

This short review should serve to convince you that robotics is a technology very much in its infancy. The same impression can be gained even more immediately by looking at a typical robot arm (Fig. 1), or at a typical hand (see Fig. 2). Figure 3 is a sketch of the hand on the International Business Machines (IBM) RS-1 arm, one of the most

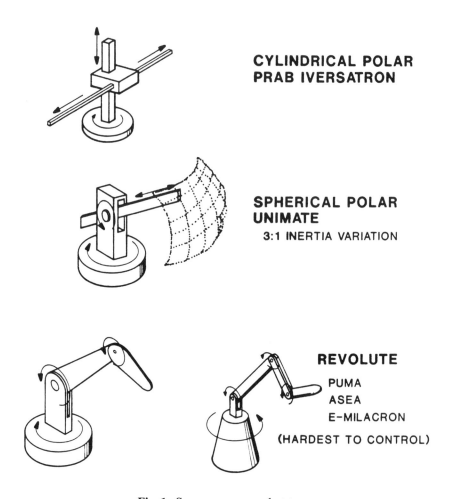

**CYLINDRICAL POLAR
PRAB IVERSATRON**

**SPHERICAL POLAR
UNIMATE**
3:1 INERTIA VARIATION

REVOLUTE
PUMA
ASEA
E-MILACRON
(HARDEST TO CONTROL)

Fig. 1. Some common robot types.

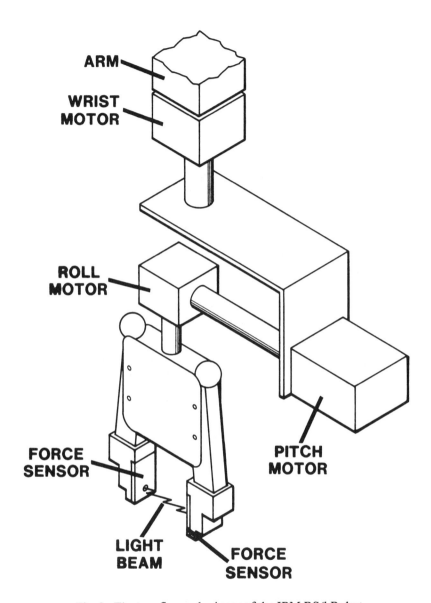

Fig. 2. The two-fingered gripper of the IBM RS/1 Robot.

- Paths planned in moving frames
- Force-controlled motions
  — Improved tactile sensors
  — Force-controlled adaptive grasping
  — The multifingered hand as gripper and limiter
- Control of multiple manipulators
- Proximity sensors
  — Assured collision avoidance after intrusion
- Improved vision systems
  — Additional uses of structured light
- Debugging systems
  — Collision detection algorithms
  — Path planning for recovery to safe positions
  — Collision avoidance protocols

Fig. 3. A list of desirable robot capabilities.

sophisticated grippers now commercially available. As seen in the figure, the hand consists of a simple plier-like pair of fingers, whose tips are equipped with strain gauges that allow pressures to be sensed rather crudely. A light beam passes between the fingers so that the robot can sense when an object passes between its fingers. This unsophisticated hand represents the leading edge of present commercial robots.

If one contemplates current robotic technology and reflects on what is missing, a very long list of desirable capabilities emerges, which includes things that go a little bit beyond the state of the art to things that lie far beyond our current abilities. Figure 3 is an excerpt from this extensive laundry list. Let me comment on a few of the items that appear. A capability that poses no special technical problems but that goes modestly beyond the present commercial state of the art is the ability to transpose motions automatically into moving coordinate frames, so that, one can handle objects to enter the robot's workspace on a conveyor belt. One wants the robot to adjust its manipulations automatically to the motions of the conveyor belt, and one wants this capability to be built into the programming language used to control the robot. This capability already is available in a few languages; however, it is not standard, though it ought to be. In general, one wants a much richer repertoire of primitive motion control commands. A typical class of useful primitives that goes beyond the present state of the art is the family of force-controlled motions: for example, primitive "grip and squeeze" command that instruct the robot to grip until it feels something and then squeeze until it reaches a certain gripping force. A moment's reflection on human manipulative actions shows the potential importance of the class of manipulative actions that this hypothetical instruction exemplifies. For example, curling one's fingers around the handle of a suitcase and lifting it up is a typical force-controlled adaptive grasping action. Attempts to create commands of this type raise many interesting problems in control, e.g., mastering the ability to grasp a tennis ball or an egg with four fingers and then twirl it in the way that people do for amusement with their own hands would represent a substantial advance in the robotic art. I will return to this issue later in my remarks.

Improved sensors must rank high on the roboticist's list of desiderata. Robots need much improved visual sensors, among which three-dimensional vision sensors appear to be particularly appealing. Such sensors would allow a robot to look at an object and to read out not merely the illumination of each point on the visible part of its surface, but also the true geometric distance to each surface point, and perhaps also the normal orientation of each point on the surface. This additional information may assist greatly in determining what the surface is.

Improvement of geometric modeling systems is another important area. This is crucial to our ability to manage the very interesting problem of debugging large, complex robot systems. To see the importance of this issue, one has only to imagine the dilemma of a responsible administrator standing at the start button of a newly constructed, large assembly line involving dozens or hundreds of robots driven by hundreds or thousands of program fragments that have been assembled separately and carefully tested by a staff of programmers. The administrator knows that as soon as he starts these arms moving, they may self-destruct in a very short time. The administrator clearly requires some better way of testing his control software! Plainly, robotics research does not lack for stimulating research challenges.

I now want to talk about a few assorted topics from our own recent research that convey a bit of the technical flavor of robotics. Let me preface this review by emphasizing that I believe robotics to have very broad significance for computer science. It will be the role of robotics to lead computer science in much more mathematical directions than have been typical until now. Current computer science does have important mathematical aspects, but aside from numerical analysis, these have been largely finite and combinatorial in flavor. Robotics will strengthen the connections of computer science with continuous mathematics, a point that will be apparent in some of the things that I want to say about specific points of research.

The first specific research area that I want to talk about—one that I am fond of because it was the area in which my own work started—is the so-called "piano movers' problem." This is the problem of planning the motion of a rigid body, or even of a body with internal degrees of freedom, in the presence of obstacles that it must avoid. This is the problem one actually faces when one knows the geometry of a couch and has to carry the couch through a narrow corridor. Almost everybody has faced this problem in daily life and many have noticed that, when one gets into tight spots, a rather intricate pattern of combinatorial motions sometimes becomes necessary to achieve a given global motion. That common observation reveals the presence of some mathematical phenomenon.

For a sharp formulation of the motion-planning, suppose one has a robot system of some known geometry and that the geometry of the obstacles among which the robot is to move, from point A to point B, is also known. Does there exist a continuous path that will take it from A to B (see Fig. 4) without touching the obstacles? Here we have a mathematical question: either a path does or does not exist. We and other universities, notably the Massachusetts Institute of Technology (MIT), have groups totaling roughly a dozen people working on this problem in its many different variants. This is really a practical problem in algebraic topology. We can define the space of free positions, that is, those positions in which the robot is not touching any obstacle, which is an algebraic manifold with boundary. What we need do is to decompose this manifold into its connected components. However, because this decomposition must be realized by a computer calculation, the problem as originally given must first be reduced to a discrete combinatorial form to allow precise calculation on a computer.

Initially the complexity properties of this problem, that is, the time and space required to solve it, may give one pause. As initially put, it is not clear a priori that the problem is recursively solvable. Indeed, many rather similar looking computational problems are known to be recursively unsolvable. Nevertheless, recent work has shown this motion planning problem to be solvable. Of course, solvability alone is not

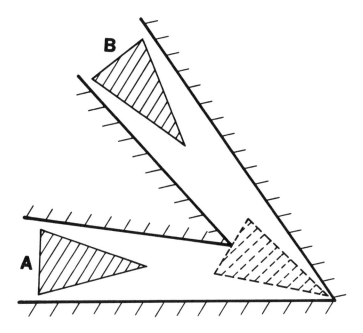

1. Given A, B ε F, find a continuous path in F from Z_1 to Z_2 (if one exists).

2. Given A, B ε F, do the paths lie in the same connected component of F?

Fig. 4. The "piano movers' problem" or how to move an oversized object through corridors.

sufficient; we want efficient solutions. For example, if you are selling an arm and want to supply automatic motion routines that will simplify the problem faced by the user of your equipment, you require efficient algorithms rather than just algorithms. At our laboratory, we have studied numerous cases of this problem and have developed methods ranging from simple but relatively efficient schemes, to more complex but efficient techniques for handling it. I would like to give you some idea of the methods used.

The simplest case that is at all challenging is the case of a rigid rod moving in two dimensions in an environment of polyhedral obstacles. Without trying to give the complete analysis of this problem, I shall just try to indicate its flavor. In Fig. 5, the two ends of the rod are marked P and Q, respectively, and we fix the point P at a given position X in the plane. With P held fixed at any such X, there will be certain angular orientations that the rod can take without colliding with the walls. In effect, by fixing P we project the three-dimensional space of positions and orientations of the rod onto the first two coordinates of the rod position, which have the crucial advantage of being purely nonlinear. That leads to a motion-planning solution that is summarized in the next few figures. Specifically, if you think of the angles accessible to the rod after P is fixed at the point X, then the set of positions the rod can assume without touching the walls always breaks up into a finite number of angular sectors (Fig. 6). This observation gives the correct hint that what one wants to do is consider the critical positions at which the pattern of these sectors changes qualitatively. At a position like that shown in

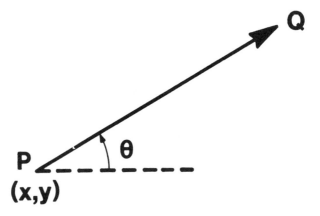

The case of a line segment ("rod") moving in two-dimensional space amidst polygonal obstacles:

Three degrees of freedom (x, y, θ)

- Project F onto AcV by $\pi(x, y, \theta) = (x, y)$
- Hold P fixed, let B rotate about P.
- "Fiber" $\pi^{-1}(X) \equiv P(X) \equiv [\theta: (x, y, \theta) \, \varepsilon \, F]$

Fig. 5. The space of free positions for the "piano movers' problem."

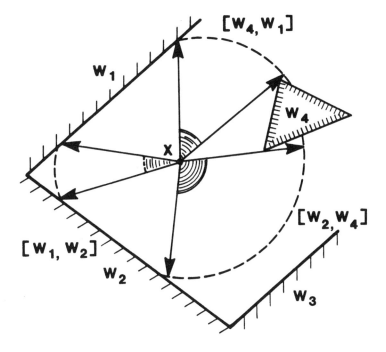

- P (X) has three components (arcs) with labels $[W_2, W_4]$, $[W_4, W_1]$, $[W_1, W_2]$.
- The same will continue to hold in a small neighborhood of X (X is noncritical).
- X is critical if the combinatorial structure of P(X) changes discontinuously at X.

Fig. 6. Basic mathematics of motion planning by the "projection method."

Fig. 7, the pattern doesn't change qualitatively; that is, if we move it a little bit, we will still have three disjoint sectors accessible to the rod. However, at certain more critical positions of P, qualitative changes will occur at positions just the right distance from a corner. For example, the ladder will suddenly swing free of the corner. One way of analyzing this kind of problem is to look systematically for such positions. Part of our work exploits this projection and critical curve approach.

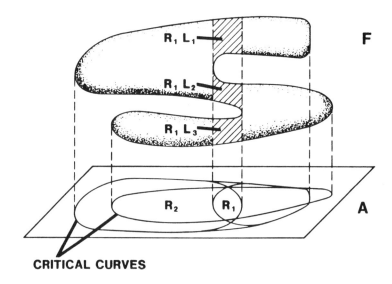

CRITICAL CURVES

Topological interpretation:

- Projection onto a lowered-dimensional space A.
- Partition A into noncritical regions by critical submanifolds (critical where the structure of the fiber P(X) changes discontinuously).
- Obtain cells of F of the form (R,L) and compute adjacency of cells by crossing rules through critical submanifolds.

Fig. 7. An abstract view of the "projection method."

Another different approach is suggested if we think of a disk moving in two-dimensional space amidst polygonal obstacles. For this very simple case, it is easy to conjecture that the best way to move a round object is always along a path of maximum clearance from the walls. Such paths can be defined as paths in the space of accessible positions that lie at equal distance from at least two walls. These constitute the so-called Voronoi diagram (named after the 19th-century Russian geometer Gregory Voronoi) of the walls. In Fig. 8 we see a case where the walls are indicated by cross hatching and we simply plot out all the points that are equal distance between two walls, or between a wall and a corner. This is plainly a set of straight line segments and parabolic segments. The

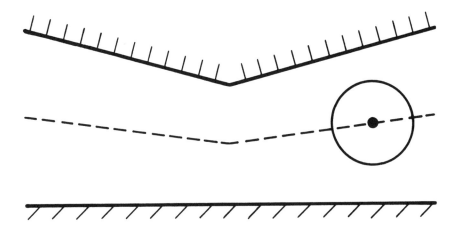

- For a disc moving in two-dimensional space through polygonal obstacles.
- It is safest to move a disc so that its center will never become close to only one obstacle.
- Move the center only on the Voronoi diagram of the set of obstacles.
- Voronoi diagram V or (S) for a set of planar objects S : set of points X simultaneously nearest to two objects in S.

Fig. 8. Motion planning by the Voronoi method.

question of how rapidly this diagram can be calculated is an interesting problem in computational geometry. This is all I have time to say about the motion planning problem, which typifies a large group of purely geometric problems that arise in robotics. Concerning the subject of computational geometry, I will say nothing except that it is a lot of fun and is developing very rapidly. Several hundred geometric algorithms of remarkable efficiency have been discovered over the last 5 years.

The even more important problem of manipulation is particularly interesting in that it crosses over into a problem domain where not only geometry but a much headier mixture of geometry and force is involved. Problems of this kind inevitably arise when a robot must actually touch other objects. To gain an understanding of this area, we can consider the very interesting problem of using the fingers of one or more dexterous hands to grip and manipulate an object whose shape is not exactly known. This includes the problem of using several robot fingers to grip and turn an egg, a screwdriver handle, or some other kind of tool. Many such manipulations are part of the ordinary repertoire of motions. For example, I can request you to grasp a handle that is geared some way that you don't know and to push the handle around and around in whatever manner the gearing allows. I don't have to give you a completely accurate spline curve representation of the orbit that the handle will follow; you can easily use sensed forces to adapt to whatever the motion turns out to be. At the present time no robot can do this very well.

The key issue here is to master the mixture of geometry and force involved in adapting to bodies of imprecisely known shape. An important subproblem is how to classify exceptions and to react to them appropriately, which raises interesting problems of software design. For example, suppose I direct a robot to move at a certain rate along a tabletop, maintaining a certain downward pressure. If it is to behave sensibly when it comes to an edge, the robot can no longer maintain the specified downward pressure, and the robot control software will have to include appropriate software interrupts and use them to invoke appropriate exception handling statements within some larger software context. This makes it clear that increasing sophistication of robot manipulative capabilities will require new language and software structures, which will have to include features to help the robot user handle the widely varying empirical situtations that he will face.

Manipulation raises many very challenging control theory questions. For example, suppose that I attempt to control a four-fingered robot hand. With such a hand, and assuming that each fingertip can move anywhere in three-dimensional space, each finger must have at least three degrees of freedom. This implies a total of at least 12 degrees of freedom. The present control theory of 12-dimensional systems is not very satisfactory; control theorists have been happiest in dealing with systems of one degree of freedom. Robotics will place more strenuous requirements on control theory and I expect that this will encourage interesting, new developments. Figure 9 shows just a little bit of what is involved. The two-dimensional manipulator apparatus shown in Fig. 9 has two fingers, each of which can move in two dimensions to grip a two-dimensional object of unknown shape. Even this highly simplified hand involves four degrees of freedom; to drive it, I have to control four independent motors. Because the shape of the object is not known a priori, purely positional control cannot be used. To emphasize this point, suppose that the object is fragile, for example, an eggshell, and that I attempt purely positional control. But if the control is a little inaccurate

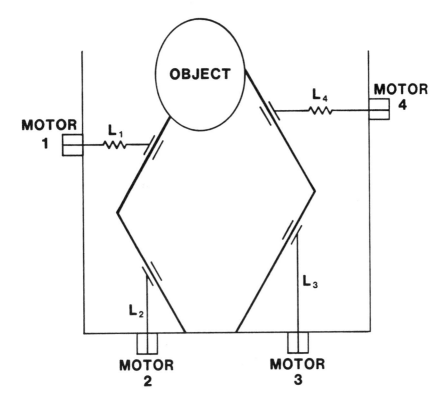

- L_1, L_2, L_3, and L_4 are controllable lengths.
- Motors are regarded as sources of position.

Fig. 9. A simple two-finger planar manipulator.

in one direction, the hand will drop the object, while if it is a little inaccurate in the other way, it will crack the eggshell. Thus, as shown by springs represented by wavy lines in the figure, all possibility of success depends on incorporating some degree of compliance in the robot system. Another useful observation is that, because the object being manipulated is a rigid object moving in two dimensions, it has three degrees of freedom, whereas the two fingers shown have four degrees of freedom. This specifies how we want the object to move. The computer controlling our simplified manipulator must then calculate how it is to control its four motors in terms of sensed force and position readings. What are the mathematics involved, and in particular, what is the role played by the fourth degree of freedom available to the pages but not to the body?

These problems clearly become yet more substantial if one tries to manage four fingers in three-dimensional space to move an object with six degrees of freedom. Here one needs to control 12 motors and a complicated mixture of force and position is involved. These are interesting issues, but having only minutes, I will say no more about them.

The final research problem that I wish to review reflects another aspect of our desire to incorporate some rudimentary intelligence concerning real world objects into our robot control algorithms. Robots need to know something about the frictional phenomena that are crucial to some real life situations. For example, when you try to push a drawer into a tightly fitting chest of drawers, it will sometimes wedge and refuse to go in. What does a person or a robot do then? What accounts for this kind of wedging? What is the general theory of these frictional effects? The peg and hole problem, shown in Fig. 10, represents the simplest case in which these wedging and jamming effects can be explored. Because it is a rigid body that appears in the figure, only a force and a torque can be applied to it. Given this force and torque, how will the frictional forces that result cause the body to move? Although this seems about as trivial a problem as one can propose to a roomful of physicists used to working with Tokamaks, it requires a surprisingly complex analysis. Surprisingly, existing literature includes very little discussion of friction except for one-dimensional situations, and things that I would have guessed had been done by Euler, were in fact worked out in Matt Mason's 1982 MIT doctoral dissertations. It is interesting to note that physics seemed to have abandoned friction as a subject of study roughly at the time of Newton. Analysis of frictional problems is just now being revived.

A study of the peg-in-the-hole problem shown in Fig. 10 begins with the observation that a large number of qualitatively different motions are possible. For example, the object can simply wedge and refuse to move at all; it can slide on the two points of contact it makes with the wall, thus moving into the hole; it can pull free of both walls and start moving in empty space. Moreover, it can be held frictionally at one corner and can roll around that corner, pulling free of the other wall. A complete catalog of these alternatives would list eight possible motions. After writing out this catalog, one needs to understand the region in force-torque space in which each of these motions would result. I have

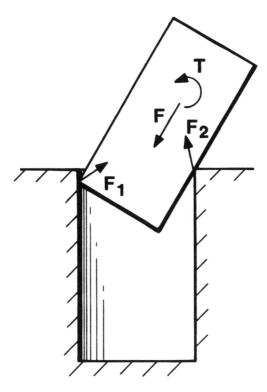

- What reaction to given (F,T)?
- Three-dimensional case?
- Wedging and jamming.
- Little understanding of friction except in one-dimensional situations.
- Newtonian mechanics; nondeterministic in presence of friction.

Fig. 10. The "pen-in-the-hole" problem.

rarely had the experience of starting to work with what appeared to be so simple a problem and finding so many unexpected complications in it. Even the analysis of the two-dimensional case is nontrivial, and analysis of the three-dimensional case, in which we push a cylindrical peg into a cylindrical hole, looks quite challenging. In this three-dimensional cylindrical case, the relevant space of forces and torques is five-dimensional, and one must therefore decompose a five-dimensional space into the many critical regions corresponding to a complete set of peg motions.

As a final unexpected complication in this harmless-looking problem, it must be noted that Newtonian mechanics is simply not deterministic in the presence of friction. When a given force and torque are applied to a body in frictional contact with a wall, any one of several motions can result. Close analysis shows that this is an ill-posed, hence nondeterministic, problem. This fact is concealed by almost all texts on mechanics, even though it is clear that the authors know it, because inspection of problems given at the end of each chapter shows that the problems are carefully formulated to avoid the ambiguous cases—an amusing conspiracy of textbook authors!

Training roboticists will pose interesting problems for computer science departments. Specialists in this area will have to know much of classical mathematics and science, some of which they went into computer science to avoid. In lecturing on robotics to our own graduate students, I can sometimes see them silently thinking, "I went into computer science to avoid Lagrange's equations, and here they are again!" It is plain that its classical mathematics content will result in robotics having a major curricular impact on computer science. Universities will have a central research and educational role to play, in part because industry is short in the theoretical and conceptual skills that it needs to operate in this field. Mathematics, computer science, and engineering departments will have to cooperate to accomplish the necessary work.

Let me make just one concluding comment on artificial intelligence (AI), of which the field of robotics is often regarded as a branch. It was interesting to me in starting to go to robotics conferences about 2 years ago to see that robotics researchers generally don't regard themselves as AI researchers. I think this is because AI is simultaneously an inspiration and a source of peril to the robotics researcher. Its role as a source of inspiration is obvious; the peril comes from the fact that the general but loose, "weak methods" that characterize almost all AI research are rarely the most appropriate for robotic application. As our very brief discussion of the motion planning problem illustrates, a good algorithm tailored to the problem at hand can be hundreds of times more efficient than any generalized tree-searching paradigm, attaining hundreds of orders of magnitude greater efficiency. The roboticist wants to begin by finding all the optimized geometric and dynamic primitives that he can; this defines the agenda for the next few years or decades of robotics research. As this search succeeds, we may start building weak-method AI superstructures on the resulting base of powerful algorithmic primitives.

22

Programming Language Support for Supercomputers*

R. T. Hood and K. Kennedy
Rice University
Houston, Texas

Introduction

From the very first automatic compiler project, efficiency of the executed code has been an extremely important consideration. In his reflections on the project at the History of Programming Languages Conference in June 1978, John Backus reflected on the motivation for much of the FORTRAN I compiler design:

> It was our belief that if FORTRAN, during its first months, were to translate any reasonable "scientific" source program into an object program only half as fast as its hand-coded counterpart, then acceptance of our system would be in serious danger . . . To this day I believe that our emphasis on object program efficiency rather than on language design was basically correct. I believe that had we failed to produce efficient programs, the widespread use of languages like FORTRAN would have been seriously delayed. In fact, I believe that we are in a similar, but unrecognized, situation today: in spite of all the fuss that has been made over myriad language details, current conventional languages are still very weak programming aids, and far more powerful languages would be in use today if anyone had found a way to make them run with adequate efficiency.[1]

In this passage, Backus clearly reflects the concern that it may not be possible to compile a high-level language into code that is comparable in

*Support for this work was provided by the National Science Foundation, grants MCS-8104006 and MCS-8121884, and by the IBM Corporation.

efficiency to code that can be produced by a competent assembly language programmer.

Since we cannot expect that modern scientific applications will be programmed in assembly language, the concern of the machine designer is that all the advantages of a clever machine architecture may be voided by a poor compiler that is unable to take advantage of them. From a different viewpoint, the potential performance upper bound of a machine means nothing if that upper bound cannot be achieved or even approached in code generated from the standard language compilers. This is a sobering thought to most machine architects, which probably explains why so few of them seem to think about the problems of compiling to their architectures.

The fact of the matter is that optimizing compilers are hard to write and hard to adapt to radical new machine organizations. In the words of Neil Lincoln:

> There was, in 1964, no great body of theoretical work to guide compiler developers in dealing with the multiplicity of CDC 6600 functional units and its many asymmetrical registers. After nearly *ten years*, a truly optimum match between language features, compiler, object code reliability, and machine organization was finally achieved. To expect less of an effort for similar results with new supercomputer schemes is fatuous.[2]

Extending this observation to tomorrow's supercomputers, it is clear that a software initiative will be needed if such machines are really to achieve their potential.

In this paper, we speculate on how some of the current trends in programming systems and programming language compilers may evolve into programming systems for supercomputers—systems that will be well suited to help the programmer take advantage of the performance of parallel machine architectures while not sacrificing the convenience of high-level language programming. A survey of the standard techniques used in optimizing compilers and an example of how they are used to support machine-dependent optimization are given in the next section. The section on Software Support for Vector Computers surveys the existing techniques for automatic vectorization. Under Extension to Parallel Computers, we discuss how these techniques might be extended to detecting parallelism for multiprocessor-based supercomputers and the problems that must be solved if we are to be successful. The

Programming Environment section introduces a new model for programming language systems in which all the tools for program preparation and testing—the editor, the debugger, the compiler, and the file system—are cognizant of the specific programming language being used and work together to assist the programmer in his or her task. It is shown that such an environment offers clean and effective solutions to some of the problems from the section on Extension to Parallel Computers. Finally, in Implications for Multiprocessor Supercomputers, we speculate on extensions to current programming environments that may be particularly useful for programming supercomputers.

The conclusion is not surprising: current work in programming support software can be naturally extended to effectively support supercomputers, but there is much to be done if we are to make that come about.

Optimizing Compiler Technology

A problem with any machine architecture is that there are special features that the assembly language programmer will naturally take advantage of, but the programming-language compiler must be adapted so that it makes use of these features in the code for every program it generates. The compiler writer is faced with the task of reasoning about the code that will be generated when various input programs are presented. The optimizing compiler must be able to analyze the whole program and tailor the generated code to the special features of the machine.

To do this, the compiler must thoroughly analyze the program to discover enough about it to transform it into efficient code. The analysis is usually partitioned into two phases. First, the *control-flow analysis* phase subdivides the program into *basic blocks* of straight-line code and builds a directed graph representing program flow, called the *control-flow graph*, in which vertices represent the basic blocks and edges represent the possible control-flow transfers. The control-flow graph is then used by the *data-flow analysis* phase as an auxiliary data structure to help determine the data relationships in the program.

As an example, consider *live analysis*, which is the determination at each point in the program of which variables may be used again. The standard approach is to determine which variables are live at the beginning of each basic block and to propagate this information forward to the instructions contained in that block.

A variable A is said to be *live* on entry to block x if there exists a control-flow path, free of any redefinition of A, from the beginning of block x to some block y that contains a use of A before any redefinition of A. Let LIVE(x) be the set of all variables that are live on entry to block x. We can compute LIVE(x) as follows. Suppose we have, for each block y, the sets:

IN(y)—the set of all variables for which there is a use in y prior to any definition in y.

THRU(y)—the set of all variables for which there is no assignment in block y.

These two quantities can be determined for any given block by simply scanning the block. There are two ways that a variable A can be live on entry to block x:

1. Block x can have a use of A that is not preceded by a definition, i.e.,

   $A \varepsilon IN(x)$.

2. Block x has no definition of A, and A is live at some block y to which control may transfer after x is executed, i.e.,

   $A \varepsilon THRU(x) \cap LIVE(y)$.

These observations lead to a system of equations describing the LIVE sets:

$$LIVE(x) = IN(x) \cup_{y \varepsilon S} (x) \cup (THRU(x) \cap LIVE(y)).$$

Systems like these can be solved using any of a number of efficient techniques.[3]

A particularly useful data-flow relationship is captured by *use-definition chains*, which link instructions that use a variable with the instructions that might compute the value used. Use-definition chains can be applied to the problem of dead code elimination by marking all instructions that are known to be useful (e.g., output instructions) and then tracing back on use-definition chains to mark new instructions that compute values used by instructions that have already been marked. When there are no more instructions that can be marked, the unmarked instructions are useless.

Use-definition chains can be computed by solving a set of data-flow equations to determine the set of defining instructions whose result may reach a given block x without being redefined. Once this information is available for block entries, the construction of use-definition chains is straightforward.

The usefulness of global data-flow analysis is illustrated by considering an example. The *register allocation* problem is to determine the best assignment of variables to registers, where "best" means the one that produces the most efficient program. Because the cost of memory references is high relative to the time required to get an operand from a central processing unit (CPU) register, register allocation is an extremely important machine-dependent optimization. Unfortunately, the problem of finding an optimal register allocation scheme is NP-complete in all but the simplest of cases.[4,5]

A particularly good register allocation scheme is employed in the PL/8 optimizing compiler at IBM Research in Yorktown Heights, New York. The approach is as follows:

1. Generate low-level machine code for the target machine (a reduced instruction set computer) using an infinite number of symbolic registers. In other words, do everything normally done in code generation except register assignment.

2. Perform live analysis on the symbolic registers.

3. Build an *interference graph* reflecting which symbolic registers cannot be assigned to the same real register. Two variables cannot occupy the same register if one is live at a definition point for the other. In the interference graph, each vertex represents a symbolic register and each edge connects two symbolic registers that cannot share a real register.

4. Using a heuristic algorithm, attempt to n-color the interference graph, where n is the number of available registers. If this succeeds, we are done—all variables have been assigned to registers. Otherwise, we must find the regions with high register requirements and generate instructions to write certain symbolic registers to memory to reduce those requirements. This process is known as *spilling*.

This method is incorporated into an experimental compiler and is extremely effective in allocating scalar variables to registers.[6,7]

The main problem with the data-flow analysis techniques used in most optimizing compilers is that they do not attempt a systematic analysis of array subscripts. Instead, any use or definition of a subscripted variable is treated as a use or definition of the whole array. This oversimplification makes it extremely difficult to adapt these techniques to support vector machines because on such systems it is important to determine when loads and stores from arrays access the same elements. Thus new techniques are needed.

Software Support for Vector Computers

A more precise treatment of array dependences can be obtained by observing that most subscripted code occurs within DO-loops. The indexes in DO-loops follow a regular pattern. We can use that regularity to analyze dependence within arrays.

Many investigators have examined the problem of array dependence in loops,[8-10] but perhaps the most complete job has been done by Kuck and his colleagues at the University of Illinois.[11-14]

Consider two statements in a program, such as the ones shown below.

DO 100 I = 1, 50
S_1:   A(I) = X(I) * 10
.
.
.
S_2:   B(I) = A(I − 1) + 3
100 CONTINUE

We say that statement S_2 *depends upon* statement S_1 if

(1) S_2 can be executed after S_1, and

(2) On some execution, S_2 uses as input a value that has been computed by a previous execution   of S_1.

There exist reasonably precise tests for this condition, such as Banerjee's test.[15]

How can this form of dependence help us to vectorize programs? Consider the following loop:

DO 100 I = 1, 100
    X(I) = X(I) + 10
100 CONTINUE

This loop can be directly converted to a vector statement in FORTRAN 8x or some other language supporting vector notation:

$$X(1:100) = X(1:100) + 10 .$$

However, if we consider a slight variation on this loop,

        DO 100 I = 1, 100
            X(I + 1) = X(I) + 10
    100 CONTINUE   ,

we cannot directly transliterate to the corresponding vector notation:

$$X(2:101) = X(1:100) + 10 .$$

This is because the semantics of FORTRAN 8x require that the vector statements behave as if all quantities on the right-hand side of the statement are extracted from memory before any stores occur on the left-hand side. These semantics reflect the reality of vector machine instructions that attempt to gain speed by streaming data from memory—hence the loads cannot wait on the stores.

The reason that the transliteration cannot work is because the instance of the statement on the second iteration of the loop uses a value computed on the first iteration. Hence the statement *depends upon itself.* No statement that depends upon itself either directly or indirectly can be transliterated to vector form.

This idea can be extended to a general procedure for vectorization.[12]

1. Build a dependence graph, using a precise test for dependence such as Banerjee's, in which each use-definition link is treated as an edge from definition to use.

2. Find all strongly connected regions in this graph.

3. Any statement that is not in a strongly connected region may be vectorized directly.

An extension to these ideas can greatly increase the amount of vectorization possible in a given program. It is possible to connect each dependence edge with the DO-loop that gives rise to it. To understand this, consider the following example:

```
DO 200 I = 1, 100
    DO 100 J  = 1, 100
S₁    A(I,J)    = B(I,J) + C(I,J)
S₂    B(I + 1,J) = A(I,J) * D(J)
100   CONTINUE
200 CONTINUE
```

The two statements in the inner loop form a recurrence. S_2 depends on S_1 in a way that is independent of any loop because it uses A(I,J), which is textually identical to the output of S_1. However, S_1 depends on S_2 because it uses a value in the array B that was created on the previous iteration of the loop on I. Hence this dependence is tied to the variation of the outer loop. If we hold that loop constant, the recurrence does not exist.

Thus, we can vectorize both statements in the example if we run the outer loop sequentially:

```
DO 200 I = 1, 100
    A(I,1:100)      = B(I,1:100) + C(I,1:100)
    B(I + 1,1:100) = A(I,1:100)* D(1:100)
200 CONTINUE
```

The recurrence is broken because we do not attempt to run in parallel the loop that gives rise to one of the essential dependences.

This concept, known as *layered dependence* is at the heart of the successful vectorizer we have produced at Rice University.[16] The highly effective Parafrase Compiler at the University of Illinois incorporates a similar idea.[13]

Another important transformation from the point of view of vectorization is *loop interchange*. This is perhaps best illustrated by an example.

```
DO 100 I  = 1, 100
    DO 100 J  = 1, 100
        A(I,J + 1) = A(I,J) * B(K,J)
100     CONTINUE
200 CONTINUE
```

This code cannot be vectorized, because the statement depends upon itself by a dependence edge associated with the inner loop. However, if we interchange loops to make the loop on I the inner loop, the recurrence will be associated with the outer loop and we can vectorize as follows:

```
DO 200 J  =  1, 100
    A(1:100,J + 1)  =  A(1:100,J)  *  B(K,J)
200 CONTINUE
```

Both vectorizers mentioned above incorporate very aggressive loop interchange transformations.

In the next section we will discuss how this technology can be applied to detecting parallelism for multiple-processor supercomputers.

Extension to Parallel Computers

Let us consider the problem of automatically detecting sections of code that can run on multiple processors without complex synchronization. As a base, we will assume that we are dealing with a parallel machine with a shared memory and local caches. In such an organization, it is extremely efficient to run different iterations of the same loop on different processors so long as one processor does not store into any location used by another processor. In other words, if there is no dependence between different iterations of the same loop, we can achieve maximum parallelism by loading each of the processor caches with the data needed by a particular iteration and running each iteration in parallel. If we know that no dependence exists, we need not worry about synchronization.

To illustrate this, consider the following example, which applies a rotation to a matrix A.

```
NM1 = N - 1
DO 200 J = 1, NM1
    DO 100 I = 1, NM1
        TEMP   = COS*A(I,J) - SIN*A(I,N)
        A(I,N) = SIN*A(I,J) + COS*A(I,N)
        A(I,J) = TEMP
100 CONTINUE
200 CONTINUE
```

If each processor has its own copy of TEMP, the iterations of the inner loop can be run in parallel because the array accesses in each iteration are to different rows. However, the outer loop on J cannot be run in parallel because the element A(I,N) is computed on one iteration of the outer loop and used on another.

Clearly, the sort of analysis done as a part of vectorization can be useful for this. We can use the ideas of layered dependence and loop interchange introduced in the previous section. If we can identify a loop that gives rise to no dependence cycles, the iterations of that loop can be run on different processors. For example, consider the following loop:

```
      DO 100 I = 1, 100
      DO 50 J = 1, 200
      A(J+1,I) = A(J,I) + B(J)
   50 CONTINUE
  100 CONTINUE
```

Here there is a recurrence carried by the loop on index J, but none carried by the loop on I. Hence, we can run the different iterations of the loop on I in parallel because they have no store conflicts. In parallel loop notation, this would be written:

```
      DOALL 100 I = 1, 100
      DO 50 J = 1, 100
      A(J+1,I) = A(J,I) + B(J)
   50 CONTINUE
  100 CONTINUE
```

where the DOALL indicates that the outer loop may be run in parallel.

It should be noted that there is a difference between the kinds of transformations one does to support vectorization and the kind used to support multiprocessor parallelism. In the example above, the vectorizer would move the recurrence to the outer loop so that the inner loop could be vectorized. However, in a multiprocessor system, one assumes that the overhead for scheduling is nontrivial, so that it pays to get more code into the body of the loop being run in parallel. Hence, for the multiprocessor, the parallel loop is moved to the outside. If we apply this idea to the example at the beginning of this section, we would interchange the two loops and run the outer one in parallel to yield the following:

```
NM1 = N - 1
DOALL 200 I = 1, M
  DO 100 J = 1, NM1
    TEMP(I) = COS*A(I,J) - SIN*A(I,N)
    A(I,N) = SIN*A(I,J) + COS*A(I,N)
    A(I,J) = TEMP(I)
100 CONTINUE
200 CONTINUE
```

Now instead of having each processor running three FORTRAN statements, we have each processor running a whole loop.

In general, it is desirable to move as much code as possible into the body of a parallel loop to insure that the multiprocessor system functions efficiently. However, this leads to another difficulty. Suppose there are externally compiled functions or procedures in the body of a loop we wish to run in parallel, as in the example below.

```
DO 100 I = 1, 100
  A(I) = USERFN (A(I), C)
100 CONTINUE
```

In the absence of better information, we must assume that any location in A might be changed by the call to USERFN, especially if A is in COMMON storage. Without some information about what happens inside of USERFN, we must assume that we cannot safely run this loop in parallel. This difficulty is not as serious for the vectorizer, as the following example will illustrate:

```
DO 100 I = 1, 100
  A(I) = B(I) * 10
  A(I) = USERFN (A(I), C)
100 CONTINUE
```

If B is not in COMMON, the first statement can be vectorized to yield the following code:

```
A(1:100) = B(1:100) * 10
DO 100 I = 1, 100
  A(I) = USERFN (A(I), C)
100 CONTINUE
```

Here at least some vectorization has been achieved, but for the multiprocessor case, single-statement parallelism may not be sufficient to compensate for the scheduling overhead.

These problems and others have convinced us that, if language systems for parallel computers are to be truly effective, they must incorporate some sort of interprocedural analysis. But one major reason why few compilers incorporating such analysis have appeared is the reluctance of the typical FORTRAN programmer to turn over all the modules of a program to the compiler at once. Usually, such programs are developed incrementally, a module at a time, and the cost of recompiling the entire program at once would be intolerable.

In the next section we will discuss a new type of programming support system in which interprocedural analysis can be done naturally and efficiently.

The Programming Environment

How can we do an effective job of interprocedural analysis without requiring that the whole program be compiled together? The answer is to provide a system that will automatically keep track of all modules in the program being developed and remember optimizing information from one compilation for use in another. Such a system, which would oversee all activities related to development of the program, would permit incremental development and compilation while making inter-procedural optimization possible.

Over the past several years, programming language research has turned to a new paradigm in programming systems—the *programming environment*. A programming environment is a collection of programming support tools that understand enough about the task at hand to give rather specific assistance to the programmer. Typically, these tools include a language-oriented editor, facilities for management of the program source, debugging tools tailored to the programming language being used, and facilities for making consistent executable modules. Examples of environments abound in the literature. The *Cornell Program Synthesizer* is an environment to support development of small PL/I programs by introductory programming students.[17] *Mentor*, one of the earliest environment projects, supports programming in Pascal.[18] The *Interlisp* system contains many LISP-specific tools to assist the programmer.[19] The *Gandalf* project at Carnegie Mellon University is building an environment-generating system that can be used for any of a number of languages.[20] Finally, a group at GTE is working on a programming environment for the *Chill* language.[21]

A programming environment provides the ideal vehicle to support interprocedural optimization because the various tools can record information in the data base for later reference by other tools. If this approach is to be successful, the system must be so convenient to use that it is easier for the programmer to turn over all of his program for the system to manage than it is to manage them himself. In other words, by providing a rich system of programming assistance tools, we encourage the programmer to let the system manage his program source. We are then free to record in a program data base whatever information we find useful for interprocedural optimization or other purposes.

As a part of the R^n project at Rice University, we have been developing a programming environment for FORTRAN that will support interprocedural analysis while providing a powerful collection of tools to the FORTRAN programmer. It is intended for use with FORTRAN systems for fairly conventional machines, but we will indicate how it can be very effectively used to support multiprocessor supercomputers.

Overview of the Environment

Our conceptual view of the environment is depicted in Fig. 1. First, it is a major component of the R^n project at Rice University, which is building a network of high-performance workstations designed to provide the modern scientist, engineer, or numerical analyst with a computational resource tailored to his needs. The specifications for such a workstation are summarized in Table 1. Thus, the environment is designed from the outset to run on such a workstation and to take advantage of the high-resolution graphics, the graphical input device, and the local computational power. The environment may also run on simpler graphics devices, such as dumb terminals, but we have not compromised the design to accommodate such devices. We envision that the network will have other resources connected to it, such as a computation server, a long-haul network gateway, and a file server.

The programming environment will be partitioned between the file server and the workstation, as depicted in Fig. 1. At the heart of the environment is the project data base, which resides on the file server. It records all information about the programs and modules in a project, including source, specifications, test data, documentation, interprocedural information, and much more. All access to it is made through the *project manager software*, which stores and retrieves the source files in the project, answers questions about the programs and modules, insures that project rules are obeyed, and makes consistent versions of

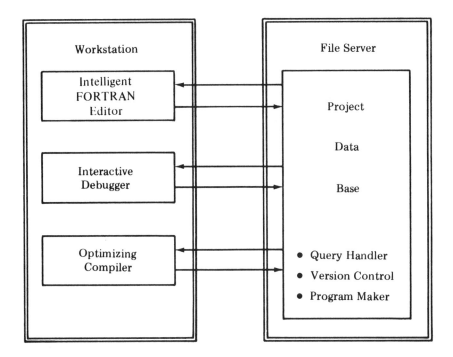

Fig. 1. The R^n programming environment for FORTRAN.

the programs for execution. The project manager stores information from and provides information to three main tools in the environment:

1. An *intelligent FORTRAN editor* that not only helps the programmer build syntactically correct programs, but also warns of possible run-time anomalies that can be detected at compile time.

2. A *debugging interpreter* that can step through parts of the program and allow the programmer to interrupt and monitor execution. With the help of the project manager, the interpreter would be able to handle a hybrid program consisting of some compiled and some interpreted modules. Thus, control could be made to pass quickly through most of the program to the module under development, which could then be interpreted.

3. An *optimizing compiler* that converts the partially compiled version of the program maintained by the editor to an optimized form

TABLE 1
WORKSTATION SPECIFICATIONS

1-2 mip CPU
High-speed floating point
Large virtual address space
1-2 megabytes real memory
≥ 20 megabytes local disk
800×1000 pixel bit-mapped display
Graphic input device (mouse or tablet)
Network interface
— file servers
— print servers
— compute servers
— gateways to other networks
Unix software base
Reasonable cost ($5K-$15K)

suitable for integration with the rest of the system. With the help of the project manager, it uses the system data base to do a thorough job of interprocedural analysis and optimization.

These tools work together to assist the programmer in preparing, documenting, and testing the program. They also cooperate to make the final programs as efficient as possible. We will discuss each of them in more detail.

Project Management

A *project manager* program will control access to all programs and modules within the project and maintain a data base of semantic information about them that can be used by other tools in the project. The basic framework is depicted in Fig. 2. In this scheme, the largest entity is the *project*, which may be thought of as a collection of programs that are being worked on by a common pool of programmers and that may make use of a common group of subprogram modules. A project might contain one program that is the central focus of the work, along with a collection of test versions, or it might include several central programs.

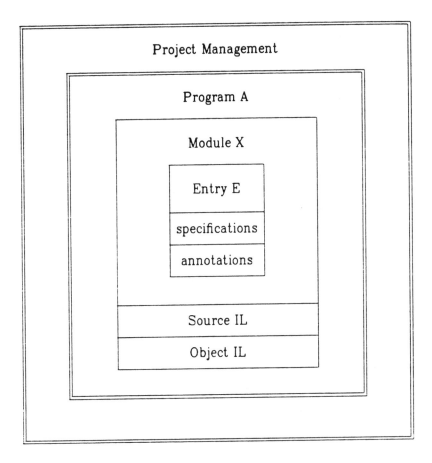

Fig. 2. A conceptual framework for project management.

A *program* is simply a collection of modules that, when integrated into a whole, may be executed. Several programs in a project may share the same modules, so the system must support some mechanism for sharing. A program may have several named *versions*, each using a different set of modules.

A program may be viewed as nothing more than a recipe indicating how to *compose* the modules (with versions specified) that it incorporates. Indeed, this is how programs are implemented in our preliminary system.

A *module* is a collection of entry points that is always edited and compiled as a whole. Modules may also have named *versions*. For example, there will usually be both an "official" and a "test" version of any module that is being modified. Presumably, the programmer will be working on the test version.

Associated with modules are various kinds of information, including source and compiled intermediate language. Each module also contains some number of *entry points*, which are the names by which the module is accessed externally. This will include all the callable entry point names. Associated with each entry point will be two kinds of information. *Specifications* are properties of the entry point which are entered by the programmer. In the first system, the specifications will consist only of the number and types of parameters. Later this may include other information about the intended behavior of the entry. *Annotations* are facts about the behavior of the entry that are gleaned by any of the tools in the environment. For example, the editor might add an annotation that indicates which other entries might be called as a result of a call to an entry point.

To conveniently provide the facilities of standard groups of modules, such as LINPACK or IMSL, the system will need to understand the concept of a *library*, which is an external project in which some modules have been declared to be "public." Single modules may be incorporated into a project from any of a number of specified libraries for the project.

Finally, any system that supports versions of its basic components must also support defaults. The environment we are developing would always have a *standard* version of every object for which versions are supported.

It is the role of the project manager to maintain the project data base, to maintain the consistency of programs within the project, and to provide information about the project or any of the programs and modules within it. For example, the manager must keep track of which programmers are working on which versions of a given module. Also, the manager will provide tools by which new programs can be constructed from modules in the data base. Finally, the project manager will provide the interface through which all queries about the project must pass.

To understand the role of the project manager, it is helpful to consider a selection of the functions we envision it performing. There are essentially three main functions performed by project management.

1. *Query Answering.* In this category, we include any operation that provides information about the project in a nondestructive fashion; in other words, any operation that does not cause a change in the current project state. Examples are requests to browse source modules, questions about specifications or annotations for a given entry point, and questions about the structure of a given program, such as a request to display the call graph.

2. *Module Creation and Modification.* In this category are all operations on modules in the project that lead to new or changed modules being stored in the data base. Examples are requests to edit a given module or to create a new one.

3. *Program Creation.* In this category we find the function of program composition. In the system, programs are created by specifying a collection of modules to be incorporated in the composition. The project manager then adds enough modules to make a complete program or until it must report that the program is incomplete.

An issue related to program composition is the *current context program.* In the process of working on a project, we envision that the programmer will establish a program as the one in which he or she is currently working. The current context program establishes the default for many operations of the project manager. For example, when a query asks for information about a given entry point name, the project manager will assume that the query refers to the version of that entry point in the current context program. Similarly, in performing a composition, the program is completed by adding modules from the current context program.

The project manager will also be responsible for maintaining the project privilege rules. We use a very simple mechanism for deciding the authority of project programmers to perform certain functions. Each module and program has a *creator*, a *status* (public or private), and a *reference count.* A private program or module belongs to its creator and may be modified or released by that programmer. A program may be made public by its creator. By doing so, the creator relinquishes his or her authority over the program and every module contained in it. The creator may not modify a public module or program. He or she must create a new version of the module and build a whole new program composition to make such a change. Presumably, this composition will be private.

This mechanism insures the stability of public programs. Only the chief project programmer may release a public program; it then reverts to private status. Modules released by the chief project programmer revert to private status only when all references to them are by programs owned by the creator of the module.

Intelligent Editor

The *intelligent FORTRAN editor* will serve as the programmer's home environment from which all activities are invoked. It will permit the programmer to browse through projects and programs; it will acquire modules and other information from the data base; and it will make heavy use of a sophisticated graphics interface featuring multiple windows, highlighting, structured region hiding, and the use of a pointing device such as a mouse.

The editor will be language-oriented and will assist the programmer in entering FORTRAN by providing commands that generate templates for the major language constructs. For example, to insert a DO-loop, the programmer need only invoke the DO-loop command and the cursor will be replaced by a DO-loop template with *place markers* in the positions where further text should be entered.

```
DO  <iterator>
    <body>
    REPEAT
```

The syntax displayed above is taken from FORTRAN 8x.

Not only does the editor help a programmer enter syntactically correct programs, it also obviates the need for a parser by directly constructing the abstract syntax tree for the program. All components of the environment can then use the abstract syntax tree as the standard program representation. The display is constructed by unparsing the abstract syntax tree. The abstract syntax permits the editor to provide both textual and treewalk cursor movement. Thus, there will be separate keys that allow the programmer to move quickly to subparts of a larger language construct. For example, if the cursor is positioned at an IF statement, there will be a cursor move function that will quickly move to the condition field.

The high-resolution display on the workstation permits a particularly convenient view of the program to be presented. Typically, the display will have three windows, as in Fig. 3. The main window will display the current region on the screen, with region hiding as appropriate. A

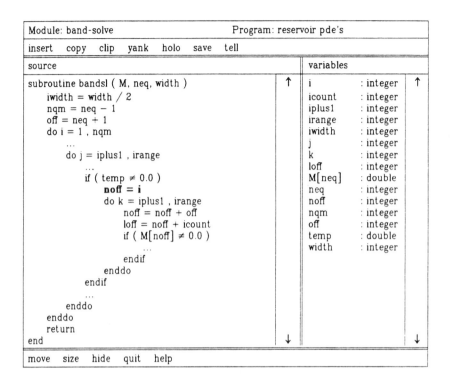

Fig. 3. A typical editor display.

parallel window will always display the current declarations for each variable used in the region of program on the screen. Finally, an option window will show the functions that are available at the current cursor position. For example, in Fig. 3, the cursor is positioned at a statement location, so any statement may be inserted. An option may be selected using the mouse or by explicitly entering the command.

Note that the program is displayed in a notation that is somewhat different from that of standard FORTRAN. In an environment such as this one, the user will have the opportunity to tailor the display format to his taste. The program is shown in a format similar to the one used for Ratfor or C on Unix* systems.

In our system the editor will also be able to detect and report many subtle semantic errors such as uninitialized variables. It will make use of

---

*Unix is a trademark of AT&T Bell Laboratories.

information stored in the project data base to help construct subprograms that are consistent with the program being developed. For example, when a programmer wishes to insert a call to an external subroutine, the editor will query the data base to provide a template for the parameters that are required.

CALL S (<integer ncases>, <real array x>, <real array>y)

In this statement, the programmer inserted CALL S and the system provided the parameter template.

There are several documentation functions that the editor will perform, including prompting the programmer for certain kinds of specifications and maintaining a modification history. The editor will also compute and record summary data flow information for each module that it creates or modifies; such information can be used in both optimization and error detection.

In advanced versions of the editor, we will experiment with incremental data-flow analysis. New results by Reps,[22] Wegman,[23] and Zadeck,[24] lead us to believe that use-definition chains (pointers from statements which use variables to the statements that might create the value used) can be efficiently created by the editor in an incremental fashion. If this is true it will be possible to provide some powerful diagnostic features.

For example, it will be possible to have a function that scrolls back from a usage point to successive points of definition for the value used (see Fig. 4). This facility would be extremely useful in debugging because most errors are detected when a bad value causes some fault to occur. The point of fault is easily located. However, the real error probably occurred where the bad value was *created*. Use-definition chains can help us quickly find all possible creation points.

Debugging Interpreter

The *debugging interpreter* will enable programmers to step through parts of a given program and allow them to interrupt and monitor execution.

The debugger, like the editor, will also make effective use of the high-resolution graphics. As we envision it, the programmer will be able to monitor execution using a display similar to the one depicted in Fig. 5. While highlighting the statement being executed in one window, the debugger will simultaneously display the changed values of variables in a second and the program output in a third window.

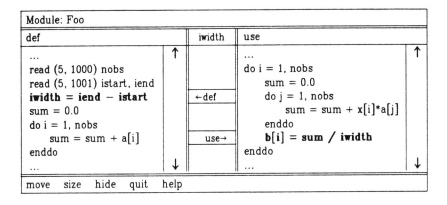

Fig. 4. Scrolling back to definition points.

```
Module: fib
run   continue   set break   remove break   step   next   pause
┌──────────────────────────────┬─────────────────────┬──────────────────┐
│ source                   ↑    │ variables       ↑   │ output       ↑   │
│ program fibonacci             │  [ 8] current       │   i    fib(i)    │
│   read n                      │  [ 7] i             │   1    0         │
│   i = 0                       │  [10] n             │   2    1         │
│   current = 0                 │  [13] next          │   3    1         │
│   next = 1                    │                     │   4    2         │
│   print 'i', 'fib(i)'         │                     │   5    3         │
│   while ( i ≠ n ) do          │                     │   6    5         │
│     i = i + 1                 │                     │   7    8         │
│     print i, current          │                     │                  │
│     next = next + current     │                     │                  │
│     current = next − current  │                     │                  │
│   enddo                       │                     │                  │
│ end                           │                     │                  │
│                          ↓    │                 ↓   │              ↓   │
└──────────────────────────────┴─────────────────────┴──────────────────┘
move   size   hide   quit   help
```

Fig. 5. Execution monitoring in the debugger.

An important design goal is to support *hybrid execution,* in which compiled and interpreted modules are intermixed. This will permit interpretive testing of a module that may not be executed until many minutes of execution of the whole program. To support this feature, it is absolutely critical that compiled and interpreted programs maintain a consistent layout of data in the program. This strategy will also make it more likely that the compiled and interpreted versions of the same module will behave identically.

Another important debugging feature we intend to support is reversible execution. There is no special difficulty to this. Because the abstract tree is doubly linked, we can easily move backward in it. A problem arises at three main points of ambiguity: assignments, gotos, and calls to compiled code. Traditionally, these are handled by saving on some file the value of the changed variable or the location from which control came. The big problem is caused by calls to compiled code. At these, the interpreter must save the values of every variable that might be changed before control returns. In the absence of better information, this means every variable in common and every parameter.

In the R^n environment, the burden will be much smaller because the interprocedural analysis will provide the interpreter with a much more precise estimate of what might be changed by a call. Thus fewer variable values will need to be saved.

Debugging is an extremely important programming activity that has received too little attention from FORTRAN implementers. Here is an area where the graphic capabilities of the personal workstation will be especially valuable. One aspect of numerical debugging is common to non-numeric debugging: the elimination of semantic errors in the program, errors that cause the program to behave in an incorrect manner. There is another type of debugging common in numerical programs—elimination of the errors of precision and accuracy that make the answers incorrect or the algorithm fail to converge rapidly enough. It is here that debugging truly takes on the flavor of experimentation, and the ability to interactively follow execution while monitoring the output may permit enormous savings of research time.

Optimizing Compiler

The *optimizing compiler,* which is really an optimizing code generator, will convert the partially compiled version of a module maintained by the editor to an optimized form suitable for integration into the program of which it is a part. The main advance in this tool over previous optimizing compilers for FORTRAN is its use of interprocedural analysis and optimization.

Compiler optimization researchers have long believed that the interprocedural effects are the last remaining major source of inefficiency in languages with optimizing compilers. Why then are there so few compilers with any interprocedural analysis and optimization? The answer is that the compiler would need access to all the code in a program to do a good job. It is unreasonable to expect to compile whole programs at once—the cost in computation time would be too great. It would be almost as impractical to perform data-flow analysis on the whole program at each module compilation.

The solution is to save the interprocedural information needed for optimization between compilations in the project data base. This requires that the interprocedural information be updated each time a module is edited.

We intend to use the environment to attack two problems. First, we will investigate the use of interprocedural information to do *linkage tailoring*—the construction of efficient subroutine linkages tailored to the actual caller and callee. An example of linkage tailoring is in-line substitution, but there are many less dramatic forms.

A second area is to compute the patterns of data usage and definitions as a result of procedure invocations. An example is the computation of *mod(s)*, the set of variables that might be changed as a result of the procedure invocation at call site s. There are two components to this information.

1. First there are the immediate effects of the procedure being invoked. These can be recorded in the data base by the editor—on putting a module away, the editor need only store the list of variables that are changed in some statement in the program.

2. To this list must be added the secondary effects due to calls to other routines from within the called routine. These must be handled by solving a data-flow problem on the call graph.[25-32] A recent dissertation by Cooper describes fast algorithms to solve this problem in an incremental fashion.[33] The basic idea is that whenever the editor puts away a module that is incorporated in a program, a demon is invoked to update the interprocedural information. This demon makes use of comparisons of old information with new information to keep from doing redundant work.

As a result of the actions of the demon described above, several modules may need to be recompiled because of new interprocedural information. Thus, the environment will permit us to at last mount a concerted attack on interprocedural optimization and analysis.

Implications for Multiprocessor Supercomputers

As indicated in Optimizing Compiler Technology, interprocedural analysis will make it possible to do a much more aggressive job of analyzing vector dependences. This will in turn lead to compilers that will be able to construct very precise dependence information about arrays of the sort described in the section on Software Support for Vector Computers. Such a compiler might well attempt to automatically assign different iterations of a loop to different processors. It is conceivable that this might lead to parallel programs that are acceptably efficient on a parallel machine.

Even more exciting is the possibility of interactive parallel programming. If the workstation on which the programming environment is implemented is powerful enough, it could interactively compute the dependence edges and display them on the screen in a manner similar to the one depicted in Fig. 6. In such a display, color or shading could indicate the loop to which specific dependences are attached. In Fig. 6, the dependence edge is confined to the inner loop so it is laid out completely within the inner rectangle.

If this were accompanied by a flexible facility for loop interchange that could automatically or semiautomatically interchange loops and report

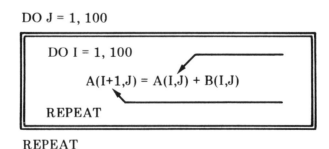

```
DO J = 1, 100

    DO I = 1, 100

        A(I+1,J) = A(I,J) + B(I,J)

    REPEAT

REPEAT
```

Fig. 6. An interactive parallel programming environment.

when this might lead to a semantic anomaly, the environment would be a powerful laboratory for interactive parallel programming. The laboratory could be further enhanced by the provision of an interactive diagnostic facility that would answer questions (such as why a loop cannot be run in parallel) and interactively assist the programmer to recast the loop into parallel form.

With the advent of programming environments for supercomputers, the programmer will be able to sit down at a graphics workstation and conduct a dialog with the system in which he crafts a parallel code while the environment advises him on the semantic implications of what is entered.

Summary and Conclusions

It has become obvious to all those who program parallel computers that the task is a hard one. If the programmer is to do an adequate job, he must be able to factor out all but the most essential details. This implies that we must have strong programming support systems—languages, compilers, and environments—to support high-level constructs for parallel programming that are free of artificial constructs arising from the specifics of the underlying machine.

However, such languages will need powerful optimizing compilers to tailor individual programs to the available hardware. We hope that we have convinced you that the technology of compiler optimization and vectorization is sufficiently advanced to expect that, in time, we will be able to develop those compilers. However, the need for concern with larger granularity of parallelism makes the need for interprocedural analysis and optimization even more pressing.

Programming environments, which have been the subject of much recent study, promise to provide a vehicle for increasing programmer productivity while permitting cross-procedural information passing among the tools of the environment. In particular, the tools of an environment can easily be adapted to aid in the process of inter-procedural information gathering. The R^n programming environment project at Rice University is attempting to develop the techniques for interprocedural analysis in the context of an environment.

In addition to their other advantages, programming environments can be adapted to provide interactive programming support for parallel programming. It is easy to envision these environments as powerful programming laboratories for crafting supercomputer programs.

However, the outlook is not completely rosy. Work has only just begun on programming and much software remains to be developed. Only if we start to actively pursue the goal of a truly interactive parallel programming environment now will we be ready to support the multi-processor supercomputers when they reach the market in the second half of this decade.

References

1. Backus, J. "The History of FORTRAN I, II, and III." *ACM Sigplan Notices* **13**, no. 8 (August 1978):165-180.

2. Lincoln, N. R. "It's Really Not as Much Fun Building a Supercomputer as it is Simply Inventing One." In *High Speed Computer and Algorithm Organization*, edited by D. J. Kuck, D. Lawrie, and A. Sameh. New York: Academic Press, 1977.

3. Kennedy, K. "A Survey of Data Flow Analysis Techniques." In *Program Flow Analysis: Theory and Applications*, edited by S. S. Muchnick and N. D. Jones, 1-54. New Jersey: Prentice-Hall, 1981.

4. Sethi, R. "Complete Register Allocation Problems," *SIAM J. Computing* **4**, no. 3 (1975):226-248.

5. Bruno, J. L., and Sethi, R. "Code Generation for a One Register Machine," *J. ACM* **23**, no. 3 (1976):502-510.

6. Chaitin, G. J., Auslander, M. A., Chandra, A. K., Cocke, J., Hopkins, M. E., and Markstein, P. W. "Register Allocation via Coloring." *Computer Languages* **6** (1981):47-57.

7. Chaitin, G. J. "Register Allocation and Spilling via Graph Coloring." *ACM Sigplan Notices* **17**, no.6, (June 1982):98-105.

8. Cohagen, W. L. "Vector Optimization for the ASC." *Proceedings of the Seventh Annual Princeton Conference on Information Sciences and Systems*, Department of Electrical Engineering, Princeton, New Jersey (1973):169-174.

9. Myszewski, M. "The Vectorizer System: Current and Proposed Capabilities." Massachusetts Computer Associates, Inc., report CA-17809-1511, Wakefield, Massachusetts (September 1978).

10. Higbee, L. "Vectorization and Conversion of FORTRAN Programs for the Cray-1 CFT Compiler." Cray Research, Inc. publication 2240207, Mendota Heights, Minnesota (June 1979).

11. Kuck, D. J. "A Survey of Parallel Machine Organization and Programming." *Computing Surveys* **9**, no. 1 (March 1977):29-59.

12. Kuck, D. J. *The Structure of Computers and Computations*, Vol. 1. New York: John Wiley and Sons, 1978.

13. Kuck, D. J., Kuhn, R. H., Leasure, B., and Wolfe, M. "The Structure of an Advanced Vectorizer for Pipelined Processors." *Proceedings of the IEEE Computer Society, Fourth International Computer Software and Applications Conference.* IEEE (October 1980).

14. Kuck, D. J., Kuhn, R. H., Leasure, B., Padua, D. A., and Wolfe, M. "Compiler Transformation of Dependence Graphs." *Conference Record of the Eighth ACM Symposium of Principles of Programming Languages.* ACM, Williamsburg, Virginia (January 1981).

15. Banerjee, U. "Data Dependence in Ordinary Programs." Department of Computer Science report 76-837, University of Illinois, Urbana-Champaign (November 1976).

16. Allen, J. R., and Kennedy, K. "PFC: A Program to Convert Fortran to Parallel Form." Department of Mathematical Sciences report MASC TR 82-6, Rice University, Houston, Texas (March 1982).

17. Teitelbaum, R. T., and Reps, T. "The Cornell Program Synthesizer: A Syntax-Directed Programming Environment." *Comm. ACM* **24**, no. 9 (September 1981):563-573.

18. Donzeau-Gouge, V., Huet, G., Kahn, G., Lang, B., and Levy, J. J. "A Structure-Oriented Program Editor: A First Step Toward Computer-Assisted Programming." *International Computing Symposium 1975*, Amsterdam: North-Holland Publishing Company, 1975.

19. Teitelman, W. "A Display-Oriented Programmer's Assistant." *Proceedings of the Fifth International Joint Conference on Artificial Intelligence,* Carnegie-Mellon University, Pittsburg, Pennsylvania (1977):905-915.

20. Habermann, A. N., and Notkin, D. S. "The Gandalf Software Development Environment." Computer Science Department research report, Carnegie-Mellon University, Pittsburgh, Pennsylvania (January 1982).

21. Rudmic, A., and Moore, B. "The Chill Compiling System: Towards a Chill Programming Environment." *Proceedings of the Fourth International Conference on Software Engineering for Telecommunications Switching Systems,* IEEE Conference Publications ISSN 0537-9989, no. 198 (1981):187-190.

22. Reps, T. "Optimal-Time Incremental Semantic Analysis for Syntax-Directed Editors." *Conference Record of the Ninth Annual ACM Symposium on Principles of Programming Languages*, Association for Computing Machinery (1982):169-176.

23. Wegman, M. N. "Summarizing Graphs by Regular Expressions." IBM Research report RC 9364 (41252), Yorktown Heights, New York (April 1982).

24. Zadeck, F. K. "Incremental Data Flow Analysis in a Structured Program Editor." Ph.D. dissertation, Department of Mathematical Sciences, Rice University, Houston, Texas (August 1983).

25. Allen, F. E. "Interprocedural Data Flow Analysis." *Information Processing 74.* Amsterdam:North-Holland Publishing Company, 1974.

26. Allen, F. E., and Schwartz, J. T. "Determining Data Relationships in a Collection of Programs." IBM, T. J. Watson Research Center report RC 4989, Yorktown Heights, New York (August 1974).

27. Banning, J. P. "An Efficient Way to Find the Side Effects of Procedure Calls and the Aliases of Variables." *Conference Record of the Sixth Annual ACM Symposium on Principles of Programming Languages*, San Antonio, Texas, Association for Computing Machinery (January 1979):29-41.

28. Barth, J. M. "A Practical Interprocedural Data Flow Algorithm." *Comm. ACM* **21**, no. 9 (September 1978):724-736.

29. Myers, E. W. "A Precise Interprocedural Data Flow Algorithm." *Conference Record of the Eighth Annual ACM Symposium on Principles of Programming Languages*, Association for Computing Machinery (1981):219-230.

30. Rosen, B. K. "Data Flow Analysis for Procedural Languages." *J. ACM* **26**, no. 2 (April 1979):322-344.

31. Spillman, T. C. "Exposing Side Effects in a PL/I Optimizing Compiler." *Information Processing 71*. Amsterdam:North-Holland Publishing Company, 1972.

32. Weihl, W. E. "Interprocedural Data Flow Analysis in the Presence of Pointers, Procedure Variables, and Label Variables." *Conference Record of the Seventh Annual ACM Symposium on Principles of Programming Languages*, Association for Computing Machinery (1980):83-94.

33. Cooper, K. D. "Interprocedural Data Flow Analysis in a Programming Environment." Ph.D. dissertation, Department of Mathematical Sciences, Rice University, Houston, Texas (May 1983).

23

CAD/CAM: Ford Motor Company Engineering and Manufacturing

R. W. Heiney
Ford Motor Company
Dearborn, Michigan

Ford began computer-aided manufacturing in the early 1960s with numerical control machines that cut templates, die models, and stamping dies. Let me describe how we used to do our job. Before computers came into use at Ford Motor Company, the steps to get from the clay models in the Design Center to the final stamping dies were very time consuming and laborious.

Then, as it is today, vehicle design began in the Design Studio, where full-sized clay models were developed to show the appearance of all surfaces, shapes, and finishes (Fig. 1). Then cardboard patterns or templates were cut to fit these clay models. Using these cardboard templates, master surface layout drawings were created to show surface contours (Fig. 2).

By using manual techniques, the lines were smoothed to refine and complete the surface drawings (Fig. 3). Draftsmen added holes and attached flanges and reinforcements to the surface panel drawings; they also designed the component's inner panels, hardware, and ornamentation. This procedure was followed so that production parts would closely match the appearance, shape, and surface texture conceived in the Design Studio.

Next, metal templates were constructed to develop the wood die model. Template construction was a very time-consuming process. The completed templates were used to finish the wood die model surface. This was another very time-consuming process because we made a template for every 5 inches of the vehicle. Figure 4 shows some of the templates that were required. Back in old days, several storage rooms like this were jammed with literally thousands of templates.

Fig. 1. Cardboard patterns or templates were cut to fit clay models.

Fig. 2. From cardboard templates, master surface layout drawings were created.

Fig. 3. Draftsman designed inner panels, hardware, and ornamentation.

Fig. 4. Metal templates.

The final result of this laborious process was a master wood model (Fig. 5). These models were used not only for tooling, but when they were blocked together—what is called cubing—the surface of the complete car could be viewed. Then, plaster casts were made from the master models and were used for cutting dies (Fig. 6). Other plaster casts were needed to make fixtures for welding the panels together and for checking to make sure that resulting assemblies were properly made.

In the early 1960s, Ford began the development of a system to optically digitize the draft, and through a computer program, drive the numerical control machines for cutting aluminum templates, master wood models, and production dies for outer surface or skin panels (Fig. 7). It was not until we introduced the electronic scanner at the Design Center and the Ford Computer Graphics Design System in 1968 that we began to realize the potential for an integrated system—that is, a process that develops digitized scanner data from a stylist's clay model electronically and transfers these data to an engineering design graphic station and eventually to manufacturing (Fig. 8). This electronic sharing eliminated all templates and the laborious smoothing techniques. Let us look at the major elements of the integrated process.

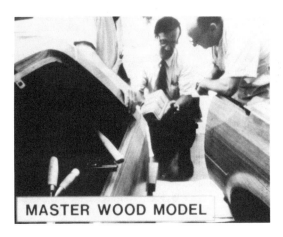

MASTER WOOD MODEL

Fig. 5. The final result was a master wood model.

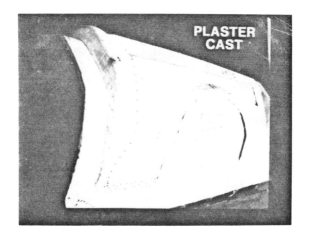

Fig. 6. Plaster casts were used for cutting dies.

Fig. 7. Numerical control machine.

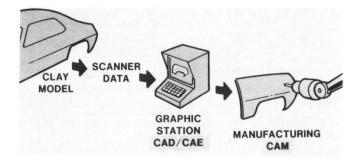

Fig. 8. Ford Graphic System (FGS).

Computer-aided design (CAD) relates to the application of computer graphics during the process of conceptualizing, defining, and verifying surface, form, and design geometry (Fig. 9). Basically, it makes the drafting board obsolete and lets designers and engineers create and analyze design alternatives using computer graphics.

The next phase is computer-aided engineering (CAE). Engineers use it to help them specify and evaluate function and performance before

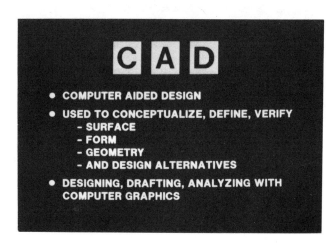

Fig. 9. Computer-aided design.

completing a design and before a prototype or production parts are made (Fig. 10). This is where high-powered computing really comes into play.

Computer-aided manufacturing (CAM) involves the use of computers to run production machinery. Applications include numerical control, robotics, and computerized monitoring of production operations (Fig. 11). Through the use of CAM techniques, computer-controlled machines are able to provide speed, accuracy, and dependability that human operators usually cannot match. In addition, by using the electronic data base created by product engineering, manufacturing operations are able to build tools, dies, and molds to produce parts exactly as specified.

I would like to stress that our computer-aided design, engineering, and manufacturing applications are very much interrelated (Fig. 12). There is no distinct boundary for each. As represented in this figure, there is much overlap, interplay, and feedback among these applications during the product development process.

CAD makes it easier to consider all sorts of alternatives and to make design changes on the spot. A number of alternatives can be viewed quickly and the best one selected (Fig. 13). It is also essential for the construction of the models used in CAE and "playing back" the analytical results.

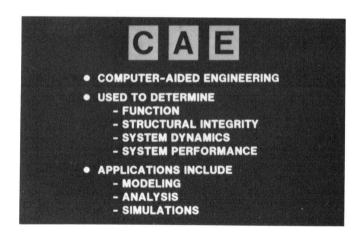

Fig. 10. Computer-aided engineering.

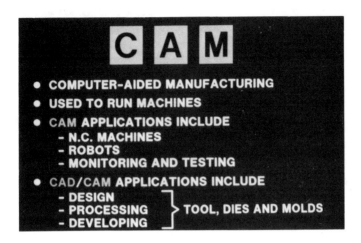

Fig. 11. Computer-aided manufacturing.

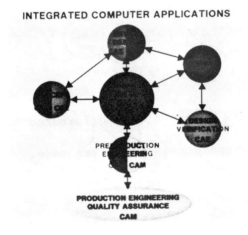

Fig. 12. Computer-aided design, engineering, and manufacturing applications are interrelated.

Fig. 13. Computer-aided design allows on-the-spot design changes.

Our CAE efforts consist of two major categories. The first approach (Fig. 14) encompasses computerized, analytical models for specific components, systems, or vehicle functions, as follows:

- analysis programs for components such as gears, catalysts, and brakes;

- simulation methods for predicting performance of systems such as engines, electronic controls, and air conditioning; and

- vehicle models such as those used for predicting fuel economy and performance based on vehicle aerodynamics, rolling resistance, and powertrain factors.

The second major CAE category is general-purpose methods (bottom, Fig. 14). These methods are expanding rapidly in usage because they are flexible and not locked into a design configuration. Their disadvantage is that they require considerable expertise and training to use. Some of the methods are as follows:

- Finite element analysis (FEA), which is the most powerful generalized method. Applied to almost any component or system, FEA can determine strength, vibration characteristics, buckling loads, and thermal performance.

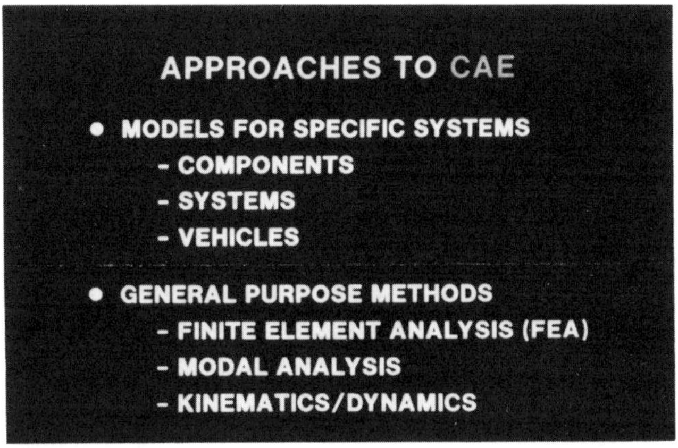

Fig. 14. CAE for specific systems and for general purpose methods.

- Modal analysis methods, which are used for the vibration analysis of various components and vehicles.

- Kinematic/dynamic analysis techniques, which are applied to mechanisms and vehicle dynamics.

We have used FEA to reduce weight and costs of metal components and to reduce vibration effects. FEA has allowed us to conduct more comprehensive safety studies, while reducing the number of prototype crash vehicles, which cost $300 000 each.

Next, I will discuss modal analysis. Modal analysis can be described as feeding dynamic inputs into a system model, as shown in Fig. 15, or a vehicle in the lab, and measuring outputs. The advantage of the computer is that outputs can be obtained and design changes made considerably faster than by an actual test. Inputs include tar strips on roads, chuck holes, imbalances in tire and wheels, and shaking forces from the engine. The model determines vehicle response for these inputs. The engineer can then equate this response to what the driver and passengers hear or feel as noises, vibrations, and shake. In contrast, Fig. 16 shows the traditional approach on the left as the car is being driven over test track cobble stones. On the right is a vehicle on a test stand, where different road conditions can be duplicated with the car instrumented to measure actual vehicle responses.

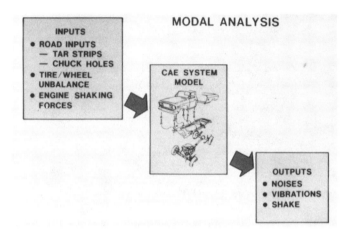

Fig. 15. Modal analysis.

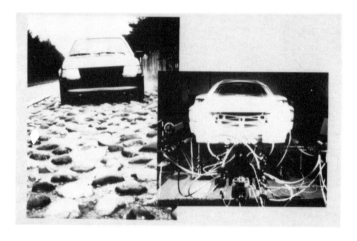

Fig. 16. Traditional road test on the left and a vehicle on a test
stand on the right.

Figure 17 shows a computer-generated response output. It is probably more personally satisfying to evaluate vehicles the old way; however, output response curves like this provide invaluable insight for improving the vehicle. Although the peaks for the modification are reduced in magnitude, which is desirable, it takes a trained engineer to assess the performance implications. The output response is calculated for points that the driver is most sensitive to, such as the steering column and wheel, the seat, the front fenders and hood, and the interior noise level. The development engineer often focuses on the body, which has 80 to 90 modes in which it can vibrate. To evaluate the body, a very accurate FEA model is developed.

Figure 18 shows a structural model that has more than 24 000 finite elements. We use a model of the body to evaluate acoustics and indicate with color graphics which parts of the body influence interior noise levels. In Fig. 19, the lighter area shows that the roof panel vibration generates the most noise at ear level. Computer graphics provide vital information to development engineers in evaluating design modifications to reduce roof panel vibration.

Our last topic is kinematics and dynamics. Software for kinematic and dynamic generalized methods has become commercially available within the last 5 years. We began computer implementation of the methods more than 10 years ago as a cooperative effort between the University of Michigan and Ford Engineering. These methods are now

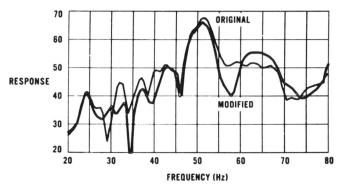

Fig. 17. Computer-generated response output.

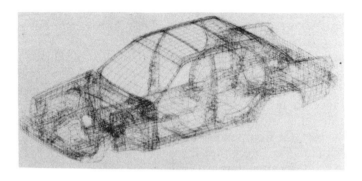

Fig. 18. Structural model.

Fig. 19. CAE plot of a 1986 Ford body acoustic model.

used extensively to evaluate suspension motion to assure acceptable system performance.

Another valuable application is to simulate test track pot holes at various speeds. The most valuable data the engineer obtains from this program are the input loads for structural analysis of suspension components.

Another example is vehicle-handling simulation. A sophisticated total-vehicle model developed for the Bronco II was used early in development to evaluate handling characteristics before the prototype was built. By graphic animation, the engineer simulated a severe 30-mph, quick, full turn of the steering wheel. The results showed a number of engineering modifications that could be implemented to improve handling. The simulation showed that, in this severe maneuver, the vehicle behaved very well. The Bronco II has received outstanding reviews on its handling characteristics—a testimonial to the engineers and their application of CAE.

Now that the vehicle is well engineered, it must be manufactured efficiently. Let us look at some examples of CAM. Time does not allow us to cover all manufacturing areas, so the focus will be on specific CAM applications related to our Stamping Operations. These operations participated in the initial venture into Numerical Control Machining 20 years ago and were involved in the start of computer graphics 15 years ago.

Stamping Operations has expanded CAM applications in line with the increasing volume of digital data from Body Engineering. Ninety percent of body sheet metal for our 1986 new car program will be designed using computer graphics (Fig. 20). CAM has completely transformed the traditional, manual methods of Stamping Engineering for processing and drawing development. Determination of the manufacturing sequence, of what we refer to as processing, is the first area where we see a major impact of CAM in stamping tooling. In the past, we relied on a plastic part, as shown in Fig. 21, to visualize and determine how to process and design the tool. Now the part is displayed on a graphic screen

Fig. 20. Sheetmetal design with computer graphics.

Fig. 21. Plastic part to visualize for determination of how to
process and design the tool.

and rotated or sectioned as required (Fig. 22). The process engineer
views the part in tipped positions to pinpoint possible manufacturing
problems and completes processing the dies.

The first operation in the stamping process, used to produce a fender,
for example, is forming the shape into the sheet of steel from which the
fender will be stamped (Fig. 23).

Draw development is the engineering method used to design the
formed shape of the stamping, as shown in the fender in Fig. 24. The
objective is to minimize the depth of draw that is the sheet metal
deformation when stamping the part. Another objective is to minimize
the gripping material that is used to restrain the sheet metal when
stamping the part, because any excess material left over after stamping is
scrapped. In the past, draw development was a trial and error process,
tedious and costly, using full size plaster study models.

The men in Fig. 25 are pressing a sheet of steel into the plaster model
to simulate the initial impact of the stamping die before entry of the
forming punch. The holes you see are drilled to measure draw depths. In
subsequent soft tool tryouts, where various depths of draw are tested
(Fig. 26), the final draw depth is established. The computer then gives
instantaneous measures of draw depth (Fig. 27). The depth of draw and
the gripping material are minimized through the skills of the designer

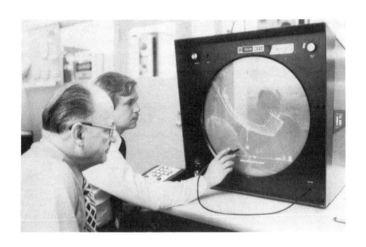

Fig. 22. Part displayed on a graphic screen.

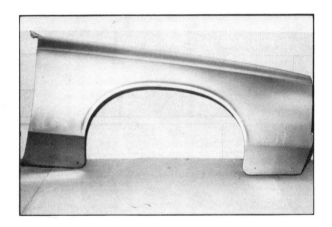

Fig. 23. Formed shape in sheet of steel.

Fig. 24. Formed shape of the stamping.

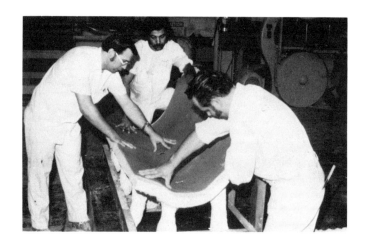

Fig. 25. Workers fitting steel part to plaster model.

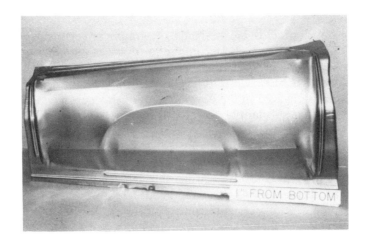

Fig. 26. Part used to test draw depth.

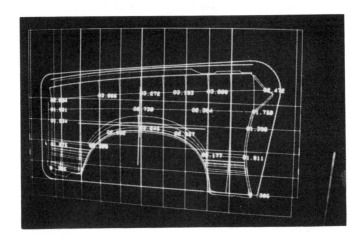

Fig. 27. Measures of draw depth shown on the computer.

using CAD and CAM. These considerations are important because the metal used for drawn stampings constitutes over two-thirds of our steel purchases.

Draw developments are designed on graphics in considerably less time (Fig. 28). The ultimate technique for draw development is to add CAE, in other words, to simulate the stress and strain of the forming process through FEA. Currently, the Stamping Engineering and Research Staff is engaged in the development of this new technology. It is clear to me that substantial power will be required to handle such an analysis. For example, to simulate front-end crashes is a substantially more complicated problem than the rear-end crash analyses.

To summarize all of these applications, the computer makes it possible to integrate the entire design through production process, from start to finish (Fig. 29). As you would expect, communication throughout the organization is significantly improved. By using a common electronic data base, our designers, product engineers, and manufacturing engineers know what each is doing and are better equipped to resolve issues concerning part design, overall product configuration, and manufacturing. The benefits are enormous in terms of improved timing, lower cost, and higher quality products.

To give you a better idea of how we have combined CAD, CAE, and CAM in the process of developing our products, I would like to show one

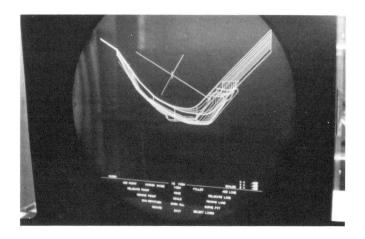

Fig. 28. Draw developments are designed on graphics.

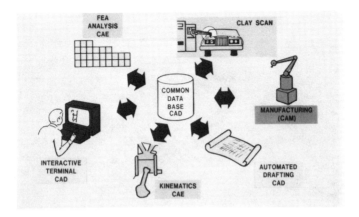

Fig. 29. Integrated computer applications.

last example. Figure 30 shows the 1984 Lincoln steering column shroud—the plastic cover on the upper end of the steering column just below the steering wheel. Figure 31 shows the Design Center's scanner data. The final design produced through the CAD process looked like that shown in Fig. 32.

When the product engineer's design specifications were obtained, the manufacturing engineer began the process of designing the mold needed to make this part. Figure 33 shows a view of the mold as designed by the manufacturing engineer. The mold is 12 by 10 inches, the general shape

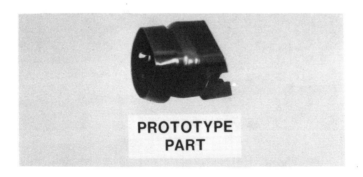

Fig. 30. Steering column shroud of 1984 Lincoln.

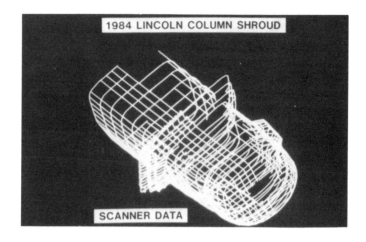

Fig. 31. Design Center's scanner data.

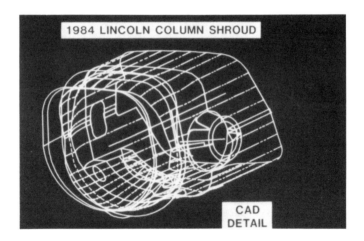

Fig. 32. CAD detail of steering column shroud.

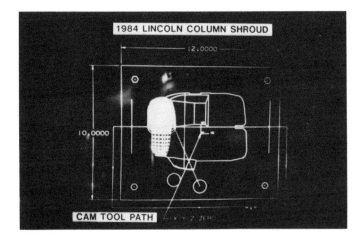

Fig. 33. View of the mold.

of the part is outlined in the center, and the tool paths are shown. These tool paths were transmitted in digital form to the prototype and production part suppliers.

The suppliers entered the design data into their graphics systems, where computerized numerical control machine instructions were created to actually cut the mold (Fig. 34). Figure 35 shows the numerical control machine actually cutting the metal mold that will produce the plastic part. Effectively, this part was designed, evaluated, and produced without need for conventional paper drawings of parts, mold, or manufacturing fixtures.

I would like to spend a few more minutes to reflect with you on what supercomputers mean for the integrated computer-aided product development process. I remember when structural analysis activities first started. There were not very many engineers trained in the process. A timely relevance to product design was almost out of the question. It was a contest to see which took longest—gathering the data for the model from blueprints, building the model, performing the calculations on the computer, or analyzing printouts of the results. You have seen what computer graphics has done for gathering data, building models, and

Fig. 34. The suppliers entered the design data into their graphics systems.

Fig. 35. Numerical control machine cutting the metal mold.

understanding analytical results; as an indirect result, we now have hundreds of skilled engineers at Ford who compete on a worldwide basis for the services of our systems.

Meeting their demands is a challenge. They want immediate access to their gigabytes of the data. They want instant response for small jobs, which are 90% of all tasks, but only 20% of demand. They want much better turnaround for large jobs, although less than 1% of all tasks comprise 25% of the demand. They also want to do more of both kinds of work. But, they do not want to spend any more money.

We have issued a purchasing information request to find out how today's supercomputers could help meet the challenge of our users. As we review the responses to this request, we will be looking for more than performance and price. Ease of use by these engineers is extremely important. We must continue to improve their productivity. Supercomputers must be integrated into our overall process.

The same challenge will face the designers of tomorrow's supercomputers. Whatever applications these supercomputers are designed for, careful attention must be paid to the whole environment of the end user. The operating system, the front end, the mass storage that somebody must manage, and all of the necessary applications software must minimize any barriers to the supercomputer's end user.

24

A View of Supercomputing

G. D. Byrne
Exxon Research and Engineering Company
Clinton Township, New Jersey

Introduction

Supercomputing is now done within Exxon. There is also an increasing awareness of and interest in supercomputing at Exxon. My goals for this paper are to tell about some of the corporate activities in large-scale scientific/engineering computing. I will also speculate about the future. Before doing so, I will begin this section by briefly describing corporate interests. Then I will narrow the view to two companies within the corporate structure. Finally, I will focus on two problem types.

The divisions and more than 500 affiliated companies of Exxon Corporation operate in the United States, as well as over 80 other countries. Their principal business is energy. This involves exploration for and production of crude oil, natural gas, and petroleum products; exploration for coal and its mining and sale; and fabrication of nuclear fuel. Exxon is also engaged in exploration for and mining of other minerals. Reliance Electric Company, Zilog, Exxon Office Systems, and Exxon Chemical Company are examples of members of the Exxon family engaged in other activities. These nonenergy companies are involved in the production of a broad line of industrial equipment, computer chips, electronic office equipment, and chemicals.[1-3]

Two of the companies that provide research, development, and engineering support to this large family are Exxon Production Research Company (EPR) and Exxon Research and Engineering Company (ER&E). With respect to the energy business, these two companies participate in the upstream (exploration and production) and downstream (refining, manufacturing, transportation, and sales)[4] sides of Exxon's petroleum business.

In practice, these two companies share many common technical concerns and cooperate in many areas of research and development. As

336

an example, ER&E, EPR, and Exxon Corporation's Communications and Computer Sciences Department recently collaborated in a study of the opportunities in parallel processing. Findings of this study highlighted corporate interests and helped to seed several ongoing activities in supercomputing and parallel processing.

With this view of Exxon in mind, we will in turn look at two of the many possible problem areas that can utilize supercomputers. Reservoir simulation is a typical problem area for EPR, which is located in Houston. The simulation of chemical transport phenomena is a problem common to ER&E. During the course of talking about these problems, I will indicate current and future computational needs. I then will discuss a common thread that ties these two problem types together and leads to an understanding of their computational needs. These problems are difficult, but they are well worth solving, and I will explain why. I will then conclude with some personal views and concerns about future engineering/scientific computation.

Oil Reservoir Simulation

To some, the simulation of an oil reservoir may seem rather straightforward. So I will begin this section by explaining a bit about this problem area.

Some of the difficulty in reservoir simulation stems from the structure of an underground reservoir. If we took a core sample from a petroleum reservoir, it would look pretty much like a cylinder of concrete. The oil is trapped in the pores, or interstices, of the rock and looks like black sand in the concrete cylinder (Fig. 1).

Generally, reservoir models account for the movement and time evolution of oil, gas, and water phases (Fig. 2) through this underground formation. Detailed mathematical models keep track of the distribution of these phases throughout the reservoir.[5-6] There are three basic forces that control distributions of these fluids. Gravity tends to move gas upward and water downward relative to oil. Viscous forces retard the motion of the fluids. Capillary forces draw water, and sometimes oil, into regions of the reservoir that have relatively small pores.

The velocity of the phases in these models is developed from Darcy's Law. This law is centered around permeability, a measure of the ease with which fluids can flow through the reservoir. Loosely packed rock is said to be more permeable than tightly compacted rock. Darcy's Law simply states that if gravity is neglected, velocity in a coordinate

Fig. 1. Illustration of a core sample.

direction is proportional to the product of permeability and the negative of the spatial rate of change of pressure in that direction. A pea shooter illustrates the empirical law: the harder we blow, the faster the pea goes. A gravitational field complicates the picture a bit. If gravity is admitted, the velocity component is proportional to the difference between the pressure gradient and the product of phase density, gravitational force, and the rate of change of depth in that coordinate direction.

The models used in a reservoir simulator are time-dependent, and it is common to run simulations to obtain field history and projections of several tens of years. The character of a field changes as the oil is

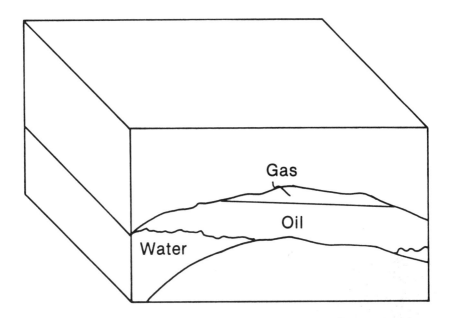

Fig. 2. Sketch on an oil reservoir.

removed—pressure of the reservoir drops, phases separate, and some-times water enters the reservoir from a surrounding aquifer.[6]

It turns out that we typically can only extract 10 to 50% of the oil from a reservoir using primary or secondary recovery.[7] Primary recovery uses natural reservoir pressure, perhaps in conjunction with pumps, to recover oil. Secondary recovery involves injection of water or gas into the reservoir to recover the oil. The next step is to use various enhanced oil recovery methods: gas flooding, steam stimulation, steam drives, surfactant (detergent) flooding, and polymer drives. Generally, these methods involve the injection of gas (say CO_2), surfactants, steam, or viscous polymers down one well and the production of oil from another well (see Fig. 3). More complex compositional models are used to model these recovery methods.[5] These models may introduce other phases and account for the interactions among the phases.

Now that I have talked about what is being modeled and the models themselves, I will turn to the numerical solution. The Multiple Applica-tion Reservoir Simulator (MARS) has been described elsewhere.[8] This

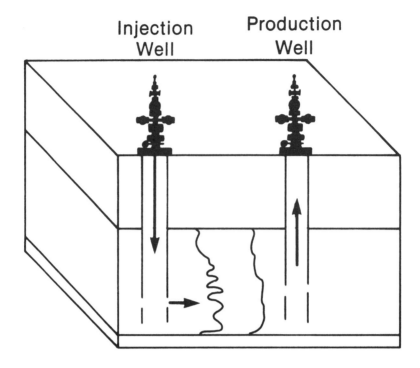

Fig. 3. A reservoir drive.

code is designed to handle both compositional and black-oil models in three spatial dimensions. MARS has several other salient features. These include its ability to run efficiently both on the Cray-1S and on scalar machines. The open literature report of a 30 000-cell model with three phases in three spatial dimensions indicates the problem sizes involved. At the time, this was believed to have been the largest reservoir simulation ever. The problem was run on a Cray-1S, so we have some feeling for current machine requirements. We can also deduce that, if the model were to cover any amount of history and future projection, the problem would require hours of run time. MARS is quite remarkable because it was used for this simulation 6 weeks after the code was released! More generally, MARS uses a few tenths of a millisecond per grid block (a "small" computational segment of the reservoir) per time step. This gives a feel for the grind time [Central Processing Unit (CPU) time per time step per grid block].

This problem area is of general interest for various reasons. Because energy in gas and liquid forms is so important to the world economy,[9] knowing the reserves and economically feasible oil recovery methods is essential. For Exxon, these are clearly vital issues. Further, careful management of reservoirs, which may even be jointly held with other oil companies, is a must.

A few years before I joined Exxon, an oil production manager colorfully described the importance of compositional models. He said, "We go to corporate management and tell them that it will be profitable to pour a million dollars worth of polymers down a hole in Louisiana. It will take time for them to see the return on the investment. Simulations help us convince management it will be worthwhile. We need to be right."

In the practical use of simulators, time can be crucial. Just 2 years ago, a reservoir simulation might have taken weeks on a sequential computer. Now, at EPR in Houston, such a simulation takes but a few hours on the Cray-1S. As oil and gas reserves diminish, it seems to me that enhanced oil recovery methods will increase in importance and that reservoir management will be more demanding than it is today. Consequently the models will be more complex, and even more detailed resolution will be required. My hunch is that EPR scientists and engineers will soon be running simulations of more geologically complex reservoirs whose fluid properties will vary significantly in space and in time. It seems to me that in 2 to 4 years they will be taxing computers significantly more powerful than today's supercomputers.

Chemical Transport Phenomena

We now turn to the downstream problem area of chemical transport. Here we are concerned with phenomena that can be modeled by some simplified form of the equation of continuity for a multicomponent chemically reactive fluid.[10,11] If we look at the time rate of change of the mass concentration of a particular component (or species) in the fluid, it depends on three things: diffusion, convection, and chemical reaction. The solution of one of these models measures the concentration of each of the several components as a function of space and time. Of course, such models can and often do incorporate the Navier-Stokes equations for continuity, momentum, and energy. At ER&E, there are several applications for chemical transport modeling, such as modeling gas scrubbers, baffled reactors, and combustion.

Gas scrubbing—removing undesirable products from stack gases of power plants or production plants—is an important application. For one gas scrubber model, my colleagues and I used the code DISPL2[11,12] to solve a small system of these reaction-diffusion-convection equations.* The reactions involved time constants differing by 8 to 10 orders of magnitude. Problems of this type are called stiff. I introduced a steep, smooth ramp to take care of a very sharp jump in the starting values of the concentrations. On a 1.2-megaflop machine, the wall clock time was about 18 minutes, and about 20 000 words of storage were needed. The 2-dimensional analog of such a problem might require something like an 800-megaflop machine and 19 million words of storage to get an 18-minute wall clock time run. By the way, not long ago, such problems were simply not solved because neither the numerical methods nor the software were available. It really was not just an issue of computing power.

Now that the problem can indeed be solved, it makes sense to talk about wall clock time. These computations were generally done "interactively." That is, one of us ran the job from a terminal and waited for the completion flag. There is some human tolerance time for waiting. Maybe it should be called antsy time. Runs that take more time than antsy time make the computational scientist/engineer impatient or antsy. One minute is the standard American antsy time. A fast response for a problem run is not just for the purpose of making a scientist/engineer feel comfortable. The primary purposes are to speed code or model development, to cut the lag between the gossamer thought about a computer run and the effect, and to eliminate the potential waste of human resources—waiting time. As demands for increased productivity of engineers and scientists increase, and as the cost of computational power decreases, really fast responses will become both necessary and feasible. Meeting the standard American antsy time would require about a 22-megaflop machine for the previous example.

A second application for transport models is in the study of baffled reactors. A cross section of an extremely simplified one is shown in Fig. 4. This type of reactor is sometimes packed with a catalyst; the feed enters one end, reactions with the catalyst take place, and the product exits the other end. Generally, we want the reactions to be complete by the time the material exits, and we want to make sure the catalyst is not dead throughout the reactor. This means that we need to keep track of

*Preliminary documentation for DISPL2 was also discussed with G. K. Leaf and M. Minkoff of Argonne National Laboratory.

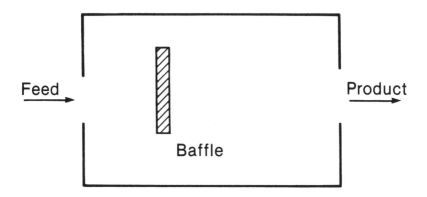

Fig. 4. Cross section of a baffled reactor.

any sharp front depicting the location of strong reactions, perhaps with the catalyst. In that way, a reactor with a dead catalyst can be cut from the production stream for replacement and a refreshed reactor can be cut into the stream. Alternatively, we may be interested in revising the feed, the reactor design, or its operation. Characteristics of such reactors vary markedly with the feedstock, catalyst, and design. The flow may be fairly slow or turbulent. We are currently looking at dynamic grid techniques for solving transport models of baffled reactors. These methods are used to resolve fronts or steep gradients without paying the computational price of resolution where it is not needed.

Let us now take up the third example—combustion. ER&E does have research activities in this area. However, what I will describe is *not* directly related to a specific ER&E project. Alan Hindmarsh and I worked with a combustion model involving nine chemical species.[13] Consequently, there were nine convection-diffusion-reaction (transport) equations, as well as three equations for continuity, momentum, and energy (temperature). This system of equations modeled a carbon monoxide burn. Some preliminary computations showed the disparity in time constants for the reactions to be around 12 orders of magnitude. A simulation of about 0.14 milliseconds of burning took about 90 seconds of CPU time on a CDC 7600 at Lawrence Livermore National Laboratory. On a Cray-1, with very light code messaging, the CPU time was about 27 seconds. In either case, the CPU time was 2000 to 6000 times as long as the event being modeled.

These runs involved just 25 computational grid cells and used a little over 7500 words of storage. A 200-cell run on the Cray-1 took about 198 seconds. We project that two spatial dimensions, with 25 cells in each axial direction, would take around 650 seconds and over 210 000 words of storage. Two hundred cells each direction would probably take 11.5 hours of CPU time and around 13.5 million words for storage. These figures are based on methods that keep storage requirements down! We were able to do these computations in one dimension interactively. It would be a very interesting mainframe that could turn around these high-resolution or two-dimensional computations in the antsy standard of 1 minute. The scale-up to three dimensions from two dimensions should be similar to the scale-up from one dimension to two.

Applications such as these do have value and do warrant the expense for modeling and calculation. ER&E's Thermal DeNOx process uses ammonia to scrub nitric oxides (NOx) from the stack gases of power plants. The process has been substantially improved through numerical modeling. In fact, this particular example involves a gas phase chemical reactor of a slightly different type than the second example. The main reason Hindmarsh and I looked at the numerical simulation of combustion was to develop new numerical strategies. We now believe that some of our results will be useful in several applications areas, including combustion and other reaction-dominant transport phenomena. Even if the antsy time requirements are reduced, future machine requirements will increase in scope. More complex geometries, feedstocks, fuels, or designs can easily stretch the hardware needs. Therefore, the use and evolution of supercomputers are critical factors in further advancement in this problem area.

Scales: A Measure of Problem Size

I have already alluded to the contrast in scales, one of the common threads that links reservoir simulation and modeling of chemical transport phenomena. I will now develop this theme and show how problem size can be roughly estimated by looking at scales.

A computational scientist may quickly and correctly point out that reservoir simulators and transport models use very similar partial differential equations in their mathematical models. These partial differential equations are coupled and nonlinear. Individually, they include terms for diffusion, convection, and depletion or production of a chemical species or phase. What makes these problems interesting and difficult is the sharp contrast in scale of these models. These scales stem directly from the physical properties of models.

In the case of reservoir simulation, we are concerned with a geological formation that may extend several kilometers. Simultaneously, we may be interested in the fingers or thin jagged penetrations of one phase into another, or the rather similar coning effects, especially in simulating miscible or immiscible displacement drives. In managing a water displacement drive, for example, we do not want to produce water when there is still oil to be recovered. To track the front, resolution near a production well must be high. In short, we see a great difference between the spatial scales of the reservoir and the smaller structures of the reservoir or the drive. Similar disparities in time scale also are evident. A reservoir simulation may well be for a 30-year period—tens of years of history and several years of projection. Yet the kinetics in a combustion drive may involve time constants or time scales measured in fractions of seconds.

In the case of chemical transport phenomena, we also observe similar contrasts in scale. The length of time the reacting species reside in a gas phase chemical reactor is likely to be measured in seconds or large fractions of seconds. In sharp contrast, we see that gas phase reactions may vary in duration from approximately the residence time (the time the material spends in the reactor) down to 8 to 10 orders of magnitude smaller than the residence time. Similarly, the length of the reactor may be measured in meters. But the grid structure needed to capture the reaction or concentration front as it moves through the reactor may well be measured in fractions of millimeters.

This contrast of scales has a dramatic impact on the computational requirements. For example, a very rough estimate of the number of time steps is found by dividing the largest time scale by the smallest time scale to yield numbers ranging from 10^6 to 10^{10}. Thus, we see that both reservoir and transport problems may require a tremendous number of time steps. Of course, the choice of method strongly influences the actual number of computational time steps—fixed or variable step schemes, implicit or explicit.

The differences in spatial scale also serve to measure the size of a problem. If we divide the largest spatial scale by the smallest, then we again obtain a large number, say 100 to 100 000. It is a rough measure of the number of equations that must be solved during each time step. Again, we can revise our estimate by getting more information about the grid strategy—dynamic or fixed, uniform or variable density.

Given these very large and complex models, we have to take steps to keep present computing costs reasonable. If we are willing to give up requirements for sharp spatial resolution, then we often do not need as many grid points. If we are willing to require less temporal resolution, then we may get away with larger time steps. Of course, we hope the solution remains sufficiently stable and accurate to adequately model the physical phenomenon. Finally, we can "cheat" by using assorted simplifications in the model—less than three spatial dimensions (perhaps a slab), simplified domains, or spatially independent material properties. This "cheating" often leads to piecing solutions together by hand, perhaps, some extra work to be sure numerical results are valid, and time lost between a computational simulation and its use in the laboratory or in the field. It is also frustrating.

These compromises and this "cheating" lead to low-quality numerical results, if they work. Quite often, they fail. This sharp contrast in scales clearly illustrates the driving force behind the need for supercomputers for two classes of problems of interest to Exxon. Needless to say, these remarks also apply to many of our other problems.

Incentives

Now that we have talked about a few typical examples in some detail, it seems natural to talk about the motives for solving them.

Modeling benefits are great. A reservoir is in production for many years. Yet its production history can be simulated in hours or days. A scrubber installed in a power plant or a pilot plant (a scaled-down facility) may take weeks of running to produce data for the future operation of the power plant scrubber. Yet, a computer simulation can be run in a few hours. Quite often computers simulate events that would not be feasible in the field, because of physical constraints, the time involved, scheduling of the data collection runs, or budgetary limitations.

At ER&E, simulations of the kind discussed have led to substantial cuts in time between process observations in the field and the introduction of revised operating procedures. I am told that in some instances the operation procedures could *not* have been duplicated in the existing pilot plant. The benefits of such modeling are extensive—redesigning a process, perhaps avoiding pilot plant construction, or developing operating procedures for conditions beyond the original design. Perhaps the value cannot be calculated.

With regard to the upstream side, I recently read that of all the estimated oil reserves in the United States, about 40% can be obtained only by enhanced oil recovery methods. Of this percentage, only 40%—about 8.5 billion barrels—can be obtained only by chemical oil recovery methods. Just recovering a small part of that oil would justify a lot of simulation.

The Future

I will now turn to some personal speculation about the future of scientific computation at Exxon.

Supercomputing is now well established at EPR. I believe that in the next several years, the critical mass of demand will lead to the acquisition of a supercomputer for our New Jersey sites. Of course, such an acquisition will need a strong cost/benefit justification. However, I do not feel this justification will be difficult. The parallel computing study identified four ER&E problem areas that would press today's supercomputers. Since then, new compute-intensive project areas have entered the picture. To be frank, we are not solving some important problems because we lack the computing power. Furthermore, we have a growing cadre of scientists and engineers with experience on Crays, big Cybers, and, yes, Stars. We know we need the computer capacity to operate productively and to lay the groundwork to close out the 20th century.

So far, this paper and this conference have dealt with supercomputers—the biggest, most powerful computers extant. The popular press has carried this theme and another—personal computers. At ER&E, we plan to tie these two extremes together.

During the next 5 years, ER&E plans to acquire engineering workstations—small, powerful desktop computers. These machines will be used for a variety of purposes including graphical displays, data acquisition and analysis, small scientific/engineering computations, code development, electronic mail, manuscript preparation, and personal computer file management and retention. These user friendly workstations will be in a network with a mainframe, perhaps a supercomputer. This network and its widespread use will be developed through the rest of this decade.

One scenario might include simultaneous collaborative efforts such as code development or process research at several Exxon sites. Each developer would use a workstation for some segment of the code and for communication with the other partners. The complete package of segments might be pulled together on the mainframe, compiled, and run there. If various networking facilities are added, the potential can be expanded substantially. True, much of the technology is now at hand. However, I do not know of such a network involving true workstations.

There are a few attendant challenges in developing such a network. Many of us have experience in transporting codes between mainframes that have substantial architectural differences. In this setting, I would think this kind of transfer would occur routinely. Algorithmic differences aside, code for a 16- or, perhaps, 32-bit workstation might need some massaging to run on, say a 64-bit mainframe. Yes, there are preprocessors such as the one in MARS or EPISODE,[14] but these put quite a load on the software programmer/designer.

The idea of developing code on a workstation and running it on a supercomputer is intriguing. Chances are that the workstation will be a sequential machine and the supercomputer will be a parallel machine with several vector processors. The algorithms that effectively make use of the architecture of the supercomputer may not even be appropriate for the workstation. A good compiler might help move code from the workstation to the supercomputer and cause it to be run there with a modicum of efficiency. However, it seems unlikely that the underlying algorithms would be redesigned by the compiler. Consequently, the power of the supercomputer would not be used to full advantage.

As for software, there are several issues. Hyman[15] has expressed serious concern for the lack of development of scientific software. Many of us at ER&E have benefited greatly from the use of such software as LINPACK, MINPACK, the SLATEC library, the MUGTAPE, the LSODE family, and DISPL2. I am not aware of any major effort to develop collections of software. That is a worry to me because of the waste in replicated effort of code development. All in all, I personally feel Mac Hyman's view is optimistic!

According to a recent magazine article, some supercomputers are being planned to run in FORTRAN with their exotic new architectures. Furthermore, most of the scientific and engineering codes and libraries I know about are written in some dialect of FORTRAN. I do not know any estimates for the value of the FORTRAN coded software inventory, but I do know that the cost to rewrite these programs is so staggering as to be unthinkable. Granted, some of those codes are ancient. Besides, FORTRAN is evolving, and it now includes the structures that made preprocessors so popular in the mid-1970s. That suits me fine, because I am comfortable with FORTRAN and I think FORTRAN is forever.

In summary, we do supercomputing at Exxon, and our awareness and needs are increasing. I think the future of large-scale computing will be exciting, and we will make remarkable strides. We will soon be modeling phenomena that we simply talked about before. We at Exxon are certainly interested in the efforts to move forward in this field. Many of us expect to be a part of these efforts.

Acknowledgments

This paper is in part a natural consequence of a study of the opportunities for parallel computer processing in Exxon that was conducted in 1982. I gratefully acknowledge the study principals, Dr. R. L. Espino (Exxon Production Research Company), Mr. R. J. Paredi (Exxon Corporation), and Dr. A. M. Lopez (Exxon Research and Engineering Company) for the use of the study reports, their continuing support, and my participation in the study. Dr. M. J. Eisner, Dr. R. S. Stepleman, and Mr. J. D. Bashe provided the management support and encouragement from Exxon Research and Engineering Company. Dr. W. J. Silliman and Dr. J. W. Watts of Exxon Production Research Company were especially helpful.

Finally, I am indebted both to Los Alamos National Laboratory for the opportunity and to Exxon Research and Engineering Company for its realization.

References

1. *Exxon Corporation 1982 Annual Report*. New York:Exxon Corporation, 1982.

2. *The Lamp*. New York:Exxon Corporation, Spring/Summer 1982.

3. Montgomery, P., Bailey, R. H., Glosker, I., and Borea, C. *Century of Discovery*. New York:Exxon Corporation, 1982.

4. *Exxon Research and Engineering Company*. Florham Park, New Jersey:Exxon Research and Engineering Company, 1983.

5. Peaceman, D. W. *Fundamentals of Reservoir Simulation*. New York:Elsevier Scientific Publishing Co., 1977.

6. Odeh, A. S. "An Overview of the Behavior of Hydrocarbon Reservoirs." *SIAM Rev.* **24** (1982):263.

7. *Improved Oil Recovery*. New York:Exxon Corporation, Public Affairs Department, December 1982.

8. Kendall, R. P., Morrell, G. O., Peaceman, D. W., Silliman, W. J., and Watts, J. W. Paper SPE 11483, presented at the Middle East Oil Technical Conference of the Society of Petroleum Engineers, Manama, Bahrain, March 14-17, 1983, Society of Petroleum Engineers, Dallas, Texas.

9. Smith, A. *Paper Money*. New York:Summit Books, 1981.

10. Bird, R. B., Stewart, W. E., and Lightfoot, E. N. *Transport Phenomena*. New York:John Wiley & Sons, Inc., 1960.

11. Leaf, G. K., Minkoff, M., Byrne, G. D., Sorensen, D., Bleakney, T., and Saltzman, J. "DISPL: A Software Package for One and Two Spatially Dimensioned Kinetics-Diffusion Problems." Argonne National Laboratory report ANL-77-12, Rev. 1 (November 1978).

12. Byrne, G. D. "Another View of Stiff Differential Systems." Computing Technology and Services Division report CTSD.3DH.82. Linden, New Jersey:Exxon Research and Engineering Company (1982).

13. Byrne, G. D., and Hindmarsh, A. C. "Experiments in Numerical Methods for a Problem in Combustion." Computing Technology and Services Division report CTSD.1DI.83. Linden, New Jersey:Exxon Research and Engineering Company (1983).

14. Hindmarsh, A. C., and Byrne, G. D. "EPISODE: An Effective Package for the Integration of Systems of Ordinary Differential Equations." Lawrence Livermore National Laboratory report UCID-30112, Rev. 1 (April 1977).

15. Hyman, J. M. "Future Directions in Large-Scale Scientific Computing." Los Alamos National Laboratory report LA-9637-MS (April 1983).

25

A Conducive Environment for Supercomputers

W. C. Norris
Control Data Corporation
Minneapolis, Minnesota

Introduction

It is a great pleasure for me to be here to participate in this important meeting. Let me begin by noting that we must increase our efficiency in developing and applying technology if this country is to reverse its steadily eroding position as the world's technological leader. Further, the most important single step in achieving this objective is a vast increase in technological cooperation. It is in this context that I want to talk about the topic of a conducive environment for supercomputers, which Dr. Kerr asked me to address today.

It is not easy to know what to say that is new, given the flood of news articles, television programs, papers in learned journals, cabinet council discussions, and congressional hearings on this subject in recent months. A few headlines will illustrate the magnitude of the concern in a broad cross section of our national leadership:

"DARPA Chief Touts U.S. Supercomputer Project" (*Computer World*, July 11, 1983);

"U.S. Companies Need Help In High-Tech Fight Congress Told" (*Washington Times*, June 30, 1983);

"Supercomputers—Can The U.S. Beat Japan?" (*Newsweek*, July 4, 1983);

"With Stakes High, Race Is On For Fastest Computer Of All" (*New York Times*, February 1, 1983);

"Land Of The Rising 5th Generation Computer" (*High Technology*, June 1983).

Speaking of Japan, we should frequently be reminded of the challenge the United States faces with respect to its competitive position in world high-technology markets in general and in supercomputers in particular. Our once strong position in technology has been steadily eroding as Japan and other countries have taken a number of steps to accelerate their development and application of advanced technology. Broadly speaking, our foreign competitors have greatly accelerated research and development expenditures, have dramatically increased the number of trained scientific and technical personnel available to them, have reduced the cost of capital for this key industry, have reduced needless and wasteful duplication of technology development, and have fostered growth in targeted areas.

Clearly, the greatest progress in advancing and exploiting technology has been made by Japan in targeted industries where the Japanese government has promoted cooperation among industry members at the base technology level as a key ingredient for success. Automobiles, steel, shipbuilding, and consumer electronics were the principal Japanese industries targeted for development in the generation after World War II. I need not remind you of Japanese success in these areas.

Today, microelectronics and computers have become the most highly subsidized industries, and the supercomputer sector has a particularly high priority within Japan's general thrust. This strategy is an ominous threat that has serious implications for virtually all modern industries because of the pervasive and rapidly growing application within Japanese industries of microelectronics and computer technology products and services. In other words, superior microelectronics and computer technologies provide the critical basis for competitive advantages in almost all other industries. Beyond the threat to industry is the threat to our national security. This country can ill afford to lag in semiconductor and computer technologies because they underpin the superiority of most of our weapons systems.

An adequate response requires myriad actions, however. Increased technological cooperation is a key element—which must include cooperation among large companies, between large and small companies, and among industry, academia, and government. I should also emphasize that to achieve the scope and depth of cooperation needed, legislation to clarify our antitrust laws will be required. Appropriate legislation has been introduced in both houses of Congress, but there is a long way to go before it can become law. Time does not permit adequate discussion of this topic tonight, but just let me say it is vital to our topic—the future of U.S. supercomputers.

Let me return specifically to supercomputers, as I have been directly involved in the supercomputer industry from its birth. Perhaps I can provide some perspective on the environment that spawned it, what history has taught us, and what needs to be done to preserve and enhance it.

First, supercomputers are not the result of a heavenly conception. They simply cannot be designed, developed, manufactured, and brought to useful application in society without a vast underpinning of research and advanced technology. Technologies that are vital to supercomputers include thermodynamics, surface analysis, mathematics, material science, device physics, very large scale integrated circuits, sophisticated manufacturing technology, robotics, computer-aided design software—and the list goes on. In other words, the supercomputer is the result of a vast spectrum of interdisciplinary research and advanced development work. The supercomputer, in turn, is a vital tool to conduct that research and the derivation of those technologies. Within my own company, for example, two Cyber 205 computers are at work around the clock, assisting our design engineers on the development of successor products.

It follows then, that any discussion of a fertile environment for supercomputers must deal in part with the more general requirement for technology development, application, and leadership in a broad spectrum of disciplines if we are to remain technological leaders in supercomputers. Perhaps the first question that I should answer is, "What is a supercomputer?" Today, I want to restrict myself to the breed that is commonly known as large-scale scientific computers. I am not going to talk about the world of artificial intelligence, as important as that may be. Such "super intelligent" machines will no doubt depend on many of the same advanced technologies as supercomputers, but the particular needs of supercomputer development are the ones that require special attention at this point.

That leaves me with the need to define the term "supercomputer" in the context of scientific computing. Perhaps the most apt definition that I have heard is attributable to Neil Lincoln, the principal architect of the Cyber 200 series of computers at Control Data Corporation (CDC). Neil says that a supercomputer is the world's most powerful computing system, but one whose power is an order of magnitude below presently defined needs. A simpler definition is that it is "today's most powerful computer." Thus, in their day, the Eniac, the Edvac, the Univac 1100 series, the CDC 6600, the CDC 7600, the Cray-1, and the Cyber 205 could be legitimately tagged as supercomputers. It is also reasonable to

restrict the title to machines produced in quantity once we got through
the first flurry of invention that occurred in the decade immediately after
World War II. Also, I believe the term first came into widespread use in
the 1960s with the introduction of the CDC 6600.

The Environment That Gave Birth to Supercomputers

History shows that each of these computers was designed and developed
by small teams of highly capable technologists, usually in an environment of high risk. But none of them would have succeeded without the
underpinning of advanced technology that resulted from years of federal
government research and development funding nurtured in an environment of cooperation between the federal government, universities, and
industry. It is no mere coincidence that the rate of supercomputer
innovation has declined during the last decade with a time lag of 5 to 10
years behind the decline of the federal government support of the base
technologies required for supercomputer development, which was high
in the 1950s and 1960s but declined in the 1970s.

In the 1940s and early 1950s, the direct federal government funding of
supercomputer development leaned heavily on the vast reservoir of
electronic technology developed under government auspices during
World War II. In the late 1950s and 1960s, the pattern changed to
government-supported base technology development and the placing of
government orders in advance of development by small companies that
risked their future on technical success with supercomputers.

During the most recent decade, the federal government's approach
has been to buy its supercomputers at arm's length from established
suppliers who take the full risk for their development, and it is no
coincidence that the rate of progress has slowed. Examples of this three-
phased evolution abound.

This "try-before-buy" policy is now common in government procure-
ments and superficially seems equitable in protecting government interest. But it places too much of the risk for developing new supercomputer
technology on the manufacturers without any assurance of a market. In
addition, because the market for supercomputers is relatively small, the
major manufacturers are increasingly unable to justify the necessary
investments to achieve the best performances in the timeframe needed.

Let us look now to a brief history of supercomputer development to
see what it can teach us. The Aberdeen Proving Grounds funded
Brainerd, Eckert, and Mauchly to develop Eniac at the University of

Pennsylvania. Eckert and Manchly started their own company in 1944 to design and market Univac, the first commercial electronic computer. Early on, the government contracted to buy three machines, but the onus was on Eckert and Mauchly to achieve specifications before payment was made—a significant change to the prior procurement pattern. In 1950, they sold out to Remington Rand, which subsequently merged with Sperry in 1955. From then on, while they continued to introduce improvements, their creative genius atrophied in the environment of a large company.

After World War II, I helped form Engineering Research Associates (ERA) to retain a technical resource of vital national importance to the Navy after the war. We had been developing special-purpose electronic systems for cryptology. It was suggested that instead of forming our own company, we should attach ourselves to a public institution such as a university or a research foundation, but we felt the need to better control our destiny by running our own company to avoid the lethargic and often unsupportive environment of a large institution.

ERA was formed in 1946 and in August 1947 a cost-plus-fixed-fee contract was developed for the design of a general-purpose stored computer called Atlas, which was shipped in December 1950. I am convinced that, if ERA had been part of a large institution, development, if it could have been completed at all, would have taken several more years. After ERA was acquired by Remington Rand, out of the Atlas development grew the ERA 1101 and 1103 computers, the first of the Univac 1100 series. In those days, the government customers accepted responsibility for software development. They knew their problems far better than we did; they had the resources, and they made a tremendous contribution to the software art during that period and for many years after.

The National Security Agency (NSA) was a vital catalyst to supercomputer development in those early days. A few of many computer firsts at NSA, all funded under cost-based contracts in the 1940s and 1950s, were the following:

- Demon, the first practical use of magnetic drums;

- Atlas I, the first parallel electronic computer with drum memory;

- Atlas II, delivered by ERA in October 1953, with vastly enhanced input/output capabilities compared to Atlas I;

- LIGHTNING, high-speed circuitry research aimed at a 1000-megacycle computer; and

- Solo, the first completely transistorized computer.

All of these systems were followed by commercial counterparts or exerted a major influence in industry progress.

The LIGHTNING program deserves special mention because of its influence on the development of base technology. In July 1956, NSA launched a series of research studies aimed at a future 1000-megacycle computer with a budget of $25 million for a 5-year effort. Many companies and universitites were involved. Research topics included the following:

- Magnetic thin films with access time of 150 nanoseconds;

- Tunnel diode logic and memory subsystems operating at a 200-megacycle repetition rate; and

- Further development of the cryotron, culminating in a test vehicle with switching speeds of 2 nanoseconds.

The results of Project LIGHTNING were widely communicated in 160 published articles in technical journals, 71 university theses, and 320 patent applications. Fallout from the project is evident in a broad spectrum of subsequent commercially developed computers.

It is clear that the 1950s and 1960s were a most fertile time for the advancement of supercomputers. The environment was characterized by enlightened self-interest and financial support from knowledgeable government agencies working with small entrepreneurial teams of computer engineers focused on the creation of a single product. The work was underpinned by a vast reservoir of base technologies derived largely by government funding in the national laboratories, universities, and major company basic and applied research organizations.

In the late 1950s and 1960s, assistance from the national laboratories was very important. The orders from Lawrence Livermore National Laboratory for the first CDC 6600 and 7600 computers were of enormous help in reducing the risk for CDC. The technical assistance provided by the national laboratories, particularly in system software, was also invaluable. It should also be noted that the CDC 6600 and 7600 developments followed the same pattern of success with a small development team. Seymour Cray's development group never exceeded 30 people and, of course, in the case of the 6600, CDC was a small company.

It is also important to note that the availability of risk capital for small companies over the period since World War II has been unique to the U.S. economy and was vital to spawning the enterprises that have done most to accelerate the state of the art in supercomputers. Eckert and Mauchly, ERA, CDC, and Cray Research, Inc., are salient examples.

Lessons From History

Next, I will talk about some lessons from history after I say a few words about the market for supercomputers. In a nutshell, the worldwide market for supercomputers is small. Although growth is expected, for the next generation the market will be capable of supporting only a few competitors worldwide. Thus, the supercomputer market can be entered with the hope of a reasonable return. However, most companies opt for larger markets with lower risk and the potential for greater returns. Or it can be entered as an item of corporate prestige with the hope that the beneficial image that it carries will provide better than average returns in other product and service lines of the company. To say the least, the second motivation is too tenuous a proposition on which to bet our national survival and international competitiveness.

For whatever reason entry is attempted into the supercomputer market, I have to conclude that direct government support is necessary. It should take two forms. The first is to provide funding for national laboratories and universities to buy and use supercomputers. This will serve to increase the size of the market so that more competitors can stay in the game. Secondly, it will help enormously in the development of base technology within the national laboratories and universities, and that technology can, in part, be the catalyst for new advances in supercomputers.

The funding available for national laboratories and universities to buy supercomputers has seriously declined since 1970. For example, since that time CDC has delivered 85 Cyber 7600 and Cyber 176 computer systems, not one of which was procured for a university in this country. In contrast, we have delivered seven 7600 systems to universities abroad. Two Cyber 205 systems are installed in the U.S. universities, while three are installed and a fourth is on order in European universities, and we wonder why the rest of the world is gaining on us so rapidly in basic research and advanced technology!

To the best of my knowledge, there are only three supercomputers installed in U.S. universities today—at Colorado State, the University of Minnesota, and Purdue. Each of them is underutilized, and other university researchers are unable to take advantage of their research benefits because of lack of funds. So first let's increase government funding for the purchase and use of supercomputers within the national laboratories and universities, particularly the latter.

The second needed form of support is for the government to assume more of the funding risk for supercomputer development and the advanced technology on which it relies. Industrial cooperative enterprises, such as the Microelectronics and Computer Technology Corporation (MCC) and Semiconductor Research Corporation (SRC), can bear some of that advanced technology burden but not enough of it. The funding risk for actual supercomputer development can be alleviated by a commitment to purchase quantities of supercomputers in advance of their development.

Direct government research and development funding beyond basic advanced technology should be concentrated in the area of applications. Learning to fully use the power of new architectures is a painfully slow process, but this could be much faster if there was more directly sponsored government work in universities and laboratories to better apply these machines to important classes of problems.

The second lesson is that the product development, per se, is best done by small engineering teams working in an environment that is uncluttered by bureaucracy. The small company is undoubtedly the most conducive environment for such development. It is entrepreneurial. It is dedicated. Its personnel have fortunes to gain from success and bankruptcy to face from failure. There is no better motivation for hard and creative work. The small company lacks deep pockets and is, therefore, forced to focus on the simple, direct route to success.

More subtle, but nevertheless important, are the inevitable demands for at least "synergy" if not "conformity" in product development amongst various development groups in large companies. Almost by definition, developers of the ultimate possible at any given state of the art must be freed of such constraints. While this is theoretically possible, as a practical matter in large companies, it is difficult to sustain. Government agencies and national laboratories who place advanced orders can look forward to a far closer working relationship with a small company than is possible with a large corporation. That relationship can be the stimulus for more beneficial cooperation between the parties, if for no other reason that that the chief executive officer is inevitably more accessible—and if the small company gets out of line, the government's kick, if it chooses to kick, will be felt far more keenly in a small company than in a big one.

The government also, it seems to me, is less vulnerable to the accusation and fact of providing unfair competitive advantage to the small company than would be the case if the same contract were awarded to an established competitor. There is also enormous untapped potential that can be brought to bear on this problem by way of greatly increased cooperation between large business and small business. Studies show that small companies produce 24 times more innovations per dollar than larger ones.

By making available its underutilized technology and by offering its professional and management assistance to a small company, a large company can realize additional income from past investment; and through equity investment in and research and development contracts with small companies, large companies can gain more economical access to new products and markets. Several years ago my company started a program for making equity investments in small companies and offering other types of assistance. There are now over 70 of these companies, many of which are developing products and services using CDC technology as well as their own. In some cases, CDC markets the resulting products; in some cases, both of us do, and in many cases—especially those involving specialized markets—the company has sole marketing responsibility.

The potential of cooperation between large and small businesses, particularly in the context of supercomputer development, can hardly be overemphasized. This opportunity is not as readily available to other countries because of lack of a well-developed securities market where equity capital can be raised by small companies. Therefore, we must capitalize on it, just as the Japanese capitalize on the unique attributes of their culture.

The Future

With the history and the lessons from the past in perspective, what, then, should be the future course of action for the United States? I believe that much of the answer to that question is implicit in what I have already said, but let me try to summarize it. There are three major points.

First, cooperation is required among government, universities, and industry in the development of base technologies that are vital to effective supercomputer product development. The ingredients for success in this respect are beginning to be put into place.

It is clear that the federal government, as evidenced by initiatives of the Departments of Energy and Defense, is prepared to take needed steps with regard to base technologies. On the industry side, MCC, a consortium of large companies in those industries, has ambitious plans to derive some of the needed base technologies. MCC is probably the best vehicle to provide needed base technologies, but it clearly needs a greater resource commitment if it is to fully achieve its potential.

SRC is another important cooperative effort to stimulate basic research in microelectronics within our universities, and its work is in consonance with and complementary to MCC. MCC and SRC exist; they can be major conduits for government support of some of the needed base technologies. In addition to the concentration of intellectual and capital resources that MCC and SRC provide, they are also very important vehicles for the widespread dissemination of resultant technologies for greater national gain and enhanced competition within the industry.

The second point is the need for direct government support. One obvious form is increased funding for national laboratories and universities to buy and use supercomputers; but beyond that—and this is a crucial distinction from more recent practice—is for the government to assume more of the funding risk for supercomputer development. This can best be achieved by advanced commitment to the purchase of successfully developed supercomputer systems to assure the developers a start in a market.

Direct government support is also needed to bring about widespread acceptance of machine architectures that are different from traditional scalar machines. The government can and should do this by concentrating funding in universities on research in applying those nontraditional architectures to major scientific applications.

The third and final point is the need to foster smaller entrepreneurial companies engaged in the development of supercomputers. This is a responsibility of both government and industry. Government can clearly help by the way in which it channels procurement funds. Industry, however, has the prime responsibility, and this must take the form of greatly increased cooperation between large business and small business. The best way I know to show what needs to be done is by example, and that is what CDC intends to do. Because this is so important in the future of U.S. supercomputers, I have left its description until last.

Tonight, for the first time, I am announcing that CDC is helping to establish this month a new supercomputer company whose name is Engineering Technology Associates (ETA) Systems. CDC will take a minority position in ETA, and the rest will be held by its employees and the public. The business purpose of ETA Systems is simply to design, manufacture, and market the world's fastest scientific computers. Its initial product mission will be to develop a 10-gigaflop machine for delivery by the end of 1986. To do this, the architecture, very large scale integration technology, and software that CDC has been developing under the project for successor machines to the Cyber 205 will be transferred to the new enterprise. Thus, initially the technology will flow from CDC to the new company. We will also provide arms-length technical and management consulting services, design services, and possibly some administrative services. This will allow the organization to concentrate its financial resources and people on development of the new product. CDC will also make a commitment for a certain number of the initial machines. But lest I be misunderstood, that is only an initial supportive measure. One of the major secondary benefits of supercomputer development at CDC has been the flow of technology from that group to the main computer product line. Through cross-licensing arrangements, we will continue to enjoy such benefits. In fact, we will undoubtedly enjoy an increased and long-term technological benefit to our computer product line; so the ultimate beneficiaries of this will be CDC's customers, present and future, from supercomputers to the bottom of the line.

There is much more that could be said, but time is running out, so let me close with one last point. Through its 26 years, CDC has been a leader and an innovator in many regards, but perhaps the most important of these has been with regard to technological cooperation. We have pursued that course long and vigorously—from simple one-on-one cooperation in circuits and architecture to undertakings such as MPI, which became a billion-dollar enterprise, to MCC, which can become a major source of U.S. microelectronics and computer technology. Because of these undertakings, not only has CDC survived and prospered, but literally thousands of small companies have had access to more affordable technology and products.

With ETA we are taking yet another step—one that will not only help assure CDC's future in supercomputers, but will also help assure our nation of leadership in an arena of vital national importance.

26

The Role of Universities in High-Performance Computing

K. G. Wilson
Cornell University
Ithaca, New York

Many talks at this conference have concentrated on government or university needs. I believe our central focus should be the scientific computing needs in industry.

At the present time, industry buys International Business Machine's (IBM) 3081s the way you and I would buy cakes of soap—by the thousands. They do not buy them exclusively for scientific engineering computing; they, of course, use them predominantly for business data processing. But the scientific/engineering computing load on those machines is not trivial. IBM estimates that 15 to 20% of the load is scientific/engineering computing, and the scientific/engineering computing needs of industry are growing even relative to the growth of industrial computing as a whole. Industrial computing budgets are growing faster than inflation; that is how IBM's income grows faster than inflation. I think this means it is inevitable that at some time in the future—maybe in 5 years or, more likely, 10 years—industry will be buying $10 million to $20 million scientific engineering work horses the way they are buying 3081s today. Those work horses will have to be supercomputers in order to run the largest jobs that industrial, scientific, and engineering users will be putting on those machines.

The problem is that the supercomputer market, which today is described as small and high risk, will be neither. The question is, are we going to be ready for that? The Japanese superspeed computing projects could leave the Japanese companies in a position to be off and running and serving that huge market just at the time it develops. Whether that is due to foresight of the Japanese planners or incredible luck, I cannot tell; but the explanations that the Japanese give for why they have that project, I find, do not make sense. All their other national projects have had obvious market emphasis—trying to sell automobiles or electronics for example. Here is this project, and they say its purpose is to do a seismic map of the Sea of Japan. Are they serious? The oil industries, which make as much money as Japan, do not have a superspeed computing project even to do an entire world seismic map.

I am discussing a scientific engineering work horse; I'm not talking about a bare computer, like a Cray-1 or a CDC 205. Industry needs a complete system. It will be difficult for the Japanese to produce such a system. But what could happen is that we in the U.S. could build a complete system around Japanese hardware. If the Japanese have the hardware and they're the only people who have the hardware that U.S. industry needs, we will build a system around it, just as Cray builds their supercomputers around Japanese components.

Now I see two dangers in this. The first danger is in the technology itself. If they have the technology to build the supercomputers and we do not, that creates various difficulties, such as balance of payments problems. If we are talking about a market of thousands of Japanese-built supercomputers, that is going to be noticed in our balance of payments. But there is even a more serious danger: when our industry is ready for those scientific work horses and needs those scientific work horses, nobody will be making them. Now, we are talking about a thousand supercomputers, like today when you talk about thousands of 3081s. Industry is not going to want those supercomputers so they can play with them; they will have worked out procedures for fully justifying the costs of those machines. We are talking about tens of billions of dollars to buy these machines. That means hundreds of billions of dollars of profits are at stake. We cannot afford not to supply that need when it arises. That need is in civilian industries who are trying to maintain their position in international competition; it is in the industrial base for our military strength, companies like Lockheed, and so forth. I have listened to people from Lockheed talking about their future needs.

How do we deal with this problem? First of all, I see only one way that can lead us to a solution of this problem: we have to create a perception in the U.S. computing industry of the market to come, and we have to create that perception sufficiently in advance so that they do something about it. It is not simply a question of designing a machine that is 200 times the Cray, of which they can produce three examples, one for Los Alamos, one for Livermore, and one for NSA. You cannot get thousands of machines if you have persons in Chippewa Falls putting wires on the machine by hand. We have to create a perception of the market so that the computing industry will not simply design these machines but will make the incredible investment in manufacturing technology and all the other things so that they can crank them out like cakes of soap. I remind you that the biggest problem the computing industry has today is that, when they have a machine that sells, they cannot produce enough of them. Digital Equipment Corporation (DEC) could not produce enough VAXs and IBM cannot produce enough PCs; it is not even clear whether IBM can produce enough 3081s. Unfortunately, you are not going to solve that problem by having the U.S. government buy three of these machines in 1990. That is is not going to lead to the kind of investment that has to be made.

What is the chief barrier to supercomputer market growth? The chief barrier is the software problem. That software problem has two parts. One part that we have heard a lot about is the system software, how the machine looks to the user. The other barrier is in the development of applications, and that comes down to FORTRAN. It takes an enormous effort to produce applications software, and I do not care how good the system is. In fact, that effort is so enormous that what you see in industry is, on one hand, the running codes that have taken 20 years to develop to the present level. On the other hand, one sees problems facing industries for the future where basically the industries know what they have to do, but nobody has the guts to sit down and say, "Let's program this up." Those people have in their minds the kind of effort it's going to take to produce these new applications, and they are not about to get started. Finally, there are the problems of applications that are up and running, but are running out of computing power. At least, I have inferred from some of the development recently that there have been cases where the future of a company was at stake in getting simulations running on a faster machine, and they could not do it. That is a software problem.

What really scares me is that over the next 5 years or so, we will solve the software problem. I think there are ways of solving that problem, but if we spend 5 years doing that, we will help the Japanese sell computers. We cannot spend 5 years solving the software problem because we are going to be too late if it takes us 5 years.

What do we have to do in an organizational sense to deal with the software problem? The ideas for solving this problem exist in the computer science community. There are computer scientists in the universities, and there are computer scientists in some industries like Xerox Park. But the problem is that those computer scientists are isolated. They are isolated from the application areas and from the computing industry. Hardly any conversation or interchange takes place between the computer scientist and the application areas, between the computer scientist and the computing industry, even when the computer scientists are in the computing industry. Another very key part of the problem is the way programmers are trained. The present view in universities, which is where the primary training takes place, is that to teach somebody in science to compute, you only give them a 2-week course in FORTRAN. And the result of that attitude is directly visible in the millions of lines of FORTRAN code that are immobile.

I want to talk about the training problem because I think we can solve the training problem more rapidly than we can solve the other kinds of software problems. You all know that there are programmers who do not have a software problem; they produce a code in a week that would take anybody else a year to do. You heard Jim Glimm mention Oliver McBryan; he is one of those people. John Swanson, who is the author of Ansys, is another of those people. Now those people come in two classes. One kind of person writes code, and you look through it and cannot figure out how he did that and how he could understand what he did. But there are other people who write code that is incredibly modular. What they have done is build up libraries of these modules; and their programming consists mostly of pulling things out of library, making a few changes, and then they are up and running. Both Oliver McBryan and John Swanson are in that last category. They have learned how to plan their coding so that most of the time they do not have to code at all. In the training process, instead of teaching the students that if you've got an "if" statement and a "do" statement, you had better not put a comma in the wrong place, we should teach them how to do modular code by giving them examples of the kind of code that Oliver McBryan writes. We should tell them to write programs like that. In fact, we should tell them with their first program to bring it back and we will tell them all the things that they didn't do right; that is the way we've got to train them. We could set those training programs up in 6 months. We do not have to wait 5 years. And we had better do that.

But how, more generally, should we organize to try to attack the fundamental problem, which is to create a perception in the U.S. computing industry of the kind of market that is to come, so that Control Data Corporation (CDC) does not merely put $40 million into Engineering Technology Associates (ETA), but billions of dollars get put into creating the systems that are going to be needed in the future? We need to do two things, I think. We have got to end the isolation of computer science. It's absolutely essential that we start finding the good ideas that the computer sciences have and get them flowing into the applications areas, into the computer industry, into the big users of computing industry. And we have to do it in the right way. That means we cannot tell everybody in industry to use VAL because they are not about to be retrained to be academic computer scientists so they can use VAL. What we have to do is learn how to use the ideas from computer science so that the FORTRAN programmers in industry and government and academia can discover that all they have to do is go through the specification process for their programs. They have to do that anyway; they have no choice. When they finish doing the specification, they should be done. We've got to give them a system so that the way the FORTRAN programmers react is not, "Oh my God, not another language!" but, "When I finish writing this, it's going to work." In other words, we have got to use the computer science ideas that can help that to happen. But at the same time, we have got to package them so that the difficult part of computer science is hidden from the user and they are not forced to go through all the garbage that is involved in learning another language.

The second thing we have to do in order to drive the supercomputer market, I think, is not so much in the systems area, but to build up the reservoir of applications programs that makes the engineers and scientists in industry scream for more computing power, scream for more money to buy computers. What should the government do to try to help this process? I think the focus has to be in the university because that's the only place to get the kind of bold thinking and leaping that's going to make it possible to move fast on this problem. I've been watching what's happening in the national labs and at Cornell, and I have to be frank about it—I think a place like Cornell can move orders of magnitude more quickly in trying to create new concepts and new ways of attacking this problem than the national laboratories can. Also, the absolutely critical issue is training of programmers. Not simply how students are trained because they will enter the market too late to have the kind of impact we need to have. We have to learn how to do training so effectively that people from industry will come back to learn the new procedures. That is the only way we can get the system moving on a fast enough time scale to have the needed impact. So I think we need to have a focus on the universities; we need to get the computing power to them, not simply the Cray and CDC systems, but also the examples of the parallel processing systems to come. We need to get the applications people in universities to work side by side with the computer scientists on the question of getting applications programs running in 1 week that would formerly have taken us a year to do. We must bring in the expertise from people who already know how to do that, because I emphasize, there are people who already know how to do that; it's not something we have to invent. And we must have industrial associates programs in the universities. For example, we could have industry come to Cornell and help provide money for the machines needed at Cornell, for the computer access needed outside Cornell, and for hiring the graduate students and encouraging the faculty to participate in this stuff. You must have connections to industry in that program; you must have exchanges between people from Cornell and the people at Exxon, etc., so that what is learned at Cornell goes immediately to industry and vice versa. In fact, it's necessary for people at Cornell to see what the industrial problems are so that they can meet the industrial needs faster than if they just sit in isolation in an ivory tower.

Perhaps if you do put a supercomputer in a university, it's going to take a longer time to bring it up and get it started than if you put it at a national laboratory (although Colorado State and the University of Minnesota are past the startup stage). But, we have to put supercomputers in universities anyway to symbolize the fact that the universities are important and to give the faculty and students who do want to participate in this effort the pride of ownership. What you want out of the university faculty is incredible creativity. If you put faculty only on national laboratory computers, they react the way somebody reacts when they're renting a house. They're not creative about keeping that house fully beautiful and up to date if it's somebody else's house. The same thing happens with computers. If you want the creativity of the university faculty that you need for this process to happen, the faculty must own something. So you put some of the supercomputers in universities, even if it does take a while for them to come up to speed. And you put some supercomputers wherever you can get them running the fastest so that people can start running their jobs. You must put the experimental parallel processing systems in universities or you won't get anything; I know, because I've been dealing with experimental computing systems for 5 years now. Unfortunately, the array processors continue to be experimental even 5 years after we started them. But I know very well that if I had been told that our array processor would be put at Los Alamos and we would have access to it, we at Cornell would have refused to participate.

So to summarize, we've got a problem. It is a much larger problem than has typically been discussed at this conference, because the problem is not that there's a special interest group of a few scientists in a few national laboratories who want unlimited computing power. The problem is in industry, and the problem is the future competitiveness of the entire industry. Whenever I go to industry, I see that the situation is much more universal than anybody thinks. Among the companies I've talked to are Phillip Morris and Kraft Foods. Among those at Cornell who want access to large scale computing are the food science department people; the problem is not just in aerodynamics. I think we have to know what the problem is; otherwise, we will point our efforts at the wrong target. For instance, we talk about guaranteed government support by 1990. That's not the problem. Three supercomputers in 1990 will be a drop in the bucket. It'll be like guaranteeing IBM that we would buy three 3081s. On the other hand, it is incredibly important to buy supercomputers today. Get them into universities so we can get started on these problems today, so that in 1990 the computer manufacturers will be producing supercomputers like they produce 3081s today. Above all, we must do everything possible to enable the ideas of modern computer science to get into real use. Support the universities, do anything, but get the applications people talking to the computer scientist, because I don't think there is anybody else who can talk to the computer scientists at this point, except for people like myself in universities. We have to help the computer scientists understand what the applications problems are. They don't understand. I know because I've had a computer graduate student talking to a physics graduate student, and they've spent days just learning how to talk to each other. We need to get these computer science ideas flowing into the application areas—and I think that is going to happen in the universities, if it's going to happen any place. And we should make sure that goes on and flows into industry as rapidly as possible.

The one final thing I would mention, and it is extremely important, is that when you need cooperation, when you need technology flow, when you need people talking to people, the best way to get that to happen is computer networks. It has been demonstrated over and over again in ARPANET that the computer networks are fantastic for getting people to talk to each other. For example, they enable somebody in industry who has a problem with some compound (maybe it's gallium arsenide) to get on a computer network to find a person who knows something about that compound. The reason you get replies is that, when you're on a computer network and you want to be known as an expert, you'd better reply to those requests to demonstrate that you're the expert.

27

How To Succeed in Supercomputing

J. Rollwagen
Cray Research, Inc.
Minneapolis, Minnesota

As we move from a "make and break" experimental science to a practical, three-dimensional simulation of physical phenomena, we are already experiencing a tremendous interest in the technology—a tremendous attraction for the machines well beyond the national laboratories and universities and deep into industry. Much interest and a lot of excitement are reflected by an expanding market. We are still talking about small numbers, so I hesitate to give you numbers and try to generalize, but it may be instructive to think of them. Last year, our company received 16 contracts for 16 orders. That is not very many in terms of numbers, but it is substantial, based on what we expected when the company started. When we set out to manufacture machines, our objective was to produce four per year. We thought the maximum production for the Cray-1 would be about 25, and we have just shipped our 55th. If you count the Cray-1M, there will be at least 100 Cray-1s in the future. We got 16 orders just last year, and I will make a couple of observations about that.

Ten orders came from Europe, and six of them were from the U.S. firms. Note that we are participating in an international business. I know that I need not tell you that, but I have to emphasize the specific importance to us, as a company, in being able to participate internationally, both economically and technically.

We set an objective to sign 22 contracts this year. We thought that we could sign perhaps 10 outside the U.S. and 12 inside the U.S. However, something more is happening. I am having arguments now with our marketing people, and I am saying it cannot be true. They say, "You tell us what names to take off the list, John." Maybe I should not be saying this—because it will interest Engineering Technology Associates (ETA) and Denelcor—but when I look at the list now, I think we have an excellent chance of signing 30 contracts in 1983. That is a remarkable number, although it is not fact yet. So far in the year, we have signed 13, but we have letters of intent and provisional purchase orders that would cover the rest of the 30. I wanted to share the news because it is exciting.

Of the 30, most would be new customers to Cray Research. Two-thirds of the people would be new customers who have never had a supercomputer before, so they are starting with our smaller machine, the Cray-1M, but that is a substantial step and a significant event. Our sales involve very small numbers; they are not enough to base a whole national strategy on. They *are* enough to base a Cray strategy on, but not a national strategy. We see much of the activity in the U.S.; about two-thirds of our business will be in the U.S. and about one-third overseas, but that one-third is still important.

Something is happening in the market place, and that is very positive news for us all. I want to say quickly that, even though we see obvious growing needs in the commercial area, we recognize the significance of the leadership role that the laboratories have played in prodding us to move ahead and giving us the most challenging applications. The laboratories may not, in the future, represent as much of our business as they have in the past, but they enable our business by forcing us to move ahead and to do the most advanced operations.

Naturally, we are going to be inclined to take an incremental approach, but we also want to maintain the pace as fast as we can. Architecturally, from my point of view, we are just now learning how to use vectors. A whole range of problems is going to emerge and is already emerging in multiprocessors with only a few processors.

When you consider the massive parallel-type machines that will be developed, some very aggressive things are happening in the industry and in academia now. I think we are challenged to keep up with them. I think that machine architecture is being affected dramatically by memory technology, such that large memories will be associated with these machines. We are already talking about a memory to be available at the end of next year: 256 million 64-bit words of central memory on the Cray-2, supplemented with incredibly fast input/output (I/O) subsystems. Seymour Cray wants the Cray-2 to be able to strike files across 32 disks at the same time, with a huge memory and buffers large enough that you can operate asynchronously; he wants to be able to read off a sector or a whole cylinder from every disk into the memory. It is a practical idea and it can be done. Just think about the bandwidth to that disk system.

Furthermore, from my perspective—and mine is a little shorter than some of yours—these improvements are not inconsistent with past developments. Typically, there has been a five- to sixfold improvement in performance since the late 1950s or early 1960s, every 5 to 7 years. Production of the Cray-2 took a little longer than we thought, primarily because of the component problems. But it is progressing. The Cray-1 represented a similar step, so there is something to build on; it is not as if the Cray-2 had to be initiated from nothing.

Components, especially the memories, are changing right now. The availability of 256K dynamic chips—and soon, at least 16K or 64K static metal oxide semiconductor (MOS) chips and larger bipolar chips—is significant, making that large memory possible. We are very excited about developments in gallium arsenide and in high-electron mobility technology. We are designing a machine built of gallium arsenide to be available early in the second half of the decade. A major transformation will probably take place in the 1990s. After reading papers that Ken Wilson of Purdue University has written in the past, I think that Seymour Cray and our industry have been building left brains. These are big, dumb, but fast machines that follow one step at a time. I think that we are on the threshold of exploring at least the idea of building right brains. These massively parallel machines with new kinds of architecture and new kinds of software and algorithms perhaps can simulate how we make intuitive leaps. I think there is some promise but it will take a long time to develop it, and I think that is a major change in thinking. We cannot think serially as we have in the past. We must think more parallel structure, and I think that probably Seymour Cray, himself, will not participate. His career will probably span the development of the left-brain computer, but people like Steve Chen and others in our organization and other organizations will participate in this new kind of machine development. Prospects look very exciting, but it will be even more interesting when we marry the two types of computers: left-brain and right-brain types.

The last message I bring to you is that we are ahead. Do not panic. It is not over yet. Between us and Control Data Corporation (CDC), we have installed about 75 or 80 of the current-generation supercomputers, compared with zero from anywhere else—or small numbers from anywhere else. Certainly, none are from Japan. At the rate things are going, our sales will exceed 100 within the next 12 months. So today we are ahead. Neither the Japanese manufacturers nor anyone else can exhibit a standard system that exceeds the performance of either the 205 or the

Cray-1, including even the announced machines from Fujitsu and Hitachi. I know very little about what NEC Corporation has in mind, but I have some suspicions. In my opinion, even the machines announced for delivery within the next 24 months do not exceed and do not, in my opinion, match the performance of the latest machine that we have to offer, the X-MP. So keep that in mind; it is important. Let us not give up or throw the baby out with the bath water.

Obviously, we have very serious challenges. Customer's needs and expectations are extremely high. It is not unusual to hear people talking about the need for a machine 1000 times more powerful than Cray-1. Even the X-MP is not that, nor even the Cray-2 or the gallium arsenide Cray-2. So there is obviously an increase in requirements in the future.

I think that a machine in the average range 20 to 100 gigaflops will be necessary sometime around the end of the decade. It ought to be built, and it probably will be built. Obviously, our expectations will not build it, but somebody is going to build it. We are not the only ones who have identified the need. You all know, too, that Japan, France, and the United Kingdom (UK) have set up specific national goals to make these kinds of machines. They are spending the equivalents of hundreds of millions of dollars to do that, and I am sure that part of the European Economic Community (EEC) effort now will be dedicated to the same thing. Furthermore, alliances are being formed. Fujitsu has arranged with International Computers, Limited (ICL) in the UK to market their computers, including supercomputers. Fujitsu has arranged with Siemons, similarly, in Germany. Hitachi has arrangements with Olivetti. Hitachi has agreements with National Semiconductors, and NEC Corporation and Honeywell are very close. They have not announced an agreement yet, but I suspect that an agreement between those two companies will move ahead. These alliances are part of our future.

Furthermore, and this is probably the scariest thing from our jingoistic point of view, the technology is appearing outside the U.S. It is no coincidence that we buy more than one-half of our parts now from Japan. But that is not because our manufacturers are not trying. Our U.S. suppliers are trying. They are working very hard, and I admire them for their efforts. I think that they are committed to doing something, but we are still buying one-half of our parts in Japan.

I talked about the importance of the business to us internationally, but something else is coming too. Bill Norris gave some statistics in "A Conducive Environment for Supercomputers" that illustrate this, so maybe this is repetitive. By my count, six or seven supercomputers are now installed in European universities, counting the 205s and Cray-1s; these supercomputers are available for use throughout the system. Only three are online in the U.S; Colorado State and Purdue both have 205s, and the University of Minnesota has a Cray-1. Furthermore, the Japanese universities are very important in the development going on in manufacturing there. The University of Tokyo is a Hitachi test bed, and they are receiving new equipment all the time. The University of Nagoya and the plasma physics staff have Fujitsu equipment. We are trying to close the same deal with Osaka, but Japan's Department of Education is saying that maybe Osaka ought to hook up to Nagoya. We will negotiate. After the announcements by Fujitsu, Hitachi, and NEC Corporation in Japan, we have more prospects in Japan right now than we have ever had before. We never expect to dominate the market in Japan, but we are going to be part of that market place. We already are; we have two systems installed. In that way, all of this activity is very palliative. Again, if we sell machines in Japan, that is a good deal for all of us, I think.

I think that we have the resources to move ahead, and I think we can. As we look at the situation, we must learn from the past and try to build on our strengths. Consider Seymour Cray and what he has done over the years. He personally has played a key role in this business. He has provided leadership by working with small groups of people but with little money, with a very ambitious goal in each case, and with no backup. Each is a do-or-die effort. When the Cray-1 was developed, it was assembled in about 4 years from the first equation on a piece of paper to the machine itself. The first Cray-1 cost $8.5 million to build from beginning to end. It has the power, although it was not too realizable without software, of five 7600s.

If you will remember back to the early 1970s, many people thought that there was no supercomputer business anymore. CDC had decided to close out its production. When Cray Research was begun, CDC put up 20% of the money, and they owned 20% of the stock. They have since sold their stock very profitably. When Cray Research was established, however, common thought was strongly against financing Seymour Cray's fantasies. Rewards to investors and staff have been ample, nevertheless.

As a practical matter, to design and build this hardware, a small staff with little money seems to work. But what I am considering is hardware, and I want to return to some of the essential points that Ken Wilson ("The Role of Universities in High-Performance Computing") made about advancing the state of the art. I think there is a very specific reason why advances are made the way they are, and it is something we are very conscious of at Cray Research. No matter where supercomputers are going to be developed, at least their hardware and probably their software must be considered in what happens in a large organization. In our company many people worked with Seymour Cray to develop the Cray-1. There were probably 25 people involved in the final analysis, and it was time to start on the Cray-2. When you set out to build a machine that will be 5 to 10 times faster than the previous machine you made, the only thing you know when you start out is that what you did last time will not work better this time, by definition.

What is the real chemistry among the people in the organization? These people have worked on the Cray-1 and it is highly successful. It is being produced now and they are proud of it. They are excited about it, they feel they have accomplished something, and they want to build on that. They want to pass their knowledge to other people. So what do they do? They sit down and start writing things down. This is what we did on the Cray-1. These are the standards that we imposed on ourselves when we designed the Cray-1, and these are the manufacturing requirements that we established when we decided to build the Cray-1. We are still participating in the Cray-1, because the production staff calls us up when they have problems building it, and they ask us what we did when we designed it.

You have to establish design standards. You want to build on what you have learned from the past; and when that book is put together, do you know what you must do with it? You do not actually burn it; you keep it so that you do not regret anything in that book. That really happens in a large corporation. It happened to Seymour Cray at least twice. He keeps the book only so he can violate the rules, and that continues to be essential in our business. It must be built into the plan, and we are building it into our company. We are trying to run our company that way, and I am extremely proud and will not hesitate to brag that the X-MP now has been delivered. I claim that it is an unprecedented event in that no one else in the last 25 years has been able to substantially outperform Seymour Cray's current machine. People have caught up, people have been a little ahead in some applications and behind in other applications, but I claim that no one has been able to substantially exceed his performance. He says the same thing. By the same token, I will be extremely proud when the Cray-2 is delivered at the end of next year to its first user. Once again, Seymour will have reasserted himself as a leader by means of a piece of hardware.

Other systems can be developed, and other groups can be established to work on machines, and that is great! I have no problem with that whatsoever, but we will keep doing what we are doing now, and so far it works. When we find out it no longer works, we will switch. The market place has provided the incentive for us to develop systems, and it still can. There is no question about it in my mind, as long as you maintain your commitment to buy these machines and press us into doing more. Producing about three machines in 1990 does not really fit into our strategic plans; however, production of three machines next year gets our attention, and producing 30 machines the year after that really does. This market place must be a demanding market place, particularly from a technical standpoint.

Also, access to the foreign market is very important to us, and obviously, it needs control. We are not talking about selling these machines to the Russians. We are talking about selling them to France and to Sweden. Exporting them presents certain problems, but we must be able to find a way. What we need, and I really want to emphasize this, is not to do it by ourselves. We are not alone. There is only one nonzero-sum game that I know about, and that is when two smart people talk to each other and exchange information. When one gives information to the other, the first person still has it. They both come away from the exchange better off than they were before. Cooperation, at least at the technical exchange level, is extremely important, and we are committed to continuing that. We are trying to expand our connections directly with universities as much as we can. Naturally, we want to work closely with the laboratories and with all our users. I mean that in the most serious way, and to do that, frankly, we do not need the Microelectronics and Computer Technology Corporation (MCC). We need no special government agency through which to operate to provide this exchange. We know who you are, and we will come and find you. If we can't find you, come and find us. We want to talk, and we want to exchange data.

I want to close by emphasizing that using is much more important than making in our business. It is hard to make these computers; that is obvious. Not many people can do it. But using is much more, and we need many more trained people. That is the gating factor—the software and the application of software, particularly, but also the system software and the languages as well.

We have only scratched the surface of where these machines can be used. We know that is true, and yet when we go out now and call on a Phillip Morris or a DuPont or whoever, we are really starting a missionary effort. Remember, if you are depending on us, we have only 25 or 30 salesmen in the world. I do not know how many CDC has, but to sell the 205, CDC probably does not have many more. We cannot provide the educational processes required to fire up new customers. They know that they want something, but if you think our companies are conservative, you should talk to some of the big industrial companies and find out how conservative they are. If we can demonstrate to them that when we simulate a reservoir, they can use it to find up to $2 billion more oil and we can prove that to them absolutely, then maybe they will spend $10 million for one of our machines. Probably they will, but we must convince them. Three simulations were required to get the first oil company contract. We need help. Supercomputers will be important to industry. They want the supercomputers, but we need your help.

Anything that the government or anyone else can do to train more people who will explore new and interesting applications on supercomputers and who will gain good experience is money well spent. I wholeheartedly endorse any program of expanding access to existing machines and experimental machines in the universities and laboratories. I think the laboratories ought to open up more machines to outside users. I think the universities ought to obtain their own machines as well. I like the idea of putting everybody on the network.

We also need more people. In this country, 2000 science teaching positions in universities are open now. We graduate 1700 scientific or engineering PhDs a year in the whole country. Already there are 2000 jobs just in the universities, and we pay more in the industry than the universities do, so many graduates will go into industry. If we lack doctoral students in the universities, we cannot support the student load needed to provide these people, particularly at the graduate level. To me, that is an alarming situation, and something must be done. Support of education through any kind of government program, not just in supercomputers but in any kind of science, is absolutely critical.

I think companies can seek leverage through tax savings. For example, one of the things that we have been lobbying for through the American Electronics Association is giving preowned Crays to universities and letting us take a tax deduction for the market value. I do not mean the original retail price, but whatever they are worth today. Let us give them to the universities, and let us take a deduction for them. Right now we cannot do that. What we get is a deduction for the book value of the machine. That is considerably less than the original cost of the machine, and there is too little advantage to corporations to do this.

I want to make this last point, because it is critical to me. I do not know how you build it into a program, and I know you all believe it anyway. But please remember that what makes all of this happen is people—not a lot of people, but individual people. I think the biggest thing we have to do is provide an environment, not only in companies but also in universities and laboratories, that allows individuals to really excel in what they do—to take a chance, to take a risk, to try for major breakthroughs. If we have any advantage over a culture like Japan's, and I am not being critical of theirs at all, it is the individual creativity that still exists here in the United States. If we can keep track of that and nurture it, we can stay ahead of other countries forever.

28

Conference Summary

K. H. Speierman
National Security Agency
Ft. Meade, Maryland

You might wonder how I got the assignment to give the summary of this very interesting and intense conference we have attended. About 18 months ago when I was visiting here with some colleagues, several of us thought about having this conference, and I think the Program Committee has gotten even with me by asking me to do the conference summary. It is a challenging task. It has been an intensive week, and the material has been extremely interesting and very much directed at this problem that we all realize is so important. So I found it difficult to summarize this. The advice from everybody is that the summary should be short. I will try to give it that property anyway.

Before I actually start, I would like to explain that this week we have been talking about supercomputers, and by supercomputers we mean very large scientific processing systems. We want to distinguish those from systems that are being developed as intelligent machines. We believe that we also have to develop these high-speed scientific processing systems.

I did not take a vote on all of these things, but I tried to identify things that I felt were significant, and I think that they were felt significant by a number of the people here. I am going to say a few words about each one of these.

The first item is that there is a compelling need for more and faster supercomputers. I would just like to mention something about the talks on algorithms and applications for supercomputers. We talked about a number of applications for which supercomputers are essential: weapons design, aerodynamics and fluid dynamics, fusion energy research, semiconductor components design, automotive engineering and design, some graphic applications, and oil recovery from reservoirs. There are many other applications for which supercomputers are essential, but these are a small number that were actually addressed here in some depth.

Let me briefly mention an interesting example in aerodynamics where a supercomputer was used for simulation in the design of the Airbus A310. One of our speakers pointed out that billions of dollars will be saved in fuel costs because of the refined design of the A310, because it will be a lighter aircraft. Also, there were a number of other cases where costs were greatly reduced by having a sophisticated design capability. In fact, the oil reservoir simulation example pointed out the importance of using supercomputers to extract oil from reservoirs—residual oil. That could represent a considerable dollar savings.

I do not think I need to say a whole lot about the second item. The Japanese have a national goal in supercomputation and can achieve effective cooperation among government, industry, and academia. That has been well documented. I should point out that about 18 months ago, when we thought we should have a conference like this, we did not know about the Japanese initiatives. But even then we realized that supercomputers were important, and we realized that the Von Neumann machine was running out of speed potential.

The third item is that the Japanese are having a sputnik effect on the U.S. and Europe, for better or worse. I think it is probably for better. We were told that the European Economic Community is investing $1.5 billion in a large computer program called ESPRIT. One of the effects this has on us is simply to cause us to critically re-examine and evaluate our position in computers and, in fact, as a world leader in technology. U.S. vendors are planning evolutionary steps while the universities are working on new concepts for massively parallel systems. This was true, I believe, until last night. Bill Norris modified my briefing a little in his announcement in "A Conducive Environment for Supercomputers." I called this a gap in an earlier observation I made. It is an important gap, and we want such a gap to exist between the research going on in universities and the developments that are going on in industry. But now we need to look for ways in which to accelerate the movement of these advanced ideas from research in universities to where they can be incorporated into production systems produced by the vendors. I will say a little more about that as we go along. The Denelcor machine is a little different. It is sort of in-between because its architecture is unique.

The only evident approach to achieve large increases over current supercomputer speeds is through massively parallel systems. One of our speakers pointed out that if we could build a supercomputer the size of a grain of sand, we would have a better chance of getting more speed out of unit processors. But of course, we cannot do that. We are limited by size, heat, and the speed of light. Not everybody agrees with this next statement. We do not know how to use parallel architectures very well. The step from a few processors to large numbers of processors is a difficult problem. The second part, and I think most of us believe this, is that it is even more difficult to use multiprocessors with only 4 or 16 processing units. One of our speakers pointed out that, in the problem of vectorization of FORTRAN programs, one of the universities has spent 4 years to produce a really sophisticated tool for vectorizing FORTRAN programs; so the problems in exploiting concurrency are in fact very challenging problems. Much work is required on algorithms, languages, and software to facilitate the effective use of parallel structures. Problems need to be analyzed differently. Problems now are often looked at from a serial point of view. The problem statement itself needs to be looked at in a different way to recognize concurrency, and we need languages that facilitate the representation of concurrency and our ability to manipulate it. Then we need software to effectively map this concurrency into our architectures and to take advantage of it in highly parallel systems.

The vendors need a larger market for supercomputers to sustain an accelerated development program. It was pointed out that if we had better software for these large systems and if they were easier to use, that might help to increase the market place. To a large extent, the users of supercomputers have been fairly sophisticated users who have done a lot of their own system software and all of their applications. They were able to utilize these machines, whereas others who were not using them would need a significant quantum step to achieve the staff and the computer expertise to take advantage of these complex systems. However, a number of us feel that there really is a much larger base of applications than current usage indicates. And the range of applications that were discussed, that supercomputers are being used on now, suggests that there are a lot of related things that they could be used for. Again, it was believed that if they were easier to use and if more work were done on developing new applications, the market place might enlarge substantially. Of course, if they cost less money, it would be easier for people to get started with them. It is a fairly expensive proposition to get started with your first supercomputer. It is not just the purchase of the equipment, but you need all of the facilities, the staff, and the mechanism to use it. Some have estimated that the initial startup is $20 million or $25 million.

The U.S. computer companies have a serious problem buying fast bipolar memory chips in the United States. They are concerned that they may have to go overseas. This was a problem that was expressed by, I think, all three of the supercomputer manufacturers that were here. International Business Machines (IBM) does not have that problem because they are vertically integrated. However, the other companies are not vertically integrated with the semiconductor manufacturers. They have to rely on them for these fast bipolar memories, and the semiconductor manufacturers do not see a market that would make it profitable for them to invest in the development of these high-speed memories. The Japanese are able to have vertical integration, and they do not have that problem. That is felt to be a very significant problem.

The Josephson and gallium arsenide technologies presently have more difficult process development than silicon, and the level of effort is lower. Some believe that the Japanese are ahead of us, or at least, they have more going on in the investigation of gallium arsenide systems than we do. These are important technologies, but the level of effort on them probably is not sufficient, considering the importance that they may have for the future of high-speed technology.

There's an inadequate amount of work being done on process-related material science, and as densities increase, chip processing gets much more difficult. One of our speakers expressed the thought that these fundamental problems in materials and materials science really ought to be addressed by the universities. They could be characterized as interesting research problems in physics, metallurgy, and chemistry. But they are not being pursued now, and they really should be, because to make progress for these high-density systems for the production processes, some of these materials problems need to be understood much better.

Also, packaging was pointed out as at least half of the design effort for these high-performance systems. And it was pointed out that in many of these high-performance systems, half of the clock time is really taken up in the packaging and in transportation. An example was given that, in one of these high-performance systems, if the logic speed were infinite, it would just double the performance of the total system. So again, this problem is caused by the speed of light. And we saw some packaging work that has been done that is extraordinarily complicated.

The next point is that supercomputers are systems consisting of algorithms, languages, software, architecture, peripherals, and devices that should be developed as systems to recognize the critical interaction of all the parts. There is a lot in that. It has always been true, I think, that we should develop systems by working the hardware and the software concurrently in the architecture. It has not always been done. I think that when it has been done, we have had better systems. I believe that on these massively parallel systems, it is absolutely essential to do this because of the complexity of the systems. On these massively parallel systems—I was trying to think of a way to explain this—it is almost like going to a second dimension, as compared with systems that are largely serial, because we have a structure now to deal with what really represents the concurrency or the parallelism in the processes. It is like problems in physics. When you go from one dimension to two or from two to three dimensions, the work factors increase enormously. And I think that that same phenomenon applies here when one goes from serial computing systems to highly concurrent computing systems. The point made here by a number of people is that it is absolutely essential that all of these parts, these subsystems, be looked at together. You do not develop architectures or computational models without understanding the implications they have on algorithms, languages, and software.

Another point that was made was about peripherals. Many people pointed out that we really do need high-bandwidth peripherals, and we do not see much work going on in that area. It is important to have a complete and effective supercomputer system.

Collaboration among government, industry, and academia on supercomputer matters is essential to meet U.S. needs. It is particularly essential in developing this two-dimensional computer, if you will, as opposed to the simpler serial systems we were talking about. But perhaps the most important reason is that, as I pointed out earlier, there is a considerable difference, as there should be, between what the universities are thinking about in advanced massively parallel computing systems and the sensible, kind of incremental approach that industry takes. To facilitate the transfer of that technology and those research ideas from the university to the vendors so that we can build on a shorter time basis and on a faster development cycle with the massively parallel systems that we need, we must have a collaborative, cooperative effort among the government, industry, and academia.

Last, we do need a national supercomputer goal, and we should have a strategic plan or a program to reach this goal. I do not know how widely accepted this is, but I feel strongly about it. I think a number of people have expressed the thought that it is important for us to quantify our requirements, and I believe that. I think, beyond that, we need to have a specific plan for achieving our goals.

In summary, I feel very strongly about all of this, and I think that we are presented with an extraordinary opportunity in this re-examination of our place in technology and supercomputers. I think it is also true of the things that the Defense Advanced Project Research Agency is planning to do in the area of intelligent machines and symbolic processing. I think that is just as important and just as exciting. But I think that we have a unique opportunity now, and that we ought to view it as a significant point in history when we have an opportunity to do something quite important. I have talked to a number of physicists and mathematicians here, people who know a lot more about these things than I do. I think most of us feel that there are really two things that can come out of this, besides the things that were talked about by our keynote speaker, Senator Bingaman, and others, who pointed out the importance of supercomputers to the economic strength of the country and to our defense posture. But I want to emphasize two other things. One is the great opportunity we have here to make significant advances in science—a more fundamental understanding of nonlinear physical phenomena, for example. That was the reason John Von Neumann thought that his machine would be useful to mankind, that it would give scientists better insight into nonlinear phenomena. Some of you believe that that is beginning to happen now and that you are really beginning to understand some things. Understanding them has a marvelous effect on our technology. We can build more efficient things. We can build better things. We can build things that cost us less money. And it provides a real opportunity for us to take a positive world leadership position in technology. I think that this has been a great conference, and I am delighted to be here with you.

29

Closing Remarks

General L. D. Faurer
Washington, D.C.

To be here with such a distinguished gathering gives me great pleasure, and I feel honored to be able to say a few parting words at the close of this important conference. You started strongly with the keynote address by Bob Inman, you had a most significant enterprise announced at the banquet by Bill Norris, and you ended on a high note with this morning's remarks and panel chairmanship by Dick DeLauer. Finally, you chose a delightful location to showcase your significant deliberations.

For the past week, you have been a group of over 150 participants (from some 14 different universities, 15 different commercial firms, 12 national laboratories, and 16 different government organizations) meeting to discuss the future of supercomputing in the United States. The individuals in this group, you, were invited because you are the best and most knowledgeable in your fields. You form a very prestigious collection of researchers, designers, manufacturers, users, and policy makers; and I am delighted that you have shared your valuable time with us.

The theme of the conference, "Frontiers in Supercomputing," has subsumed a rather presumptuous intent to influence the course of supercomputing for the 1990s. That's a big goal but not an impossible one, for each of you is a trail-blazer in your field; you have intimate knowledge of the frontiers. It will be you, and your associates, that will push those boundaries and make significant advances.

This has been a conference filled with exciting and significant topics, covering broad areas such as national and industrial perspectives, advanced architecture, software, algorithms, applications, and national priorities. These topics clearly have their own inherent interest and fascination, captivating us with the wonders of supercomputing; but they also have a larger importance touching on U.S. and international interests. They relate to scientific excellence, commercial success, national defense, and technological superiority. The future of supercomputing is readily recognized to be intricately connected to both our economic and our national well-being.

With respect to these ideas, perhaps you will permit me a few moments to discuss what I believe are three main issues of supercomputing today; and then take a few more moments to discuss the future. And I mean a *few* moments because I'm mindful of the role of the closing speaker—to close.

First is the issue of providing the computer power needed. This is a technological issue that concerns such things as clock speed, packaging, heat dissipation, input/output (I/O), memory size, memory bandwidth, architecture, and software. From a user point of view, computers are never fast enough and we must beat the time-of-flight bottleneck with parallelism, large-scale integration, and better packaging. We are usually compute or I/O bound—frequently both. So the challenge exists to provide faster calculations and larger data bases to more and more customer terminals. Such a challenge is obviously being accepted by the researchers, designers, engineers, and manufacturers; but surely all of us are concerned with this aspect of supercomputing in some way or other.

Second is the issue of contending with risk and making a profit. Manufacturers of supercomputers cannot be expected to donate their services out of generosity. There must be risk protection and profit incentive. Yet even though there would seem to be several applications for supercomputing, sales tend to be limited. We are not now dealing with a volume product. However, new applications that use high-speed computation to solve important problems previously beyond our computer capacity, and also to facilitate improved man/machine interfaces, may greatly enlarge this market. Technology is in a state of transition, research and development costs are high, competititon is increasing, and markets overseas tend to be restricted. Government, of course, can do things to help. It can sponsor research and development. It can encourage cooperatives such as Semiconductor Research Cooperative (SRC) and Microelectronics and Computer Technology Corporation (MCC). It can investigate tax incentives. It can increase its own purchases of supercomputers. But we should strive to build a healthy industry—one that can be productive and self-supporting. All of us in the room are involved in this economic aspect.

Third is the issue of technological leadership—as a nation. Foreign competition is increasing, threatening to reduce our lead by technological advances and by capturing overseas markets. If that competition is successful, then the United States will lose not only its pride but also its control of supercomputing. Complete systems may go to others whose interests are contrary to our own. Loss of control risks placing us in an inferior position with respect to economics and national defense. This third issue, then, relates to the first two, and its resolution will depend on our technological advances and ability to market our super-computers. The pursuit of high-speed computation may be like the space program. The dedication to a singular goal resulted in much beneficial technical fallout that accelerated the development of new technology and products. Perhaps the same will occur as a result of our pursuit of supremacy in supercomputers. Again, government can do things to help. It can stimulate communication of ideas within the country. It can support university research by providing supercomputer use. I know that the concern for technological superiority was a major factor in convening this conference and I suspect it was also a major factor in your attendance.

These three issues, with different degrees of emphasis, have con-tributed to the reasons why the Los Alamos National Laboratory and the National Security Agency (NSA) have co-sponsored this conference. We believe that the "Frontiers in Supercomputing" are today being ex-panded and pushed back. The environment and potential for the 1990s are being shaped now. You, by your very participation in this con-ference, are helping to set events in motion that will determine the U.S. posture in supercomputing for the remainder of this century.

Perhaps, at this conference, we have talked most about providing the computer power needed. That is appropriate because our requirements and the technological art are the factors that drive the economics and superiority issues.

Our industry representatives, however, have voiced their concerns about development risks, profit margins, and the market for supercom-puters. You are aware that several commercial firms have cooperated to form such ventures as SRC and MCC to address the economic issue. I suspect many of us find it interesting to speculate when—or if—the giant, IBM, will enter the field.

There has also been some discussion about the foreign threat to U.S. leadership. We have featured a talk about the Japanese plans for high-speed and fifth-generation computers. We have heard how their govern-ment is supporting, in many ways, the supercomputer projects. The press continues to remind us of the Japanese challenge. And we must respond to that challenge.

But even if there were no such competition, our interests in supercom-puting would remain. In this room are people who need the very best that can be offered to probe the mysteries of weather prediction, fusion, weapons design, communications security, geophysical exploration, aerodynamics, astrodynamics, robotics, and ballistics; and the list gets longer. Supercomputing is so important that we should strive—regardless of an outside threat—to design, manufacture, and use the world's fastest computers.

When the computer industry was in its infancy, NSA's financial support was a major factor in influencing the course of computer development. In more recent times, NSA *and* the national laboratories have supported the development of supercomputers by purchasing early models of new computers. In 1971, NSA purchased Serial #5 of the Control Data 7600, and 1 year later, purchased Serial #9. In 1977, NSA purchased two Cray-1 computers, at a time when it was not known whether Cray research would even survive.

As an agency that requires supercomputers to perform its mission, NSA must bear some responsibility for the health of the industry and for encouraging the development of innovative computer architectures. As a continuing step in that direction, and in recognition of an imaginative approach to parallel processing, I would note to you my intention of acquiring a HEP computer according to the terms of the proposal made to NSA by Denelcor. We will need to learn how to apply this unusual machine to a number of interesting problems, but we are eager to get started.

Let me now change the subject slightly and conclude. And permit me to do it as if I had spent the whole week with you, for someone needs to express the proper appreciation. After all, significant conferences, such as this one, do not happen by themselves. They depend on the efforts of many dedicated and involved people.

First, much credit and praise are due to our co-sponsor and host, the Los Alamos National Laboratory. The Director, Don Kerr, has given his positive support and guidance to this successful event. He has provided a modern, comfortable conference facility in which to hold our sessions. He has allowed us to visit his scientific work areas and provided experts to explain the wonders of high-energy physics. His staff, together with my own, has planned and provided an absorbing agenda of talks and discussions; and almost all of the administrative details of this conference have been handled by Laboratory people. Thank you, Don, for the hard work and dedication. You and your personnel have done a superb job.

Second, appreciation and praise are due to our session chairmen and speakers. They have spent a great deal of their time preparing for this

past week. Without their participation there would have been no conference; and without their enthusiastic, informative presentations the
conference would not have succeeded as it has. Each day has introduced
us to innovative ideas. Thank you for your stimulating talks.

We, of course, had two additional speakers—not included as part of
particular conference sessions. Clearly, our thanks go to Bob Inman and
Bill Norris for their contributions as keynote and banquet speakers.
They provided just the right amount of high-level perspective to set off
our week's activities.

Finally, credit and acknowledgment for the success of this conference
are due to all of you who attended the sessions, became involved in
discussions, organized quick seminars, and shared a wealth of information with each other. Thank you for your active participation. You have
set the stage for important results to follow. I hope you will return to
your various organizations with novel ideas, increased vigor, and a
determination to set new, enviable records in supercomputing.

Actually, I believe that no one should leave this conference without
recognizing our substantial collective capabilities to meet the challenges
of this conference. You have the ideas, the intellect, the talent, the
technology, the will, and the certain confidence of your own potential.
Thank you, travel safely.